"Steve Huston is one of the most uniquely powerful artists out there . . . a modern master. [*Figure Drawing for Artists*] is a phenomenal resource. Steve's insight and love for what he does inspires. This book should be in every student's library. That being said, it's for every artist—students and professionals alike."

—Carlos Huante,
creature designer/art director for film and games, such as
the Men in Black movies, Shrek, and X-Men: The Last Stand

"I believe drawing is the most important skill an artist can have. Its greatest value lies in its power to help others see, just as Steve has masterfully done through his work and teachings for most of his creative life."

—Andrea Favilli,
chief creative officer, Favilli Studio, an entertainment tourism design
company with worldwide clients, including The Walt Disney Company,
Sony, Universal Studios, Changzhou Dinosaur Kingdom, and Wanda

STEVE HUSTON

FIGURE DRAWING FOR ARTISTS

Making Every Mark Count

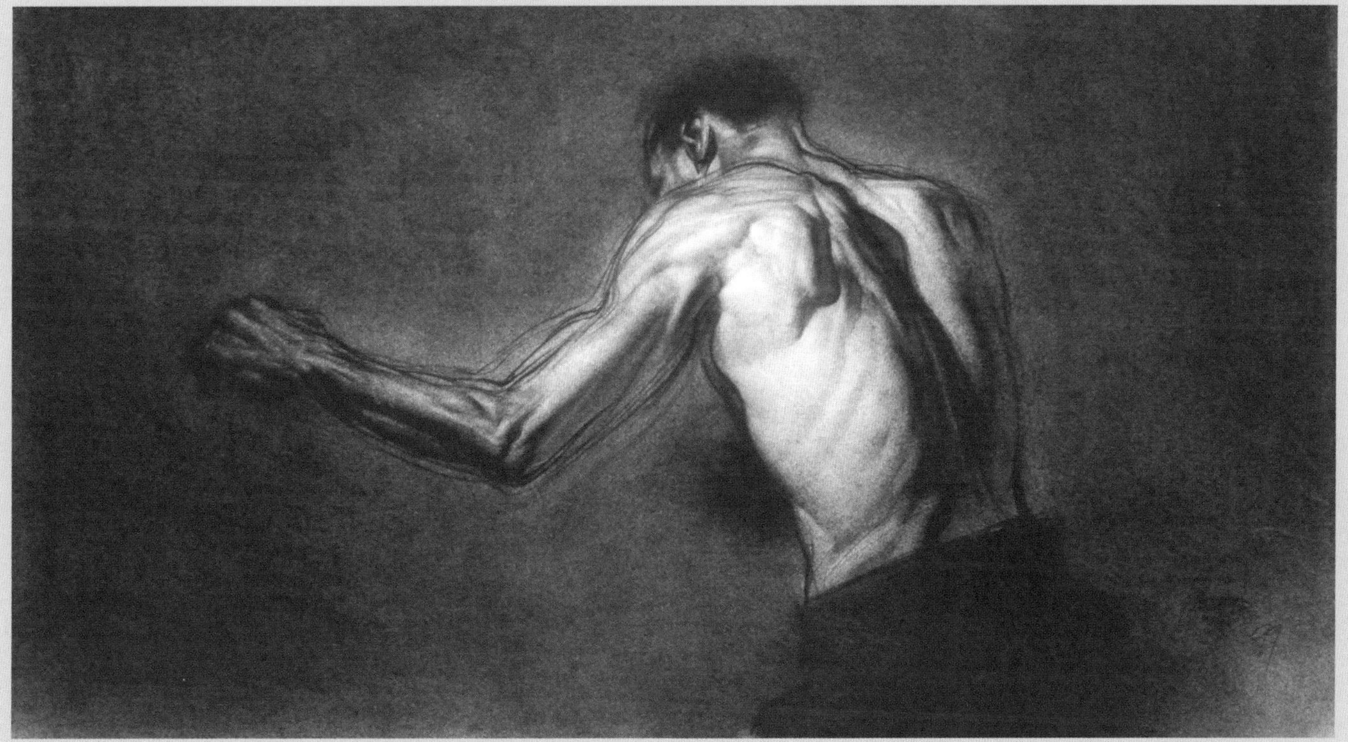

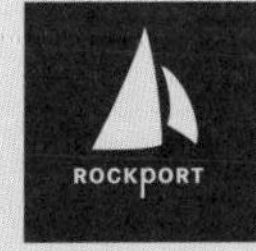

ROCKPORT

Quarto.com

© 2016 Quarto Publishing Group USA Inc.

First published in 2016 by Rockport Publishers,
an imprint of The Quarto Group,
100 Cummings Center, Suite 265-D,
Beverly, MA 01915, USA.
T (978) 282-9590 F (978) 283-2742

EEA Representation, WTS Tax d.o.o.,
Žanova ulica 3, 4000 Kranj, Slovenia.
www.wts-tax.si

22

ISBN: 978-1-63159-065-8

Digital edition published in 2016
eISBN: 978-1-63159-178-5

Library of Congress Cataloging-in-Publication Data available.

Design: Prances Design, Inc.
Cover Image: Steve Huston
Page Layout: meganjonesdesign.com
Interior Illustrations: Steve Huston, except where noted.

Printed in Guangdong, China TT032026

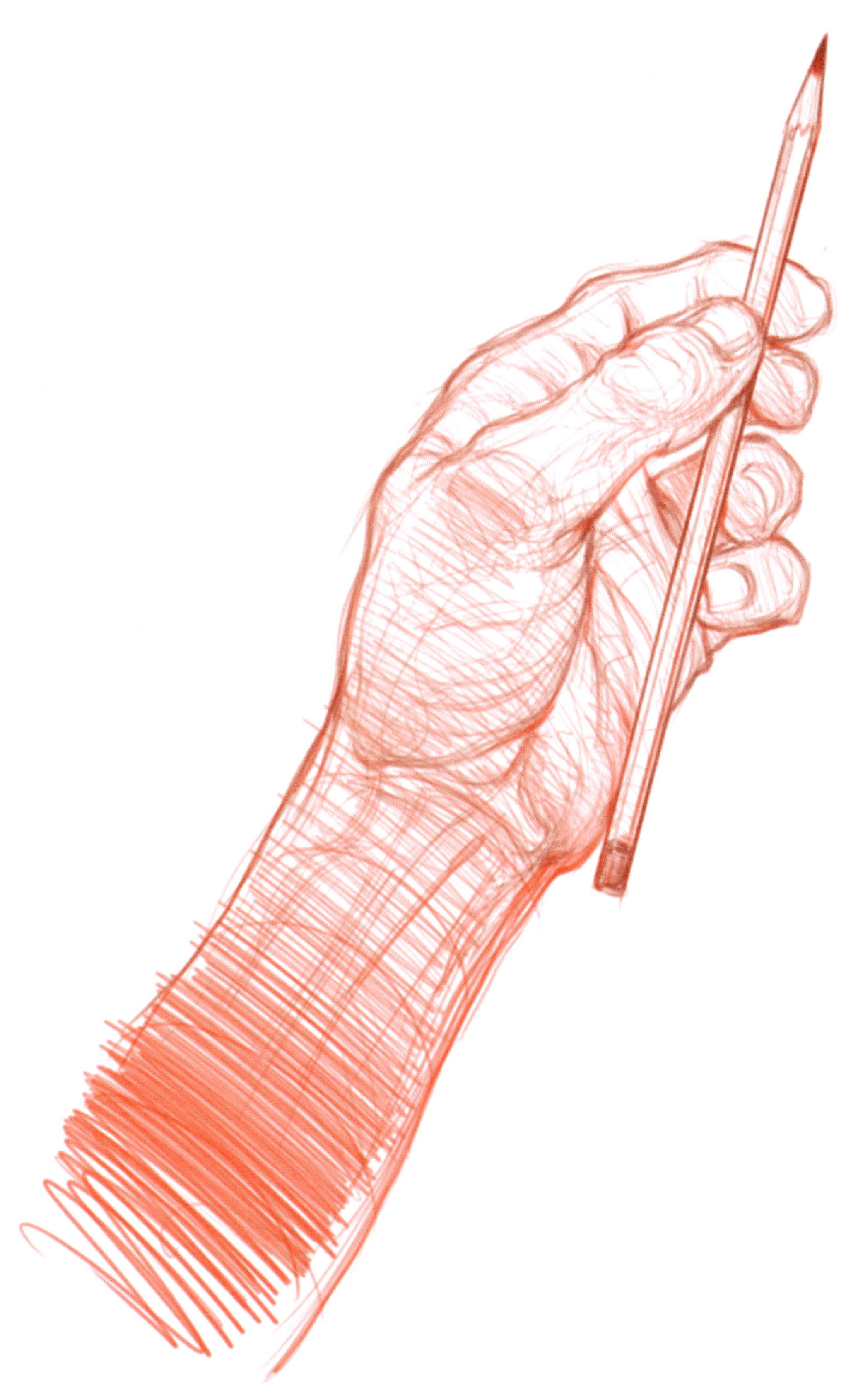

Contents

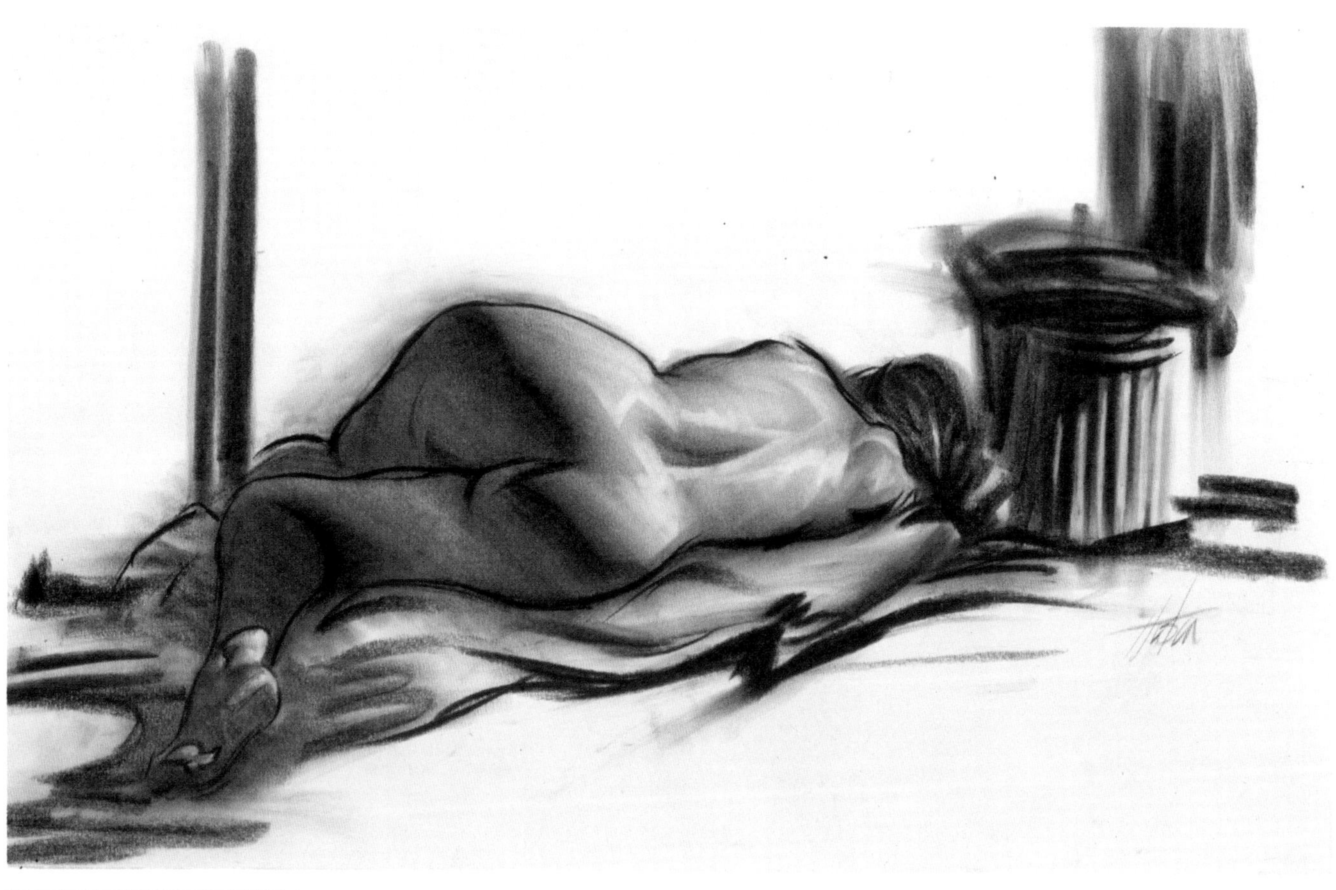

Karen, c. 2001, by Steve Huston. Charcoal drawing of a reclining female figure.

GETTING COMFORTABLE WITH YOUR MATERIALS

What is art? It could take this whole book to answer that question. In fact, it could take a whole library—and does. Critics and theorists continuously add to the canon exploring and explaining art. Their essays are thought provoking in many ways, but their theories don't turn us into better artists. Their theories don't coax the pencil into making better marks.

Art Is an Idea

I love drawing, always have—so, I chose it as a career. That made the whole "what is art" thing an important issue for me.

I needed an answer that made my thumbnail sketches, life studies, comps, and finishes excellent. And more, I needed an answer that led me toward a process that spoke with one voice, one vision—one style.

Art criticism helped me, but not in that pursuit. So, I did what any self-serving, creative type would do: I made up an answer that would.

I didn't care whether my answer held up to the rigors of critical thinking. In fact, it doesn't. I'm here to tell you what I'm offering is pure make-believe.

And I *believe* that's exactly why it works.

Fantasy, myth, make-believe: none is true for the head. But, they are all true for the heart—and the heart is where art thrives. Art is not designed to convince the rational mind. Science handles that. Art, at its most powerful, appeals to the emotions, as mythology does.

And mythology has only two requirements:

1. No matter how fantastic the world or worldview is, it needs to be absolutely consistent. Only then, will the head relax and let the heart take control.

2. The hero (and audience) takes a journey that shows the world works through some secret, simple truth. A truth such as it's sometimes an upside-down, absurd place we live in, or magic hides in plain sight, or, even, there's no place like home.

Make-believe truths like these are important—critical, really. They act as emotional road maps, helping us navigate our messy day-to-day affairs. Adults need them in some ways more than children do. The best road maps show us how to become the hero of our own lives. After all, even switching jobs or starting a new hobby is a real adventure.

Right this moment, you're reading a make-believe story for adults. You're nearly to the part about the secret truth—two, actually. As the pages turn, you'll read that the world of drawing, though it presents ogre-size problems, is a far simpler place than you suspected. Simple doesn't mean easy, though. Where's the adventure in easy?

This yarn says the craft of drawing the human body succeeds through only two ideas (here are two of the secret truths): **gesture** and **structure**. It says these two ideas work for the biggest parts of your drawing, and for the smallest.

You'll read about things like the eye socket is a whistle notch, the arm is a cleverly curved tube, the many parts of the body are connected through invisible design lines—these are the designs of life. These are all lies as far as the scientist is concerned—and yet, I bet you'll see that they ring true. And they'll allow you to draw with a vision and control you can't get any other way.

My promise to you is this: If you're willing to wear out a few pencils, this book can help you navigate the difficult landscape of the drawn figure.

The last truth I'll share for now is that I didn't make any of this up. The Old Masters did. We've been staring at these heartfelt truths for countless generations, but for the last several we simply haven't realized it.

Great art with its great stylistic differences has been telling this tale since the beginning. To the Old Masters, it was common knowledge. It's just been forgotten. What a gift these two fundamental ideas—structure and gesture—in all their incarnations, give us through the greatest voices in history.

Art, then, is really just another language. Just as the words express concepts, the lines and tones artists make do the same. This book exists so we'll know what we're talking about.

With practice, a lot of practice, you can begin telling your own story. Start thinking of the frame around your artwork as a window into your world. The marks you make explain the rules of that world. They had better be consistent.

SO, HOW TO DO THAT?

Drawing the human body is not easy. We need to approach it carefully. The premise for this book, and for my entire career as an artist and teacher, is that the drawing process reduces to those two fundamental ideas—*gesture* and *structure*. To make sense of them, then, we need to plumb them systematically and deeply. Keep in mind, structure and gesture are, in a sense, two sides of the same coin. If they don't work together, they don't work.

I will begin this exploration by first explaining, and demonstrating, structure at its most basic level and follow with an equally accessible exploration of gesture. Then, we'll dig a little deeper into structure, and then deeper into gesture, and so on. This is a method that can take you from the simplest quick sketch to the most finished of renderings and make them both ring true— but only if you learn it step by step.

This method, in one way or another, is the method of the Old Masters. Somewhere along the way, it became arcane and mysterious. I don't believe it should be. That's why I wrote this book. That's the reason I think these ideas (which are not *my* ideas) are wonderful, beautiful, and, most of all, useful.

There *are* certain immutable truths in great works of art. If you know what to look for, you can see them in the masterpieces of every great art movement. You see those truths play out in various ways in movements such as Cubism and Post-Impressionism and, likewise, in many of the modernist talents of today.

What I want to give you is a chance to achieve your potential, to master your craft, and to find your voice. This planet needs more creative voices.

So, instead of being intimidated into inaction, let's break free and express ourselves. Let's learn to speak eloquently in the language of structure and gesture.

With that in mind, turn the page, dip your toes into art's deep waters, and wade toward its shining distant shore— and don't worry. I have the life preserver right here.

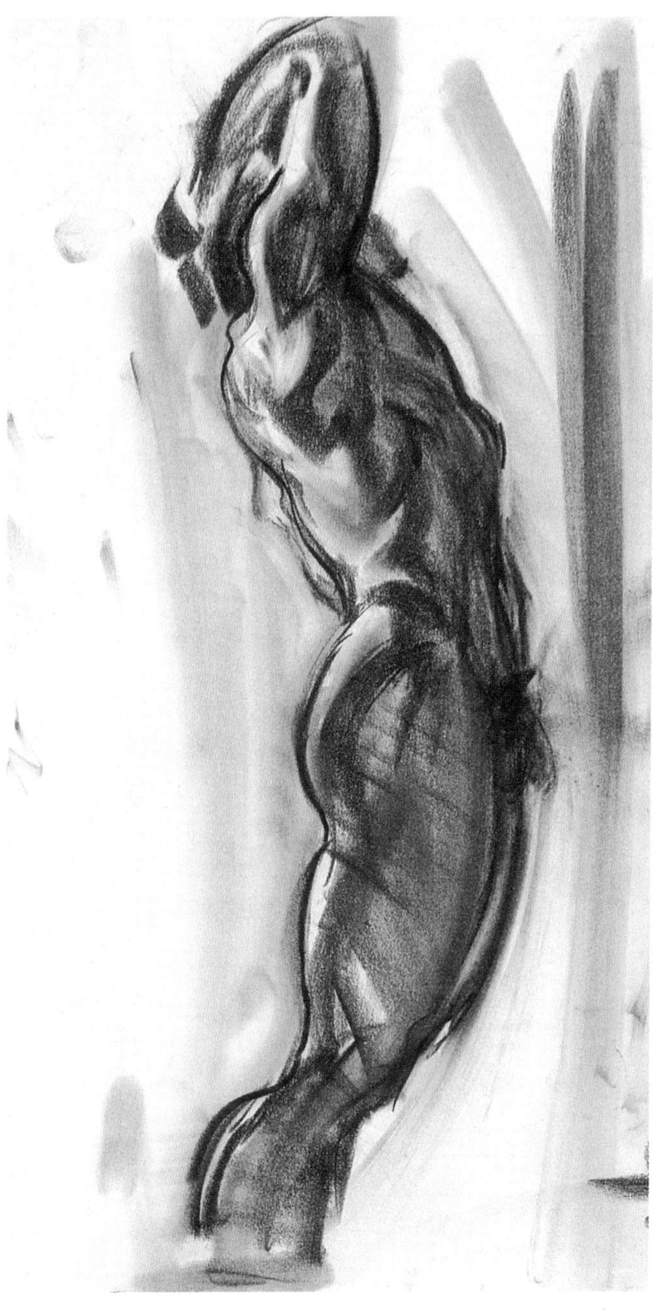

Standing Nude, 1998, by Steve Huston. Alphacolor and Conté chalk on Strathmore, Bristol finish.

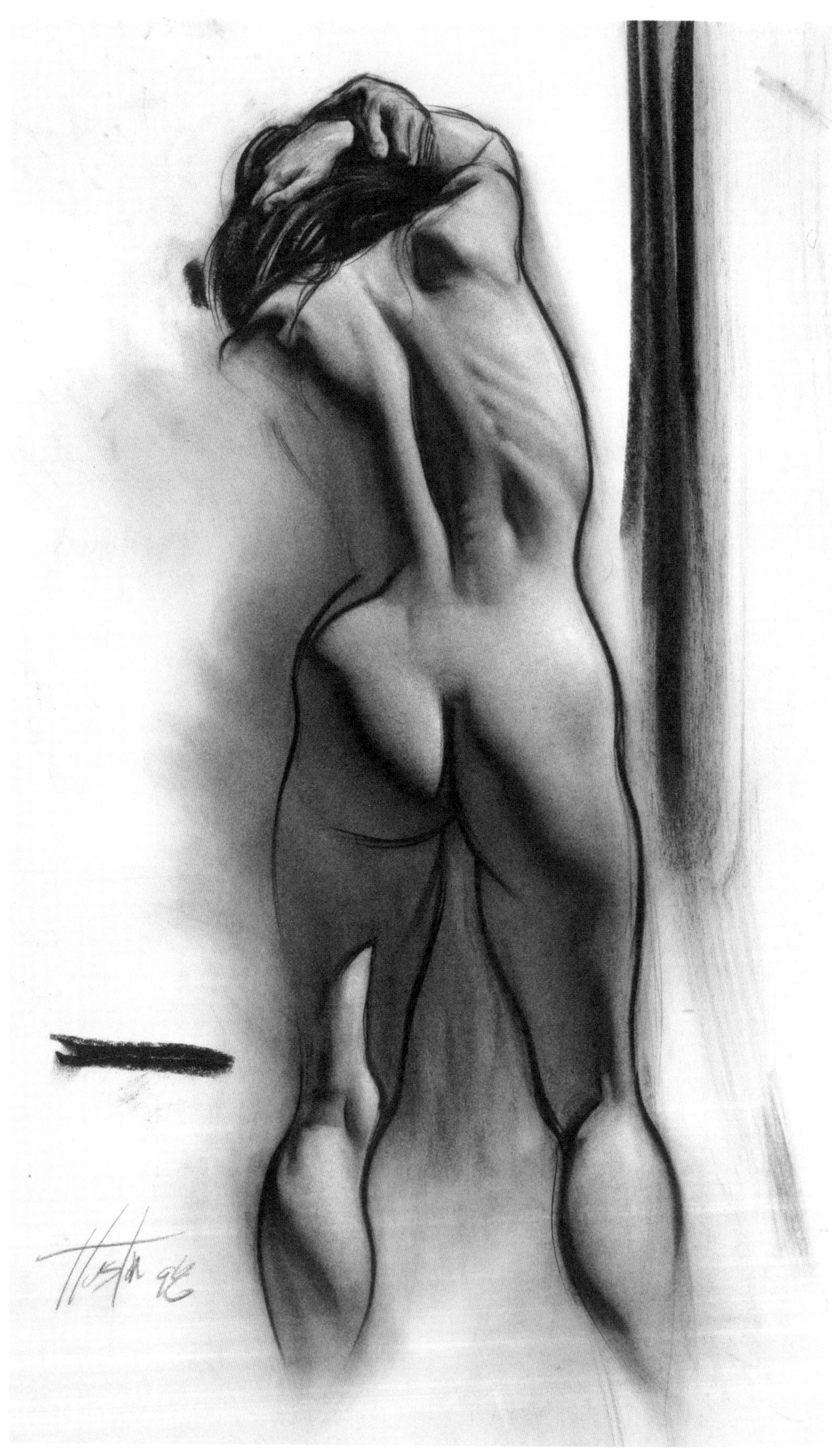

Sara, 1998, by Steve Huston.
Alphacolor and Conté chalk on
Strathmore, Bristol finish.

Making Art a Ritual

The art-making process is tied to ritual, and that repetition puts you
in the correct mind-set.

There are endless materials from which to choose. I'll give you a few of my favorites, but, every so often, grab a new pen or pencil to try out. Test new papers. Stand rather than sit.

Art is like alchemy. The alchemist attempts to make something precious from the mundane—artists, too. Ritual was all-important in alchemy—the process was connected intimately to the materials used. That's true for any spiritual or creative endeavor.

You need to develop your own ritual for making art. Clean the studio or make it messy; sharpen your pencils with a razor blade or crumble up your pastel, smear it on with your fingers, and erase it mostly away. Experiment with the process until you have a practice that works for you. That also includes the process I demonstrate in this book. But my process won't work for you unless you chop it up, mix it around, throw out some things, and add some things in; in other words, it won't work for you until you make it your own.

Where to Work?

If you don't have a studio with twenty-foot ceilings, northern-facing
windows, and a personal assistant to sharpen your pencils, use the
corner of a bedroom or sit at the dining table.

You can stand at an easel. You can sit at an easel. You can buy a tilting drafting table or have a $3/8$-inch-thick (1 cm) piece of plywood or $1/4$-inch-thick (0.6 cm) piece of Masonite cut to about 20 x 26 inches (51 x 66 cm) long and grab a couple of alligator clamps. Lay the bottom edge across your lap and lean the board against the edge of a dining table. If that's a little low, use a kitchen counter. You're ready to work.

I used to have to fall backward from my canvasback chair onto my bed to get up from my workstation. You could spend a fortune on the perfect setup, but, really, you don't need many resources to be an artist. Start simply. Start cheaply. You can always ease into massive debt later. There's no hurry.

Materials and Tools

Every material has its limitations. Don't try to get deep darks from a hard pencil. Don't do a miniature rendering with a square stick of charcoal. Take the time to experiment and learn what your materials can do. Here are the basic tools and materials you'll need.

1. **CarbOthello Pencils.** I use pencils in earth-tone colors. Why? A brightly colored pencil doesn't work well for shading. *Shadow is the absence of light.* Bright colors suggest light. The two don't mix. Other pencil brands I like are General, Conté à Paris, Faber-Castell, and Prismacolor. These last two are slightly waxy and won't work well on newsprint.

    Paper: Copy paper (any bond), newsprint, vellum, and marker paper are great. Also, I like toned paper in light to middle values and earth tones for the same reason as stated previously. I like Strathmore 500 series, Ingres, and Canson brands. Canson has the heaviest texture and, so, is a little harder to work with. You also want something with minimal tooth to it. It's much harder to do any kind of rendering or detail while fighting a rough-textured paper.

2. **Conté à Paris sticks in H, HB, and 2B.** Note that 2B is a softer chalk and gives you deeper darks, but it's also messier. H and HB are harder, but you lose the deeper values.

    Paper: You can use all of the preceding papers listed as well as Strathmore, Bristol finish, 1-ply and up, and illustration sheets, but not plate or hot press. These have no tooth to hold the chalk, and the pigment will come right off. Or use any higher-quality, acid-free paper designed for drawing. Again, you want minimal texture.

3. **Alphacolor.** Really, any brand of pastels will do. Black and earth tones work for drawing. And, of course, you can work in full color for "dry painting" pastel work. Use the better brands for painting and the cheaper for drawing. Alphacolor are big, clunky, and not designed for small-scale work or fine detail.

I did this book's cover drawing using Strathmore Bristol paper and Alphacolor for the deep darks. I used Conté chalk and a stump for the fine line and detail.

Paper: You can use all of the preceding papers listed. Canson, with its toothiness, is great for holding more pigment. Pastels build up quickly. You'll find the chalks blow away with a sneeze if you use a smooth stock.

4. **Ballpoint pen, any cheap pen, or fountain pen with brown or black ink (make sure you use fountain pen ink).** Pens are a favorite of mine for sketchbooks. I like not being able to erase. I like hatching in the value. It suggests brushstrokes to me for when I switch to paint.

    Paper: You can use all of the preceding papers listed and almost anything you can think of, such as the back of an envelope or copy paper. I use acid-free scrapbook paper a lot. It has a cardstock thickness, and I can do little painted studies in gouache alongside the ink sketches.

5. **Graphite pencils.** Any of about 3 million brands are fine. I like H or HB for hardness. You won't get charcoal darks out of it: you need 4B to 6B for that. But graphite gets a little glossy when it gets dark. I use it for under-drawing for gouache or watercolor paintings or to lay in an ink drawing. Mainly, I use it when I want a sensitive technique. It does delicate and detail like no other tool.

> One of the best ways to learn to vary your paint strokes is by using pen and ink.

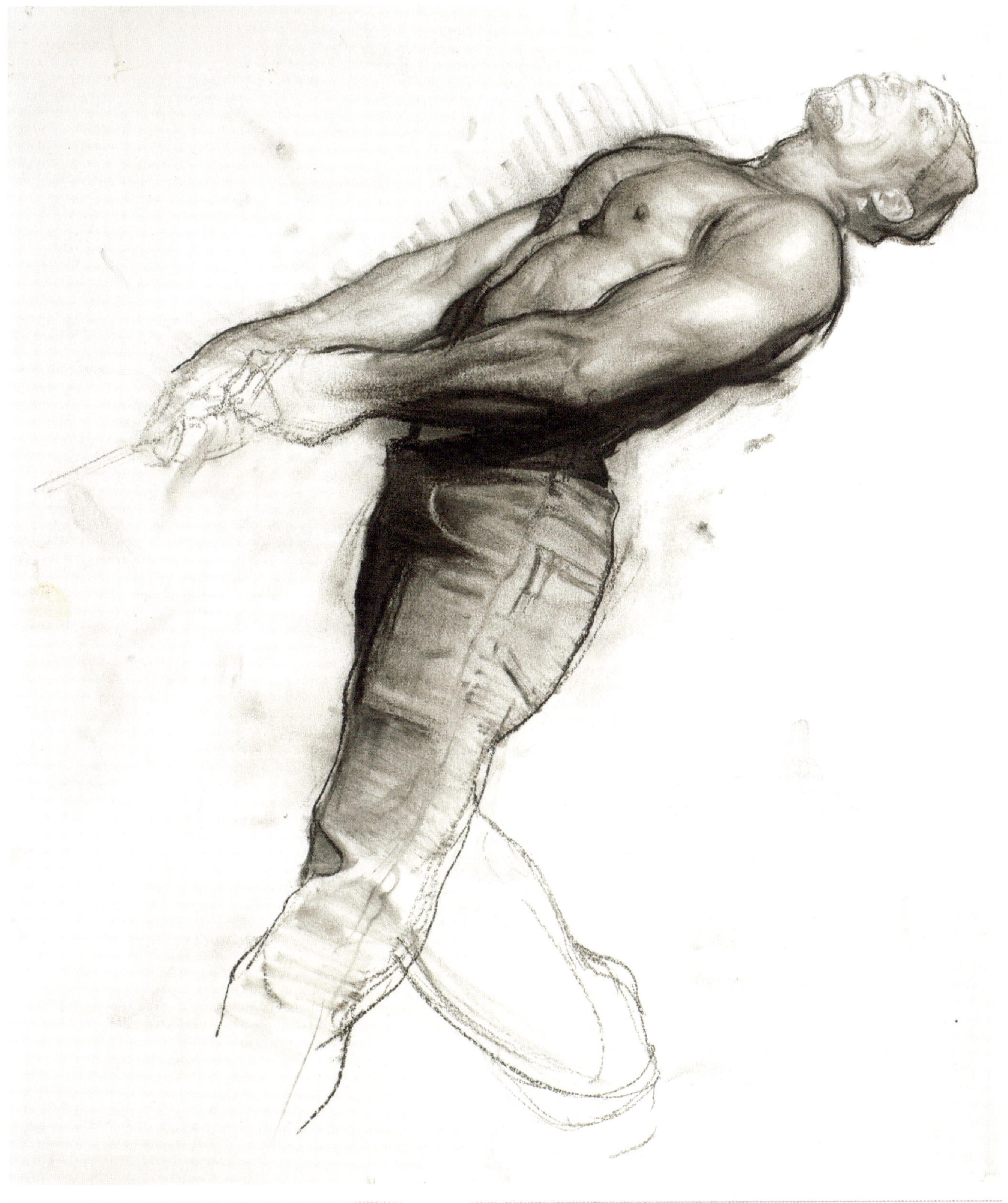

Study for *Draw*, c. 2004, by Steve Huston. Alphacolor and Conté chalk on Strathmore, Bristol finish.

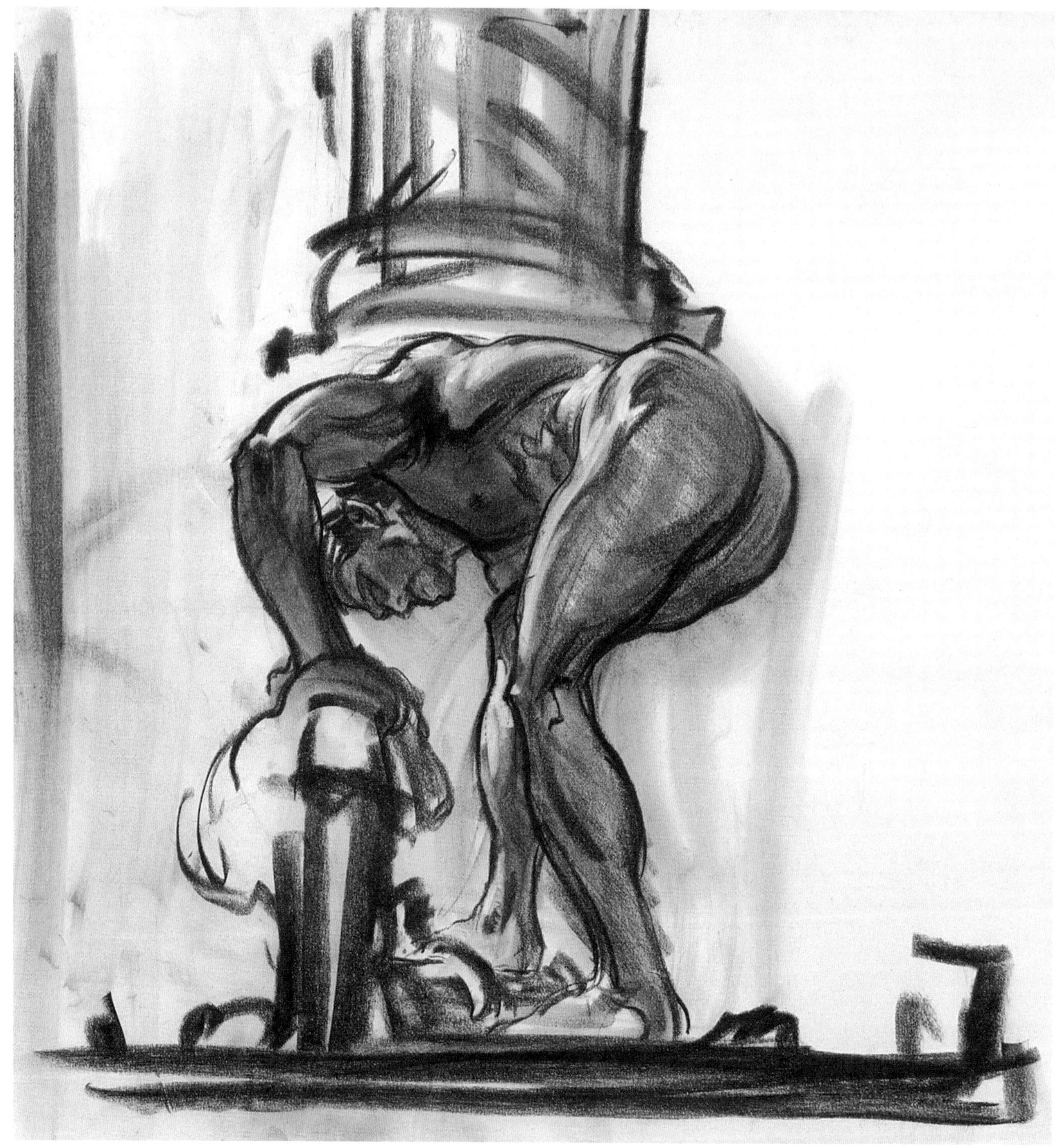

Study for *Caryatid*, c. 1998, by Steve Huston. Alphacolor on Strathmore, Bristol finish.

6. **Craft knife, sharp pocketknife, or one-sided razor blade.** You need something to sharpen your charcoal pencils with—and no, not a manufactured electric sharpener. I'll show you how the sharpened pencil should look on page 18.

7. **Kneaded eraser and hard eraser.** Either will work, but I like the kneaded eraser because it is similar to putty—you can shape it to get into tight areas. It is soft and won't take your paper back to white if there is a lot of pigment down. That's what hard erasers are for. You can even use electric erasers to buff away stubborn stains. And, yes, all the pigments discussed will stain your paper. Actually, applying pigment can damage the paper fibers. Once that happens, you may be stuck with it.

8. **Sandpaper or a sanding pad.** You can buy little sanding pads from the art store. I use sandpaper from the hardware store. It sharpens your pencils to a finer point than just using a knife. I sand down a little bit of an Alphacolor stick to load pigment onto my stump.

9. **Stumps.** These cylindrical drawing tools, made of tightly rolled paper in a pencil shape, are used to blend or smudge marks.

10. **Markers.** Choose a couple of grays to shade over your pen drawings: that's what auto designers and entertainment designers use. The thing with markers is you can start with a light gray and keep marking down a new layer over the old to get darker and darker. It's a great way to ease into the correct values.

11. **Touch display computer.** I use one for my digital teaching at New Masters Academy in California. I used a Wacom Touch for most of this book and Photoshop and SketchBook Pro for software. They mimic myriad tools.

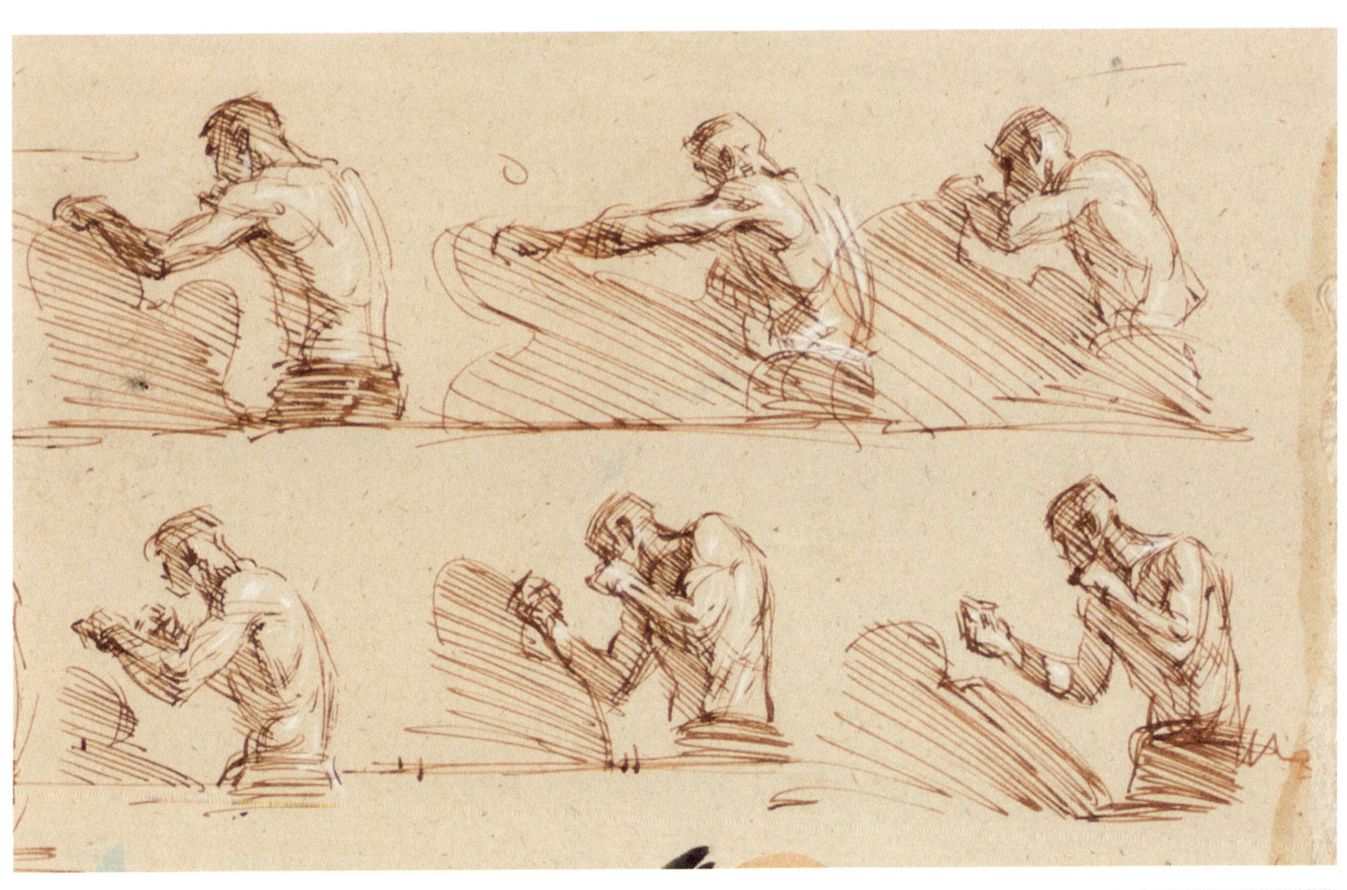

A study from my *Shadow Boxing* series. Waterman Paris fountain pen, very fine nib, on oatmeal-colored, acid-free scrapbook paper.

The Pencil Mark

Hold the pencil as if you're writing a letter but relax your fingers. Don't pinch them back in a tight grip.

A relaxed grip is so important because you want to make sweeping strokes like an orchestra conductor, meaning from your shoulder and not your wrist or finger joints. Your line quality will be nervous and scratchy if your draw from your fingers. Practice this as you would a tennis stroke.

A hard, crisp line and a thick, soft line—these are the only two marks you need. Now, for the gradation.

The zigzag technique will give you a gradation in any medium you care to use. Hard edges and soft edges—master those and you've mastered your medium.

Try these new strokes: Sketch a household item—a coffee cup, screwdriver, pencil, or a slice of bread. Learn to draw the shapes you see. Can you draw tubes, boxes, and balls from your head? We're going to practice a lot of that in the next chapter. You want a catalog of simple shapes to rely on as you sketch—the bigger the mental catalog, the better.

That's all you need to know to get started, so let's!

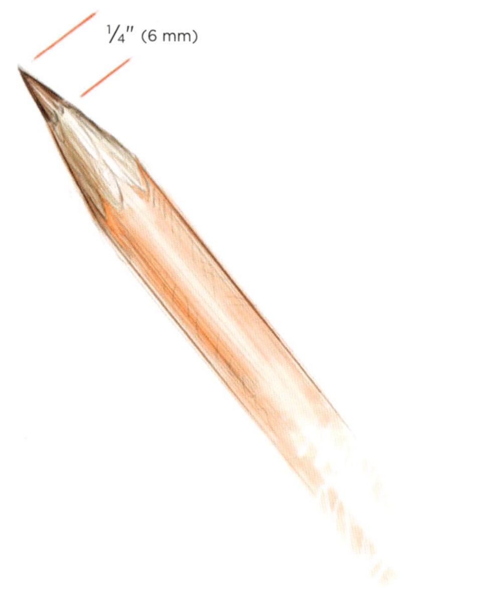

Leave approximately ¼ inch (6 mm) of charcoal or lead exposed. Some artists prefer more. I tend to break them if they get longer. You want the wood carved back at a tapered angle. This allows you to make the marks you need. I tend to use the pencil-across-the-palm grip (see right).

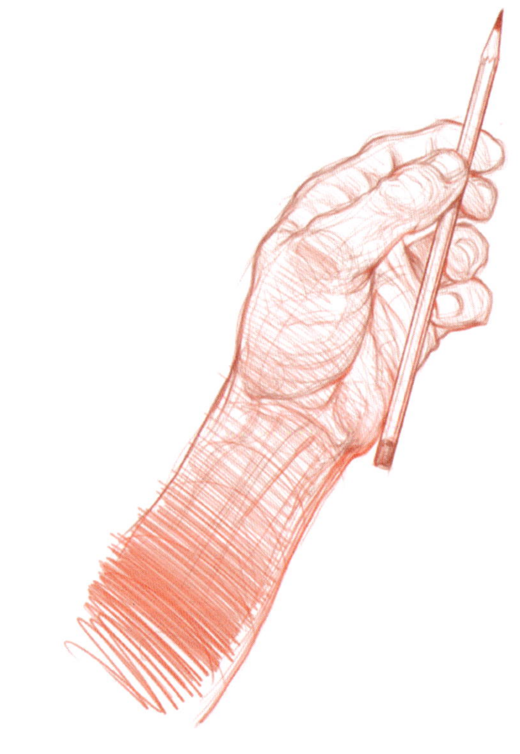

The pencil-across-the-palm grip.

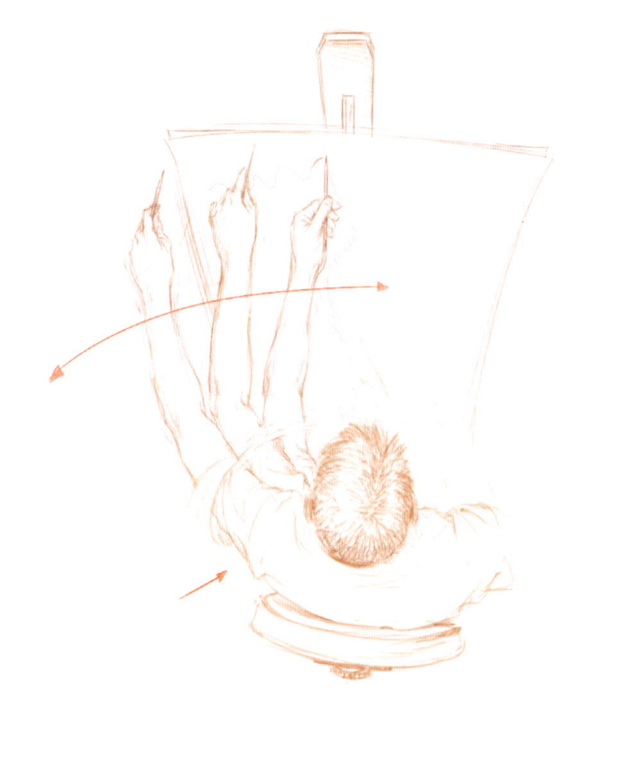

Figure drawing at an easel.

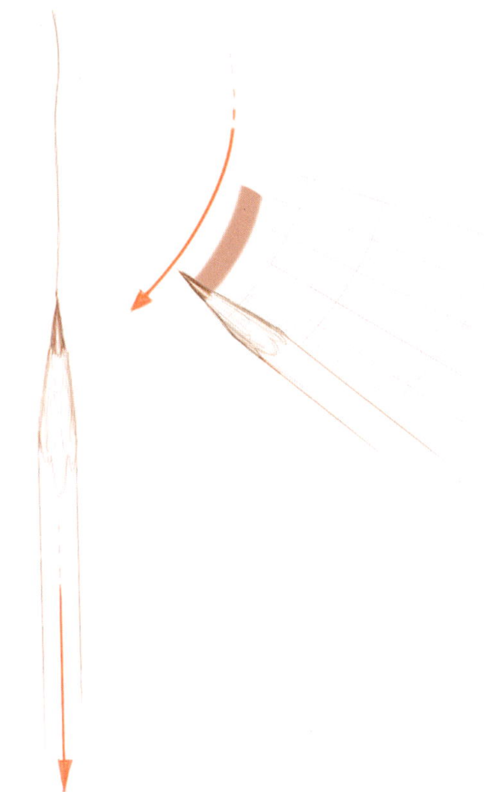

Turn your pencil in the direction of the stroke, and you'll get a hard, crisp line. Turn the pencil against the stroke, and you'll get a thick, soft line. This is why the wood has to be carved back as it is.

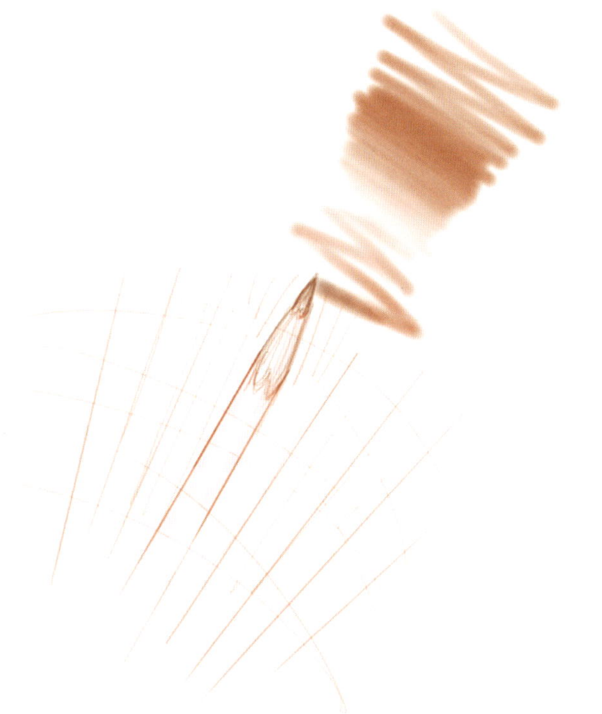

Turn the pencil against the stroke and work the pencil back and forth. You've made a soft zigzag line. Do it again. Now, compress the zigzag and slowly lighten the pressure on the page. By compressing the line on top of itself while lightening your touch, you make a gradation.

Use a layer of at least six or seven sheets of paper to draw on. The extra sheets underneath provide a slight pillowing effect that will make your mark making, especially gradations, easier. Try drawing with and without the extra sheets. Can you tell the difference?

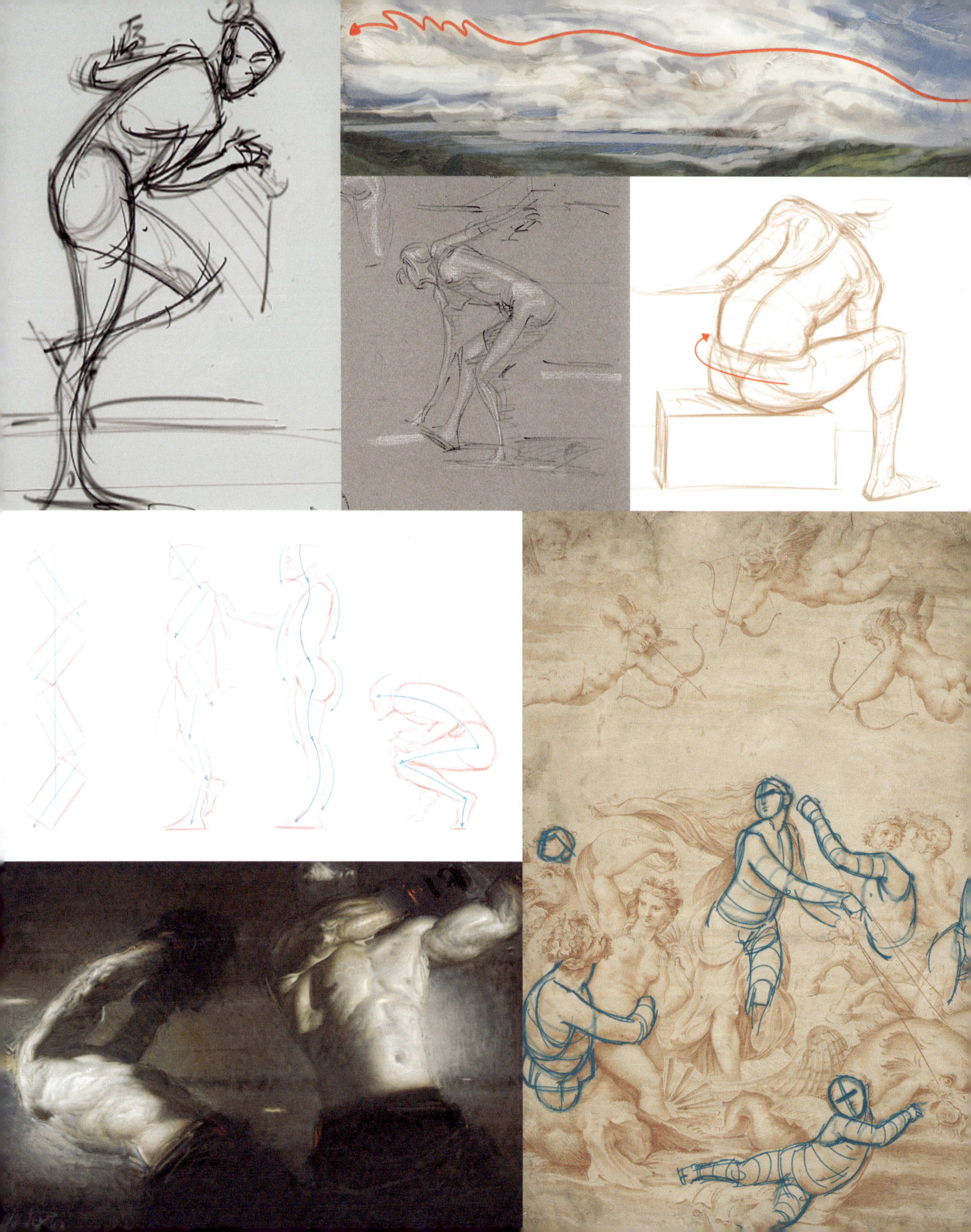

one

THE ELEMENTS OF DRAWING

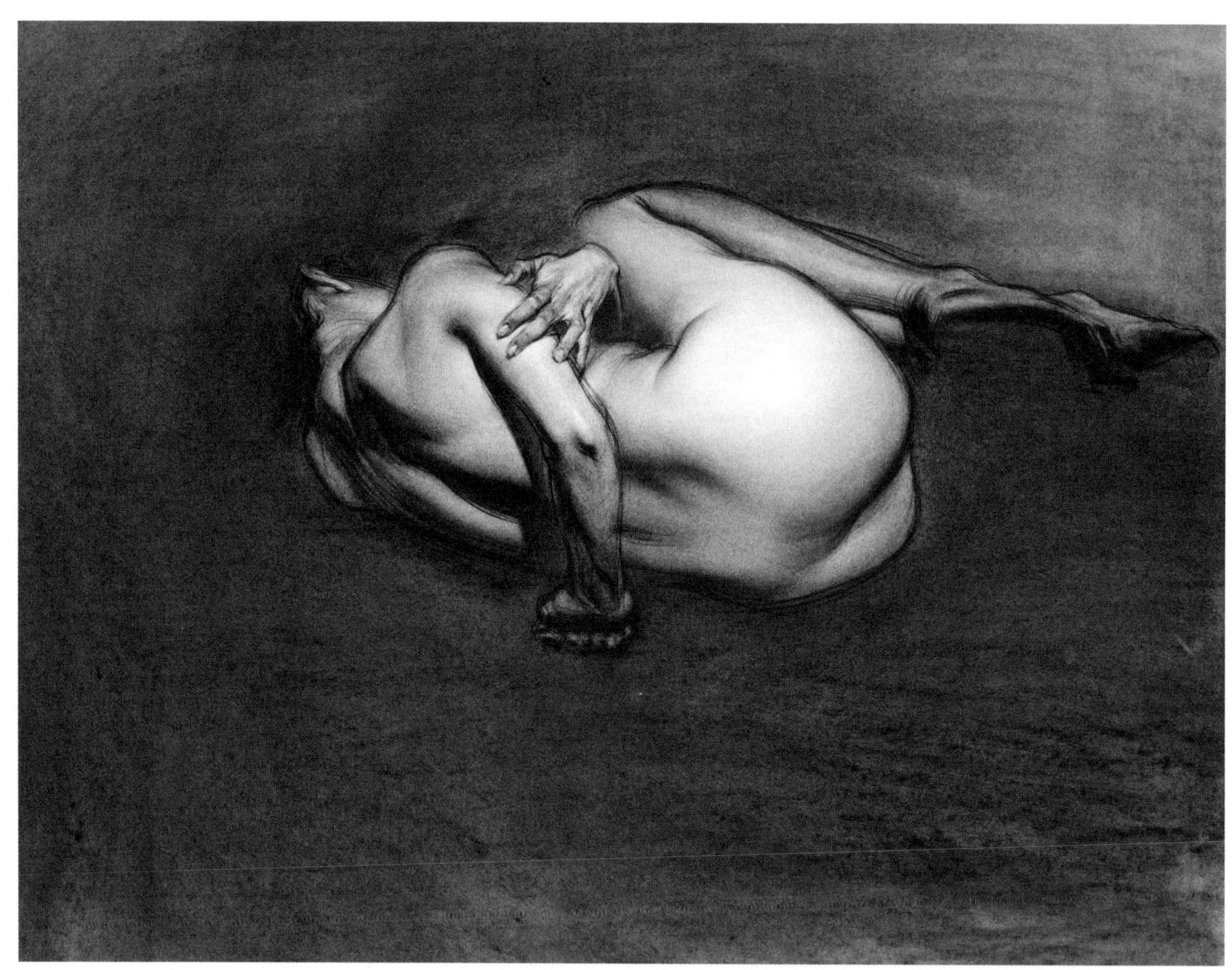

Reclining Nude, c. 2000, by Steve Huston. Alphacolor and Conté chalks on Strathmore, Bristol paper.

1 | STRUCTURE

We have ideas we want to get down on the page, but we need materials
to do that. And, we need some level of control over those materials.
That's what this chapter is about. We'll start with a review of a few
materials and then couple those with a few basic techniques. This book
is not just about making marks. It's about making the *right* marks for the
right job. And, really, it's not too difficult. We just need to make sure
the materials don't get in the way as we work through our big ideas.

Essential Ideas in Drawing

Structure and gesture are the two essential ideas of drawing. So, how
can we define them?

To understand and use the idea of structure well, it's
best to think like a sculptor, meaning we build our drawing and painting (as in sculpture) through a series
of constructed forms. Structure, then, is the *distinct
three-dimensional part(s) of any particular object*.

A tree would have a series of parts known as the roots,
trunk, branches, leaves, and, possibly, fruit or nuts.

For this book, *structure is any and all parts that make
up the human body*.

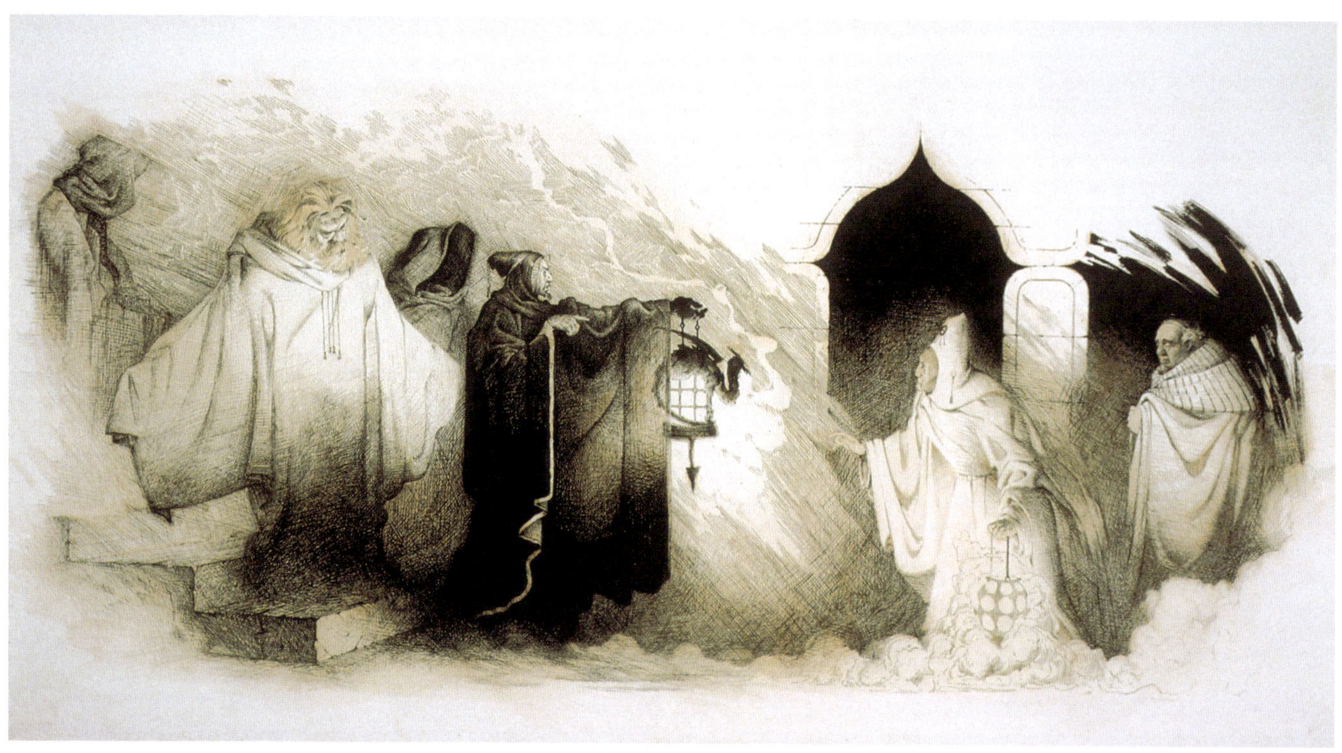

The Sages, c. 1996, by Steve Huston. Brush and ink on Strathmore paper, kid finish. To draw well from your imagination, you must be able to conceive of simple structures in space.

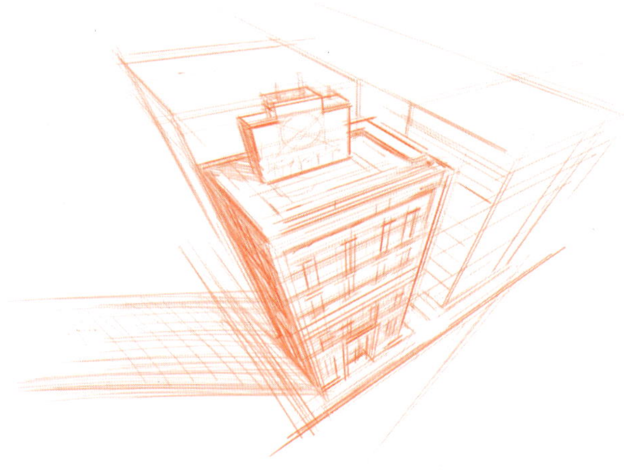

Sometimes the biggest things have the simplest structures. Even the mightiest skyscraper usually is just made of boxes.

Gesture is a different idea. Gesture is the lifeline embedded inside any living form and mimicked in most organic ones. This gestural idea makes your art look natural. You don't need to worry about gesture if you're drawing something like a skyscraper. Everything there is stiff and mechanical. The pieces just stack or lock together on a straight axis. You do still have to worry about those measuring points and vanishing points that happen in perspective, though.

If we're drawing a thumbnail sketch of, for example, a river in a landscape; or an animal; or a breakdown of the light and shadow patterns on a nude; or a study for a fine-art painting; or an aerodynamic jet airplane; or a fantasy illustration; or a thousand other objects, we need to understand something about gesture—and the more we understand, the better. We'll deepen our understanding in chapter 2.

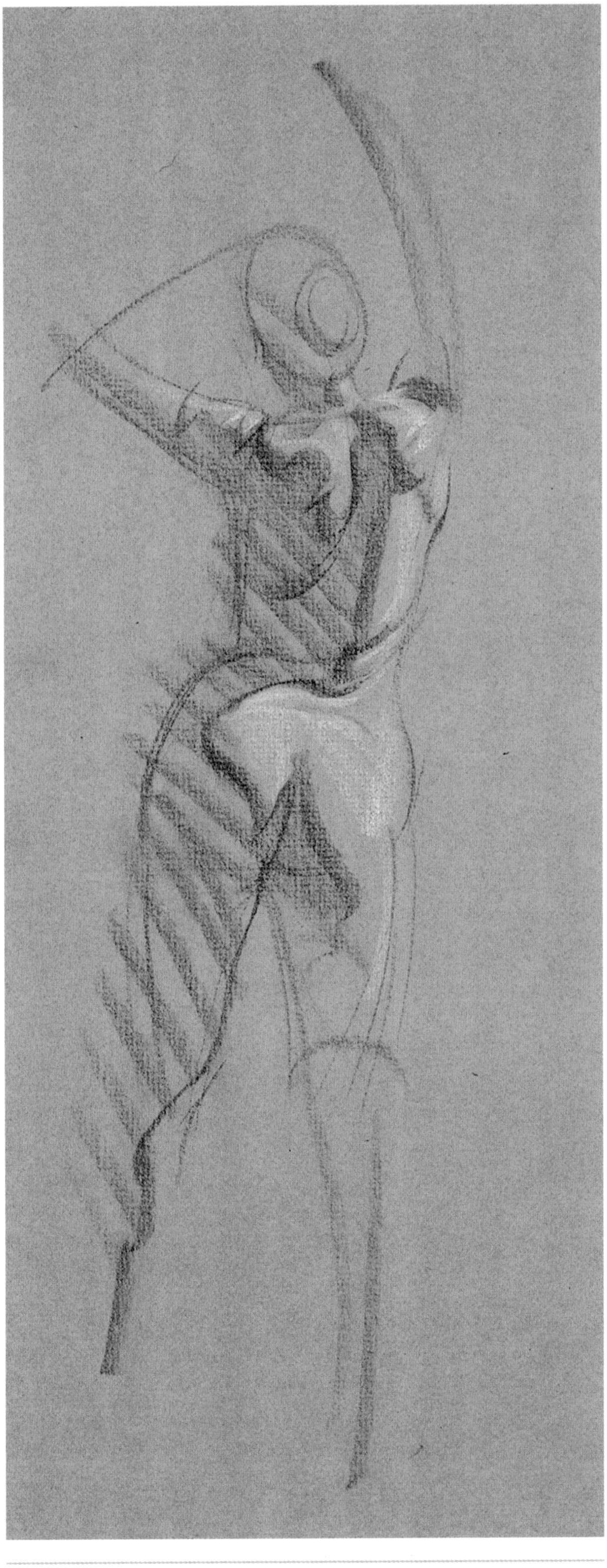

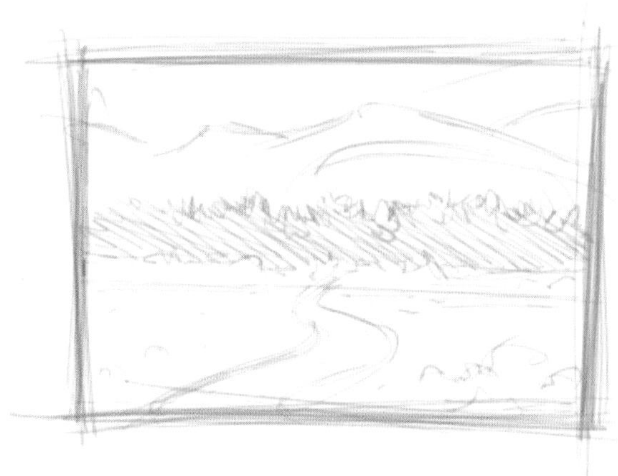

A landscape and a figure are not as different as you might think. Both contain nature's beautiful organic design.

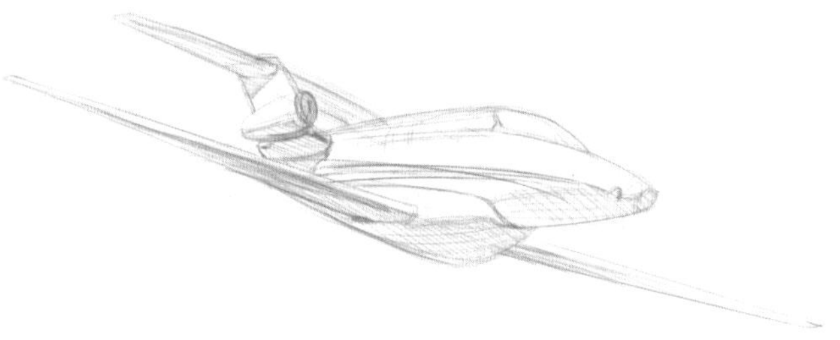

Where do you think engineers get their aerodynamic design ideas?

Every fine figure painting starts with a well-constructed figure.

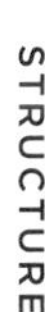

What Is Structure?

Let's take a closer look at structure.

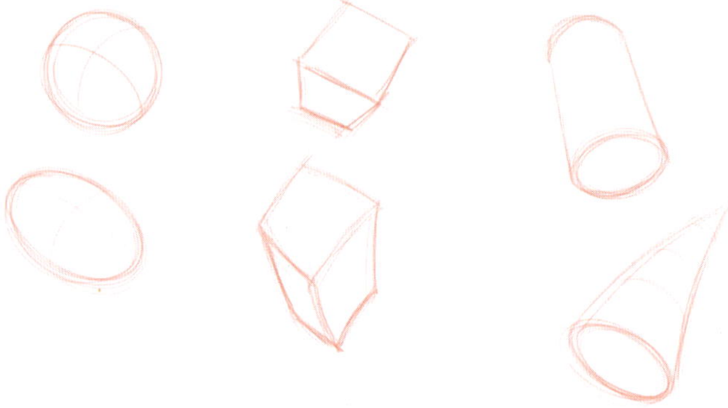

We start with the simplest possible forms.

Structure is the parts and the pieces—the three-dimensional forms. In its simplest state, structure can be reduced to balls, boxes, and tubes. The goal is to translate the world into something manageable. Only when you translate it do you have an idea of its meaning. That's structure. That's the first of our two ideas.

Structure in the human body is defined as the *jointed parts*. For example, from shoulder to elbow, that's the upper arm, from shoulders to waist, that's the rib cage, and so on. We'll get a breakdown of the full figure in chapter 6 (see page 91).

This constructed way of working can be looser or tighter, full figured or small vignettes. It works for thumbnail sketches. It works for monumental mural commissions. Structure is going to become one of your two best friends. You just need a little time to get to know each other. Let me introduce you.

Volume, mass, three-dimensional construction, form, structure: they go by many names. The names don't matter. The point is to get the idea onto the paper as simply and easily as possible, to stay in control, and to make it work for you on whatever level you need it to work. Think of it as the scaffold on which to hang your designs and rendering techniques.

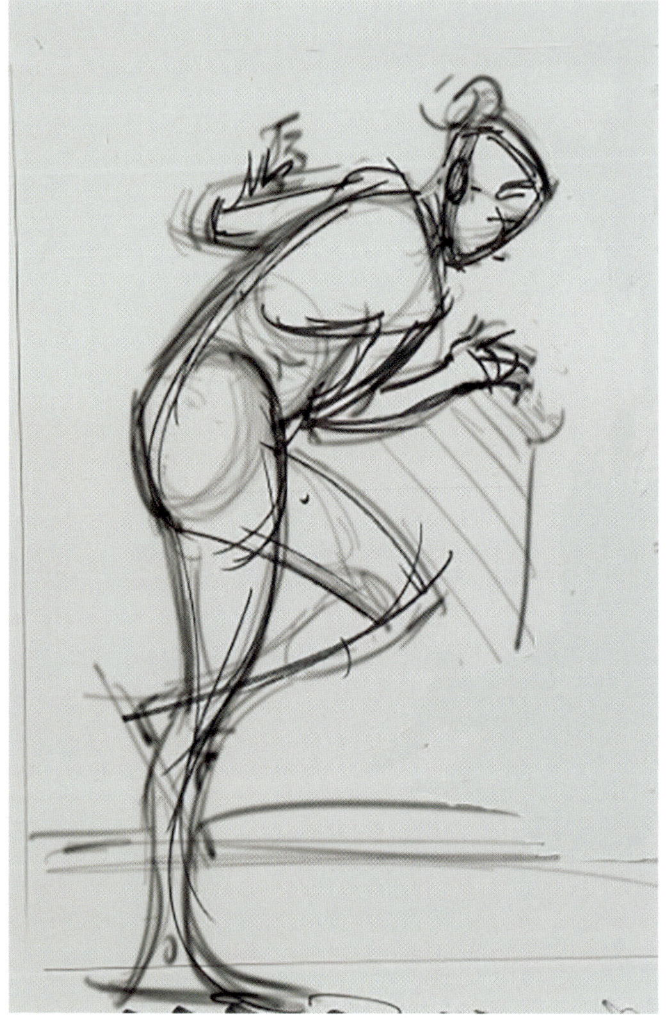

In just a few lines, we want to find all the essential elements that make up a specific pose and even the type of model in that pose.

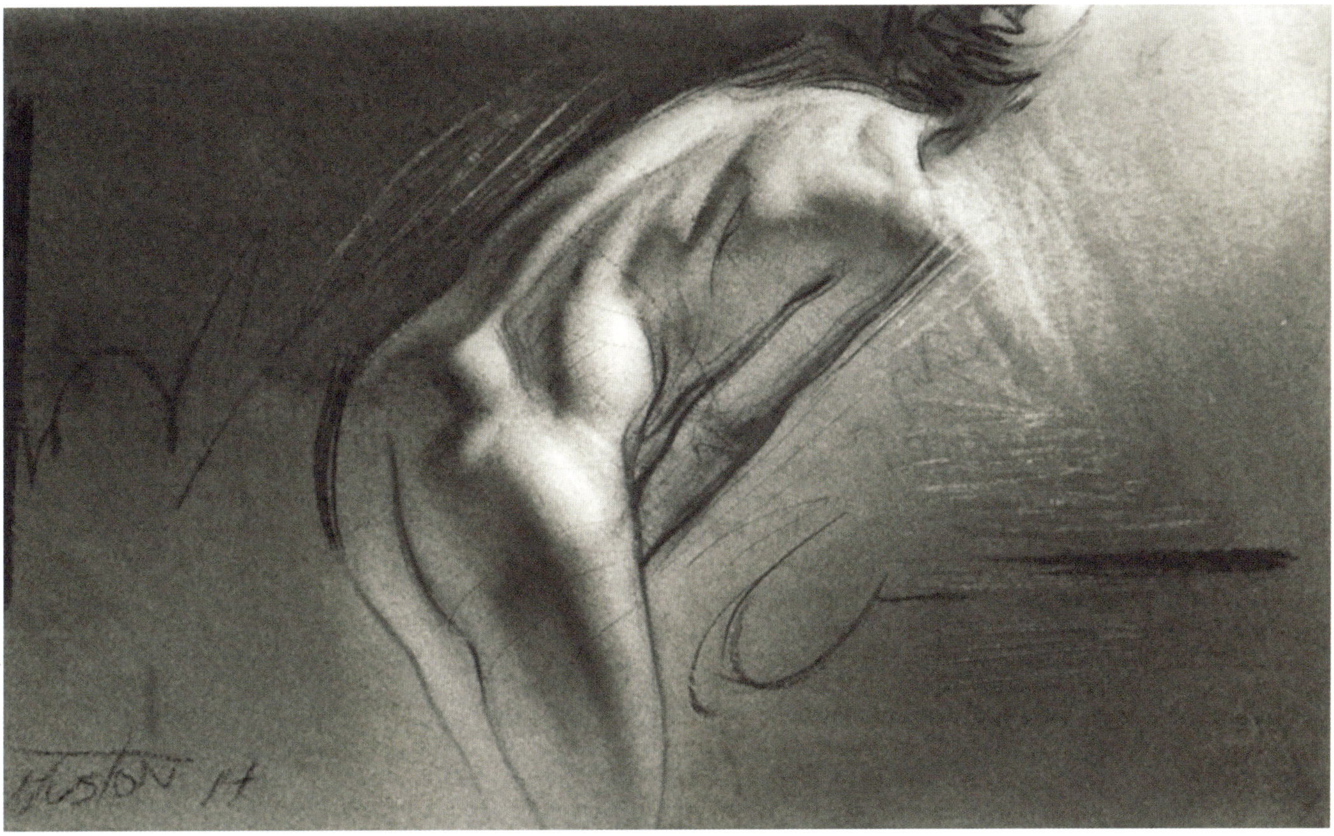

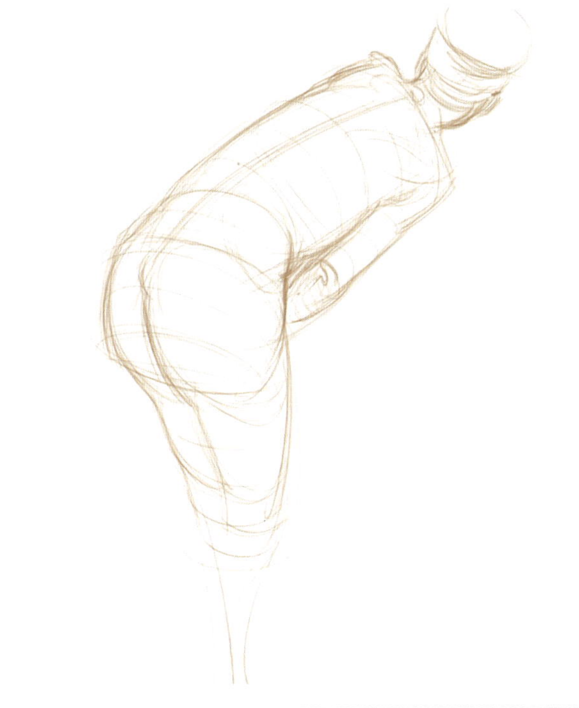

Figure Drawing, c. 2002, by Steve Huston. Alphacolor and Conté chalk on Strathmore, Bristol finish. It comes down to the fact that we won't master this with any kind of consistency . . .

. . . unless we start with something like this.

Dimension

Here's what three-dimensional structure means when working on flat paper: If the marks made on the paper move the viewer's eye over the form, then she feels a solid three-dimensional structure. Ideally, every mark we make shows the viewer structure (or, as we'll see in the next chapter, gesture). The good news is this is a lot easier than it sounds.

Turkey fingers don't work so well, do they? They lay flat because our eye goes around the finger shapes like a shadow on the wall instead of over them, as that simple cylinder drawing demonstrates.

Constructed forms automatically feel three dimensional when done well because the lines move over the form. Another way to think of it is that every mark we make, whether carefully rendered or loosely sketched, should act as a visual arrow. The more conscious we are of where the arrows point, the more successful our drawings will be in terms of structure (and eventually gesture).

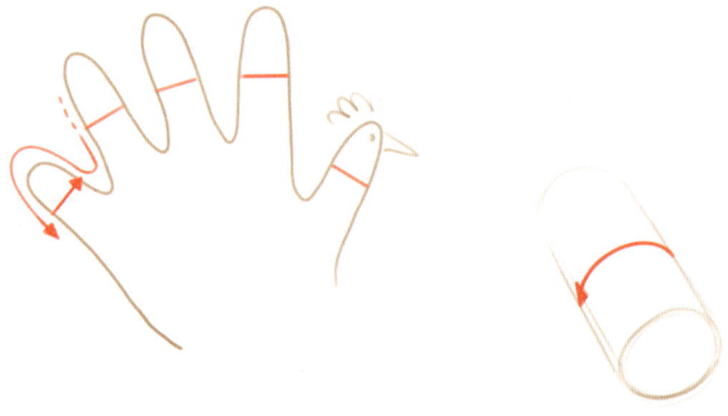

Structure = movement over the form.

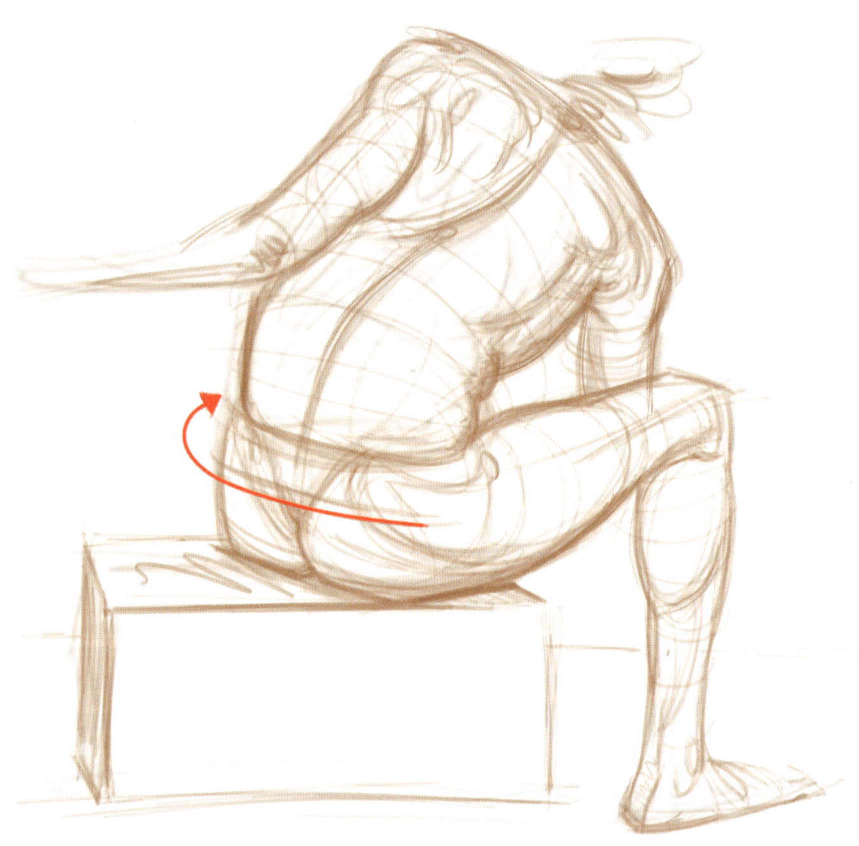

Every line we make is a visual arrow.

The Three Basic Forms

Let's look more carefully at our three constructed forms:

1. The sphere

2. The tube

3. The box

Variations of these foundational structures replace and simplify the tricky anatomy of the human body, making what's very complex simpler.

Try it. If you need to, reread the previous section to review the principles of mark making.

With practice, we can draw anything with this method. Using ever-greater variations of our three fundamental forms, we'll become ever more comfortable in the see-ing and translating process called "drawing."

If you draw a tube like I do, you start with the length, add the width, and then build on the ends. We draw the two-dimensional sides and the three-dimensional ends (the end of the tube is the "movement over the form" idea). Until we build those ends onto the constructed shape, it won't move the viewer's eye over the volume. It lies flat, incomplete.

When we work with complicated subjects such as the human figure, we will complete each structure before adding a new one.

I'll leave you to work through the other forms. But keep in mind, just as with balls and eggs, you can draw tubes and boxes without ever drawing a straight line. This is key to drawing organic forms such as the human body (more in chapter 2, see page 37).

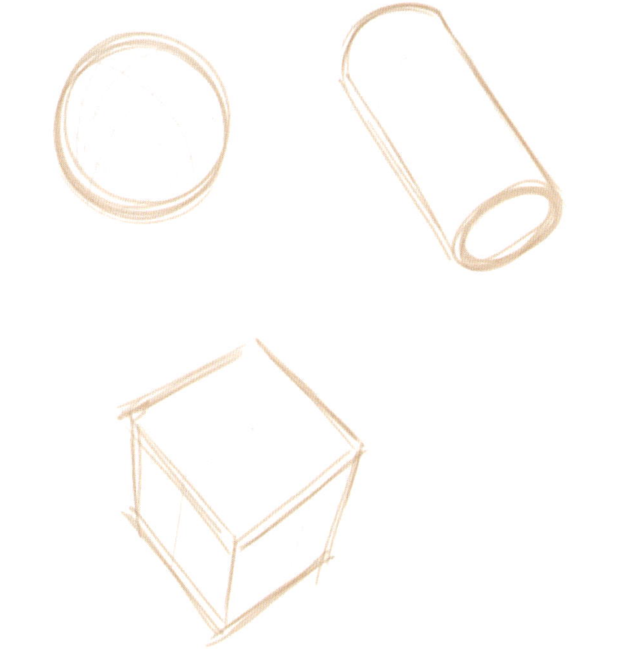

The three basic forms.

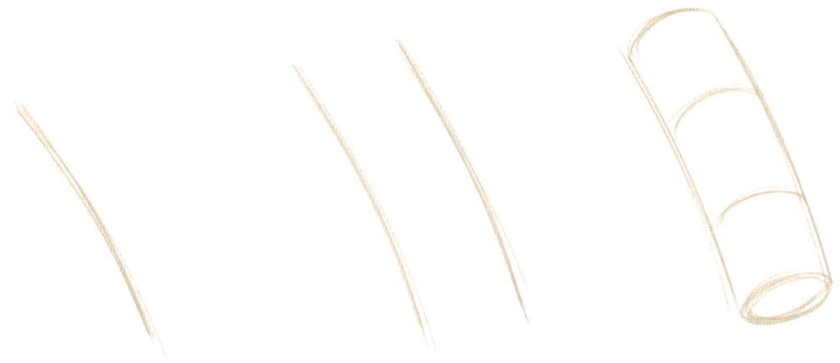

Building the ends onto the constructed shape moves the viewer's eye over the volume.

A reminder: Notice how I've drawn several lines for each step in constructing my shape. This slows me down and allows me to really see the whole structure I'm drawing and not get lost in random mark making, which is very important to avoid but very easy to get sucked into.

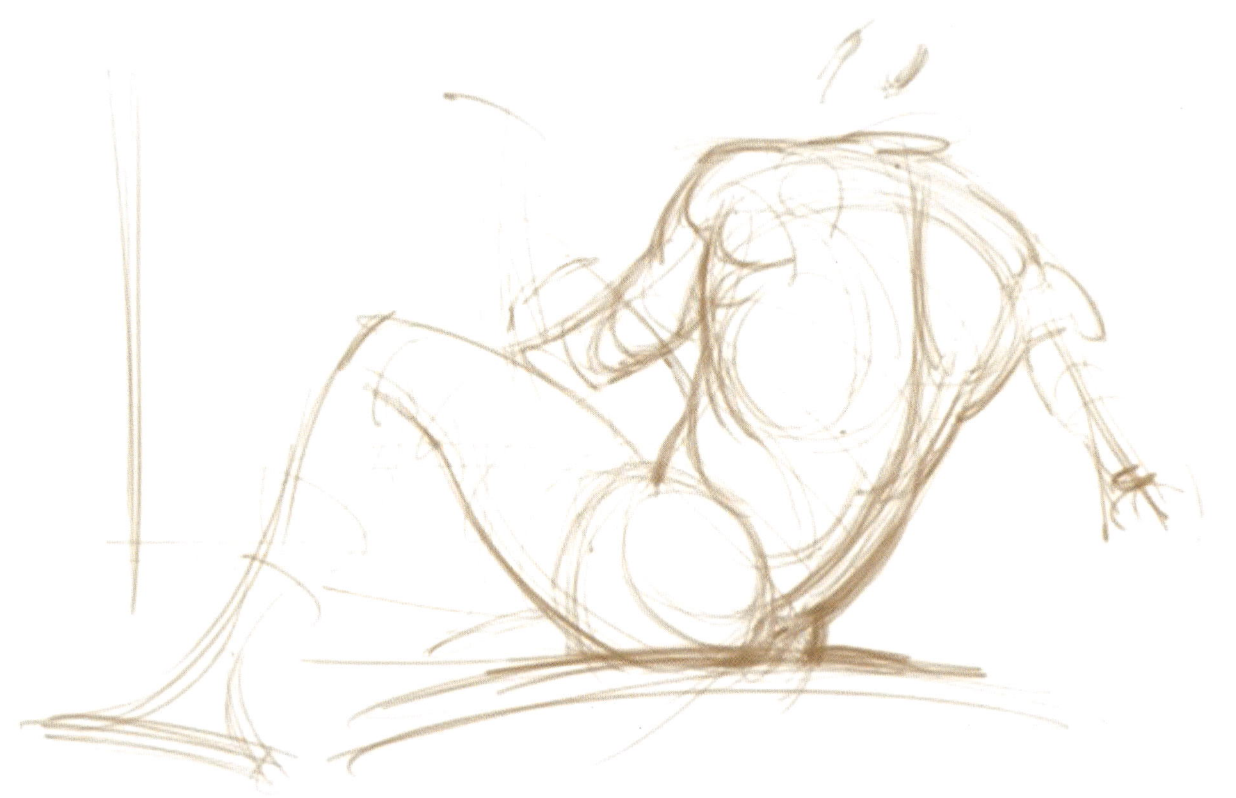

Complete each structure before moving on. When you become a master, take any shortcuts you want.

ADVANTAGES OF DRAWING THE WORLD WITH SIMPLE CONSTRUCTED FORMS

- We get our compositions or underlying drawing down quickly. I use this very method to draw bigger-than-life heroic figures on the canvas before I paint.

- We can design and redesign various elements to our heart's content, making them more fluid, more streamlined, more heroic, more challenging, or more of any quality you want to instill in your art.

- Drawing like this allows you to animate the object. That's right—this is the style of choice for almost every animation artist in the world. How else are you going to draw a character 40,000 times in incrementally different positions and get it right? And even if, like me, you aren't an animator, you can "animate" your drawing into slightly or greatly more dynamic poses.

- And, probably most important for beginners, the construction lines act as the visual arrows critical to moving the viewer's eye over the parts in exactly the way needed. They become the road map for our rendering. They give immediate control and excellent criteria for correcting a mistake.

Keep in mind that *two-dimensional structure* is just as valid an idea as *three-dimensional (3-D) structure*. We are focusing on 3-D here because it gives us a better understanding of how to translate the world and more control over rendering it in a convincing manner.

Choosing the Right Forms

We now have a sense of how to draw a beginning structure and why it's important. So, how do we choose the right structure for the right job? After all, there are nearly endless variations of our three basic structures (sphere, tube, and box).

Which, exactly, are the best choices for any particular drawing?

When should we use, say, a tube instead of a sphere? And just what kind of tube should it be? Long? Short? Tapered into a cone? Bent like a garden hose?

If that sounds a bit intimidating, it's really not. We just reduce it to two criteria: *simple* yet *characteristic*. Here's what that means.

SIMPLE

We want to pick the simplest possible form we can. Simple is simply easier—not easy. Think of it this way: Would you rather draw the orbicularis oculi, the zygomatic arch, the corrugator muscles, and a whole lot of other tongue-twisting anatomical features, or would you rather draw a ball in a hole? That is your choice when tackling the eye.

Here's what else simple does for us:

Simple is quick. That's great for deadlines or for people with short attention spans. It's also great for seeing whether you're starting your drawing well. If it's not working, it's a relatively quick fix to replace the problem area with another simple solution.

Simple allows us to construct anything with the same methods and principles. For example, it's interesting to think Ratty and Mole (top) are built through the same principles as Apollonios's *Belvedere Torso* at right.

Think about it. Rubens "animated" his models into dynamic positions just as comic book draftsmen, illustrators, and most other action- or movement-based artists do using the same principles. That sums up my thoughts on simple.

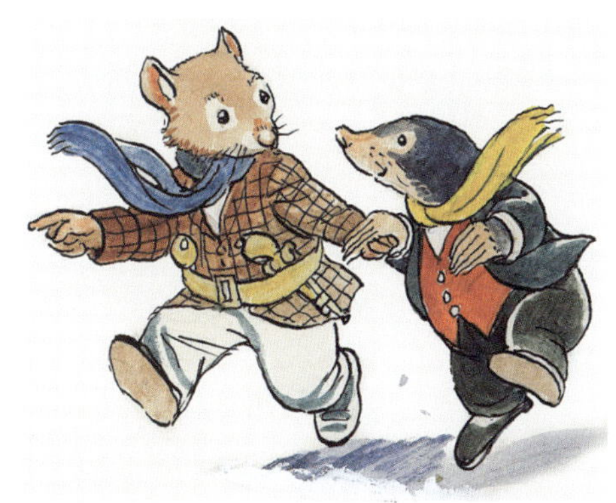

Ratty and Mole from *The Wind in the Willows*, twentieth century, Philip Mendoza (1898–1973). Private collection/*Look and Learn*/Bridgeman Images.

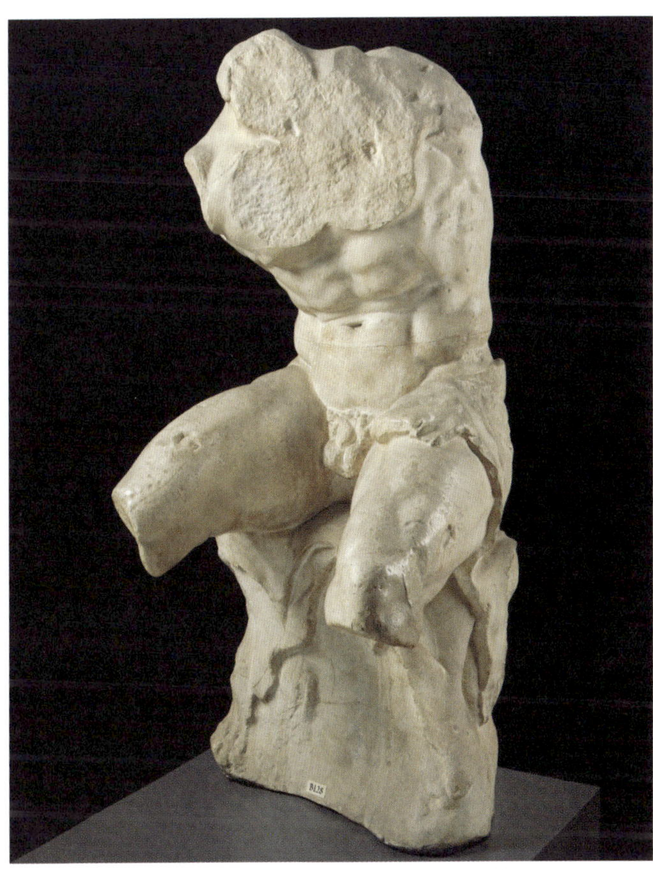

Cast of the *Belvedere Torso*, original by Apollonius (first century BCE). Plaster. University of Oxford, UK/Bridgeman Images.

CHARACTERISTIC

Characteristic is the second criteria. If simple were the only issue, we'd just draw snowmen. But we want the structure we choose for the head, or the fingers, or whatever, to be as characteristic as possible. Finding structures characteristic of what the finished product will be ensures we're on the right track. It means far less work to finish it off in whatever medium we're working. It makes sure, right away, that our parts fit together well. Fitting together, by the way, is also important for gesture, but I'm getting ahead of myself.

Take a brief look back at some of the drawings I did and look more carefully at the simple yet characteristic forms used.

Notice this Luca Cambiaso drawing is simple but not always characteristic. Something this oversimplified is fine for designing a composition—including point of view, as Cambiaso intended—but not for building figures to be rendered in charcoal, paint, or clay.

It is so meticulous that, to begin a drawing with this much detail, it is simply (pun intended) overwhelming. The other thing about focusing on too much detail too soon is it leads you to copy the subject rather than *translate* it. And then, there goes the underlying idea. This highly anatomical drawing by Albinus is certainly characteristic, but again, a little too much.

Avoid these kinds of radical stylizations or overwhelming details until you've mastered the *simple yet characteristic* principle.

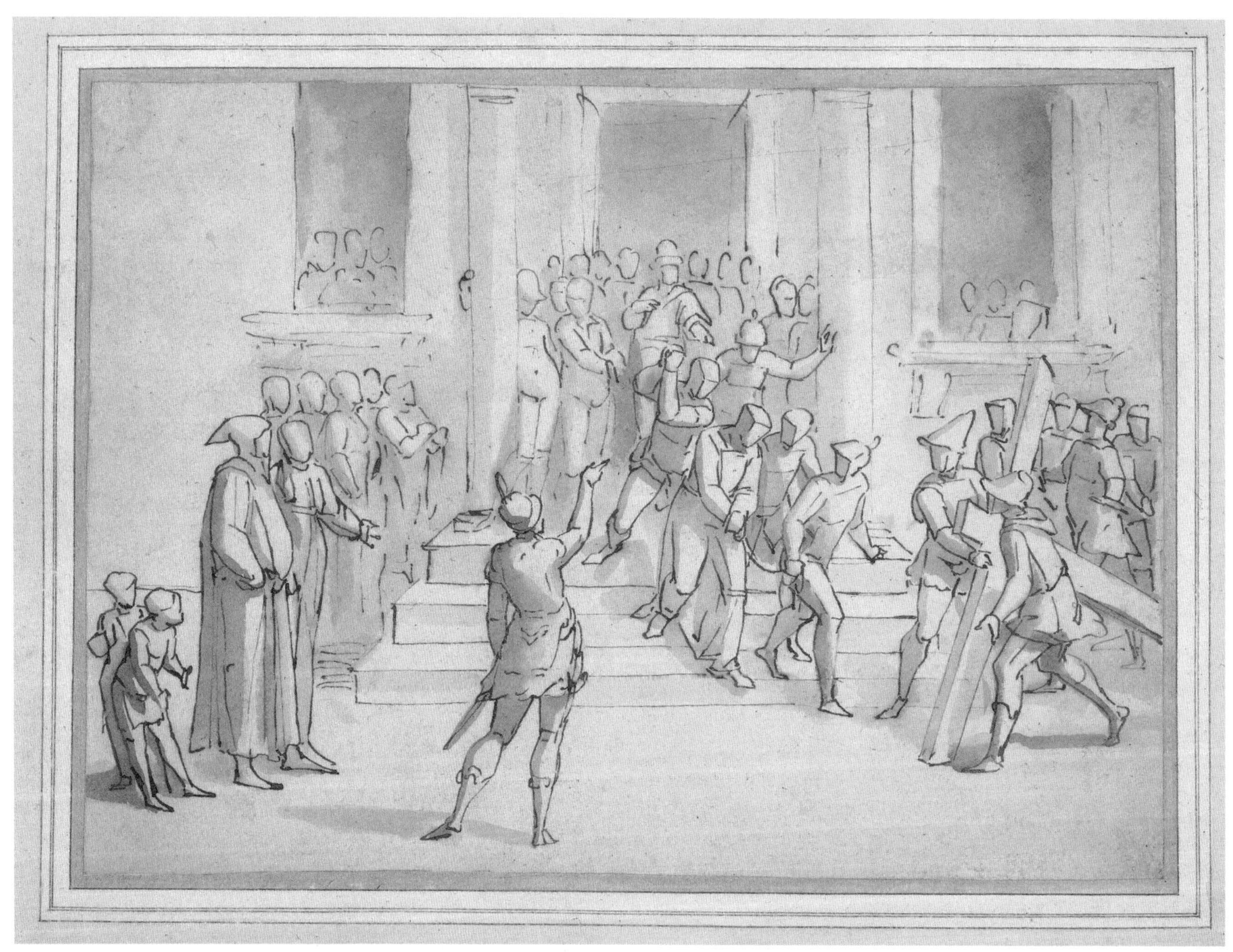

Christ Led Away, sixteenth century, Luca Cambiaso (1527–1585). Pen and ink with wash. National Museums, Liverpool/Bridgeman Images. Cambiaso is famous for his box-head compositions. We want to take things a bit further for our purposes.

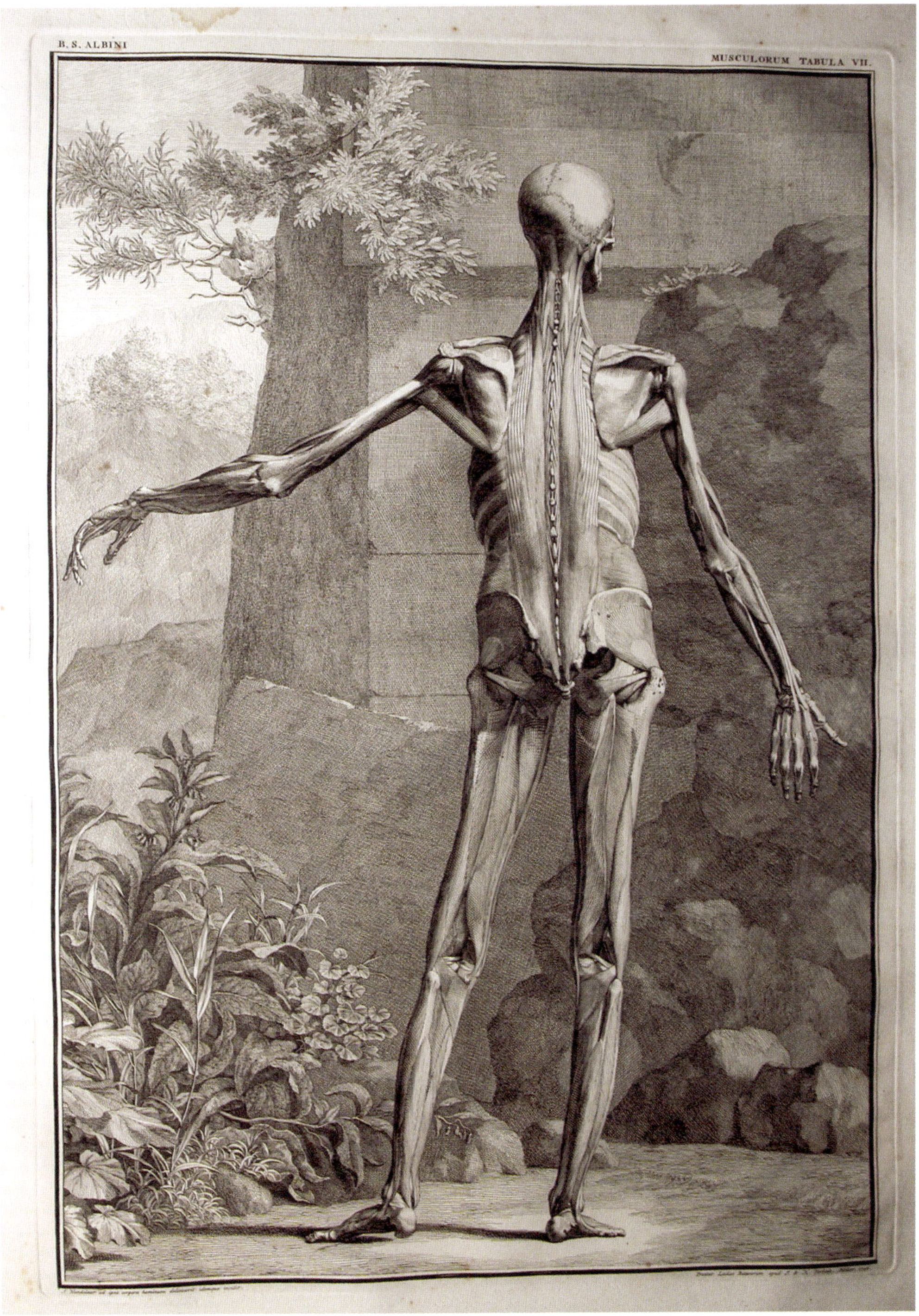

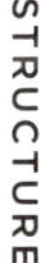

Musculature, illustration from *Tabulae sceleti et musculorum corporis humani*, 1741, by Bernhard Siegfried Albinus (1697–1770), published by J. & H. Verbeek, bibliop., Netherlands. Engraving. Humboldt University of Berlin/Bridgeman Images.

None of the great artists or art movements copied nature. In fact, Albinus was criticized for letting the engraver put in fanciful backgrounds. Their unique vision is why we recognize their work. It's why they had style! All of that embodies the simple yet characteristic principle. Each of us will do it differently, and that is a good thing.

OLD MASTER *study*

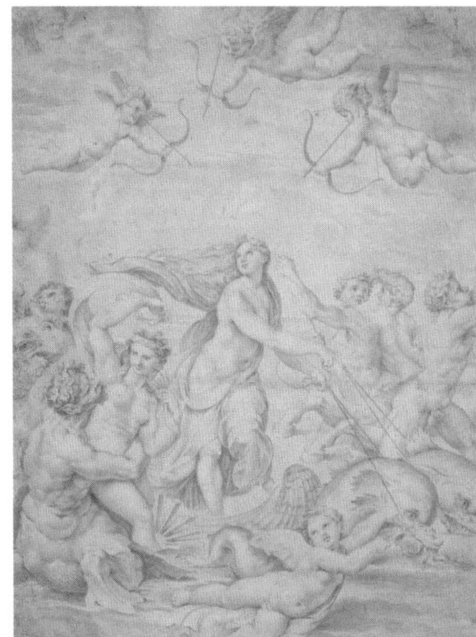

The Triumph of Galatea, sixteenth century, Raphael (Raffaello Sanzio of Urbino) (1483–1520) (after). Red chalk on pale buff paper. University of Oxford, UK/ Bridgeman Images. These simple yet characteristic choices are just right.

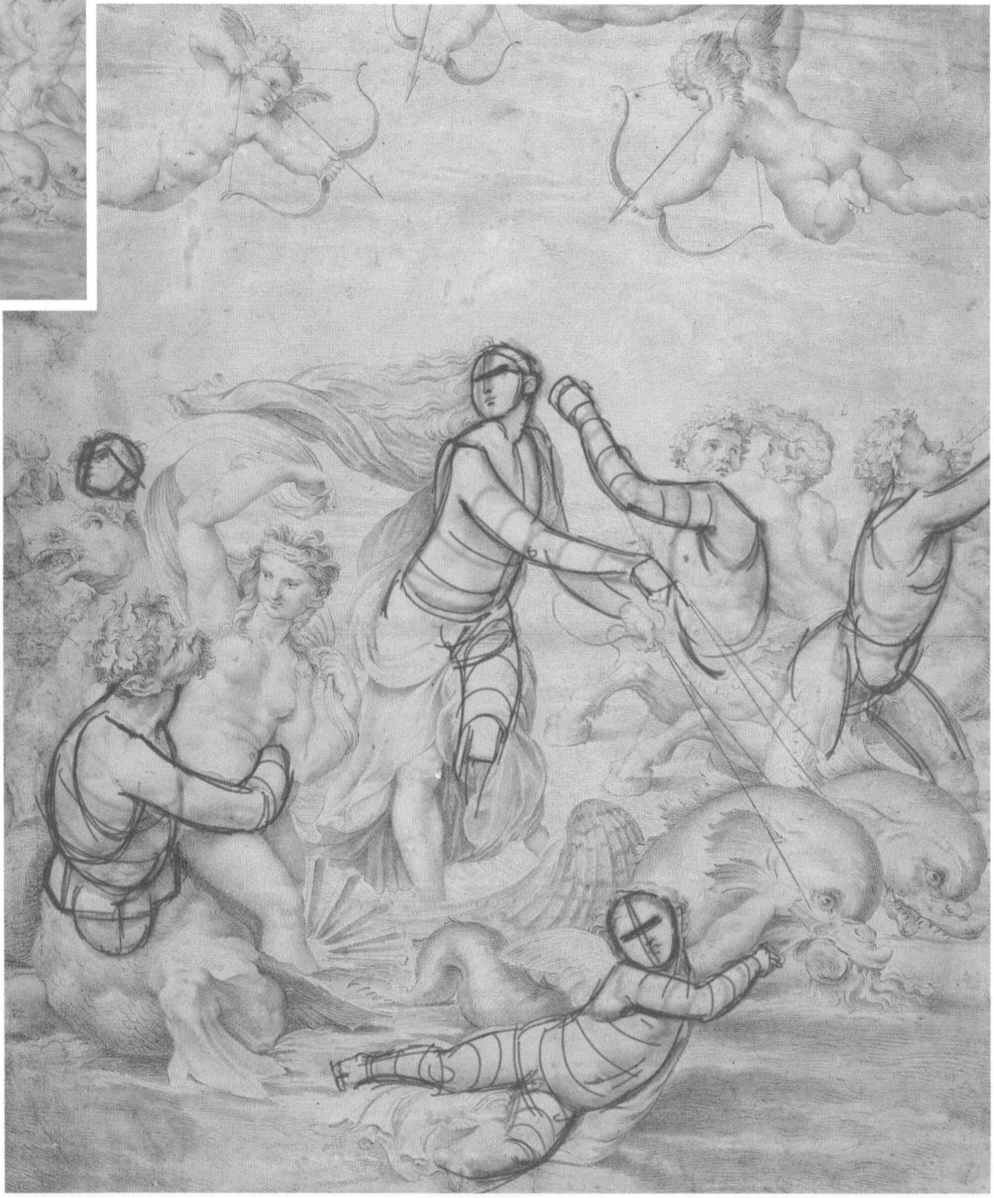

On these final pages in each chapter, we will closely examine an Old Master piece. Through the line work that I've added on top of each painting, you can see how our fundamental concepts for drawing apply. On the facing pages, you'll find suggested practice exercises that will help you apply our concepts to your work. We begin with a wonderful drawing by Raphael Sanzio.

I've marked off just a few of the balls, boxes, and tubes in Raphael's lovely composition. Can you find others by laying tracing paper over it?

GIVE IT A TRY: *Exercise 1*

Lay tracing paper over this
drawing and copy the simple
boxes, balls, or tubes. Find
the ones I didn't. Then, try
it with the Old Masters. See
whether you can find the
simple structural solutions
for all that stuff our good
friend Mr. Sanzio tossed
our way.

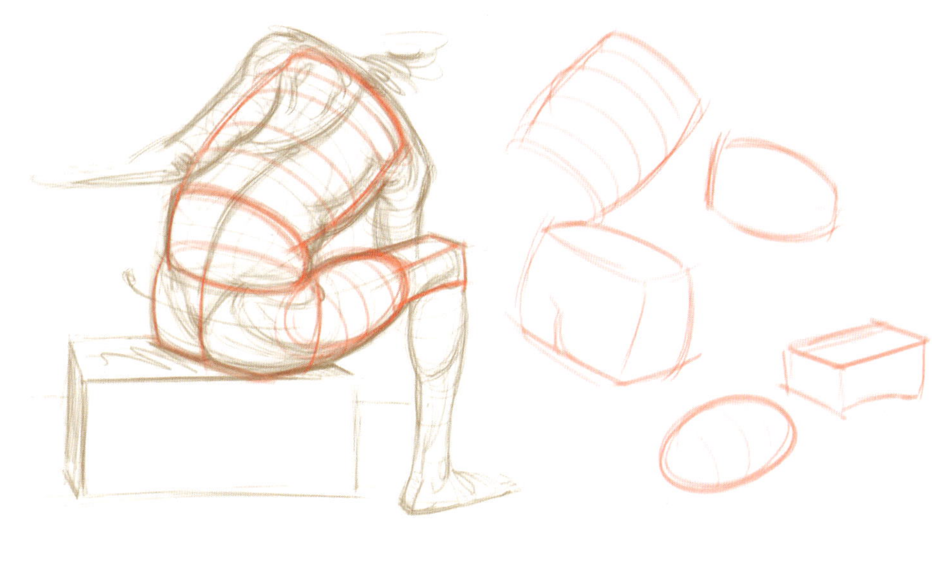

A well-constructed figure happens one step at a time.

GIVE IT A TRY: *Exercise 2*

Start a sketchbook drawing everyday objects around the house or office.

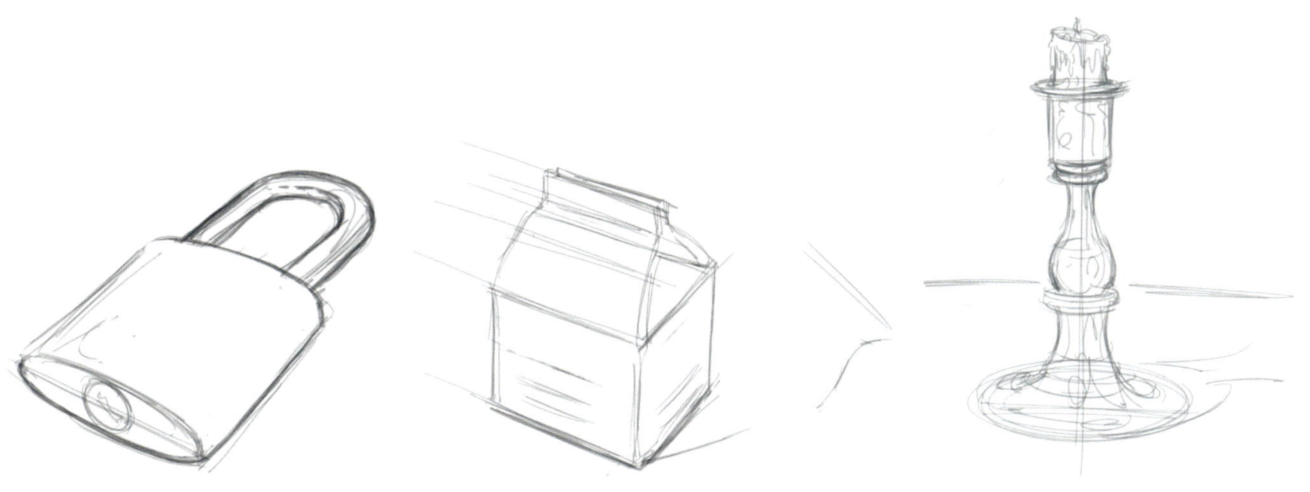

Almost anything is easier to draw than the human figure, but we get whatever we choose to draw on the page using the same method.

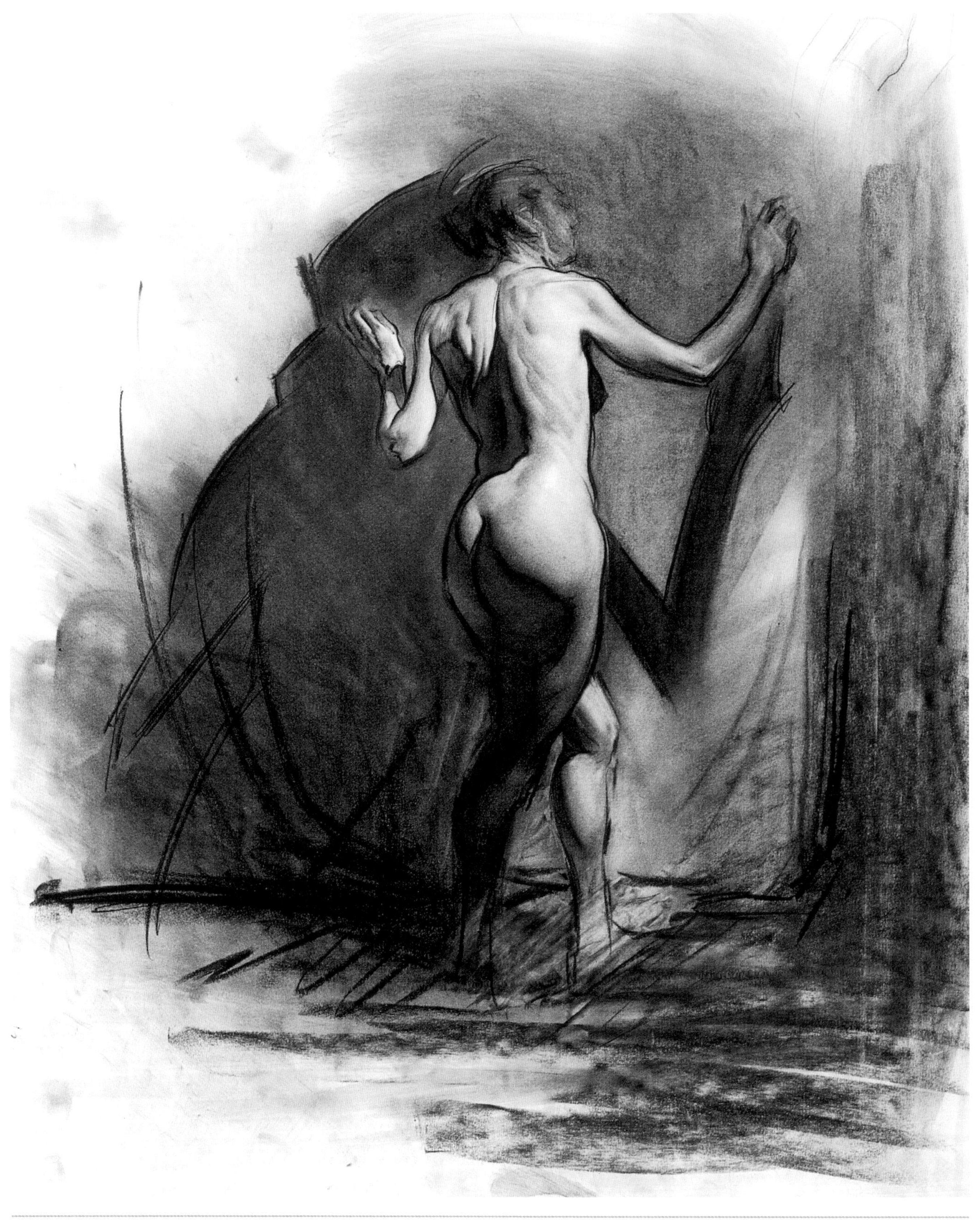

Lynn, c. 2004, by Steve Huston. Alphacolor and Conté chalk on Strathmore, Bristol finish. There's nothing more beautiful than a figure designed off a few graceful curves.

2 | BASIC GESTURE

"Structure and gesture" are fancy ways of saying the parts and the relationship between the parts. If you hold on to those two ideas, if you use them to guide the marks you make, you will execute exceptional drawings. If. Just if.

Structure is Idea 1 (see chapter 1, page 23). Gesture is Idea 2, which we focus on here.

We started with structure because it's easier than gesture. Gesture is more fundamental and more important than the simple-yet-characteristic structure we might choose. Gesture is the connection, the relationship between the shapes. Gesture is the lifeline. It keeps our drawings from looking stiff, mechanical, and pieced together. It's what gives the subject a lively and organic quality. By lively and organic, I simply mean drawing structures with long axis curves. We'll dig deep into this shortly.

Why is the curved quality of gesture so difficult and so critical? It's difficult, among other reasons, because it's sneaky. No viewers, and precious few artists, can actually explain the idea of gesture. It's like the rhythms of a fine bass guitarist. We just feel it, yet, it's critical. It's the only way to bring our drawings, paintings, and sculptures alive.

Why must it be curved?

Anything alive is, mainly, water—fluid. The human body is about 60 percent water.

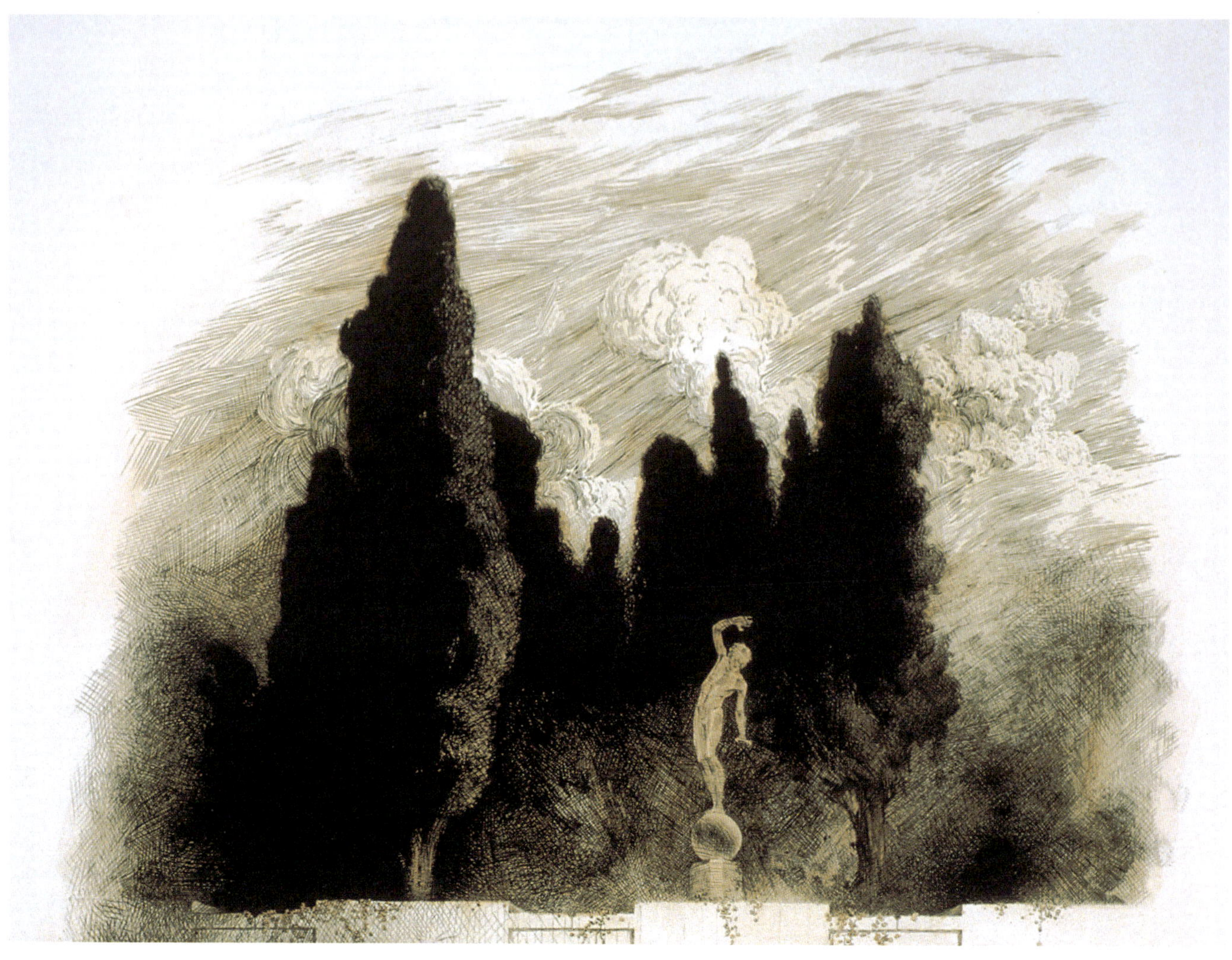

The Idyll, c. 1997, by Steve Huston. Brush and ink on Strathmore, kid finish. The world is full of watery design lines. Just look around.

Every organic thing—rivers, clouds, fire, smoke, drapery, branches, vines and flower petals, rock and soil formations, a blade of grass—has that watery quality. Organic structures evolve, stress, weather, calcify, are subjected to chaos theory and wind shear, and so almost never develop symmetrically. Organic things grow off axis, acquiring that exquisite fluidity: wandering this way and that, surprising and delighting us in their infinite variations. Of course, there are exceptions, but as long as the structure has an asymmetrical design or sits in a dynamic position, it will, in all likelihood, have a long axis curve—a gesture.

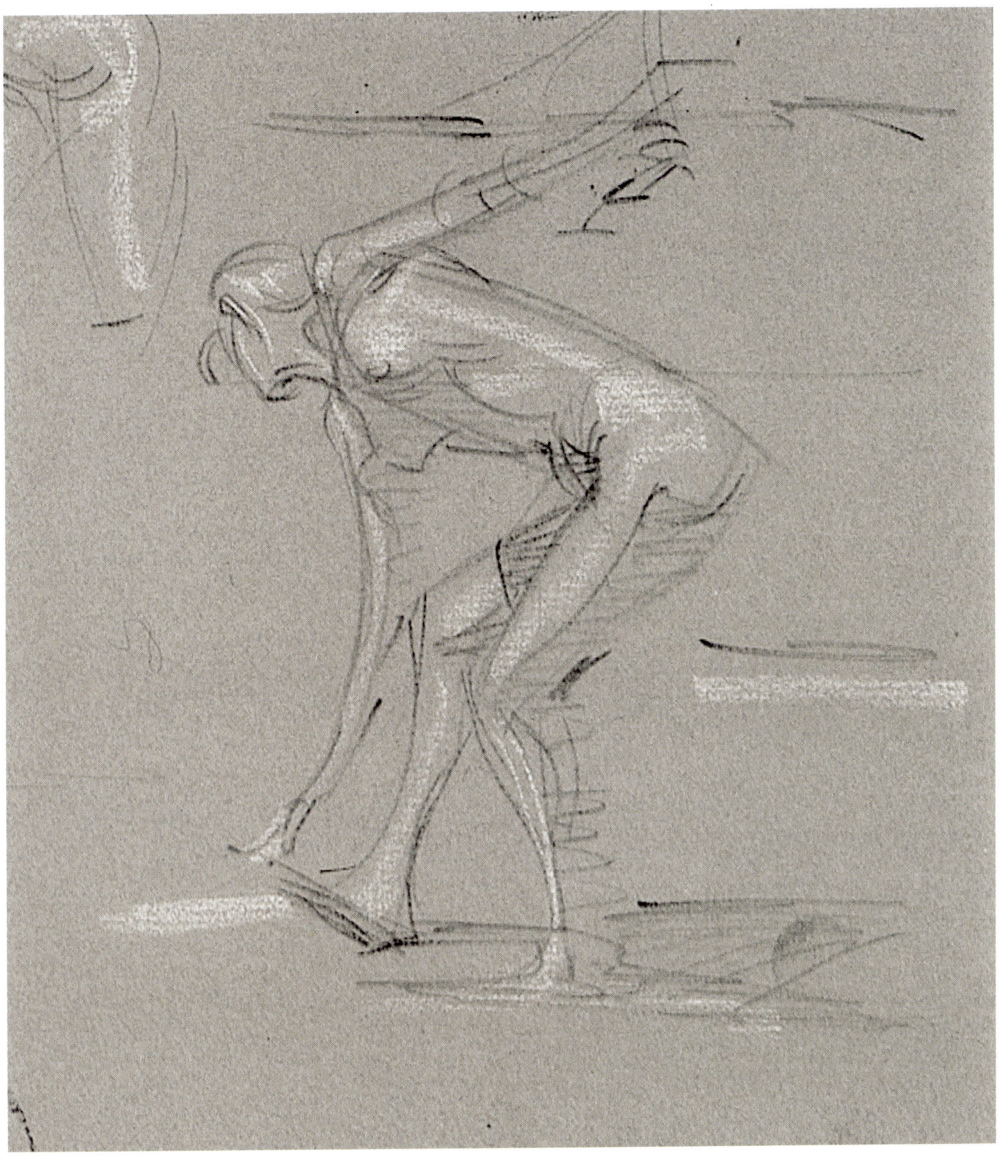

Notice that if I omit some of the lesser structures in this drawing we don't miss them. But, if I fail with even one gesture line, I may lose the essence of the figure.

For artists, this means the essential quality of any living, organic thing is its watery, fluid, graceful, curved design. Assume it has a gesture and find it. See how your forearm rises and falls along its wave-like contour. Look at the curvature of the spine.

The structure itself—the bones, muscles, and sinew of the forearm, the vertebrae of the spine—is inherently imbued with a fluid design, not just wobbly surface variations. These structures show their watery origins.

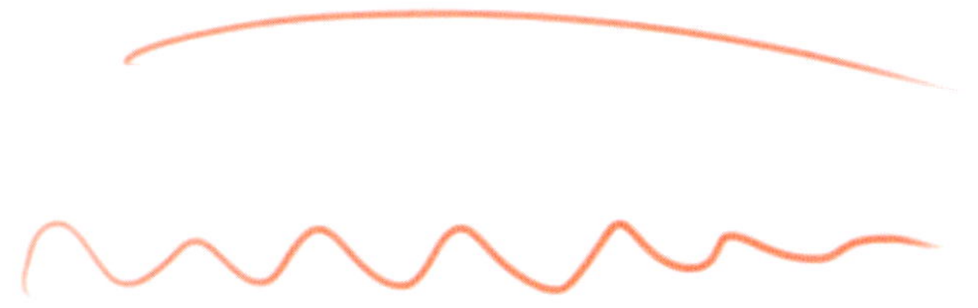

The first line shows a fundamental design. The other line shows interesting variation along what is still, essentially, a straight stretch. We always want to get the big simple ideas down before we indulge in the small, complex ones.

Even in a quick sketch, there can be a lot going on, and gesture shows up in only very sneaky ways. Trying to understand it can be blink-back-the-tears difficult if it's not approached the right way. We can do better. Let's start slowly.

The challenge for us becomes how to keep your carefully structured figure drawing from looking like Frankenstein's monster (top right). Why do you think we call corpses "stiffs?"

On the other hand, if you try to put gesture into your art without a good strategy, you end up with a stick figure (bottom right) that is mainly useless for building on. Gesture needs to accomplish two things:

1. The gesture line must act as the fundamental design line.

2. The gesture line must act as the connecting line, something to which the structure can attach.

Put simply:

gesture = the long axis curve of any structure

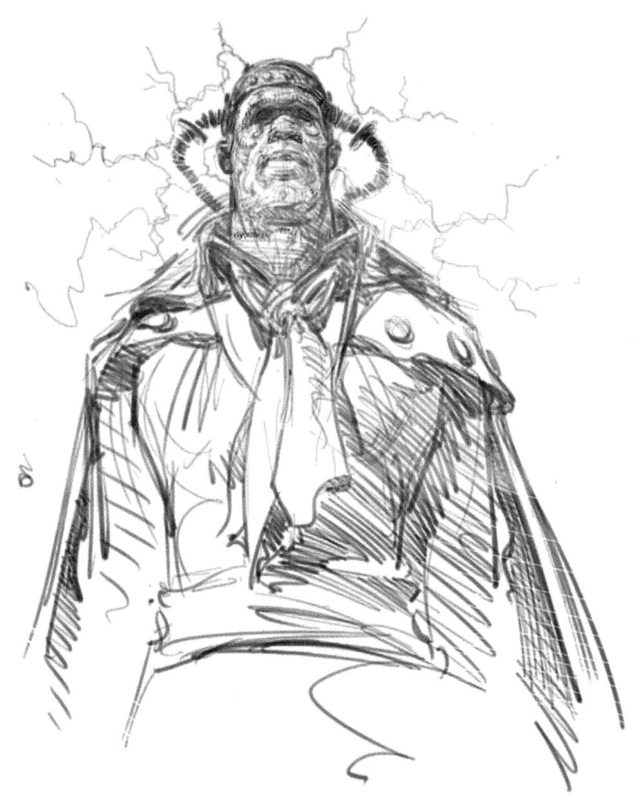

Without doubt, stiffness is the biggest knock against a constructed style—and rightly so.

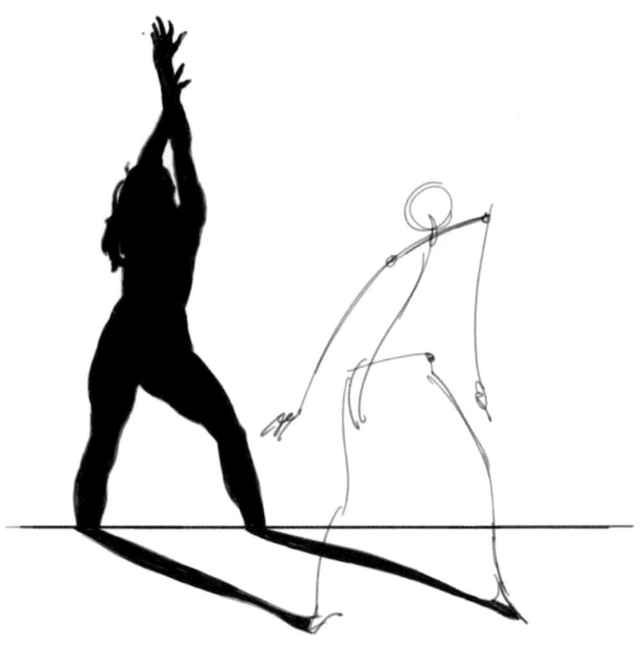

If you follow a two-step process of gesture/structure, you avoid both the stiff structures and stick figures.

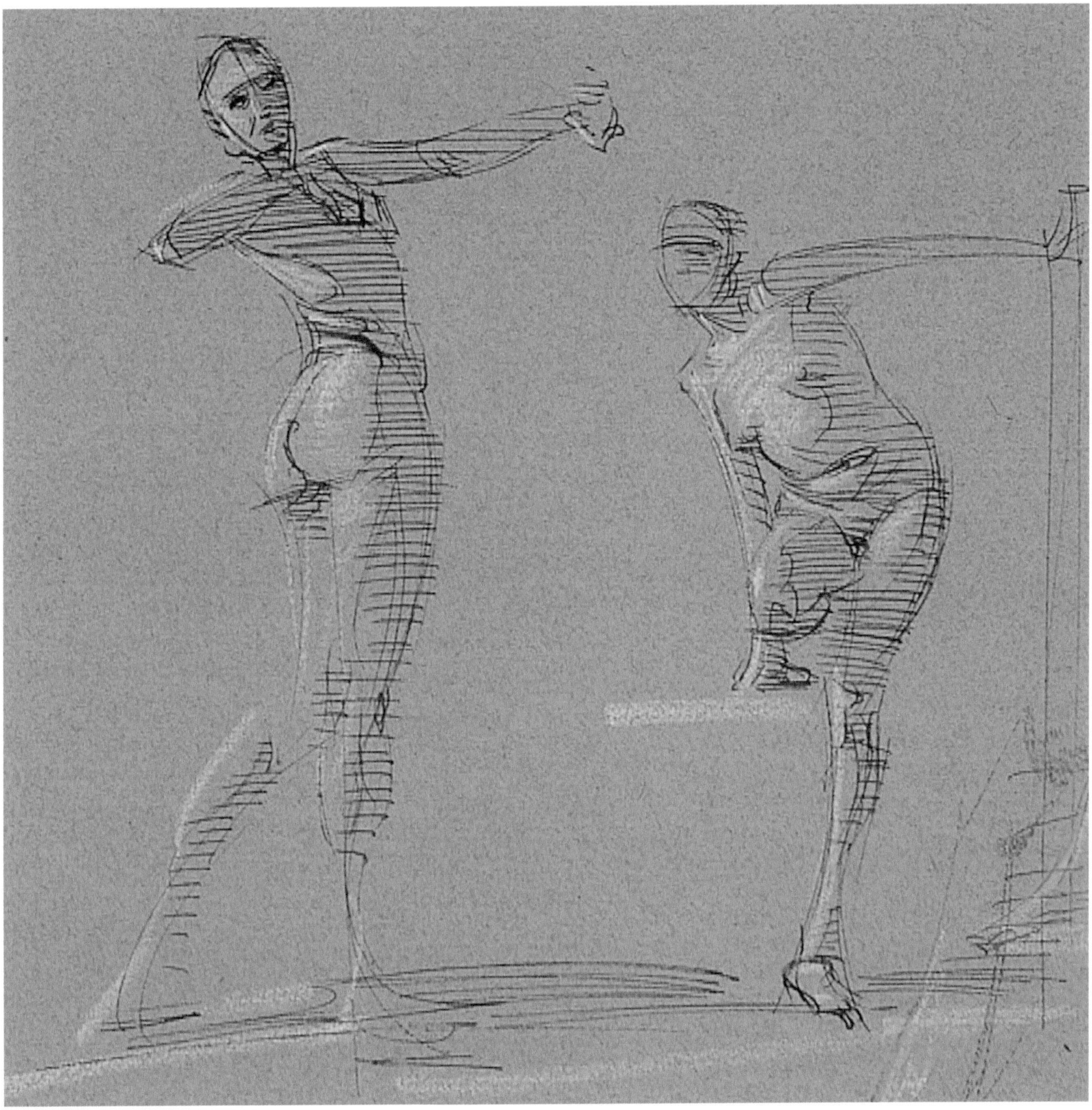

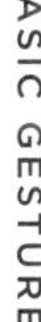

Gesture provides the fundamental design lines.

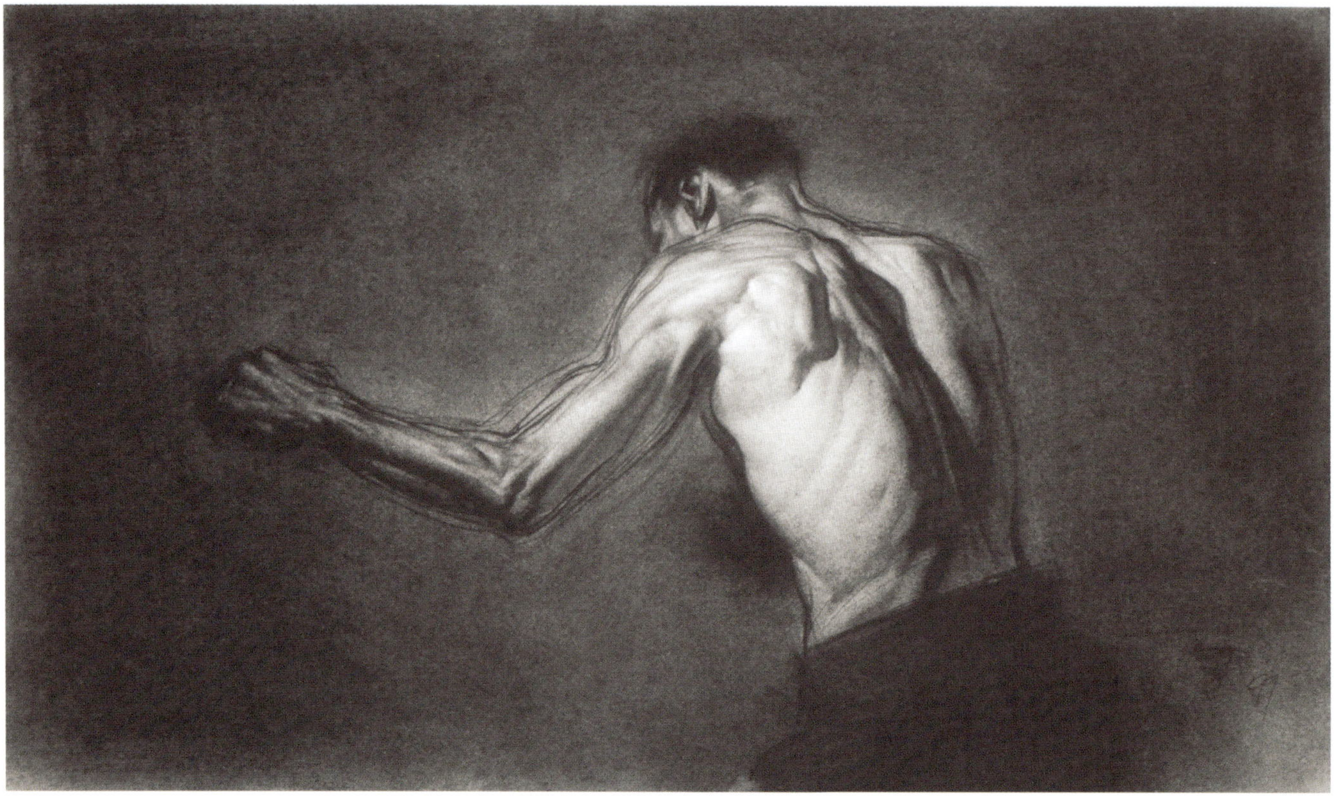

Throwing a Jab, c. 1999, by Steve Huston. Alphacolor and Conté chalk on Strathmore, Bristol finish. No matter how beautifully executed the final product is, the gesture has to be there or the drawing doesn't come alive.

Let's look again at our three basic forms.

Remember how we drew the length, width, and, then, depth to get our tube and box forms? The ball took care of itself in terms of process. For the other two structures, the tube and box, we drew the two-dimensional sides and then the three-dimensional ends. If we simply curve the sides a bit, we have gesture. And, notice, we can draw a box form without ever drawing a straight line. That makes it lively and organic—not mechanical—and that's exactly what we need.

Here are the three possible solutions for getting an overall curved, long axis—a gesture—to any form.

For each curved design, there is a bulging side and a binding side, or rather, one side is convex and the other is concave. I'm defining our gesture as the bulging (convex) side.

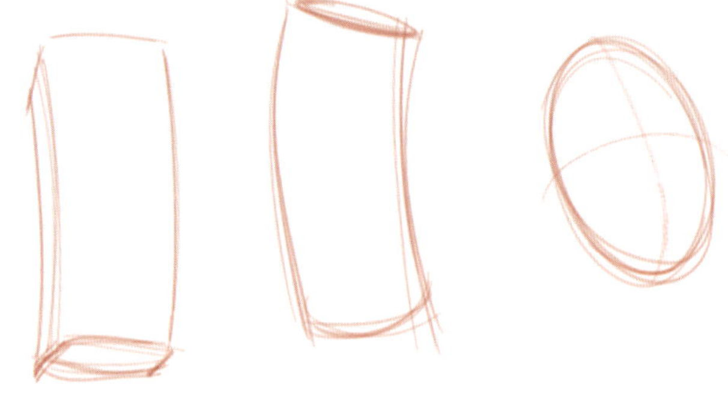

Pay attention to the red lines throughout the rest of the book. Their purpose it to help you map the structural and gestural movements in the various artworks shown.

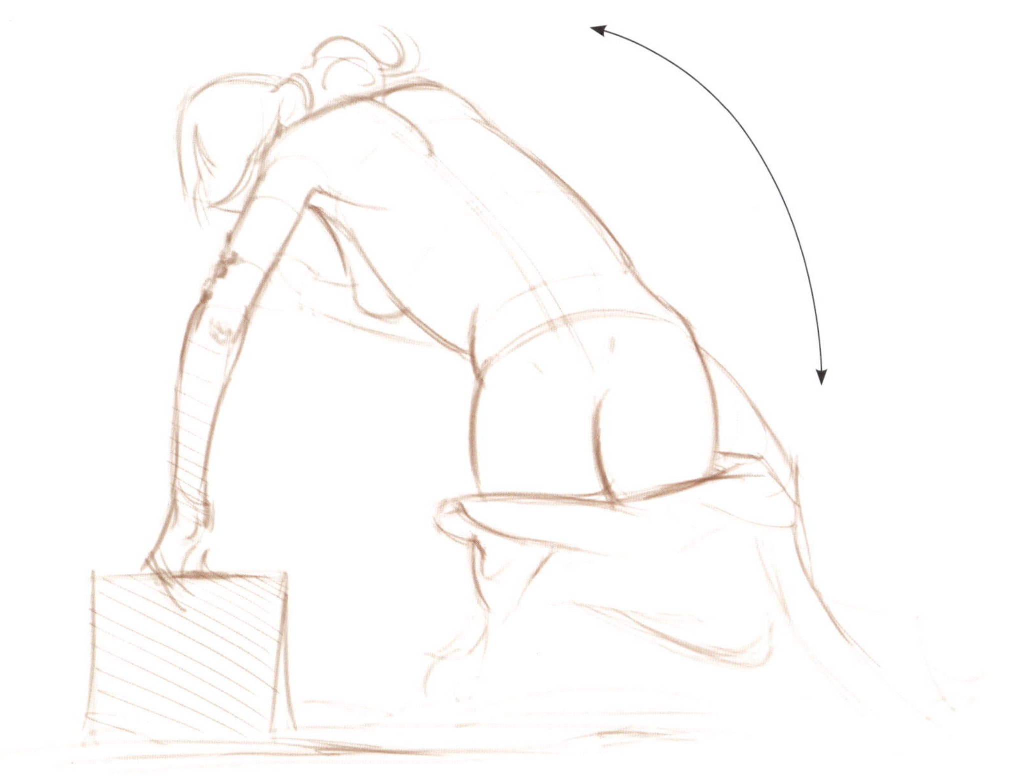

Don't allow the sides to oppose each other unless the structure is an egg shape. That will cancel out your fluid gesture.

Here's another thought about that curved, long axis, or structure: always err on the side of the more dynamic. That means, if the gesture is curved, make it more curved. If the shadow is dark, make it a little darker. Think about it: when writing a comedy, it's better and safer to make the jokes too funny. In fact, can you even imagine coming out of a theater with that complaint?

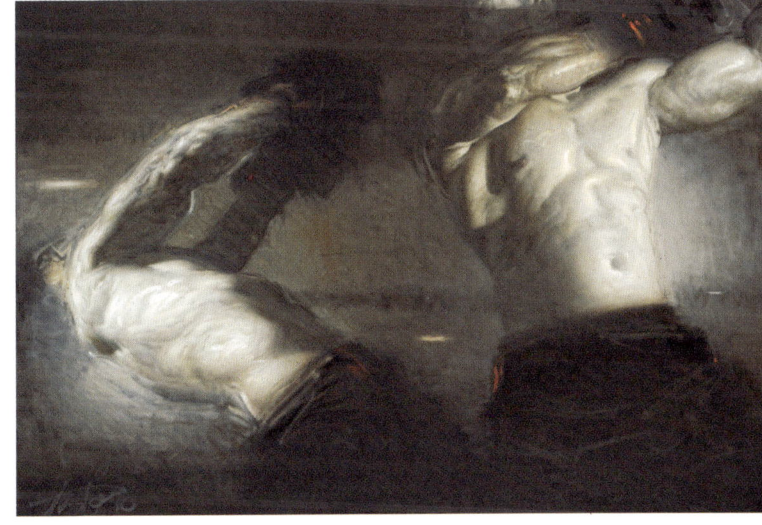

Downed, 2010, by Steve Huston. Oil on canvas. Gesture can bring not only life but action to your work!

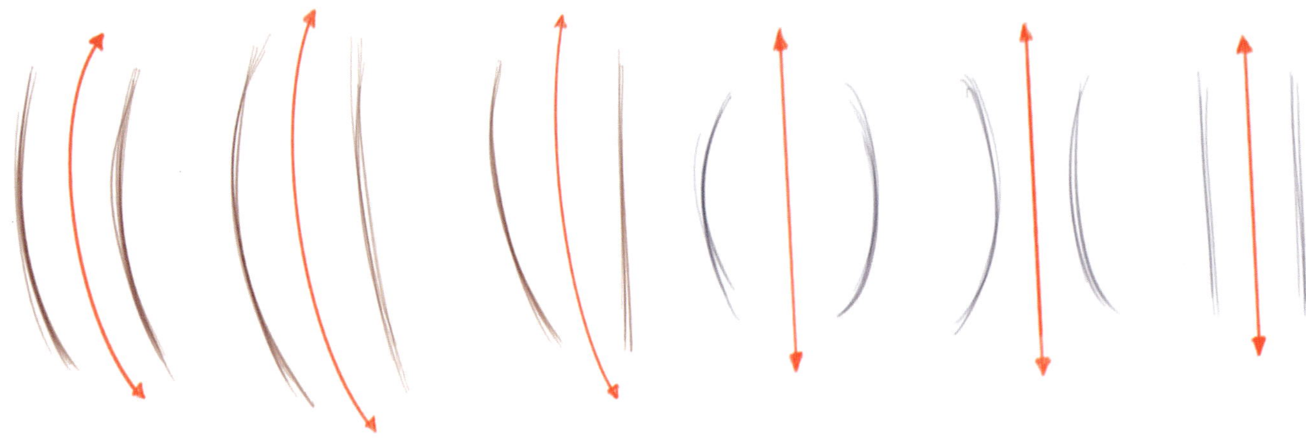

The goal is always to keep the structure while still getting the gesture.

Avoid opposing curves that take up most or all the length of your jointed part.

It is possible to bend a long axis curve too much, but odds are you won't. Ninety-five times out of a hundred, you will stiffen rather than loosen. I can almost guarantee it. And if you do overplay it a bit, even quite a bit, when you add all the lumps and bumps of detail, it will naturally stiffen up anyway. So, for now, live a little. Push that curve!

Where does that leave the ball forms?

Notice there are three ways to get a nice long axis curve. Just choose the one most characteristic of what you see. Any would look suitably alive for the human body or any such organic form.

Remember the straight, red line in that ball shape? If the sides oppose each other, they cancel out the fluid design, and there's no gesture. So oddly enough, the curviest form of all, the ball, is straight and stiff as far as gesture goes.

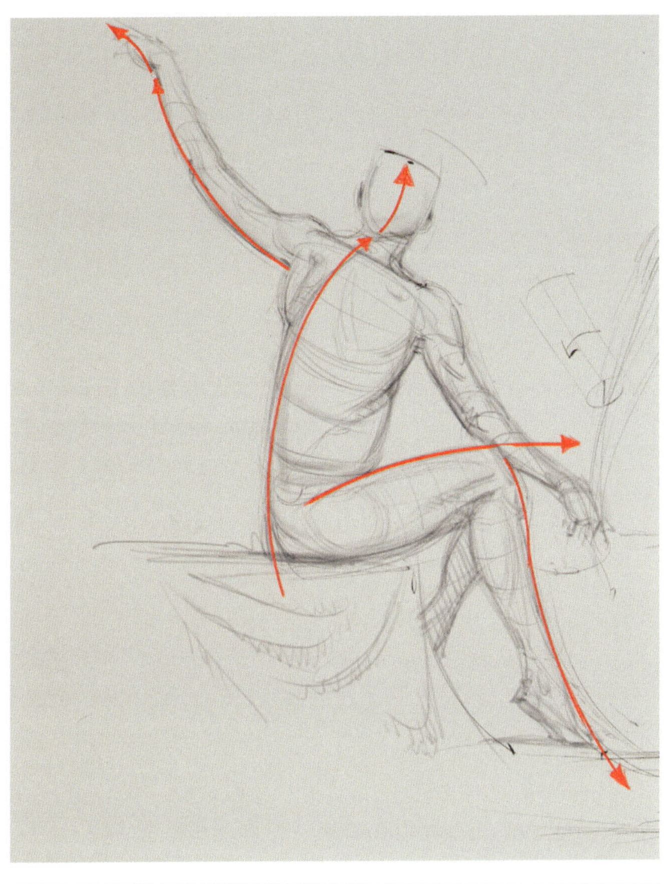

Gesture can organize several small structures under one big idea.

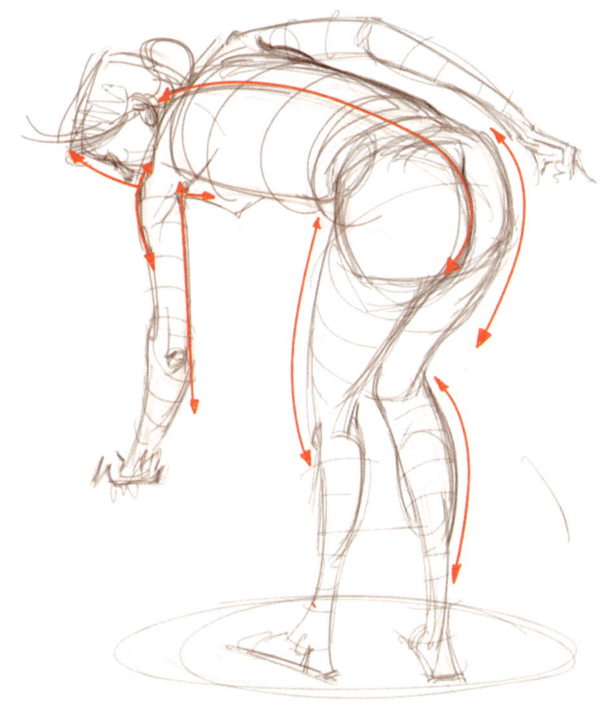

The viewer's eye flows over the forms, as over a waterfall, when the gestures are well conceived.

Take a few minutes to study these figure drawings. I've floated some red lines to show where some of the gestures are and how they track. Keep in mind that every structure with any substantial long axis has a long axis curve worth capturing. Can you find the others? Try laying tracing paper over the page. We'll build on this in later chapters as we lay out the structure and gesture of each body part.

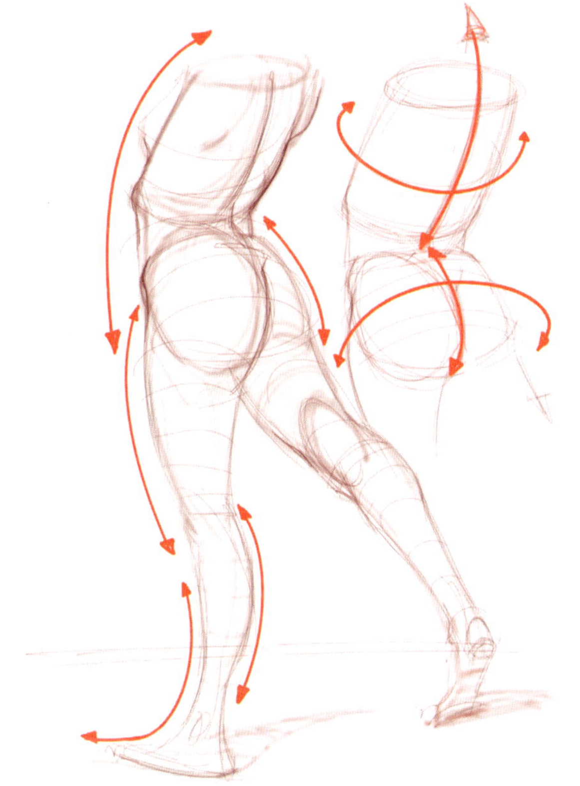

The longer and more graceful the gestural curve, the more smoothly the eye moves over the various forms.

OLD MASTER *study*

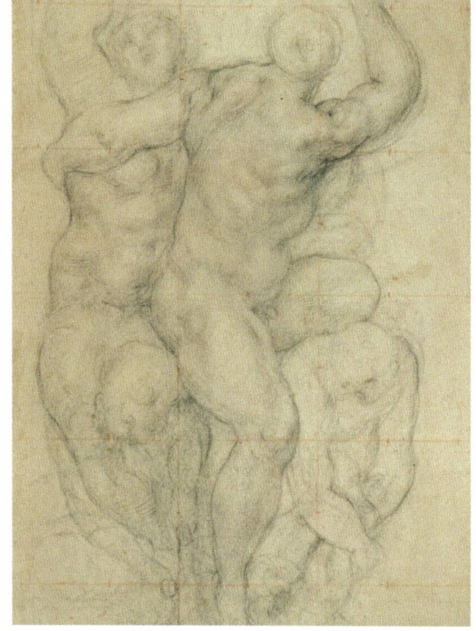

Study for a Group of Nudes, by Jacopo Pontormo (1494–1557). Chalk on paper. Gallerie dell'Academia, Venice/Bridgeman Images.

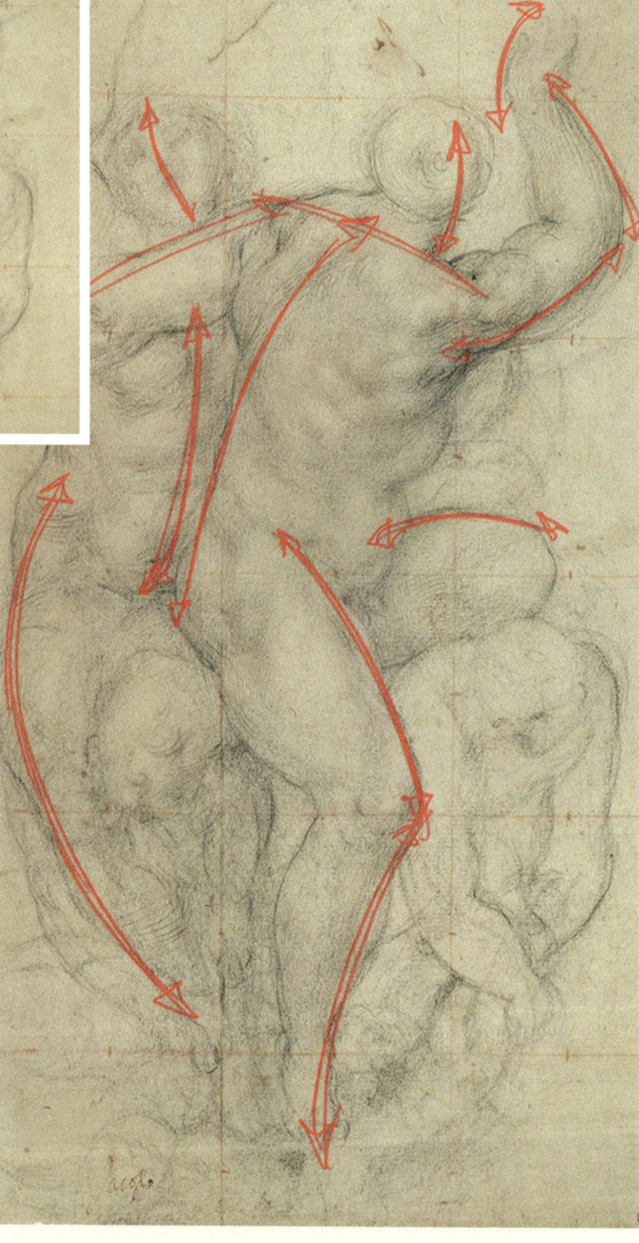

Don't be fooled by all the little wobbles. We want the big sweeping curves that define the big structures. And try to look past that incredible line quality . . . okay don't! Pontormo was phenomenal, wasn't he? Can you even find a straight line in this whole drawing? Now, this is *alive*!

Remember, use only one long axis curve for each jointed part.

Lay tracing paper over this drawing or over any drawing
in the chapter. Try to feel the long axis curve in each
jointed body part in this Boucher.

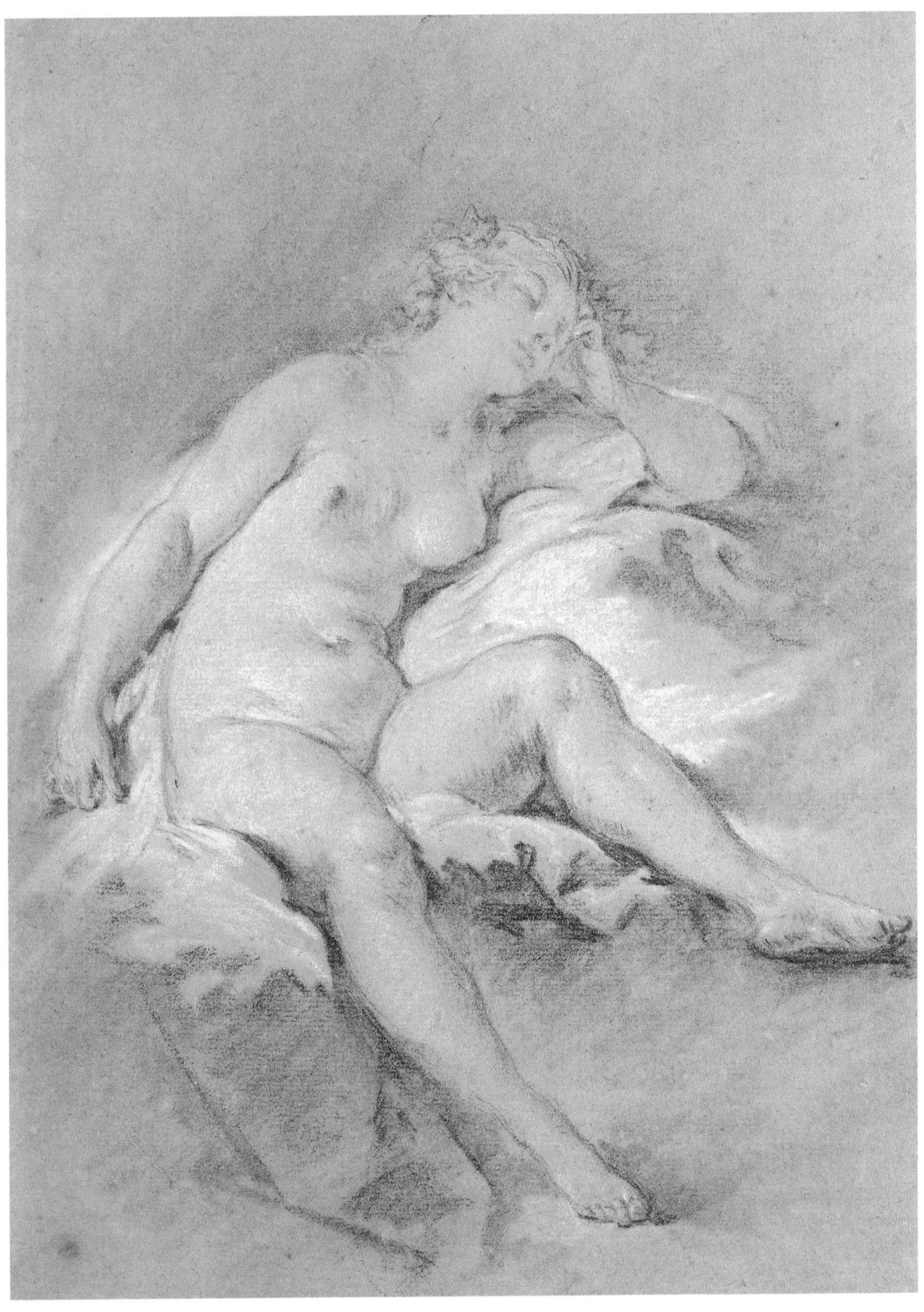

Nude Young Woman Sitting, Asleep, by François Boucher (1703–1770). Chalk on paper. Private collection/
Bridgeman Images.

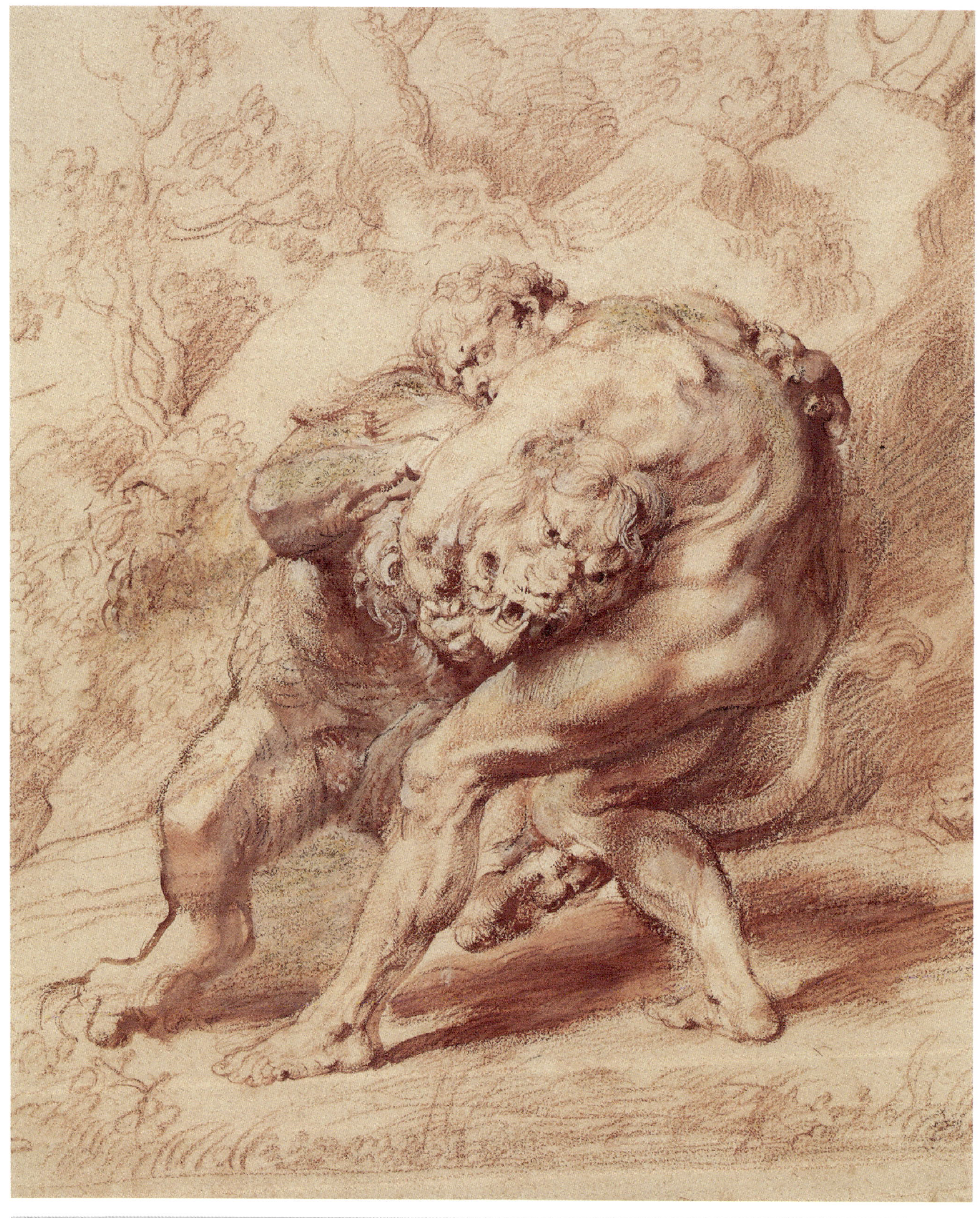

Hercules Strangling the Nemean Lion, c. 1620, Peter Paul Rubens (1577–1640). Chalk, ink, and gouache on paper. The Clark Art Institute, Williamstown, Massachusetts/Bridgeman Images.

3 | ADVANCING THE IDEA OF GESTURE

So far, we've focused on gesture (the fundamental design line) as a way to give life to each body part and link to the structure. When considering the human body, it is made up of lots of parts, and they all need to work together. In chapter 1, I defined structure as "the movement over the forms." Think of gesture as the movement *between* the forms.

The Design of Life

Gesture's greatest gift is to show, on a fundamental level, how to move gracefully and dynamically from the head to the neck, from the rib cage to the hips, all the way through the body. Gesture is what makes the separate parts one whole. In other words, gesture composes.

Ideally, a painter doesn't paint seven peaches and an apple. She paints one still life. A writer doesn't write twelve characters into sixty-four separate scenes. He writes one story. Mozart sounds like Mozart only when notes and instruments are orchestrated together. Any artist who just focuses on the pieces ends up with pieced-together results.

Art's job is to orchestrate life into something powerful, effecting, and meaningful—something greater than the individual parts. Art challenges, harmonizes, or dramatizes. It can be cathartic, it can be infuriating, but it's always, always composed. One song. One story. One dance. One meal. One figure. Gesture is the chef's secret sauce. Gesture is the design of life!

So, the next time you get out your pencil, grab hold like it's a conductor's wand and get ready to play.

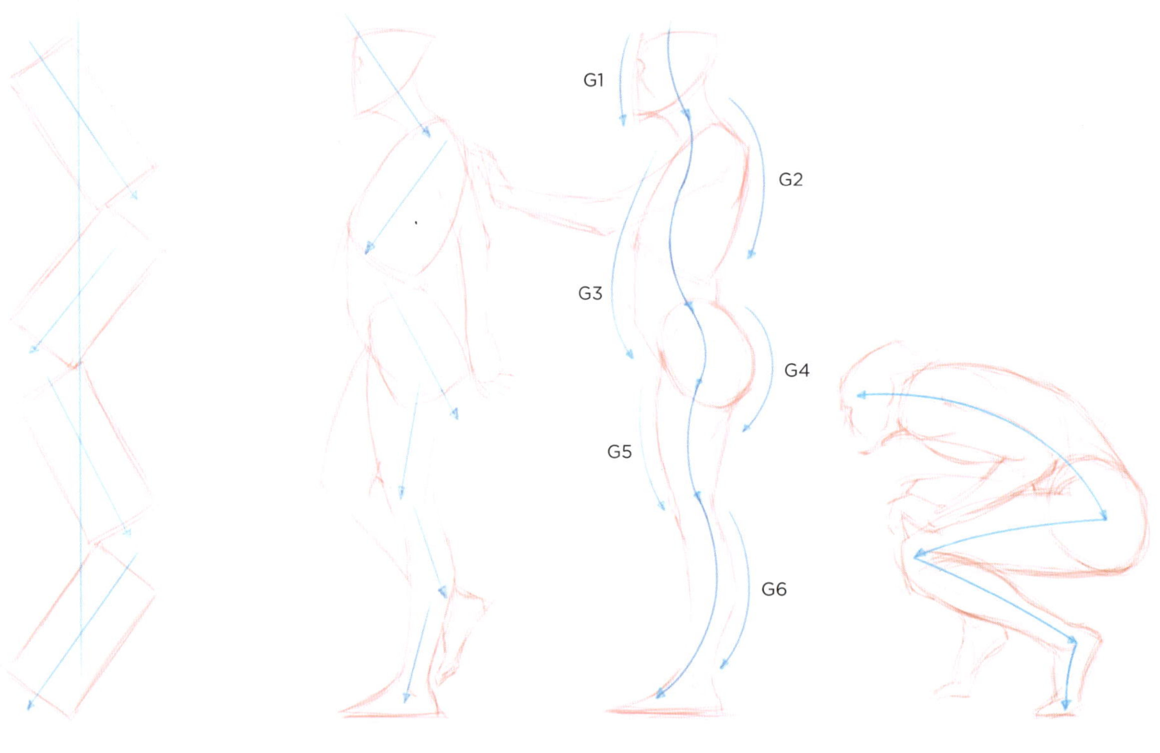

The human body is a balancing act.

THE WAVE

We've learned that anything alive is mainly water—fluid. That means life is designed, fundamentally, off the long axis curve. How does that watery design idea work in a complex of structures? It works through the wave.

Like all animals, the human animal is designed to be able to hold still in hopes the cave bear doesn't see it and then to be able to run like the dickens when it does. All animals need the stability of a tree and the explosive potential of a tension-filled spring—to go from stillness to action in the blink of an eye (or the growl of a bear). The wave design accomplishes this marvel. The wave design is the design of life. It stabilizes living forms, yet allows for quick movement.

Any set of forms with an asymmetrical design or in a dynamic pose is a balancing act. When all the forms within that set have a long axis curve as the basis of their design, the balancing act becomes a wave design.

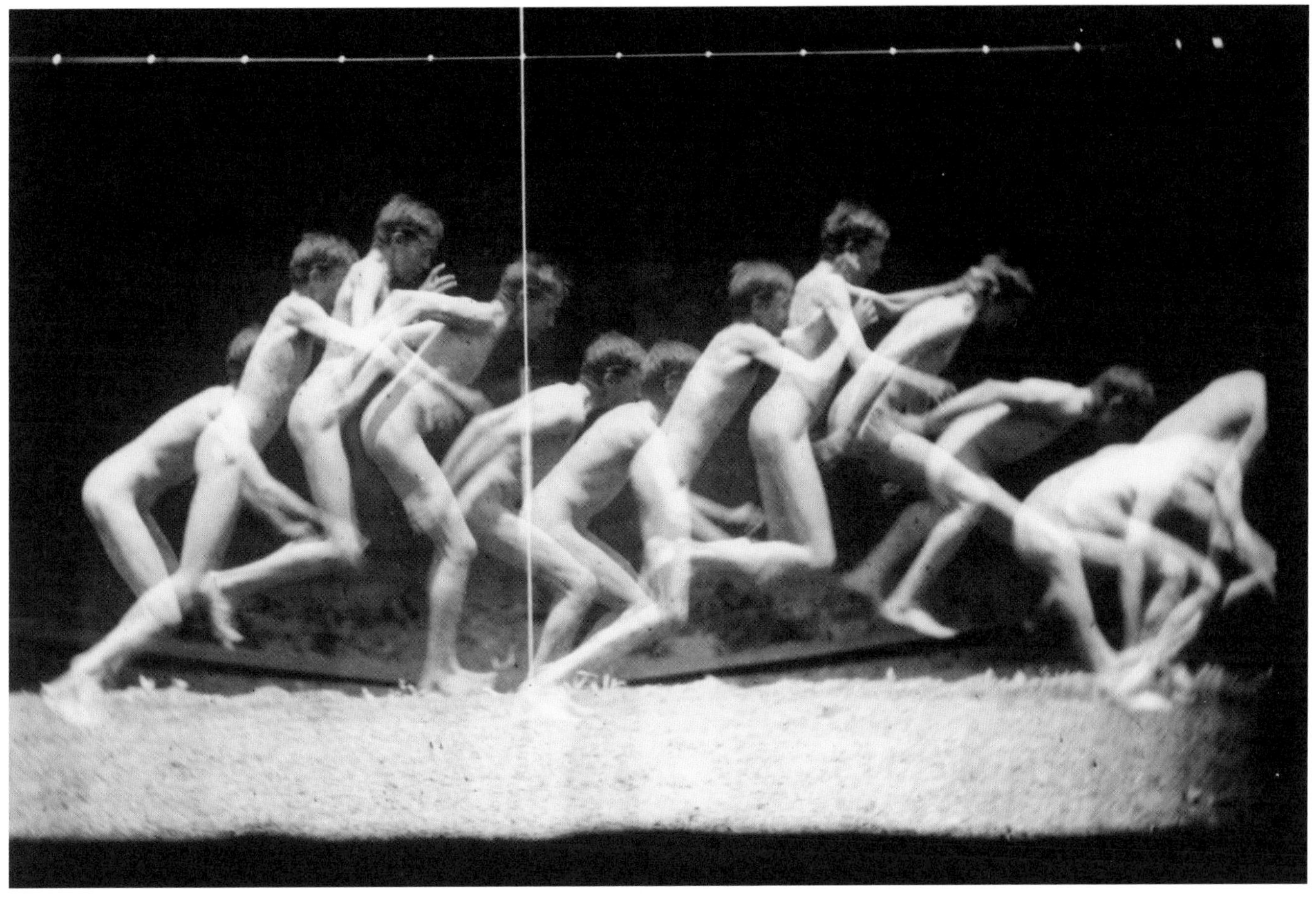

Motion Study: Boy Jumping to the Right, 1884, Thomas Cowperthwait Eakins (1844–1916). Gelatin silver print. Philadelphia Museum of Art/ Bridgeman Images. The zigzag is, generally, the essential element in getting movement into your art.

Follow the turquoise lines from head to toe in the figure at left to see all the long axis gestures for all major body parts. Notice anything interesting? Gesture 1 (G1) is high and to the left. G2 is lower and to the right. G3 is lower still and to the left again, and so on all the way down. If we take those gestures and move them inside . . . there is that marvelous, wondrous wave.

The wave becomes a zigzag if we compress it. Notice each zig and zag is still a long axis curve. The wave is life in relaxation or submission. The zigzag is life in action or aggression. There is the design of life, and we are going to find its two incarnations throughout the body underlying the big simple ideas and the small complex ones.

In the image opposite, see how the body crouches like a coiled spring. When that potential energy releases— WHAM!—it throws off gravity and moves the body into flight or fight, or dancing that Slavic kick dance.

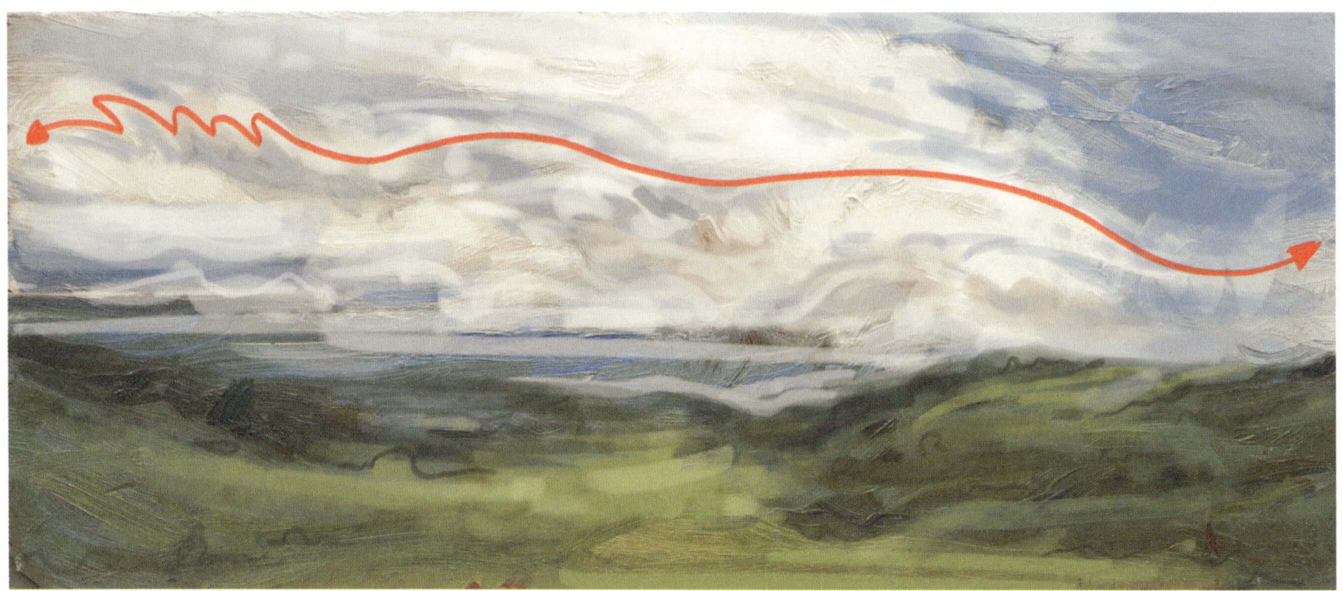

Landscape Sketch, c. 2004, by Steve Huston. Oil on panel. An example of the wave design.

The wave makes the painting above seem calm and relaxed. Artists use the wave design in many situations to evoke just that kind of feeling. (By the way, simplifying the detail and making your design horizontal rather than vertical also relaxes the mood.)

About my "calm" landscape painting: It really looks like a storm is coming, doesn't it? I tried to quiet it down even more in this oil sketch. But I can't seem to stay away from those aggressive zigzag marks. See whether you can calm the storm by sketching in more waves and pulling out most of the zigzags.

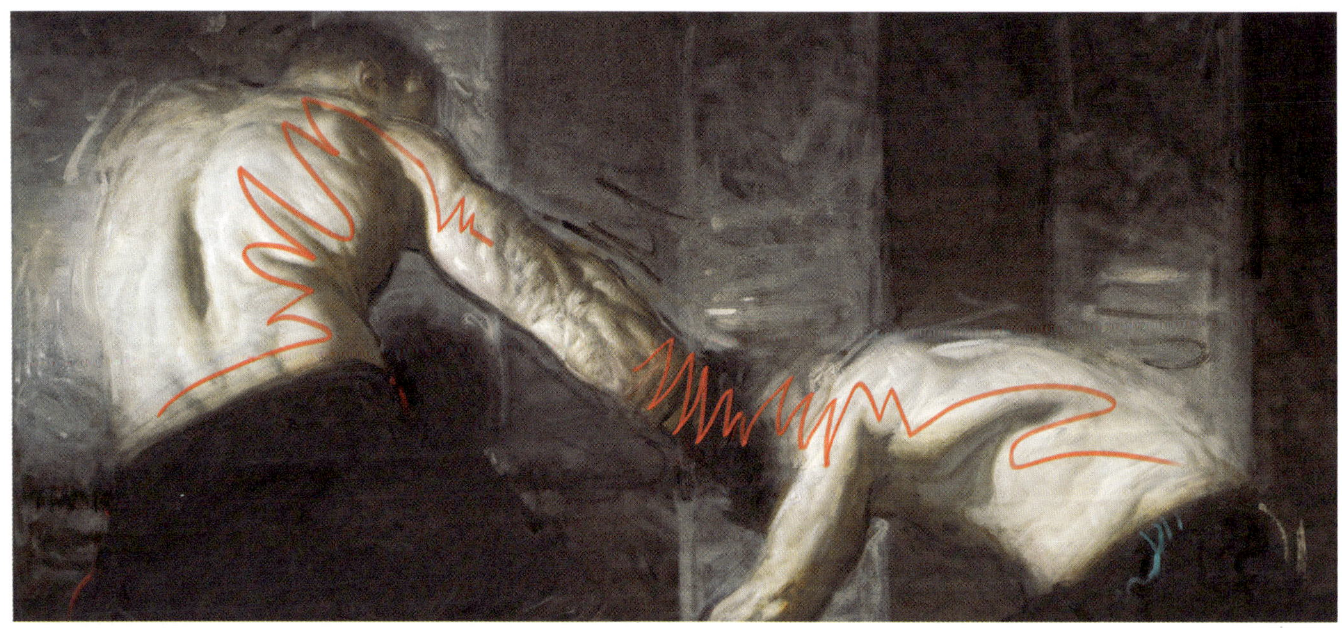

Straight Shot, 2011, by Steve Huston. Oil on canvas. You can see how zigzags are the bread and butter for my boxing paintings. Even the paint strokes themselves are mainly zigzags.

CONTRAPPOSTO

When I first heard about contrapposto, I thought it was a pasta dish. Actually, it means "counterpose" and comes to us from the Greeks and Romans by way of the Renaissance.

Let's look at the *kouros* (nude male youth) figure at right. Our early Greek friend is very proper and set in a perfectly symmetrical pose. His feet are planted squarely and his center of gravity is set right between his legs. He's stable. Life is balanced. Such balance and symmetry don't show off life's design principles very well. They don't curve. And if you walk past him for the ninety-ninth time on your way to the Bacchanalia, he's almost boring.

However, Ms. de Milo shows us something very different. I imagine some anonymous Greek genius storming around his studio, furious he has to carve another *kouros*. And being a nervous fellow (like all artists), he keeps shifting from foot to foot as he complains. He happens to glance into a mirror and sees his weight has shifted more to one foot than the other— what a discovery! The idea strikes him like a thunderbolt from his favorite deity. Contrapposto!—it's what Rodin called the classic curve.

Here's how it works: When the weight shifts, even a little, to one supporting leg, the other leg relaxes, flexes, and the hip falls compared to the supporting side. That tilt is then balanced by the shoulders tilting the other way. One side of the torso ends up stretching, the other side pinching—contrapposto. That's the wave. Exactly where each curve begins and ends depends on how the various parts articulate. But, it's there. And every artist since well before Ms. de Milo's creation has used it to compose a figurative world into a graceful and dynamic whole.

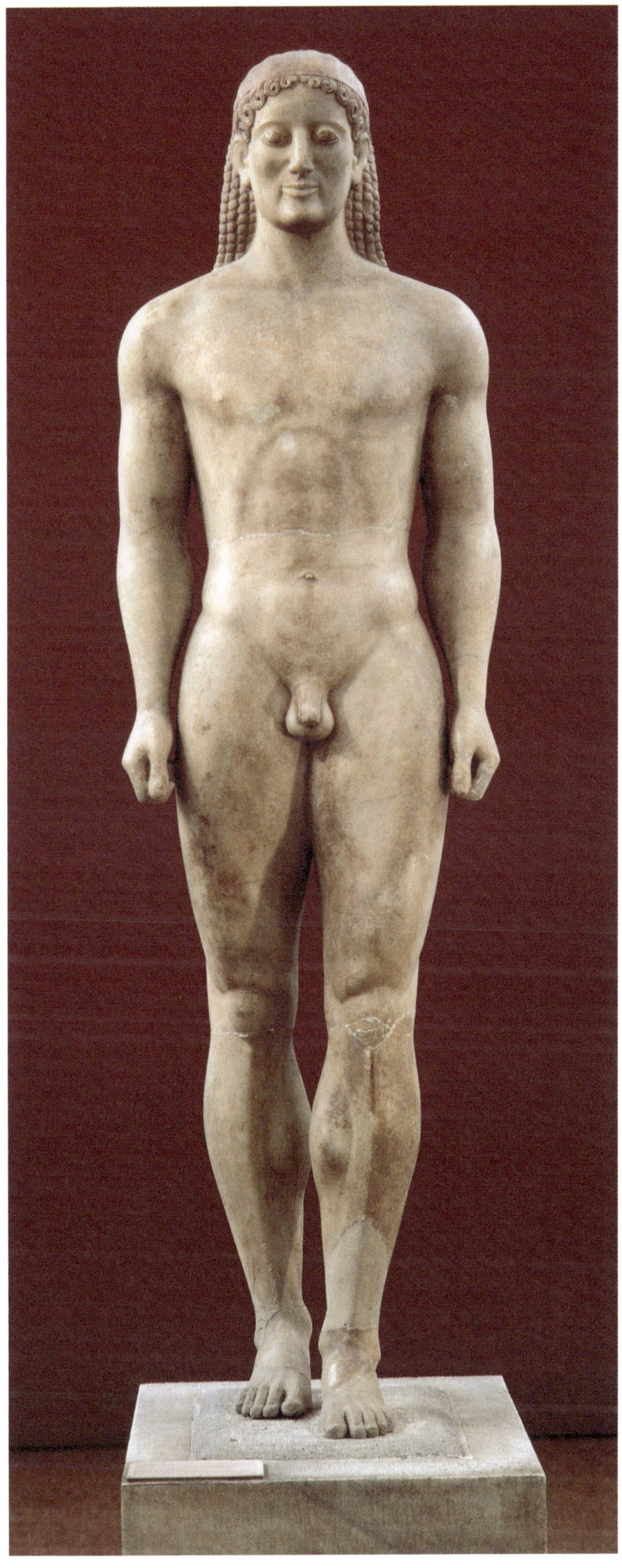

Marble Funerary Statue of Kouros, c. sixth century BCE, Greek. National Archeological Museum, Athens/Bridgeman Images. Beautiful or boring?

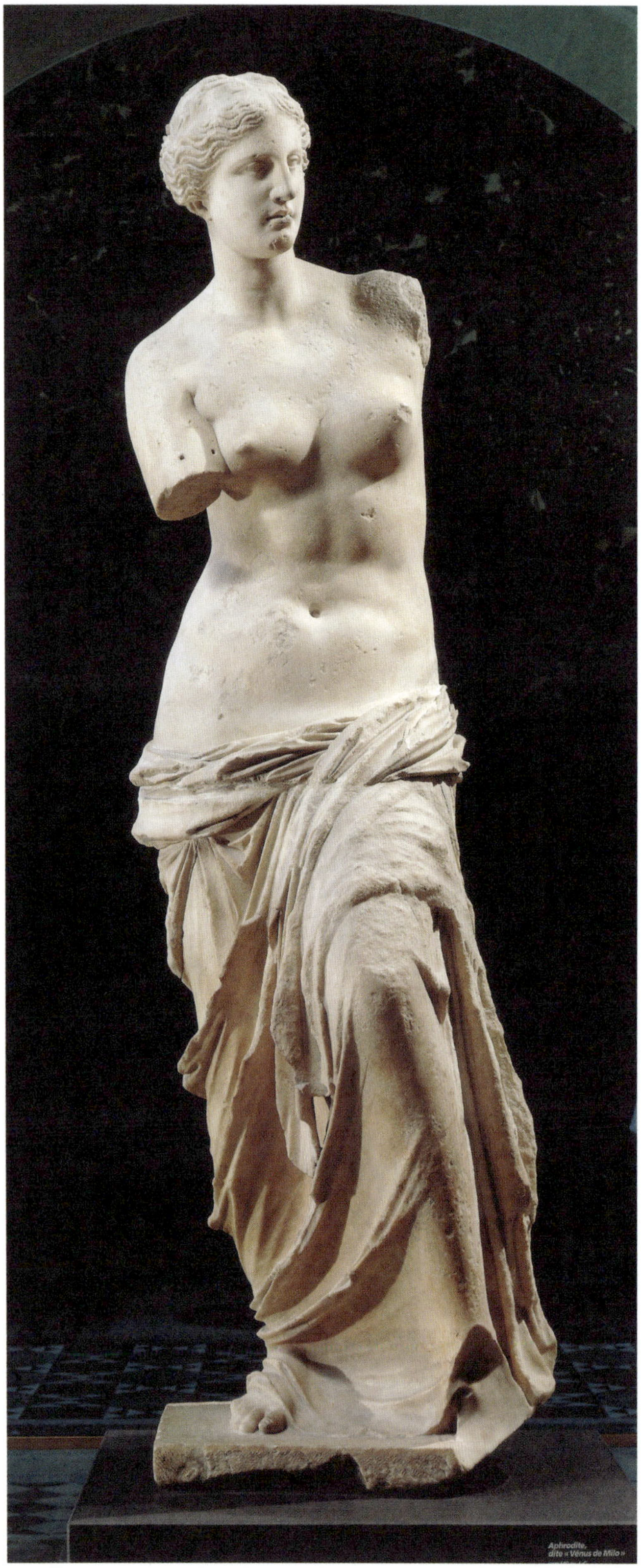

Aphrodite of Milos, known as "Venus de Milo," c. second century BCE, Greek. Marble. Louvre, Paris/Bridgeman Images. When dealing with the concept of contrapposto, it's all about symmetry, which means dynamic design. And that's the wave!

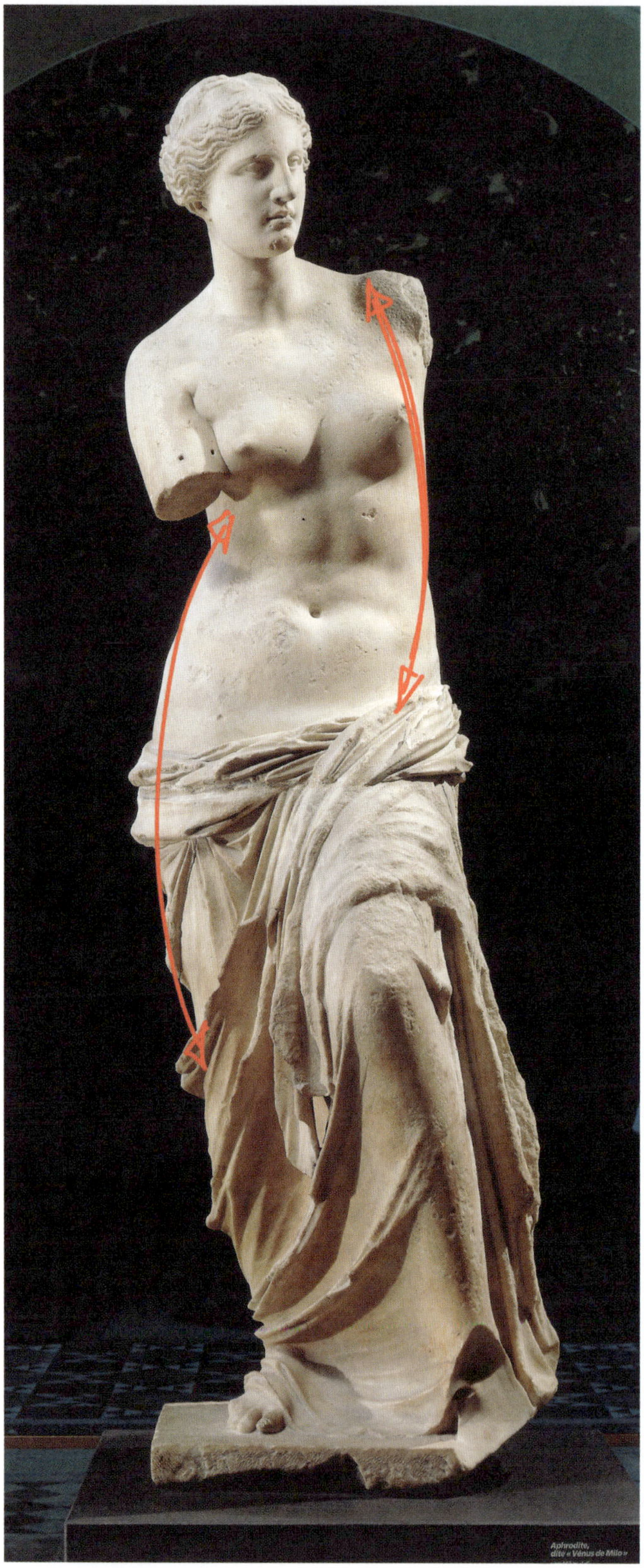

See the contrapposto now?

Here's the great thing: As you walk around the sculpture, no matter what view you take, that curve is composing the head and torso into those two, big simple, opposing rhythms. The limbs work with or against those rhythms with their own lesser rhythms like good subplots to the main story.

Why is this so important? Because as soon as the weight shifts, the pose becomes *dynamic*. It becomes asymmetrical. The pose has more potential energy, and that feels more alive to us.

It's the play between symmetry and asymmetry that's the real meat of good design. It implies change is about to happen. That's interesting. In storytelling, they call it drama, and it will keep you busy for the rest of your career.

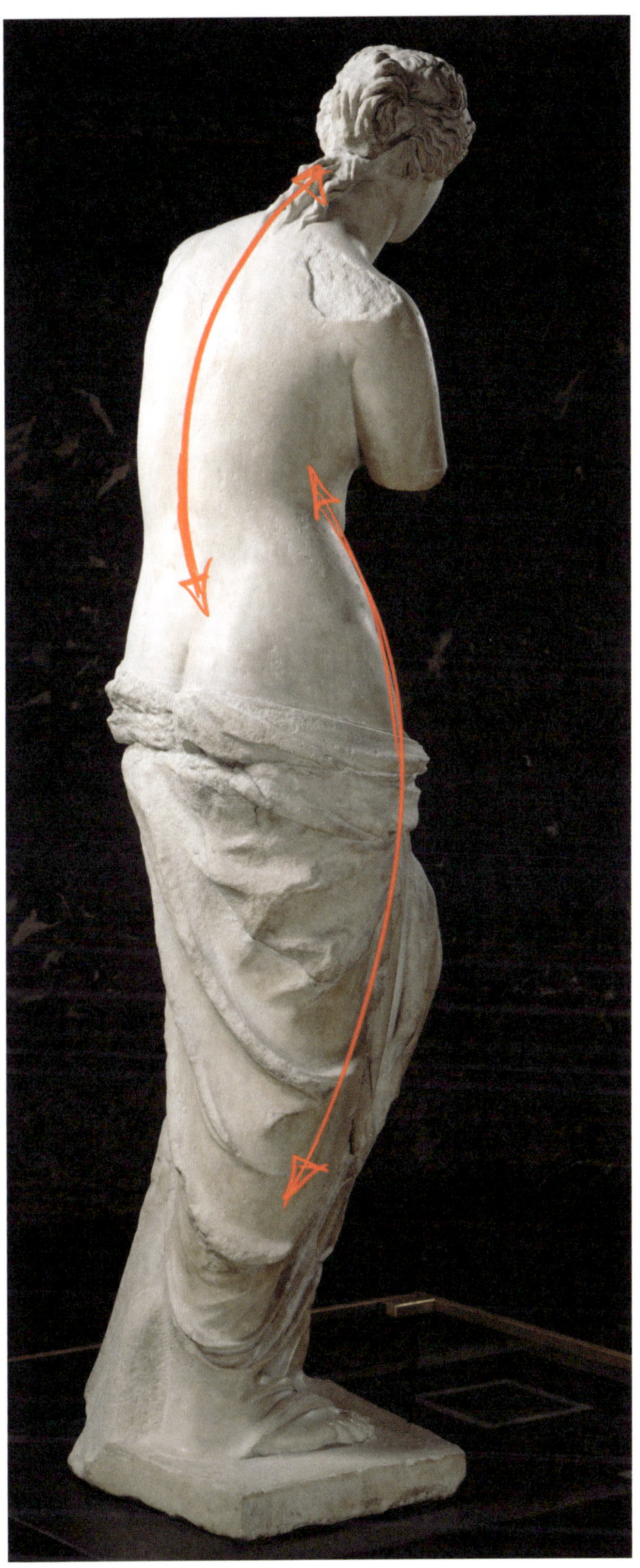

Rear View of Aphrodite, the "Venus de Milo," c. second century BCE, Greek. Marble. Louvre, Paris/Bridgeman Images. Though there are always several gestures in every pose, the two key gestures are the rib cage to the hip and the hip to the leg.

OLD MASTER *study*

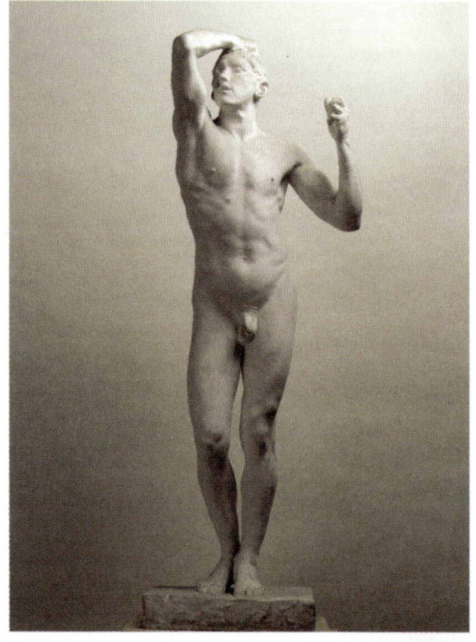

Age of Bronze, c. 1877, Auguste Rodin (1840–1917). Plaster. State Hermitage Museum, St. Petersburg/Bridgeman Images.

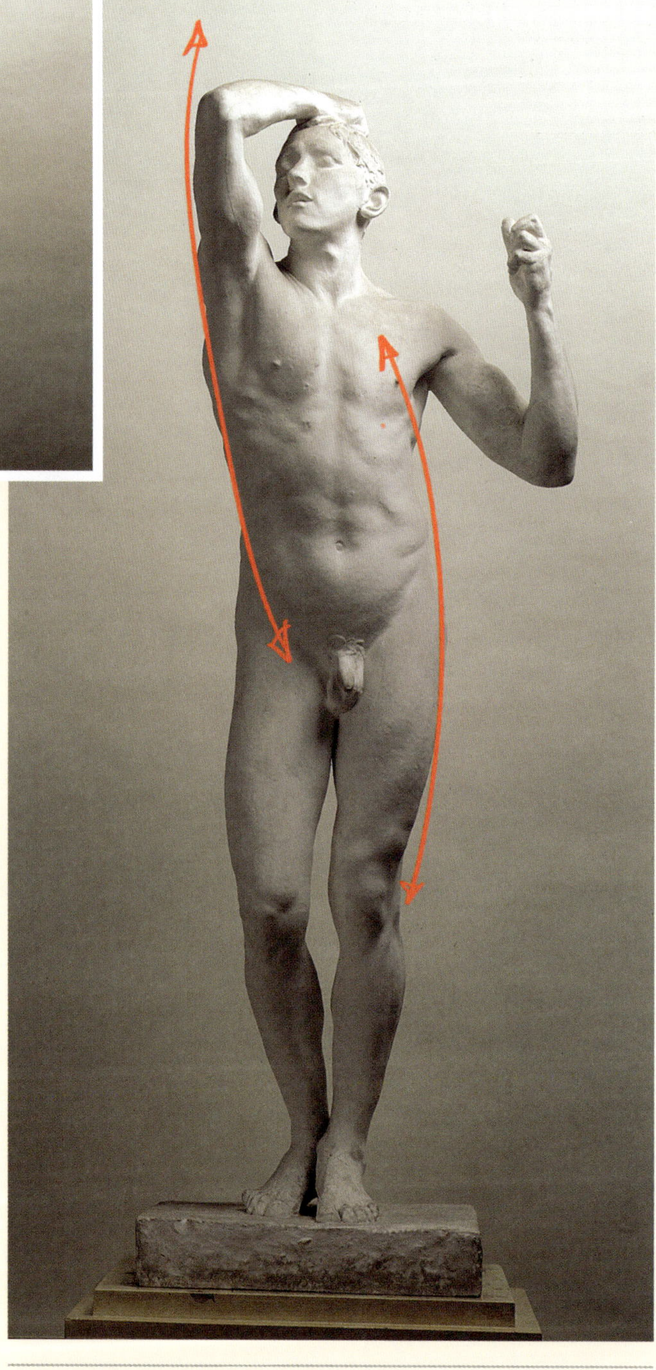

A fine example of what Rodin called "the classic curve," which is what I call "the gesture." Can you see how these two primary gesture lines were the foundations for Rodin's entire design?

Rodin (one of my favorites), was keenly aware of the Old Masters, particularly Michelangelo. As Michelangelo took from Apollonios's *Belvedere Torso*, Rodin took from Michelangelo. By the way, Michelangelo's nickname by other artists was "Il Divino," the divine one.

In *Age of Bronze*, Rodin took the classic curve a bit farther by carrying it up through that raised arm. See how the hip to elbow gesture plays oh so subtly against the opposing hip and leg? In fact, he carried that second gesture a little farther as well. It goes up almost to the chest. The divine and the august—quite a pair!

Lay tracing paper over the images on these two pages and draw well-constructed forms over the major body parts.

Don't get seduced by the bulging muscles, for example. We want to look for the single long axis curve that represents the complete part or parts. Getting that long axis gesture right is more important than picking this or that simple structure. Find as many gestures as possible with an eye on that side-to-side swing. This is how we build our all-important wave or zigzag actions.

Remember to take it one long axis curve at a time. If you have trouble, go back and review the Pontormo analysis from the previous chapter (see page 46).

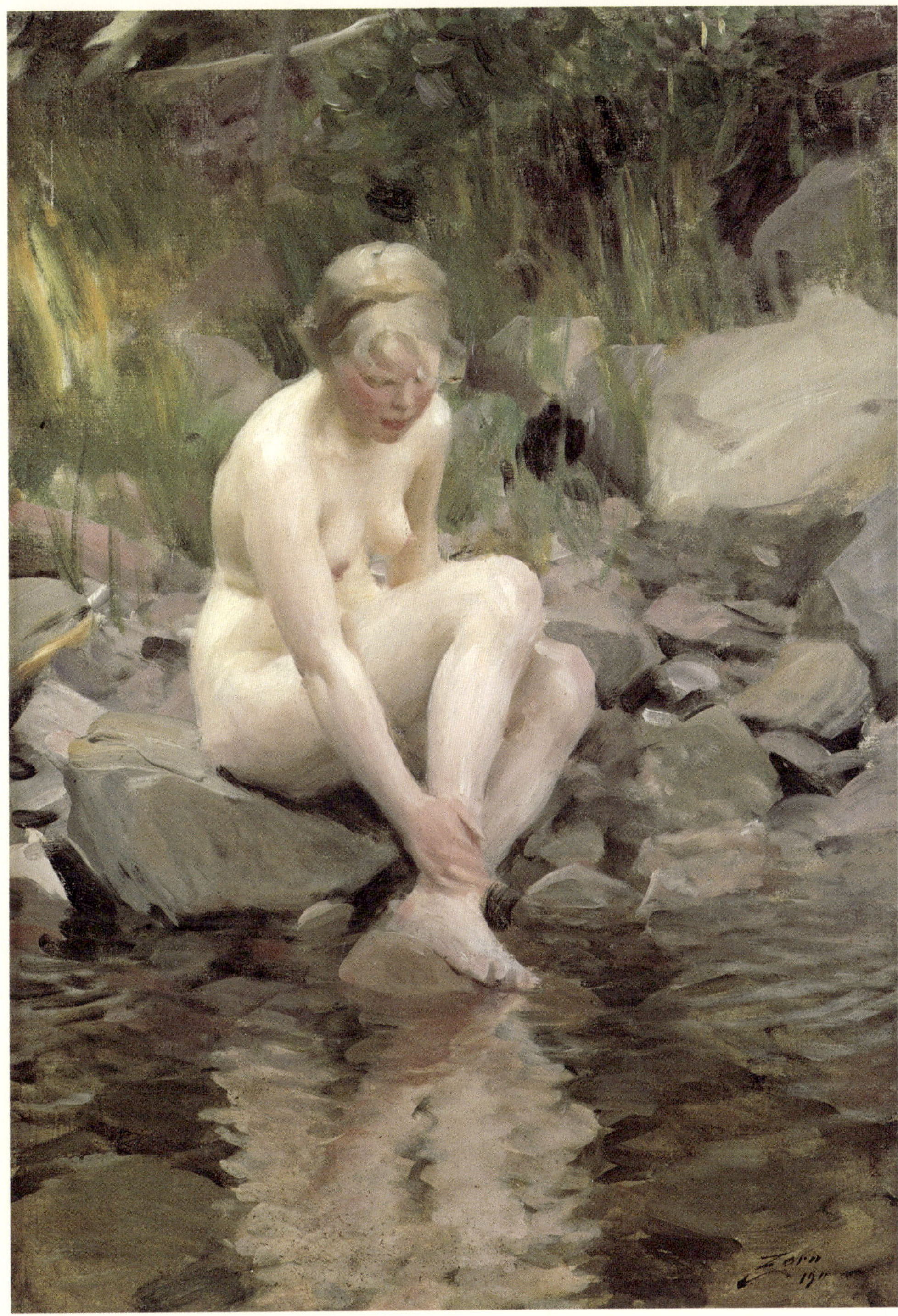

Dagmar, 1911, by Anders Leonard Zorn (1860–1920). Oil on canvas. Private collection/Bridgeman Images.

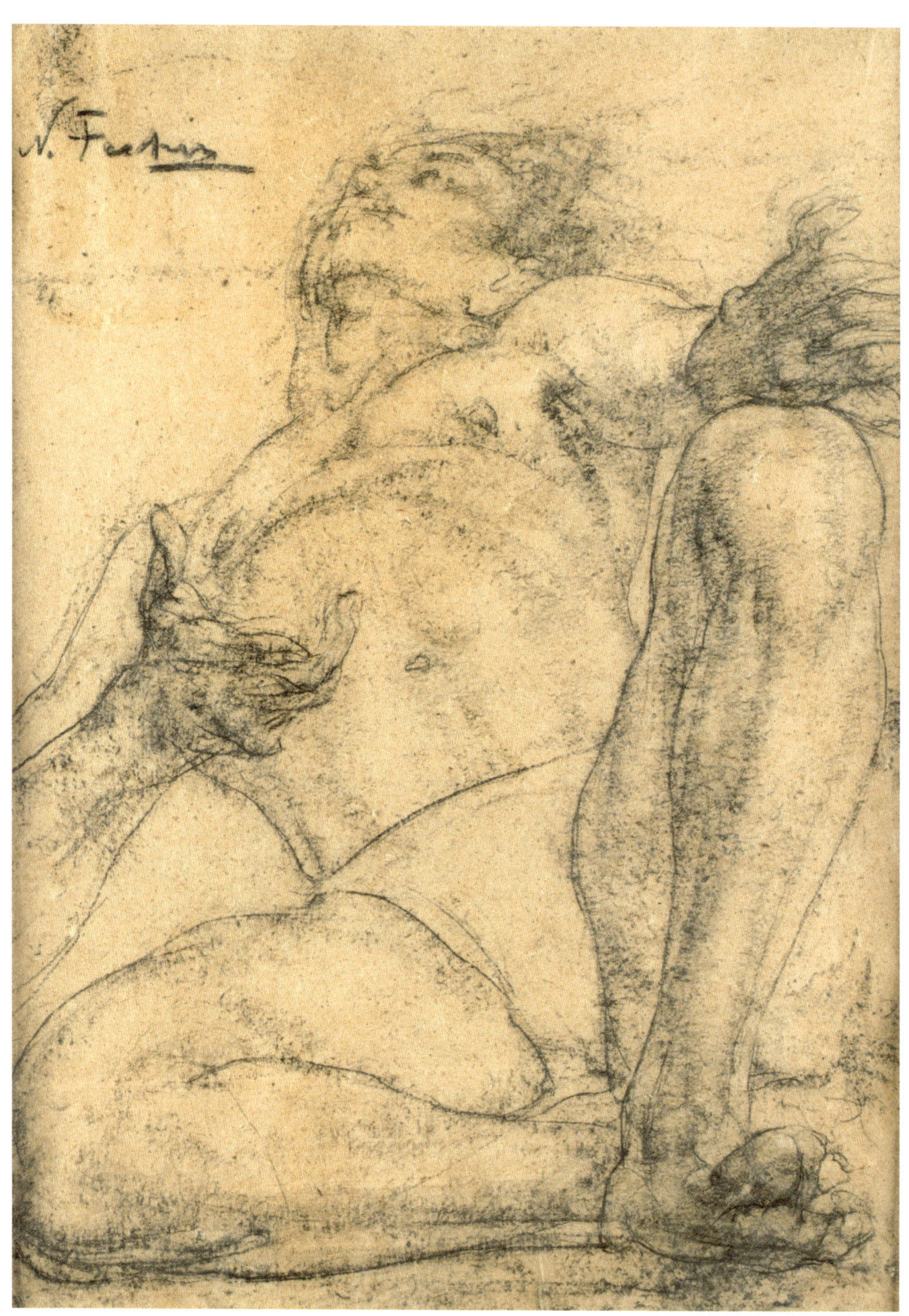

Reclining Male Nude, c. twentieth century, Nikolai Fechin (1881–1955). Charcoal on paper. University of Oklahoma/Bridgeman Images. When the pose moves into a dynamic position, proportions can change. In this case, pick a convenient structure in the pose (the head, a hand, or a foot) and use that as your yardstick—how many hands down until you reach the foreshortened belly button and so on.

4 | PERSPECTIVE

We've learned our basic approach to drawing begins with the simple-yet-characteristic idea. Now, we need to layer on perspective. Most of us think of perspective as math pretending to be drawing. But this isn't the old vanishing point perspective. It's pretend perspective.

Triangles and T–Squares Aside

Let's define our terms. Perspective is just a complicated way of saying "position." In a three-dimensional world, there are three positions in space: *lean*, *tilt*, and *face*.

Remember, we're drawing the human body. So, we're not concerned with a background with vanishing points, station points, or any of the sticky tangles of traditional perspective. All we need, in fact, is one eye and the pencil test.

To be clear, there are ways to make formal perspective accessible and, yes, even fun. And I absolutely encourage you to pursue that when you're ready to go from sketching to full-blown picture making—just not today.

You've already been doing perspective, by the way. We've been working with three-dimensional structures for a few chapters now. Three dimensions are three positions in space. And remember:

position = perspective

If you know how a structure *leans*, *tilts*, and *faces* against a flat vertical wall like the one at the end of the room you're in right now, then you have all the perspective you need. When you draw, just imagine the surface of your paper—called the *picture plane*—is a window on that wall. The model *faces away, leans against,* and *tilts in and out relative to that plane.* That's it. What follows is me reminding you what you already intuitively know. In fact, after a few short paragraphs, you won't see the word "perspective" for the rest of the book. I promise!

Let's consider our three positions. Structure is all about corners. The more corners you have, the more structure you have. To make that definition as useful as possible, I'm going to add that structure is not the same as three-dimensional form. Instead, we'll define it this way:

structure = form + position

Pretend all four forms in the image on this page have plenty of volume. In fact, they are rendered perfectly, made of titanium steel, and even weigh the same. The sphere has weight, volume, and mass. It has form.

But—by our definition—it has no structure. The box has form and it has a lot of structure. What's the difference? Corners.

In the image below, the red lines tell the tale. As we look at the lonely sphere, we can't tell whether what we are seeing is its front, side, top, or bottom. We know nothing about its position. Meaning, we can't tell if it's leaning, tilting, or facing. News flash: spheres have no corners. (I know you know that; I'm just putting it in context.)

The egg, to be an egg, has a long and a short axis. We feel the interior corner created by the meeting of the long and short axes. We know one of its positions in space. We know it leans.

The tube has the same long and short axis. It leans. We also know its top tilts into the picture plane because the bottom plane creates a corner. We now know a second position in space—and you're probably ahead of me here. The box has the leaning position *and* the tilting position. But because it has side planes, we are afforded another corner, and so we know the third position in space: how it faces.

Leaning. Tilting. Facing. Three positions. Three dimensions. That, my friends, is what we call perspective.

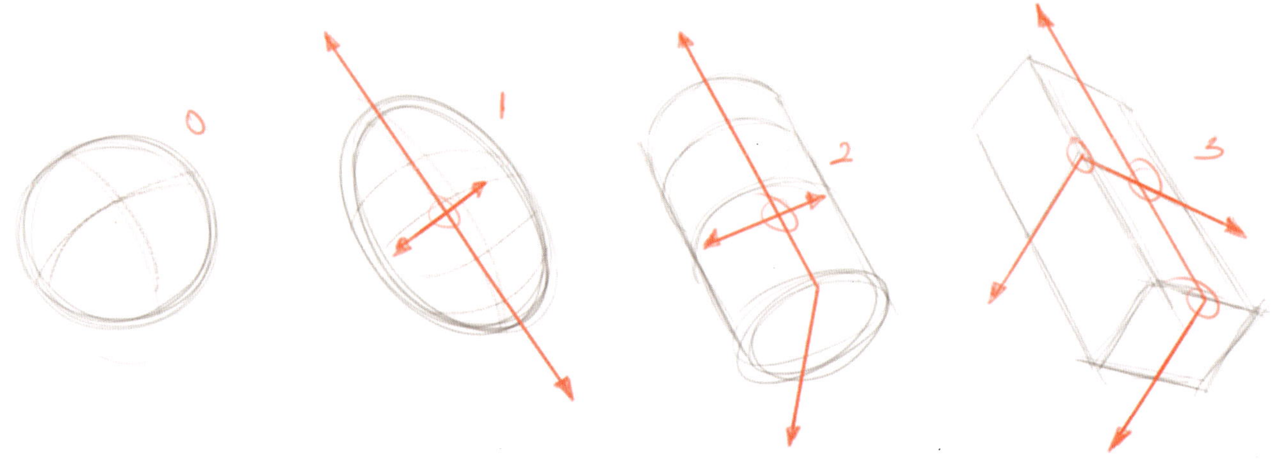

The sphere, the egg, the tube, and the box in position

THE PENCIL TEST

For this, it's best to use a tubular pencil, or marker, or such, something with a nice stripe of color or a metal eraser casing that clearly tracks around the width of the tubular structure. Now, set it down. We don't need it . . . yet.

Let's start with the facing position. Look at the center-line of the face or torso in the figure below. Both are intuitive, but, sometimes, we flub them. It's easiest when drawing the face in any kind of three-quarter position to look to the far eye socket. How much socket do you see on the far side of the nose? That's where you'll see the centerline very close to the far side of the head, and so you've nailed down the facing position.

For a back view, how close does the ear crowd the front of the face? That's about it. Profiles, front, and back views take care of themselves. We'll save the more dynamic positions for later.

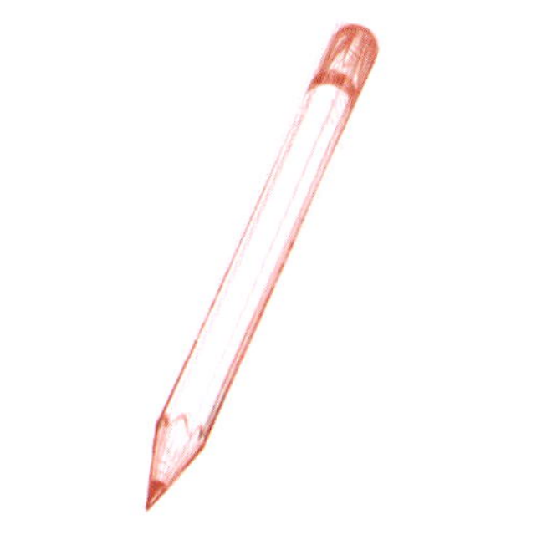

Using the pencil for more than marks

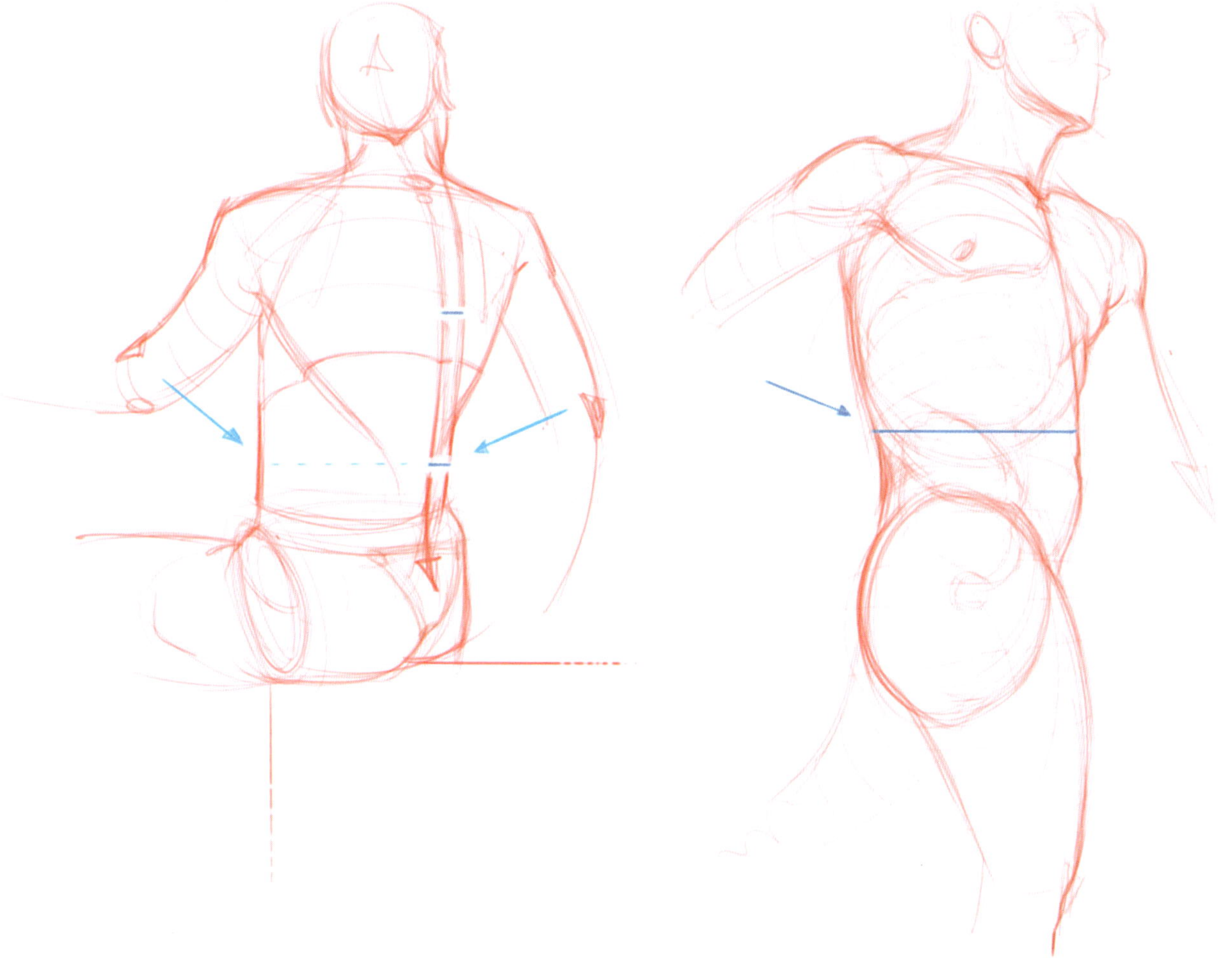

To find the facing positions of the torso, we need to look to the waist and not the shoulders.

The front, back, and profile positions of the torso are obvious. However, the shoulders can fool us in any kind of three-quarter view. Even in a profile, the shoulders can fool you into thinking it's a three-quarter view.

The trick is to look to the waist, as the turquoise arrows show. How close does the centerline (the spine or belly button to crotch) come to the far side of the waist? When you have to check proportions visually or otherwise, always measure on the short or narrow side. It's easier. No matter how wide the shoulders get, you are only concerned with drawing a waist-wide tube for the rib cage up to the pit of the neck. And, of course, it can taper into the neck by way of the bottle shape if you wish. It is not affected by the width of the shoulder girdle. (We'll look at this more carefully in chapter 9.)

What about the limbs? The limbs will orient by the correct placement of the knees and elbows and by how they attach to the torso. That's it for the facing position.

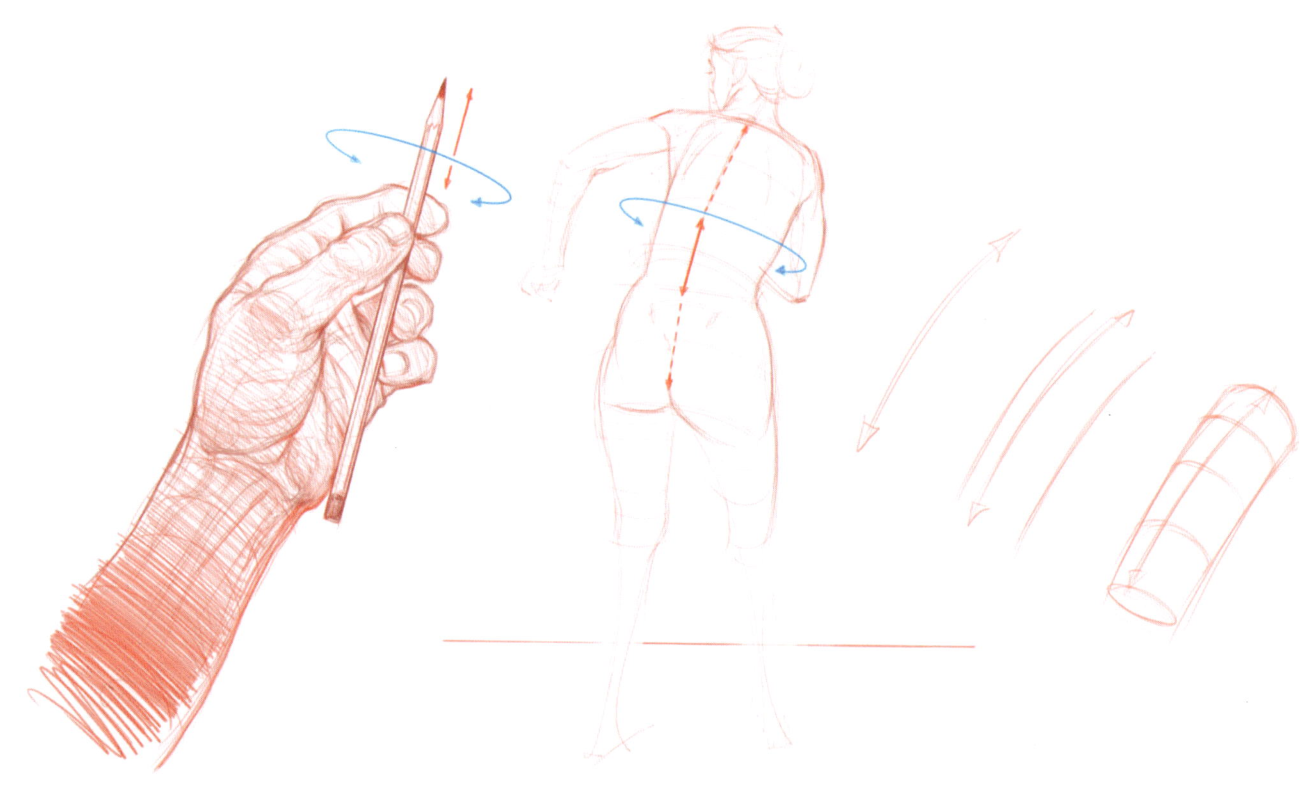

Using the pencil to find the leaning position

For the leaning position, we do need our pencils. Look to the centerlines again, in this case, for the torso. Use the long axis landmarks as shown in chapter 3. Start with a convenient section if you're dealing with a long axis curve, as you usually will be.

Close an eye. Lean the pencil to match the lean of the body part you're drawing. Bring the pencil down to your paper without altering the pencil's lean. Draw the angle. It can be the centerline or one of the sides if it's a tube or box. You can build out the full gesture, section by section, by repeating the steps. It will end with the curved idea, just a chiseled version. I've shown that on the figure opposite with the dotted red lines above and below the solid one. You're done with the lean.

The lean gives us our two-dimensional sides. With the tilt, we add three-dimensional ends. The tilt gives us the most trouble because we are telling, in effect, a lie. The paper is flat. It has no depth. And yet, we want our audience to feel the torso bending and tilting into that flat plane. As we build out the drawing, we want them to feel that muscle and bone bulge off the surface. We aren't creating depth, space, or anything like that; we are creating the *idea* of it—curves and corners, my friends, curves and corners.

Return to the figure at left. Close one eye. Line up your pencil with the top of the body part you're working on. Tilt the pencil in the same manner that the body part tilts. If the pit of the neck is farther from you than the belly button, tilt the top of your pencil that way. It's best to exaggerate the tilt a bit. So, when in doubt, err on the side of the more dynamic! Push it into a deeper tilt than you think it really is. I don't expect even a New York art critic will complain that your drawing has too much depth, do you? (Right, they probably would.) Pushing your ideas, however, can eventually become the basis of your style!

So, that is all three positions: facing, leaning, and tilting. Congratulations! You have deciphered perspective.

EYE LEVEL

There is a secret aspect to perspective that sometimes even the pros miss. There is the position of the form itself as explained by facing, leaning, and tilting. We just did that. But, there is also *our* position to the form. And by *our*, I mean both artist and audience.

This second aspect is critical. Without it, you'll never be able to place your figure drawing in a convincingly real-world environment.

Think about it. If a guard stands at attention, his three positions are fixed. We can walk around him. Obviously, the facing dimension changes in relationship to our movement. But, what if we decide to lie on our stomach to draw him? What if we climb a ladder? Both would be, should be, very different drawings even though he has not moved a muscle.

What we need to know to draw any form in a fully structured position, then, is our eye level. It's not hard. It's simply one of those quiet truths that becomes apparent only when someone points it out. Other than lining up the top of your pencil end with the top of a body part (if you're looking at something below you, you'll likely want to sight bottom to bottom), it's the same thing as our tilting test. From now on, just do them as one step. The pencil test takes care of this one, too.

The thinking goes like this (see Fig. A): If we see a tube in a perfectly vertical position in terms of tilt, in perfect alignment with the picture plane, as in schematic 1 (S1), and our eye level drops underneath it, then we draw the rib cage as I did in drawing 1 (D1).

But, if our eye level drops underneath it and it's tilting away from us at the top as in schematic 2 (S2), then the underneath-ness, the curvature of the ends, doubles up so to speak, and we end up with a more deeply tilting position like drawing 2 (D2).

Hold your pencil vertically and lift it so its flat top aligns with the top of the tubular ribs and tilt it into the picture plane as the ribs do (see Fig. B). As always, it's better to err on the side of the more dynamic and overdo the tilt. Any curving stripe across the pencil will show you how to construct your three-dimensional ends. (Test the idea against some real-world object several feet above you. A few inches might be so subtle that the pencil end looks flat.)

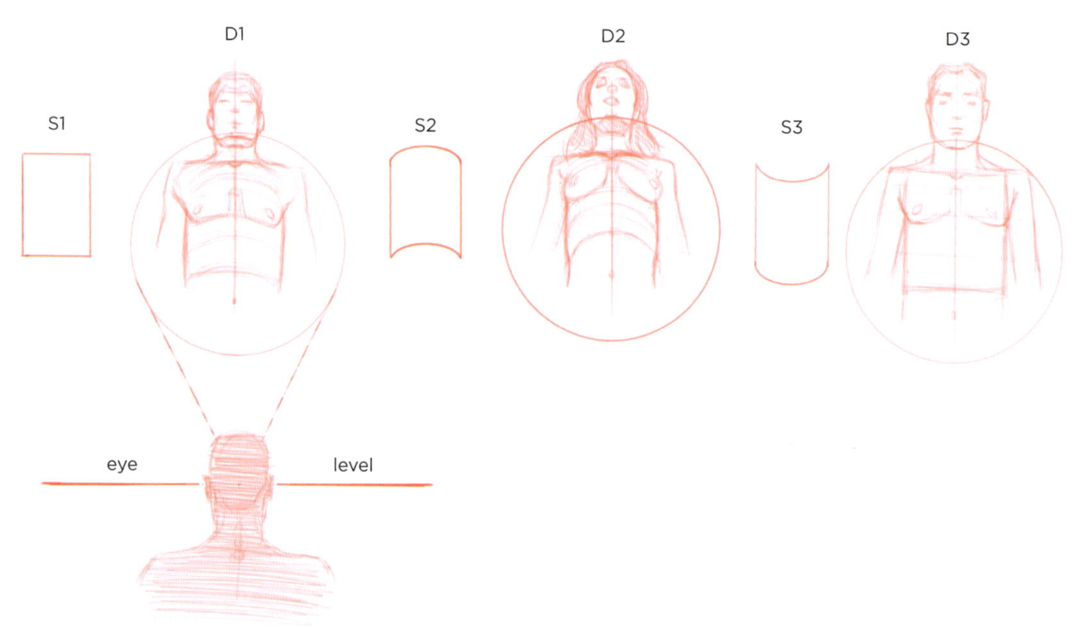

Fig. A. There are three variations to consider when underneath the subject.

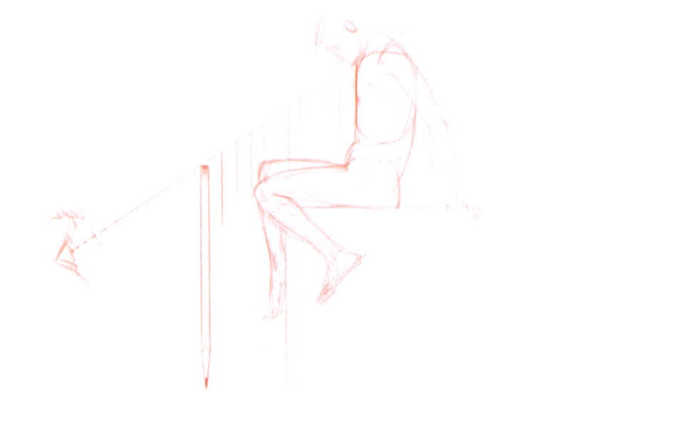

Fig. B. Drawing with the eye level in mind.

Last, if the tube tilts toward us at the top and remains above our eye level, as in schematic 3 (S3), then we end up with a rib cage that has more or less canceled the depth clues and we draw flat ends, as in drawing 3 (D3).

I hope you can see how the eye level always has an effect. The little figure before the giant Roman column in Fig. C sees each segment in a different position relative to his eye level and so must draw each segment with different three-dimensional ends. When the eye level is high, the logic is the same. For the next set, I'll just use straight tubes.

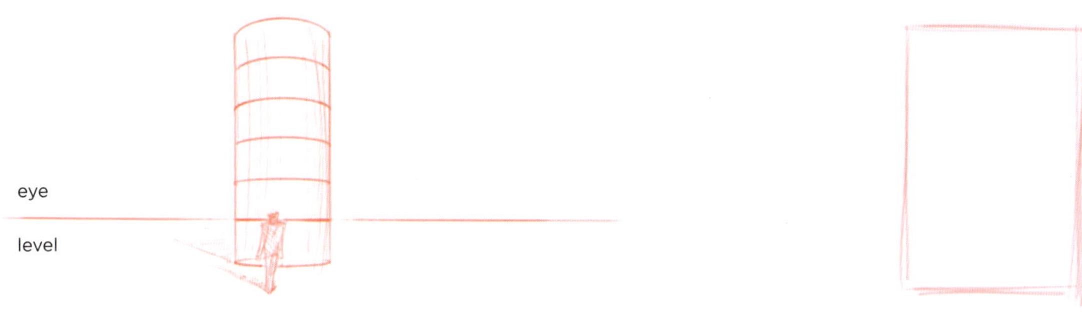

Fig. C. Using the three-dimensional ends with eye level.

Fig. E. Can you guess the problem in drawing straight lines for the three-dimensional ends?

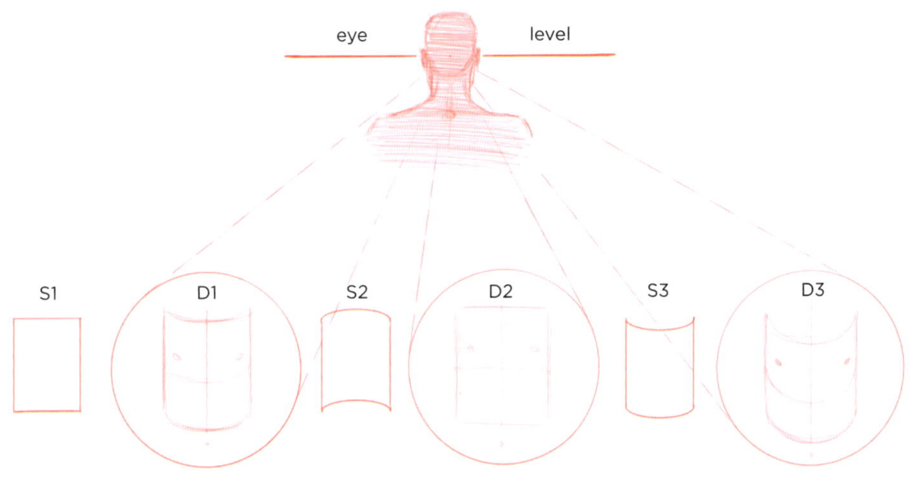

Fig. D. Drawing from a high eye level.

If we see a tube in alignment with the picture plane, Fig. D, as in schematic 1 (S1), and our eye level rises above it, then we draw the rib cage, more or less, as I did in drawing 1 (D1). If it's tilting away from us at the top, as in schematic 2 (S2), then the "on top-ness" cancels things out again, more or less, and we end up with something like drawing 2 (D2). And last, if the tube tilts toward us at the top and remains below our eye level as in schematic 3 (S3), then we end up with a rib cage that has doubled up and we draw deeply curving ends as in drawing 3 (D3).

Does Fig. E look like a tube to you? I have to tell you it's a tube because the contour doesn't say "tube." Of course, I could render it with the appropriate gradations. But, the design itself is not supporting the idea of tube-ness.

Let's revisit the tourist in Fig. C. Notice only the horizontal segment at his eye line is straight. The segment below that line curves down, and the segments above it bows up. That means only one end of that tube drawing in Fig. E would be straight. The other would be curved slightly, at least. This is a better design.

Better yet would be a more dynamic design. Tilt the whole structure slightly in or out of the picture plane. If it's so close it looks flat on the page, then pushing it one way or the other will readily be accepted by the audience. I just push it toward my design idea. For example, if it's most important to me to show viewers they're above or below the form, then I tilt it with that in mind. If it's most important to show the form breaking the picture plane, then I go with that idea. But remember, this is just for close calls. If it's clearly tilting, stick with what you see and use the pencil test to draw it.

OLD MASTER *study*

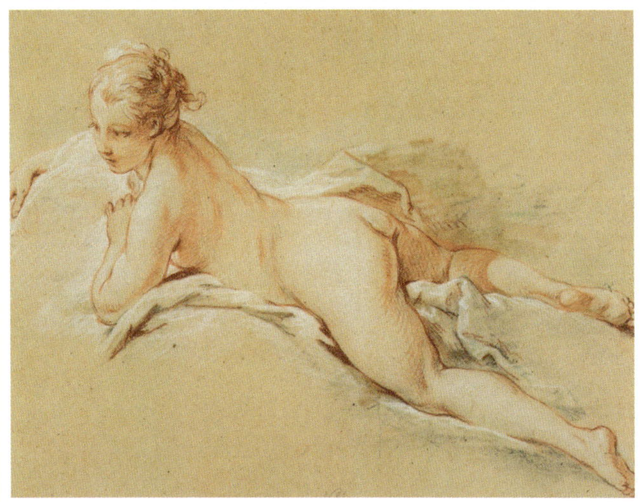

Recumbent Nude,
c. eighteenth century,
Francois Boucher
(1703–1770). Pencil
and chalk on paper.
Private collection/
Bridgeman Images.

Study this lovely Boucher. We're looking down on it, aren't we? In fact, our eye level is well above the top of the page. For fun, I've done a somewhat simpler redraw with our eye level just over the top of the figure's head, and another smaller one with an even lower eye line. In both, I've removed the drapery for clarity. The turquoise lines show the approximate eye lines. They're quite different drawings, aren't they?

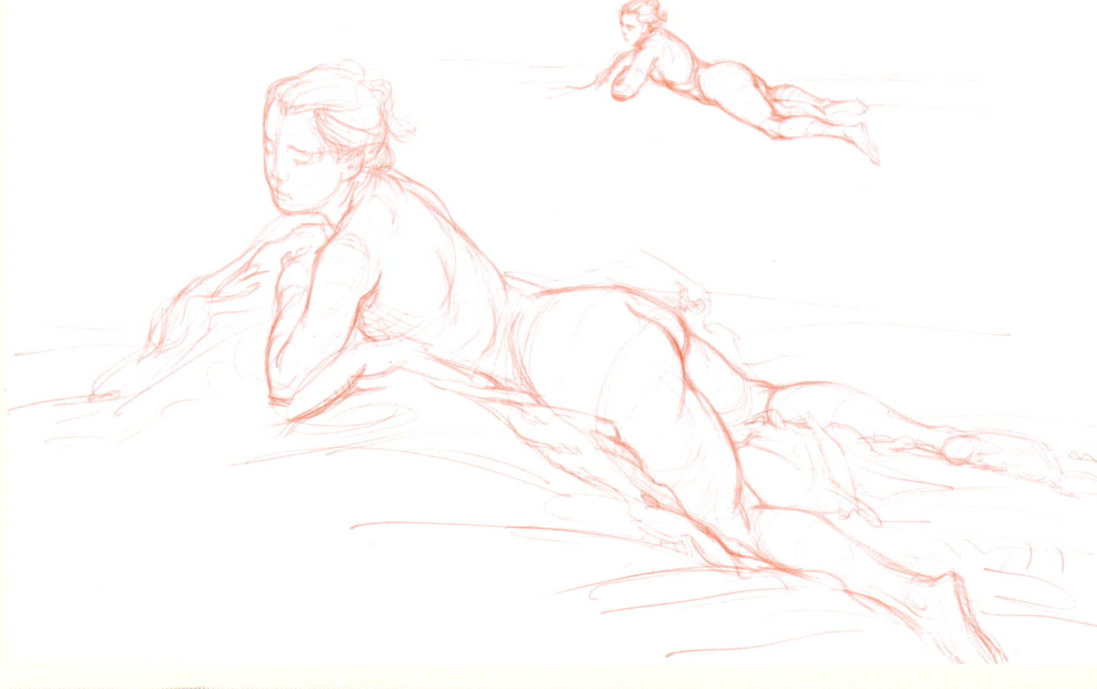

Seeing the Boucher from different perspectives.

GIVE IT A TRY: *Exercise 1*

Try the same with this Watteau. Let's say we're at the bottom of her seat. Try going even lower and exaggerate the tilt into the paper. Or try coming up higher and backing off that depth. Keep in mind, the pose itself tilts, and you would have to come way over the top to get her torso back in line with the picture plane.

The point is not to get it mechanically right, but to feel there are distinct differences in the position of the pose as our position to it changes.

If it stumps you, don't worry: it's tricky. Instead, practice a basic construction as Watteau conceived it. That's work enough.

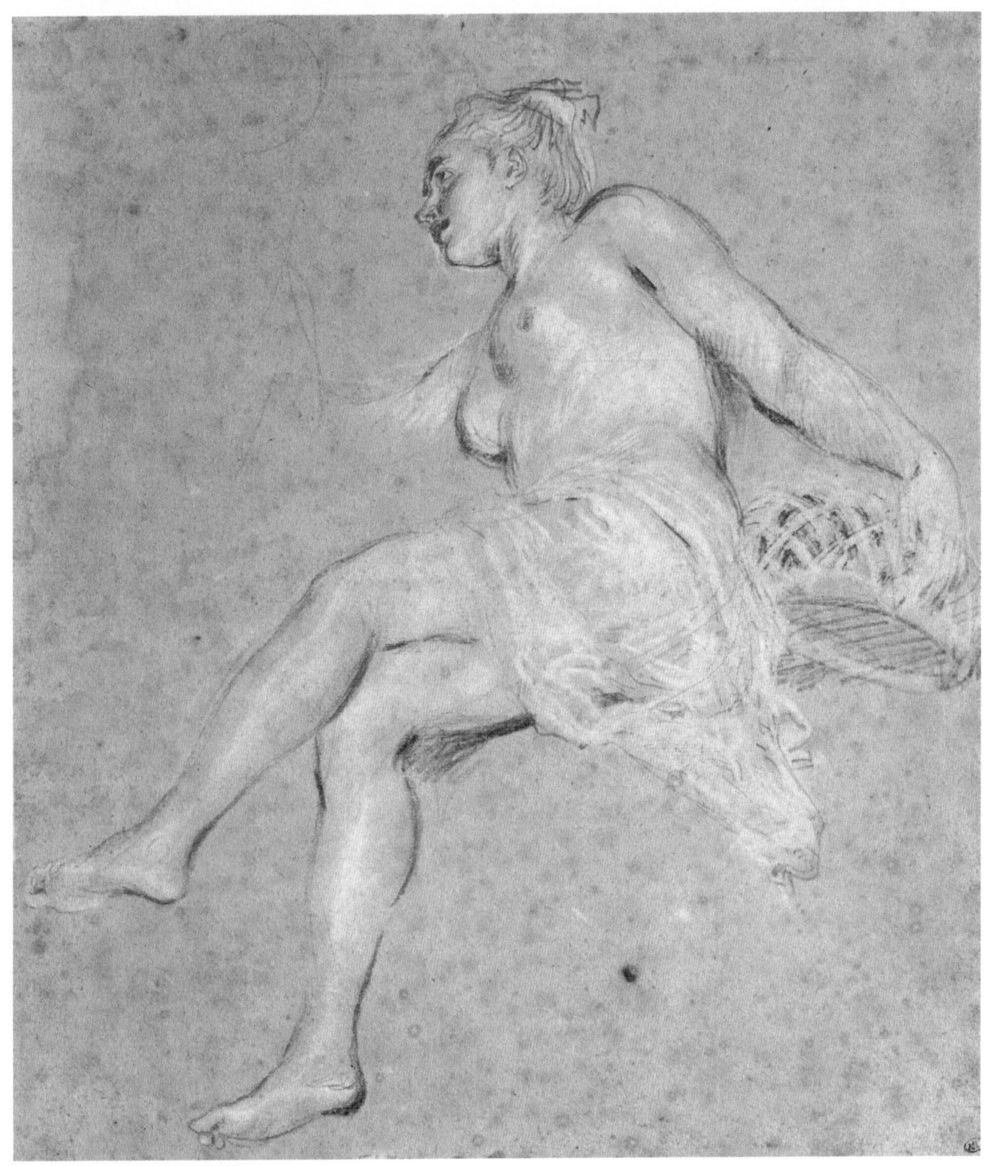

Flora, c. 1716, Jean Antoine Watteau (1684–1721). Chalk on paper. Louvre, Paris/Bridgeman Images.

GIVE IT A TRY: *Exercise 2*

Do an analysis of the Nicolai Fechin drawing (see page 58) at the start of the chapter. Can you change the eye level?

Or, draw simple tubes, boxes, and spheres with three-dimensional ends that show the forms tilting deeply into the paper. Notice the ends may be curving because the form is tilting dramatically or because your eye level is dramatically lower, or higher, to it—or both!

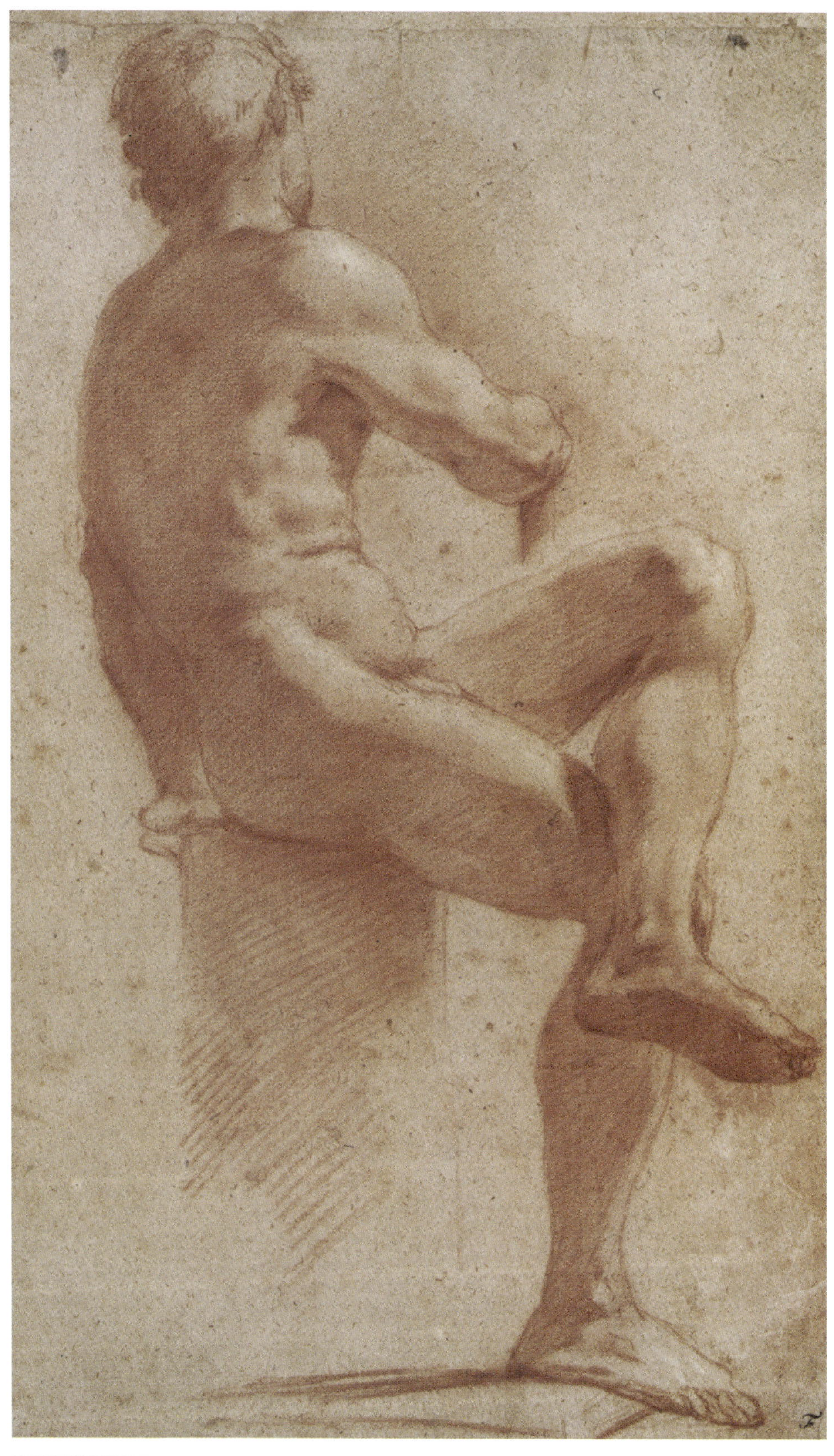

A Male Nude Seated with His Back Turned, c. sixteenth/seventeenth century, by Annibale Carracci (1560–1609). Chalk on buff paper. Private Collection/Bridgeman Images.

5 | THE LAWS OF LIGHT

I've been very clear that I devise self-serving definitions. Obviously, the body doesn't have tubes hidden inside it nor are there long axis wires flowing through it. We creative types perform all sorts of mental gymnastics to get a handle on this thing called "art."

But the laws of light are something we can take into the laboratory and prove. It's science. Nature works by physical laws. People discover them. Soon, we come to depend on them—the scientists and the artists. These laws are so constant they take us into the outer realms of space or inner realms of quantum physics. But, think about this: another word for *laws* is *rules*. Another word for *rules* is *formulas*.

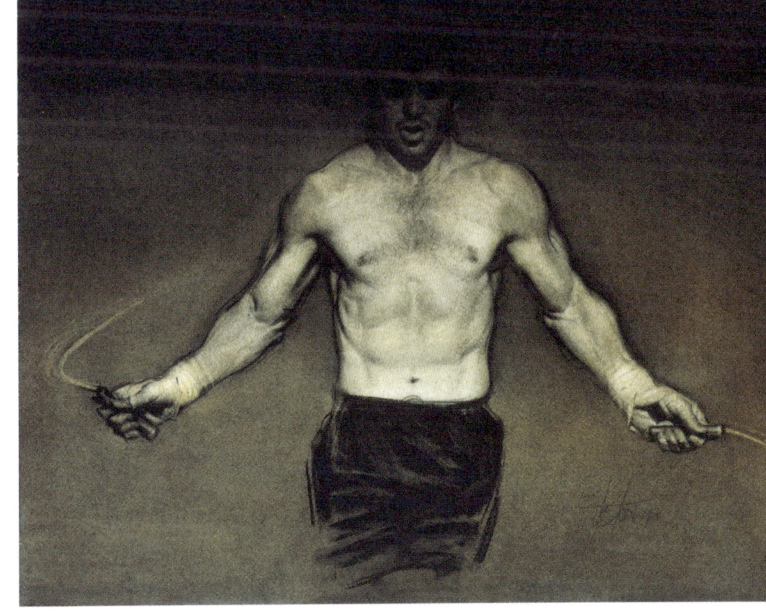

The Jump Roper, 1998, by Steve Huston. Charcoal and chalk on Strathmore Bristol paper.

Formulas Using Two or Three Values

Using formulas is considered older than old school and it's a total party killer for the cool crowd. But, it's also a very important baseline. Laws, rules, formulas—this is the mechanism by which nature acts natural. Natural is consistent. It's dependable. And if you plan to make art with even a modicum of realism, you need to know a few of the laws of nature.

You may be planning to go all Picasso after you finish this book. Fine with me. I like Picasso. The laws of nature are a great place from which to make that jump—as Picasso himself did. It's that whole "you have to know the rules to break the rules" cliché. Clichés are truisms so true they no longer surprise us. They bore. So, it's our job as artists to freshen things up. So, back to formulas: Rule 1 . . .

Rule 1: Different Value = Different Plane

All things are possible in this world. But for this book, and frankly, for most realistic artwork, the artist uses one direct light source.

Light coming from only one direction makes the process infinitely easier. Two planes equally facing the direction of the light source look equally light. But, when one plane turns away from the light, that plane gets darker.

Rule 1: different value = different plane.

From this little idea comes great things!

It may seem impossible to the uninitiated, but the rule of different value = different plane lets artists take brush or pencil to flat paper or canvas and make it look like rocks, or water, or a figure, or all of those things.

When those values are pushed toward the extremes of light and dark, as in this figure drawing at right, it's called *chiaroscuro*, a Renaissance term meaning light-dark. It means playing one value against the next for dramatic effect.

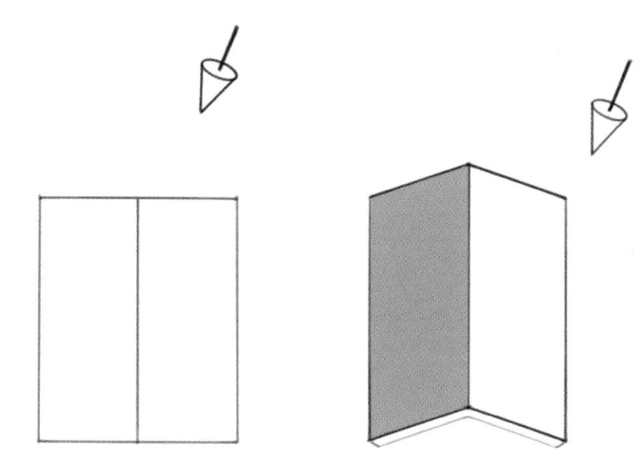

Always know the direction of the light source before beginning your shadow work.

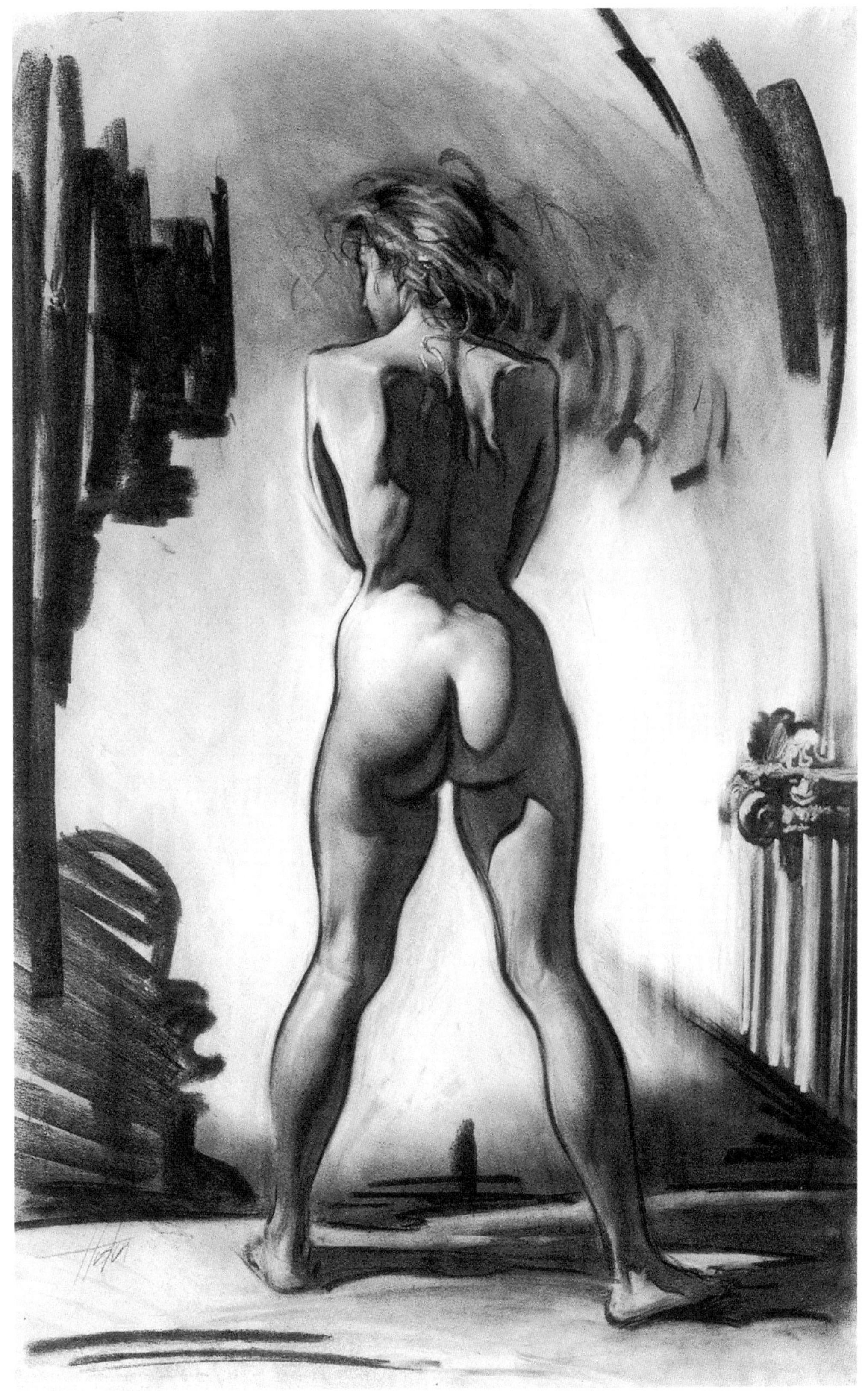

Molly, c. 2000, by Steve Huston. Alphacolor and Conté chalk on Strathmore, Bristol finish. The chiaroscuro (light and shade in drawing and painting) design is infinitely easier to render and, of course, more dramatic, than subtle lighting.

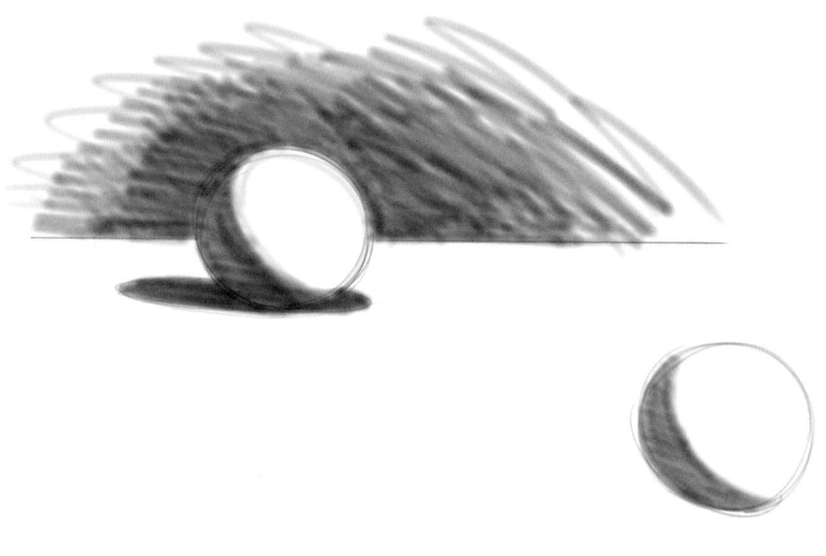

Adding a background distinguishes the foreground and roots an object in space.

If we try to capture all the subtle values one mark at a time, as we might assume Zorn did, it's overwhelming and we'll almost certainly fail. So, we fall back on one of our earliest strategies: big and simple, followed by small and complex. We start with the foundational ideas and save the subtle details for later, if at all.

We only have two responsibilities: separating light from shadow and foreground from background. That's it! And even better, this is a figure-drawing book, not a drawing-the-whole-world book, so we don't need to worry about the foreground/background relationships. Leaving blank paper around the drawn figure does all the separating needed.

It doesn't even need to be done very well. There is no line in nature. There are no hatching textures. Nature is full of color. But, because we have the big simple foundational ideas down clearly, all else is forgiven. And the loosey-goosey technique can even be charming. It's what we call a sketch, letting the process show while still respecting the big ideas.

The beauty of a solid method is we don't need to sweat the small stuff, as the saying goes. Start big—if you want to, stay big.

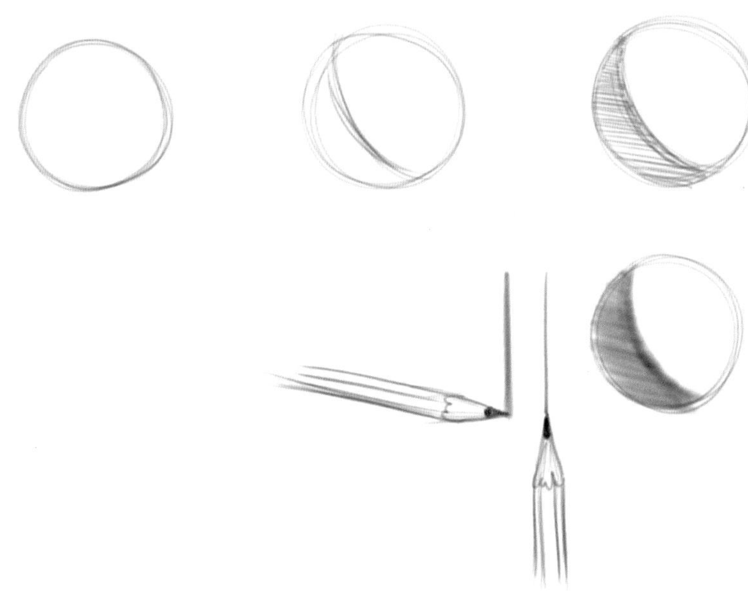

When we draw the shape of the shadow on the ball, the ball looks better (meaning a little more real). If we draw it with a soft edge, as I did in the last ball, it looks better yet. (If you need a review of how to make soft edges, reread the Introduction, page 18.)

A TWO-VALUE SYSTEM

As stated previously, the only values we're obligated to show our audience are the light and shadow values. And we're thinking big and simple, so we only need to find two values; one value for the light and one value for the shadow.

We can certainly add rendered detail onto those two values. In fact, we can add as much detail as we want.

That becomes an added step by turning the two values into two value *ranges*. Let's start, though, with a two-value system and a three-step process:

1. Draw the shape of the form.

2. Draw the shape of the shadow on the form.

3. Give the shadow a darker value.

So, you've drawn the form and the shape of the shadow on the form and then given the shadow a darker value. How do we know when it's dark enough? The best thing to do is take a cue from the chiaroscuro crowd. We use the "squint test."

Take a moment to squint at the Zorn painting, *Dagmar*, on page 57 that started this chapter. Notice that the light and shadow on the figure do not separate from each other very well. Rather, the foreground figure separates from the background when you squint at it. That one choice makes the construction of a convincing figure much more difficult. As you see, it can still be done, and beautifully.

It's still all about value. Zorn used subtler values, meaning more room for mistakes. Better to start with the dramatic chiaroscuro strategy and ensure all the shadows group against all the lights, even if there is rendered detail going on in one or both.

Now, look at Zorn's *Madonna* at the right and squint. Despite the details, the shadows look dark and the lights look light, and the two don't compete.

The master artist may choose a more sophisticated way of dealing with foreground/background and light/shadow relationships, although realism demands it be based on the rule of different value = different plane. And when sketching ideas or observations, sometimes the shadows don't separate with great contrast. Look to the earlier chapters and you'll see plenty of examples. They are still beautiful. Many are masterpieces.

However, nothing beats chiaroscuro for the dramatic effect of showing form in space. It's the easiest way to add value, complexity, and realism to your work. If the light and shadows do not separate, then the form won't pop off the page. Think about da Vinci, Giorgone, Caravaggio, Rembrandt, van Dyke, Gainsborough, or Sargent portraits, Inness landscapes, and myriad others— they all pass the "squint test." And, if you want to learn quickly and efficiently to harness the power of value, your drawings and paintings should too.

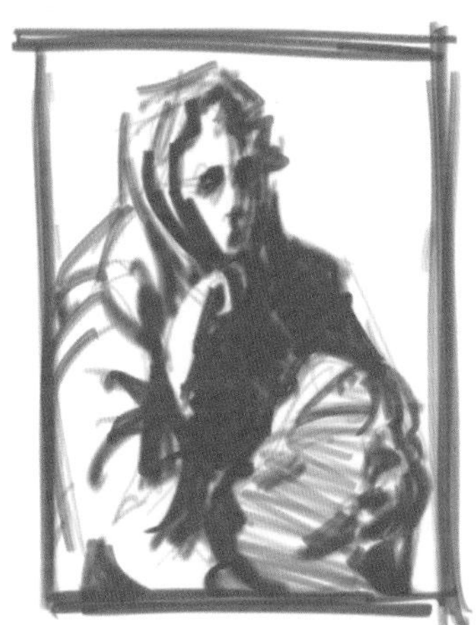
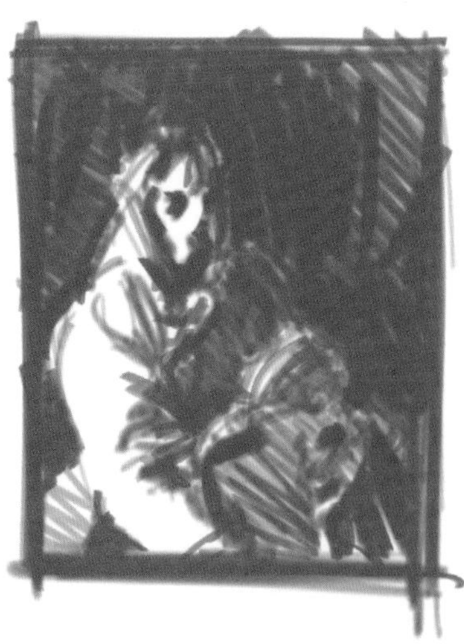

Under any lovely rendering or fantastic technique are the real bones of the work, and that is what painters call the *tonal composition*. The easiest way to put a tonal composition in place is with our two-value system: separating light from shadow through the squint test.

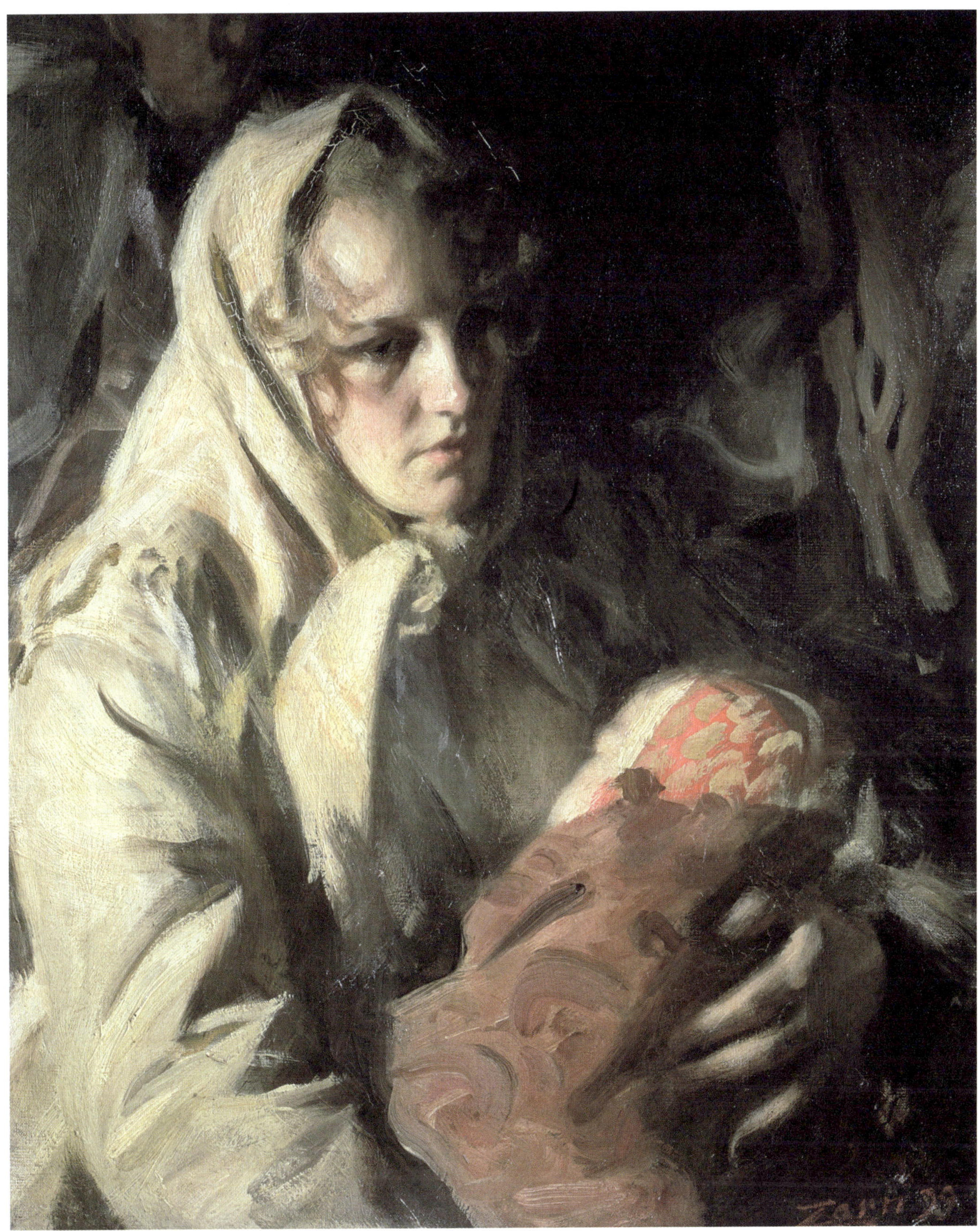

Madonna, 1899, by Anders Leonard Zorn (1860–1920). Oil on canvas. Private collection/Bridgeman Images.

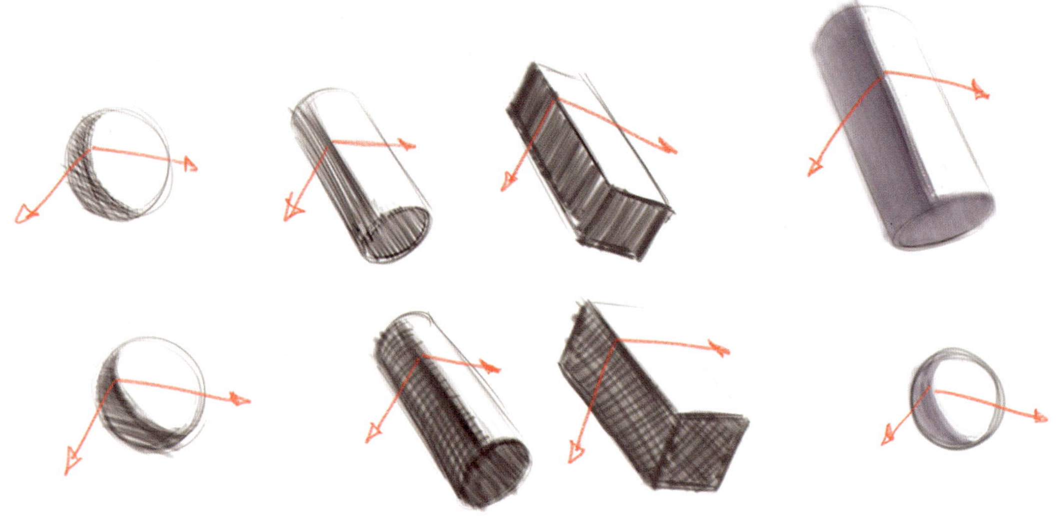

Here are some simple constructed forms done with the three-step process, but with different shading techniques.

BOX LOGIC

Look at the image above. Just so we're clear, the red lines show the corners. You can see, in term of rendered detail, the ball and tube are still very boxy. Only their contours say "round." That's often as far as we'll take a sketchbook drawing. And, oddly enough, the viewer adds the roundness for us. One of the nice things about art is if we get the beginning right, the audience will finish the rest.

Our rule, different value = different plane, turns the form, any form. Notice I drew a ball and a tube with the same process I used for the box. I call this box logic. In other words, by finding the edge between light and shadow on any form, we've found the principle "corner" for that form—another arbitrary definition, but a useful one.

By thinking of the beginning of any shadow as a corner, we have come back to our definition of structure. Corners are corners whether you create them with line or tone and whether you intend to round off those corners later. Notice, too, the drawing doesn't have to be done masterfully to get the idea across. It can be a sketch. I bet you can do it just as well, probably better.

Finding the shape of the form, finding the shape of the shadow on the form, and then grouping the shadows darker is the only responsibility we have for achieving realism. Finding the shape of the form and the shadow establishes a corner, and shadow gives an instant and deep sense that whatever you're drawing is a fully three-dimensional form.

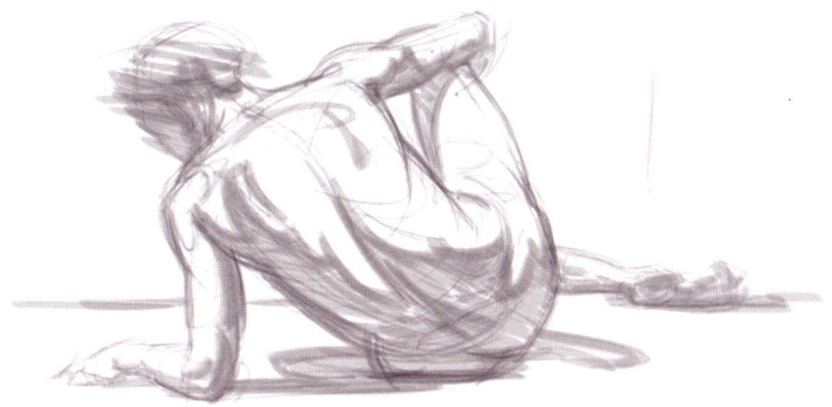

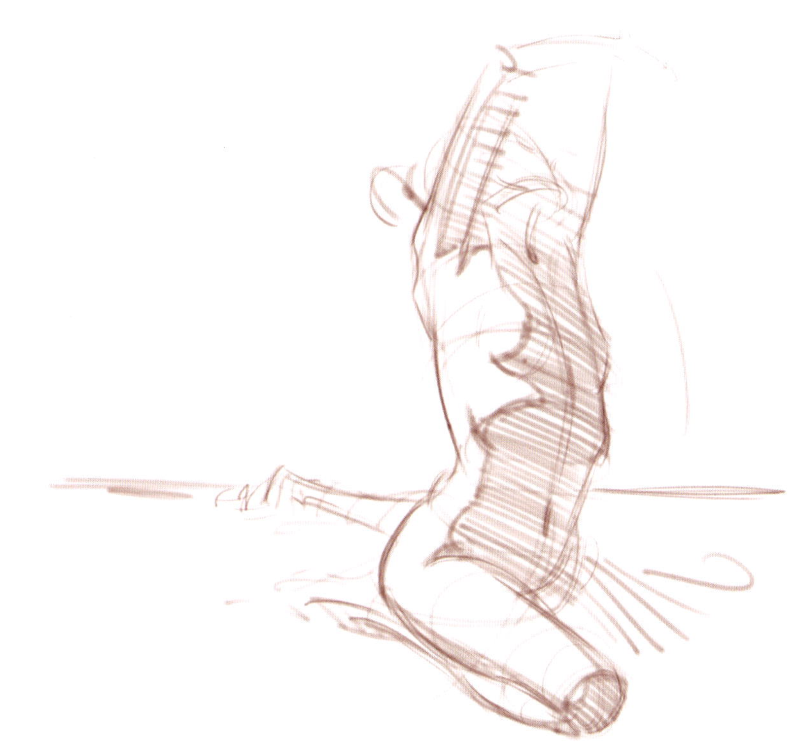

These five-minute drawings use the three-step process to add shadow shapes to a basic lay-in so you can see the application. We will walk through how to make believable shadows on full figures.

Halftones, Highlights, and a New Rule

Two types of values make up the light side of an object—halftones and highlights. Let's look at each.

HALFTONES

The halftone is everything in the light side that is not a highlight. This means the halftone can be almost as dark as the shadow and almost as light as the highlight. Whether you add a little or a lot, the character of the halftone is *gradation*.

If the beginning of the shadow is a corner, then the halftone's most important job is to round the corner. The more gradation, the rounder the form gets. That means we can render those spheres and tubes so they are completely convincing. Our two-value system becomes two value ranges once we add halftone. (By the way, it still needs to pass the squint test.)

The illustration at right shows some common mistakes artists make when adding halftones. These include:

A. Drawing the core shadow (beginning corner) with a hard edge rather than a soft edge.

B. Drawing a straight-line core to describe a round form; curved forms generally need curved details to explain them.

C. Drawing the whole shadow so light that the viewer doesn't get that chiaroscuro pop.

D. Drawing the core shadow much darker than the body of the shadow.

E. Not accenting the corner with a slightly darker beginning.

F. Making the outline significantly darker than the shadow value.

G. Making the halftone darker than the shadow.

I repeated E, F, and G in marker (H, I, and J) to make the point that it's the fundamentals we're talking about. The technique or medium has nothing to do with it.

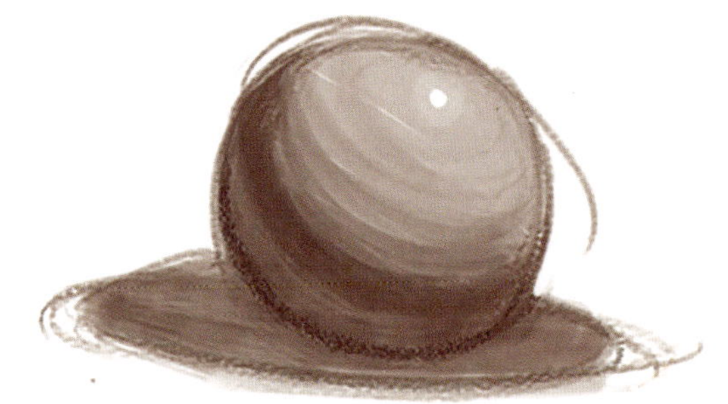

Time to make the three-step process a four-step process with the halftone added.

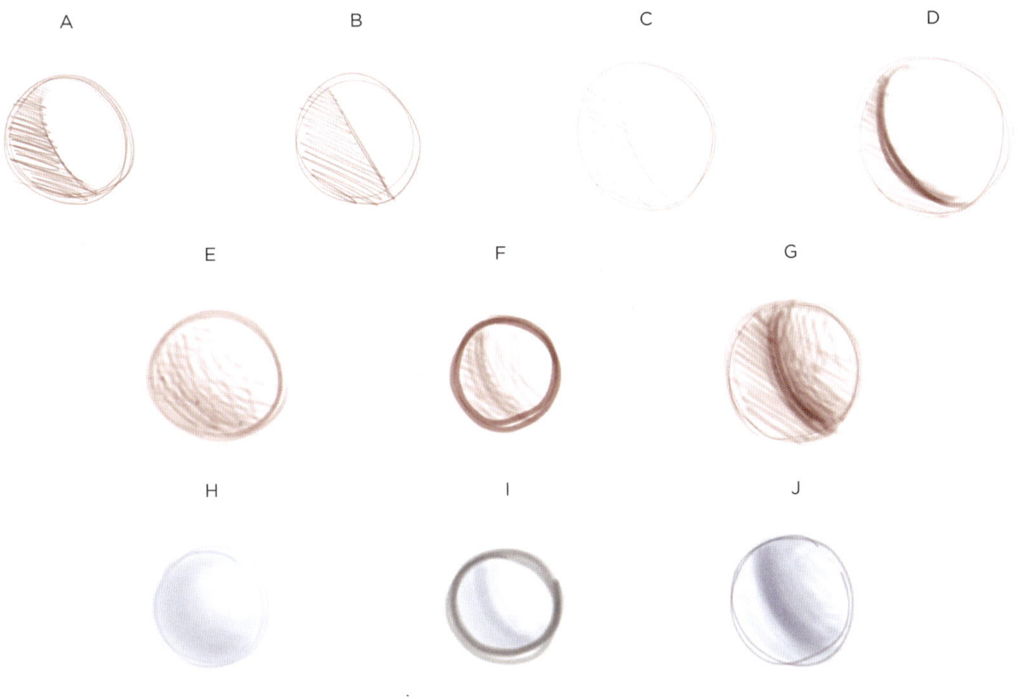

These drawings show some common mistakes.

Keep in mind, the squint test solves most of these problems. It ensures the lights stay light and the darks stay dark, and the two don't compete with each other.

It's key that you draw the beginning of the shadow shape as a nice soft edge. That sets things up for the halftone rendering.

HIGHLIGHTS

To understand highlights we need a pool table.

Light strikes an object and bounces to our eye. That's how we see both the value and the color of any object.

Study the image at right. Think of the pool cue as the light source, the ball as the light coming from the source, the far bank as the object being lit, and the pockets as the position of the artist/viewer.

The light source washes over the form. As the form slowly rolls away from the light source, the light glances off of it with an ever-weakening effect. That is our halftone gradation.

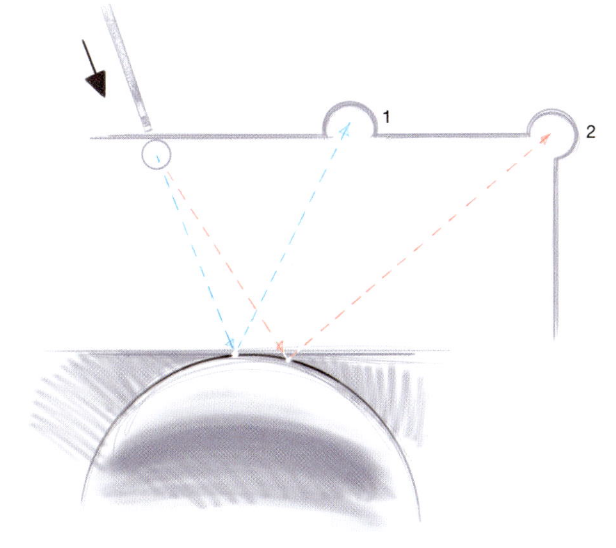

To get the ball into pocket 1, you have to bounce it off the far cushion. Light works the same way. It bounces.

The highlight is a little different—it tends to stay in the area most directly facing the light source. But, there is room for movement in that hot spot. That's going to be a good thing for us.

Notice that if neither the light source nor the object moves but the viewer changes positions, then the highlight can shift. The turquoise trajectory into pocket 1 shows this, as opposed to the red line trajectory into pocket 2.

All this is to say that light bounces. Or, as they say in the business, light *reflects*. Reflecting light explains how the highlight can move around (did I mention that was a good thing?) and it explains why shadows aren't dead black!

BOUNCING LIGHT

Light bounces. It bounces to our eyes so we see what we see. It also bounces into anything else that turns toward it. That brings us to Rule 2.

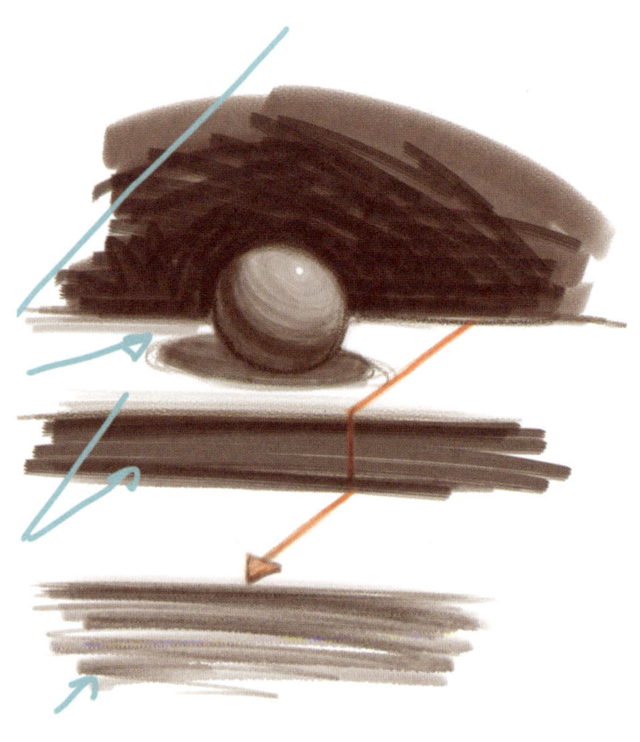

If we decide to revisit that dreaded foreground/background idea, things get more complicated.

Rule 2: Everything that Receives Light Is a Source of Light

As the light strikes the stair step or an off-camera wall, it bounces back into the ball sitting there (see the turquoise arrow), at left. It won't bounce into the light side because it's a weaker light source than the spotlight or sunlight that's powering the scene to begin with.

The way it works is, the light that bounces up off the step will lighten the planes that face down. The light that bounces to the right from the off-camera wall that faces right will lighten the planes that face left. As you see, the ball is a little lighter than the core at the bottom and bottom/left.

This can get confusing, I know. For an introduction to drawing (even a fairly comprehensive book as this is), messing around with bouncing light on a face or body is too much to handle.

There are two reasons I mention this. We need to know that light bounces so we can take control of the highlights. And we are already giving a good representation of bouncing light without even trying!

That shadow corner we accent with a core of darkness did several things for us:

- It made sure we spotted the corner for our structure.

- It was created as a soft mark to render our halftone gradations more easily out of it.

- It created a sense of bouncing light without getting bogged down with the theory.

When one mark can serve several purposes, it's a good mark.

That's more than enough to make our artwork look impressive. In fact, remember da Vinci, Caravaggio, Rembrandt, and the rest of those masters of chiaroscuro? What we just did is what they mostly did for their finishes.

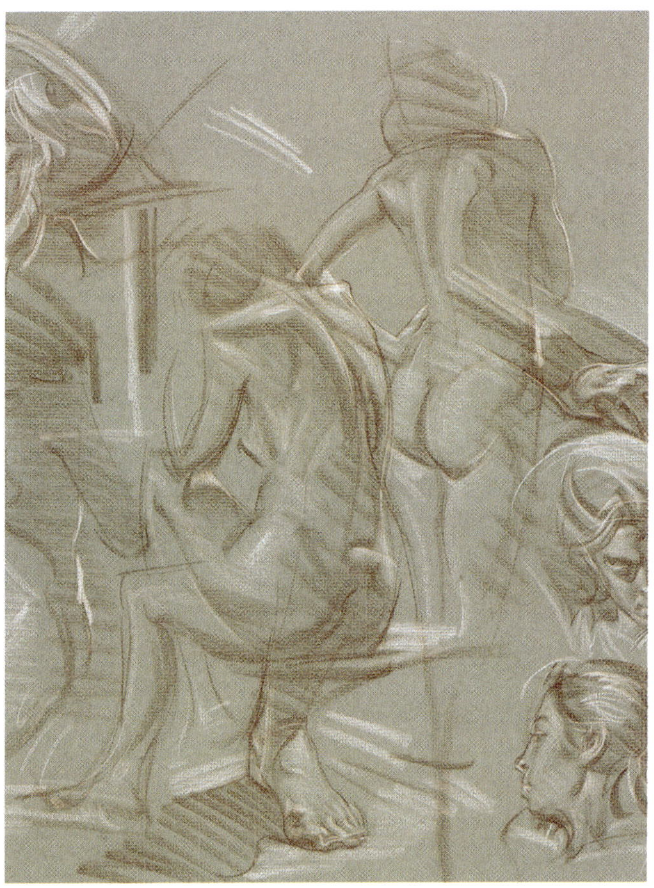

In the two central figures in this sketch, the shadows get very light and begin to compete with the light side. These lights and darks can be made to work. But in the beginning, keep to the two-value system and our squint test to determine lights and darks.

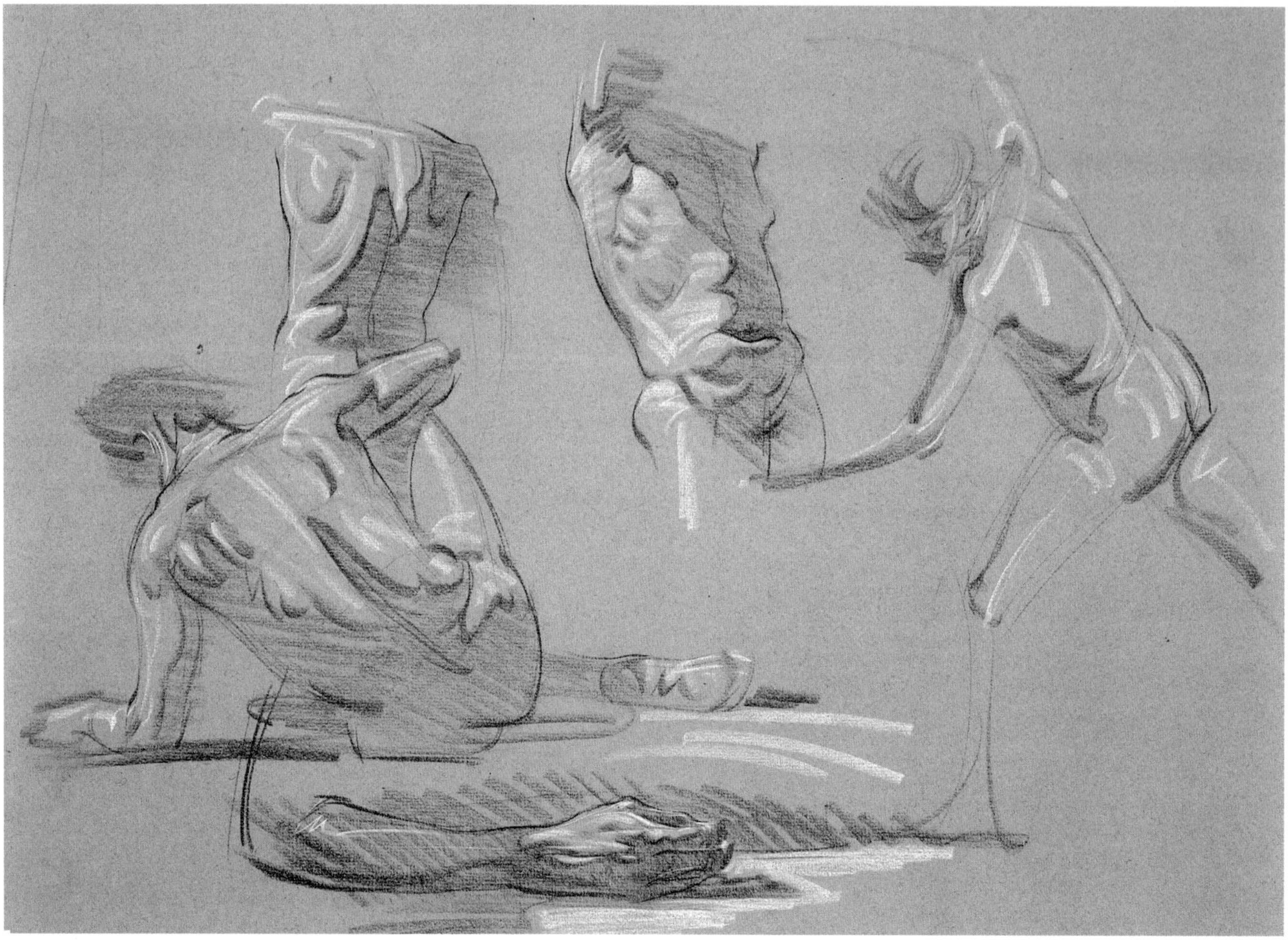

Using white and dark charcoal on toned paper is an excellent preparation for painting, and you get to play with highlights.

HIGHLIGHTS AGAIN

I'll make this quick. Because highlights move around (if you forget why, it doesn't matter), we are going to make them work for us.

As we can see in the image to the right, highlights are corners. Highlights are structure!

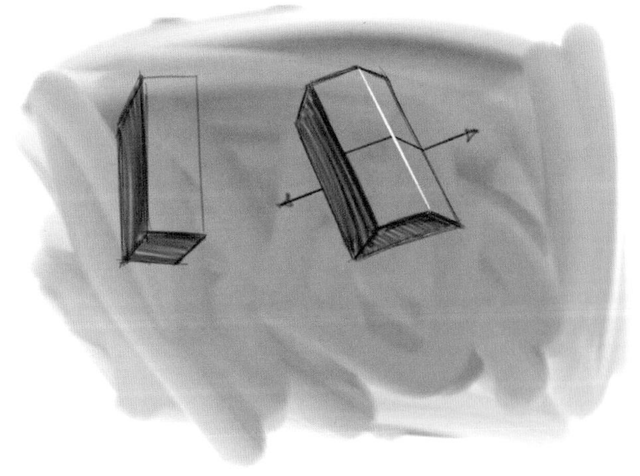

The beginning of the shadow is a corner. We know that. Well, the highlight is a corner as well. It's just a corner between two planes in light.

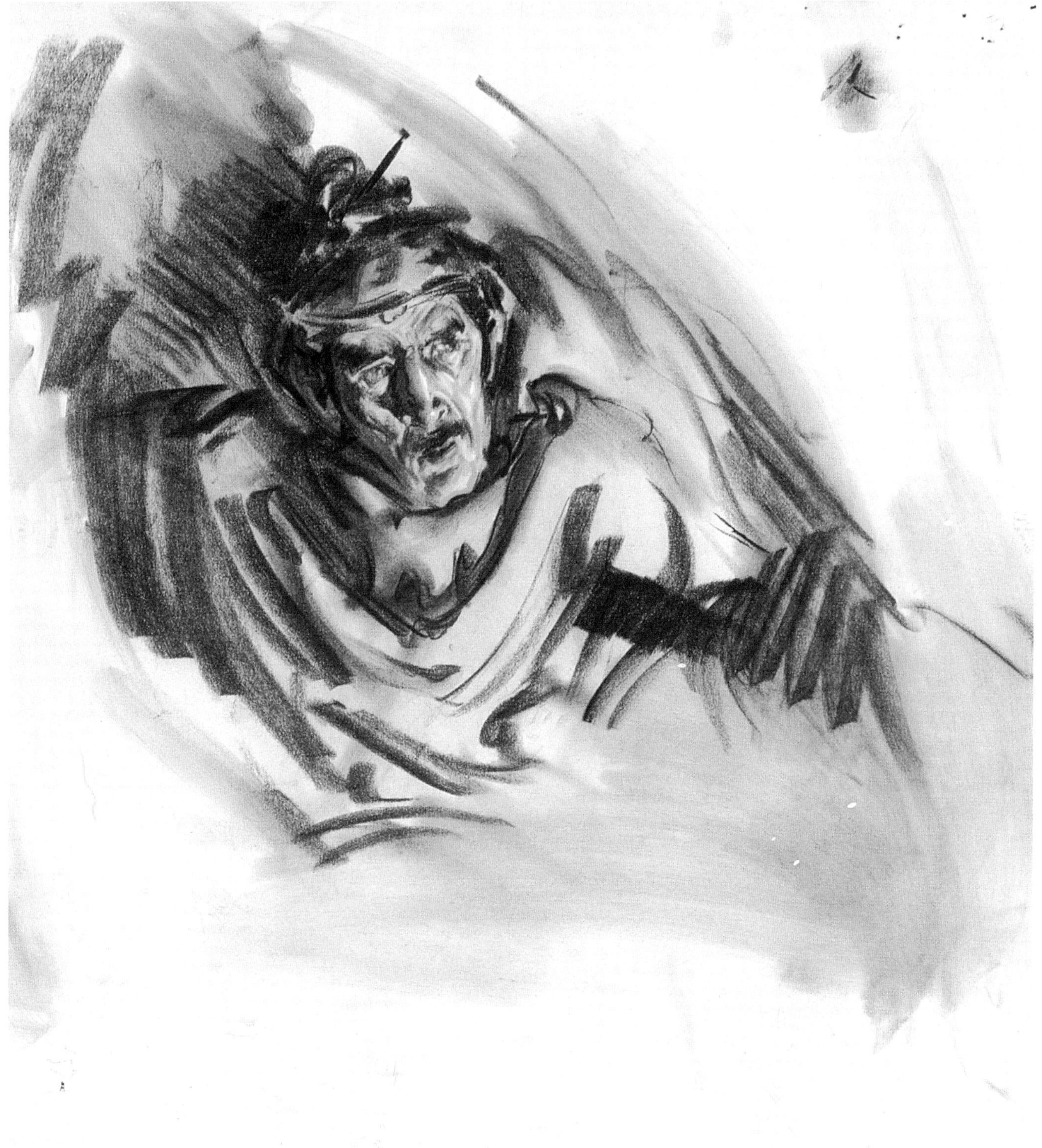

Joe in Costume, c. 1999, by Steve Huston. Alphacolor and Conté chalk on Strathmore, Bristol finish. There are lots of highlights on the head drawing I did. How many you can map out? I'll go first. Where the side of the nose meets the front of the nose on the bridge, we have a highlight. Three planes come together where the top, front, and corner planes meet at the highlight on the tip of the nose!

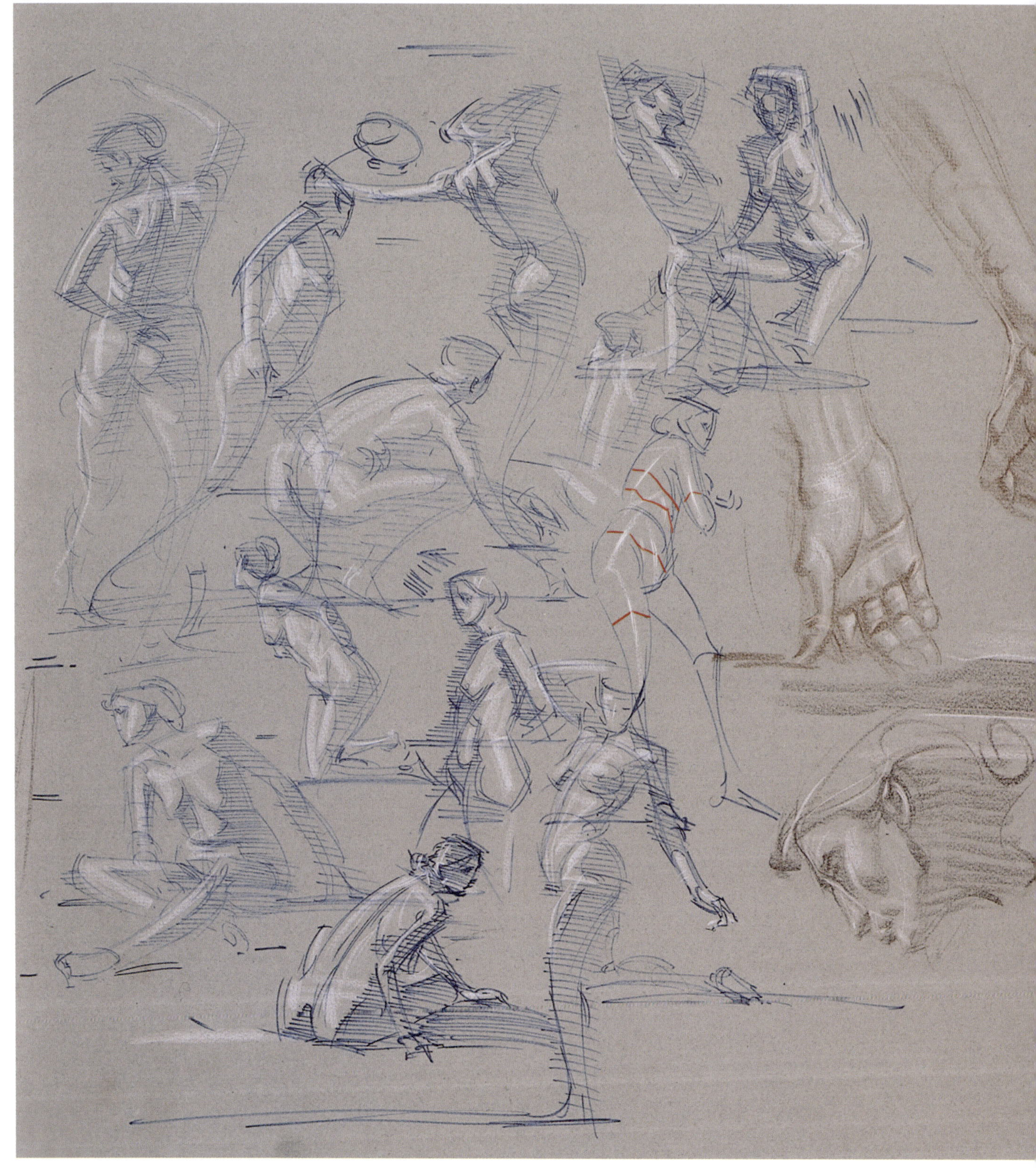

Track those highlights. If they are not quite at a perfect corner, it'll most likely be close enough.

Remember, highlights move around. The trick is to keep them away from the shadow corner. That way, the highlight always suggests two planes in light. The process should be shadow, halftone, and highlight, each having its own space.

Highlights do other things, too. They can blast out a halftone area to make it pop away from the shadows even more. Highlights and halftones can gradate down a curve to show it's fading out of light. They can also gradate across a flat plane such as a tabletop to move the eye in and out of space a little more naturally.

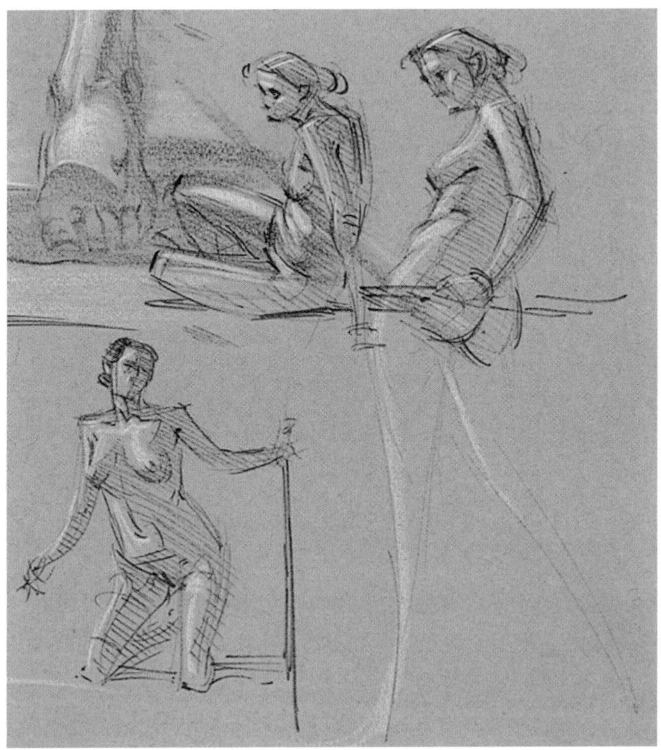
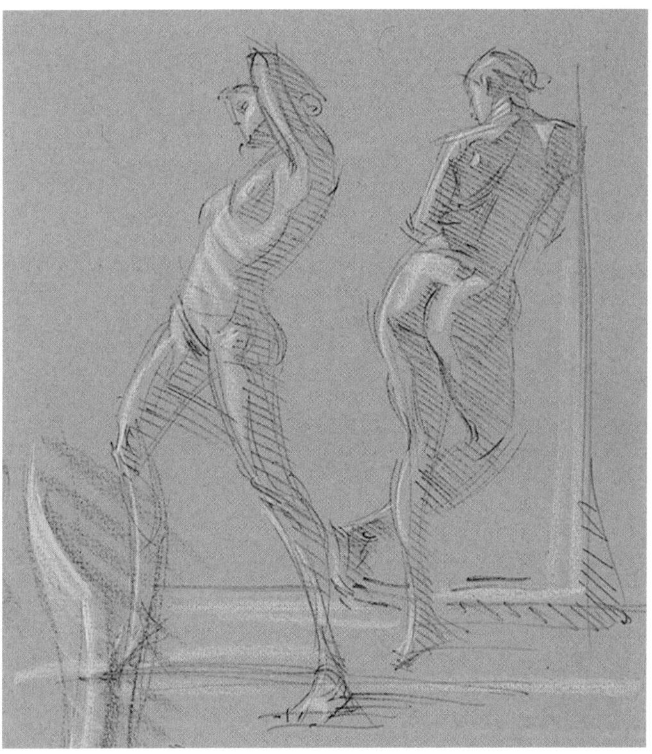

Notice that even in the quick sketches on these two pages, I keep a little of the paper's tone between the pen and ink shadows and the white chalk highlights.

OLD MASTER *study*

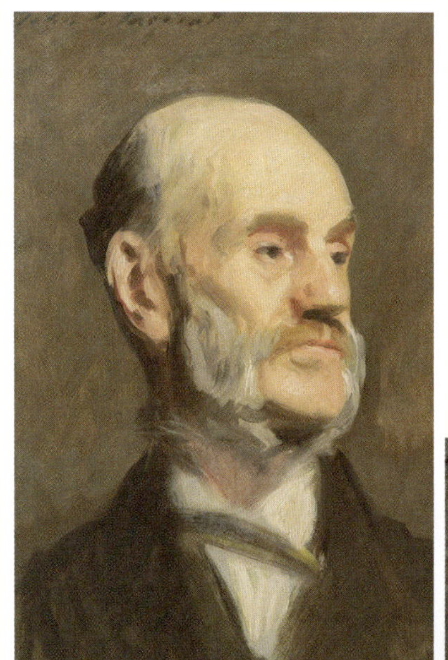

Hercules Brabazon, c. twentieth century, John Singer Sargent (1856–1925). Oil on canvas. National Museum Wales/ Bridgeman Images.

This portrait by John Singer Sargent features a well-constructed head. Imagine all the little details Sargent left out and you'll begin to appreciate the vision involved. As always in chiaroscuro pieces, the shadows anchor the image. Look how the darks pull the cheek and skull into side planes—likewise for the bottom planes.

And look at that fine highlight tracking down to the corner of Mr. Brabazon's nose. Look how the highlight on the chin stays away from the core shadow corner on the chin. Also, the highlights on the chin and lower lip are much reduced compared to that on the nose, which I've accented for emphasis.

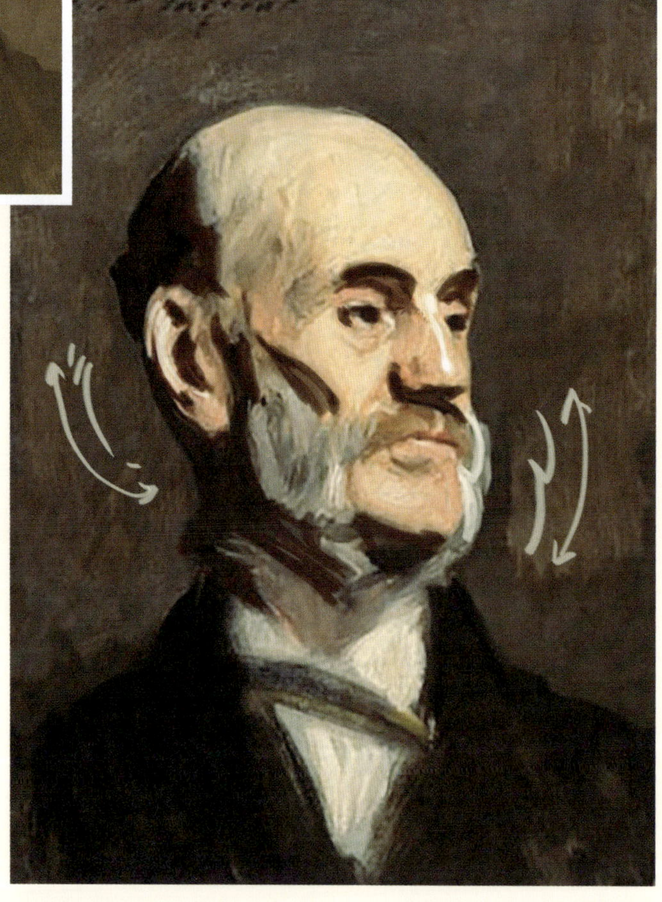

The ear highlight is a long gesture finishing in staccato strokes at either end. The far mutton chop and mustache highlight is a long zigzag that ties the two forms together—there's a great deal of variety to keep our interest. Fine work throughout.

Lay tracing paper over this drawing and try a little trick: thicken up the highlight on the nose so it's a bit fatter. Do the same for the core shadow that helps describe the hollow of the cheek. Now, both the highlight and the core have become little corner planes in and of themselves. Are you starting to see the possibilities?

GIVE IT A TRY: *Exercise 1*

Find one simple shape in some of the drawings from this chapter. Maybe it's a tube for an upper arm or an egg for a hip. And then, add the shadow shape to your simple conception. If you choose well, your shadow shape should be very close to the shadow shape in the source drawing. If not, try another simple shape.

GIVE IT A TRY: *Exercise 2*

Get some tone paper and white chalk. See the supply list in the Introduction (page 14) for suggestions. Draw simple balls, boxes, and tubes. Draw the same way you would on white paper. Add the shadows. Then, add a little white. Keep away from the shadow corners. It's better to add too little than too much.

When you get comfortable with that, try a body part or two from this chapter's drawings. Remember, we still have to figure out how to compose the shadow on mashed-up body parts.

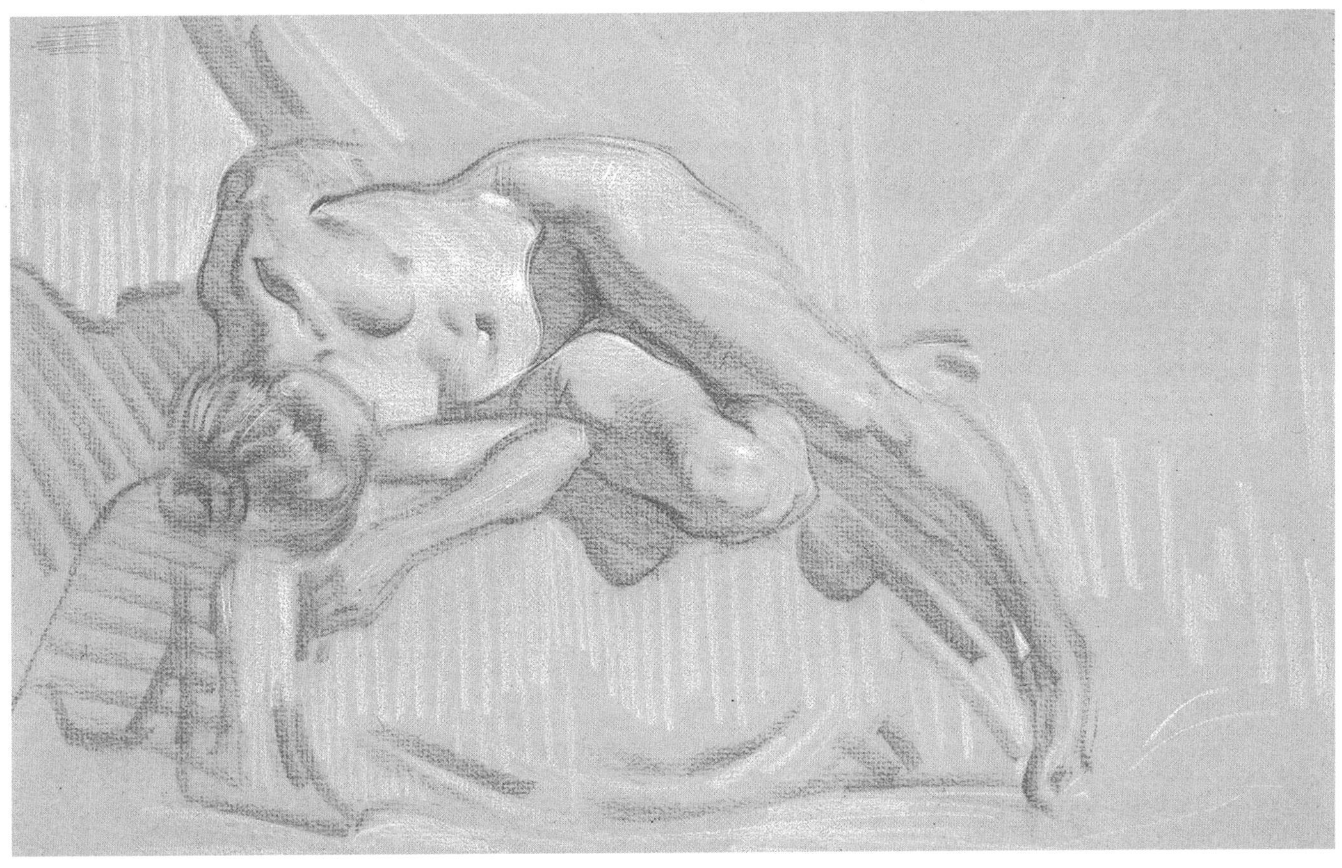

Reclining Nude, c. 2002, by Steve Huston. Carb-Othello pencil on Strathmore toned paper.

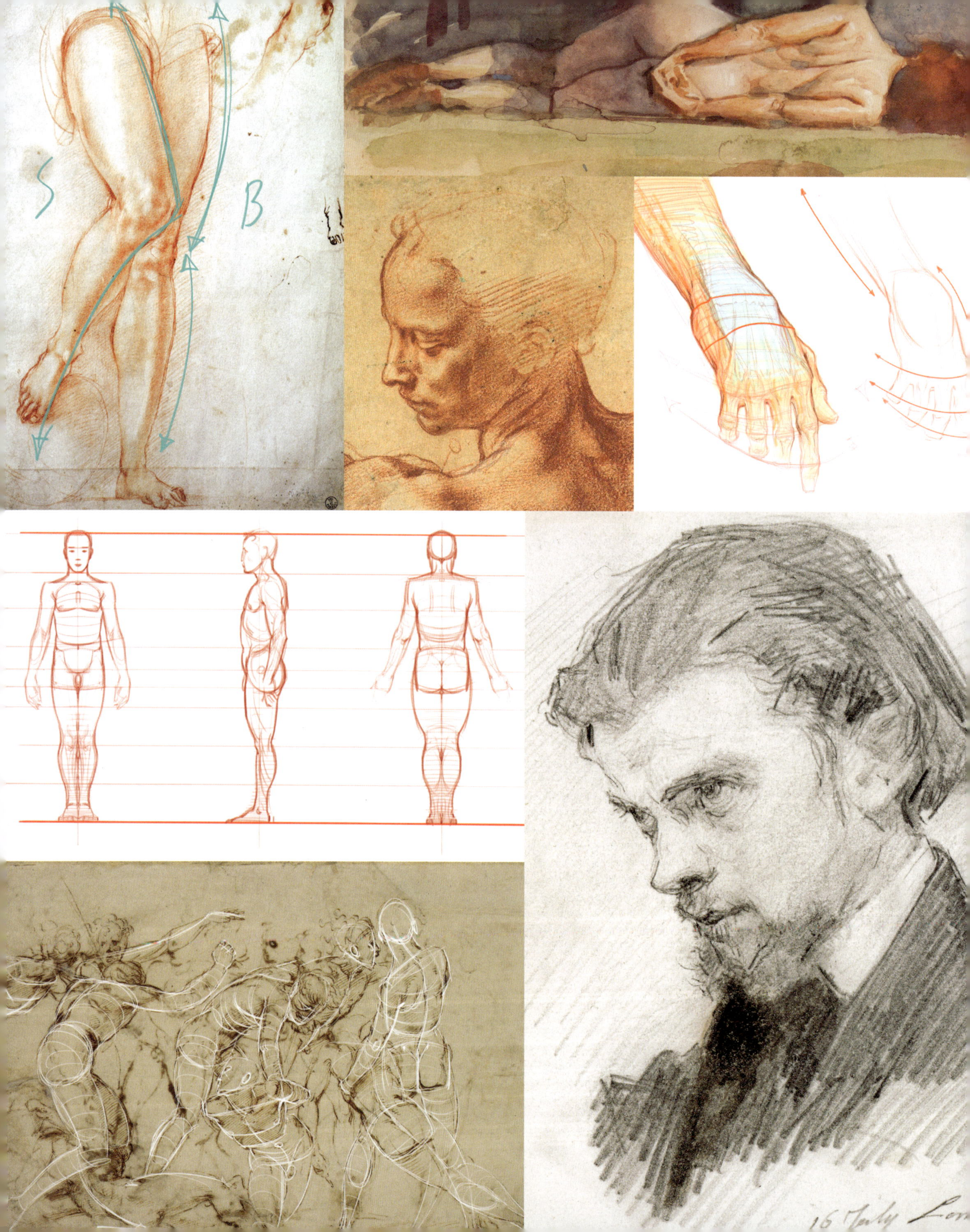

two

BREAKING DOWN THE HUMAN BODY

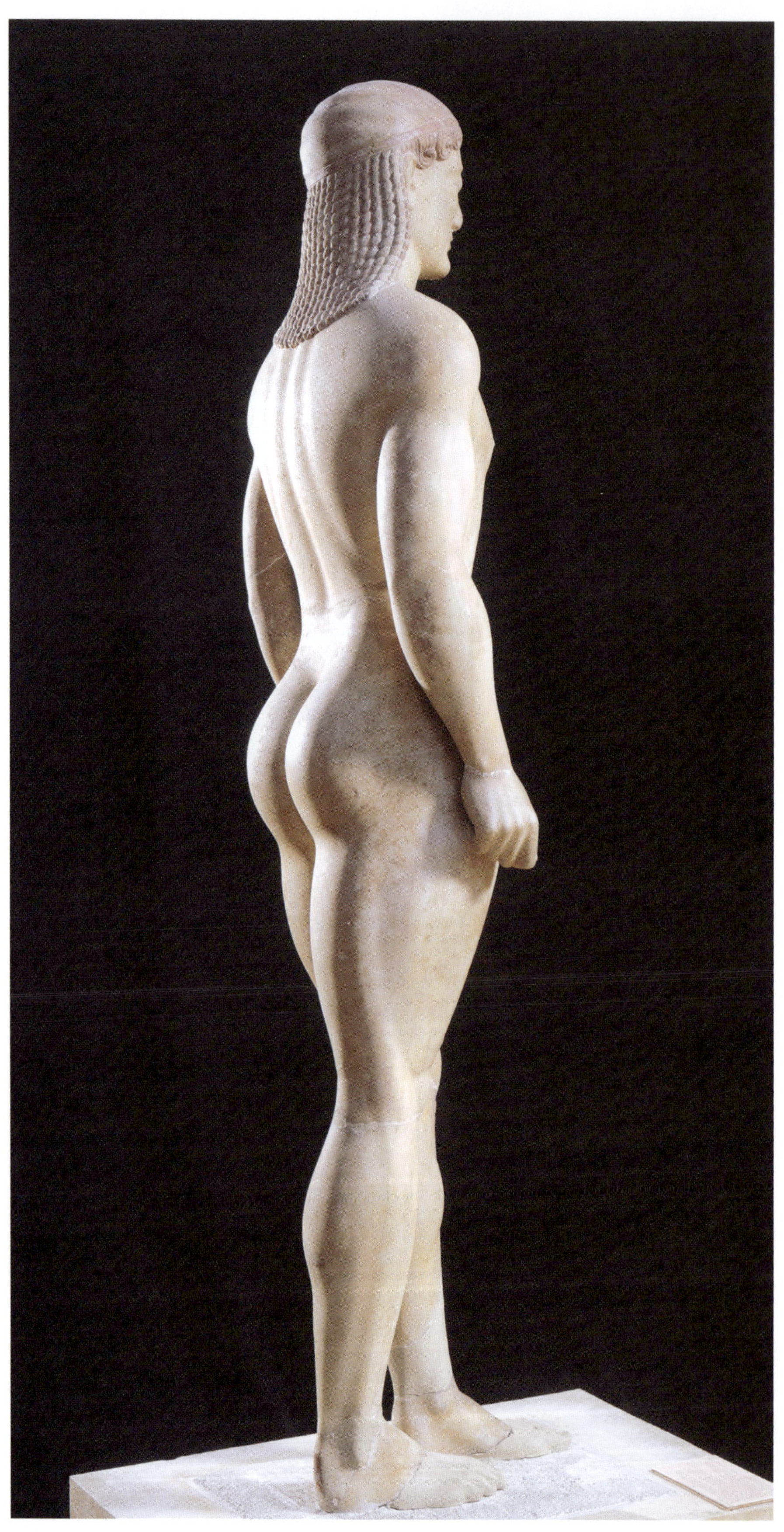

Kouros (side view), 525–550 BCE. Greek. Sculpture. National Archeological Museum, Athens/Bridgeman Images. We will primarily analyze our figures from formal positions, like this Greek kouros.

6 | THE HUMAN BODY: AN OVERVIEW OF BASIC FORMS

To capture the essence of the human body, even in basic poses, we need a strategy for dividing it into manageable pieces. It's how the Old Masters conceived of the figure, and is the same technique used by today's animators.

How to Begin

I'll take you through the body from jointed part to jointed part, always with an eye to our method: gesture/structure, gesture/ structure. This chapter is our practical beginning and lays the foundation for progressing from simple to detailed, from formal to dynamic, and from line to tone.

A word about the challenge of proportions: the looking, the measuring, the measuring, the looking, well, I've saved that until the end of the chapter. Measuring is the last thing we need to worry about while jumping headfirst into the complexities of the human body. For now, just observe and draw. Do your best with the information at hand. Part of our goal here is to build good instincts so the art comes naturally.

Here's a suggestion as you read: Stop and sketch a few of the instructional drawings after each section to test these new ideas; it is only by drawing that you will soak up the material in a lasting way. If you want to go the extra mile, after each new section go back and review some of your drawings from earlier sections to see how you did—and celebrate your progress and improvement.

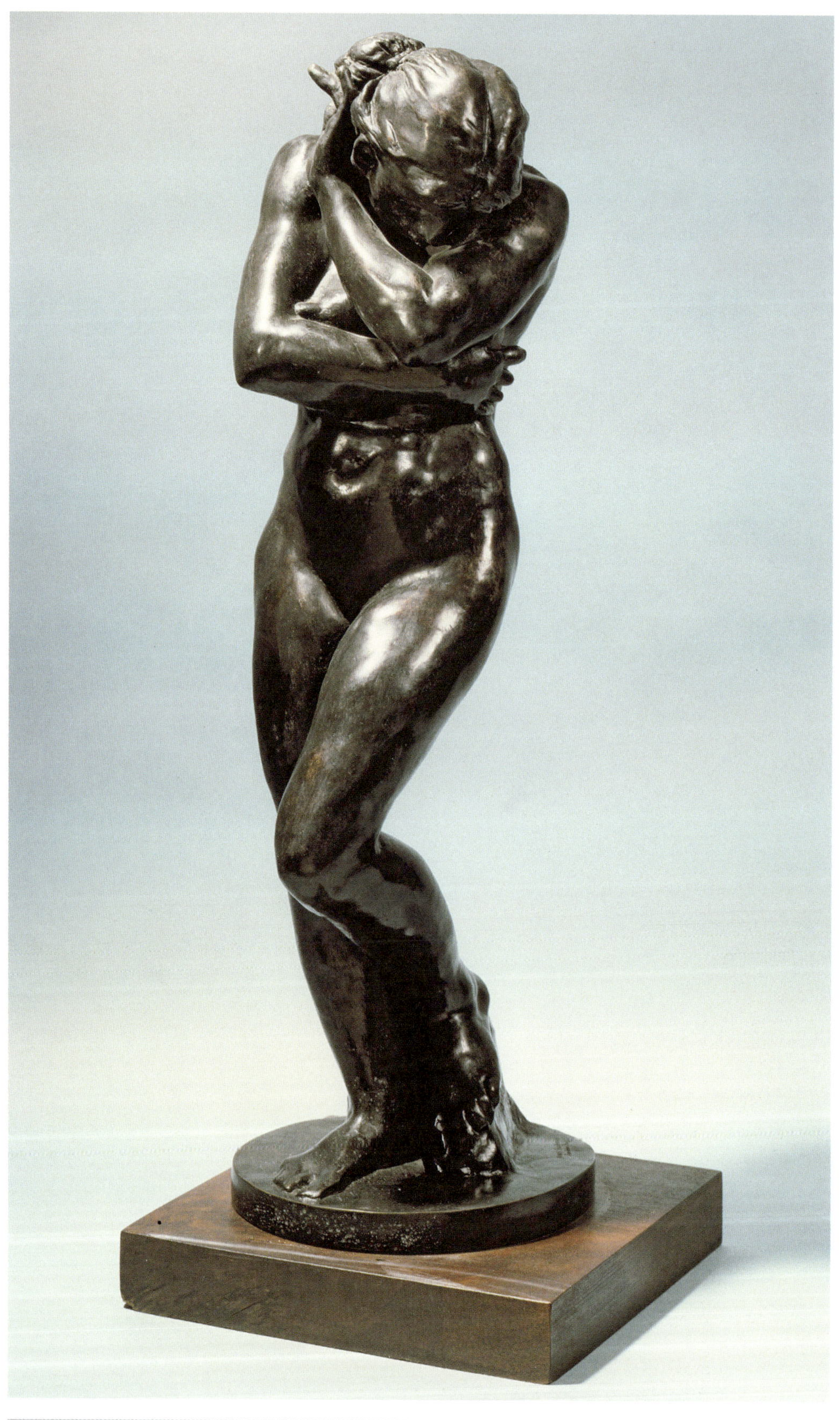

Eve, c. twentieth century, Auguste Rodin (1840–1917). Bronze. Private collection/Bridgeman Images.

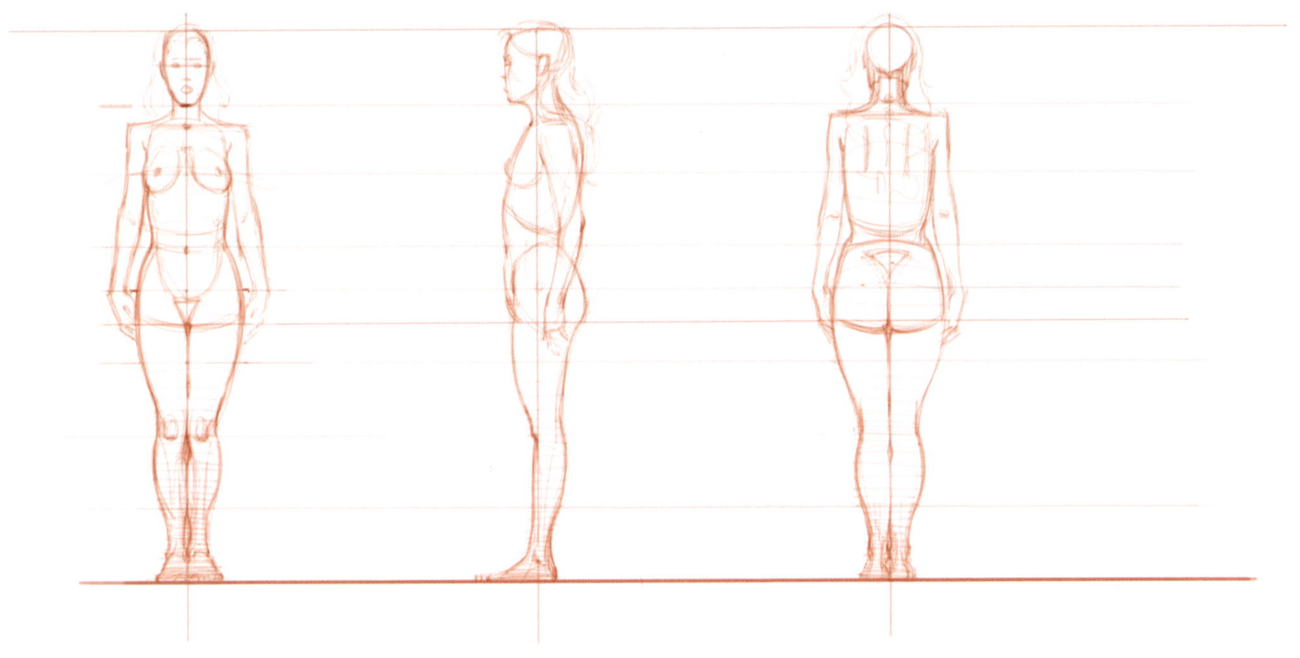

As we begin, scan these figures and mentally tick off the big simple forms you see. The artist has an eye that constantly sees and translates.

This kind of dedication teaches you to see what's in front of you in a deep way. You'll be amazed by what you missed before and at your gains as you move forward. Work those creative muscles, and you will see as you've never seen before!

As I point out the differences between male and female structures, keep in mind the number and character of the bones and muscles in both sexes are the same. The proportions and constructed forms of each simply vary a bit due to differing fat deposits and muscle masses.

However, the gestures stay substantially the same, though with the generally less-muscle-bound female those gestures can show some subtle variations in the curves of the limbs. There is a huge amount of diversity in the world, making for amazing variations on these themes. What I'm giving you here is, of course, the basics. The specifics for each body part are tackled in detail beginning on the next page.

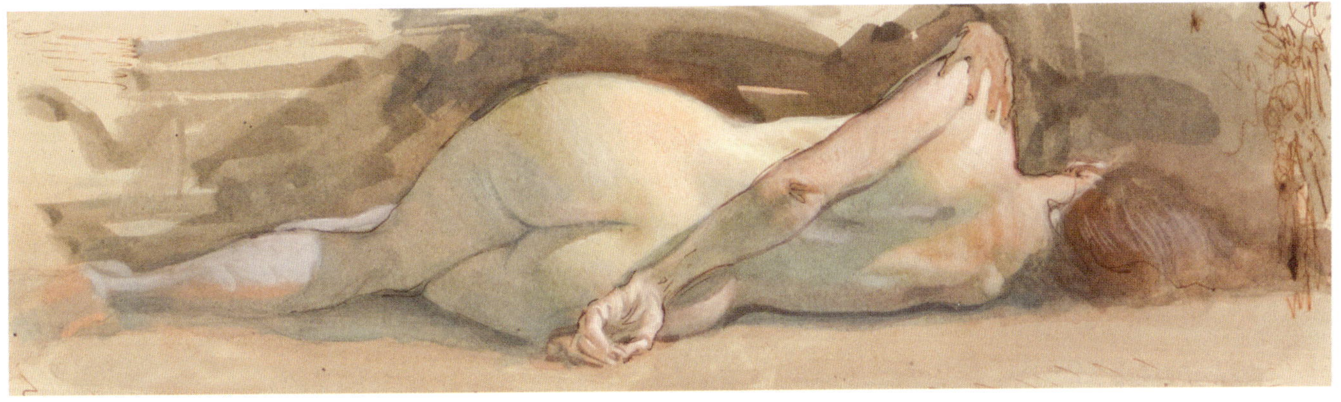

Reclining Redhead, c. 2005, by Steve Huston. Gouache and pen and ink on scrapbook paper.

The Head, the Neck, and the Shoulder Line

Because I said that the gesture is more important than the structure, we won't look at each part in total isolation. Remember, the ideas of structure and gesture really mean the parts and the relationship between the parts. Getting everything to fit together is what's tough. We need to consider that right from the start.

FRONT VIEW

As we find the first structure (S1), we want already to have drawn the first gesture (G1). So, the process becomes: G1/S1, G2/S2, G3/S3, and so on.

This, then, becomes the two-step process that is our drawing method. Got it? Good. You master this basic approach, and it will help keep Frankenstein from kicking down your studio door.

For the head, the gesture line is conceived as a vertical centerline that runs through the spot where the eyebrows meet the bridge of the nose to where the underside of the lower lip meets the chin (see Fig. A). The head is built onto its gesture as an egg with a horizontal centerline for the eye level—gesture/structure. Notice how the tilt of the head torques the neck and coaxes our beloved curve back into existence.

When you have a symmetrical situation, as in the frontal or back positions, the gesture line becomes straight and stiff for the head, neck, and torso. You are forced to sacrifice the curved gesture idea—a great, but necessary, loss. Of course, you have all sorts of chances to go crazy with the limbs or even have the hair blow in the wind. You can also make the egg into a capsule shape with flat sides as Fig. A shows. It tracks the gesture line better, which is not a bad idea.

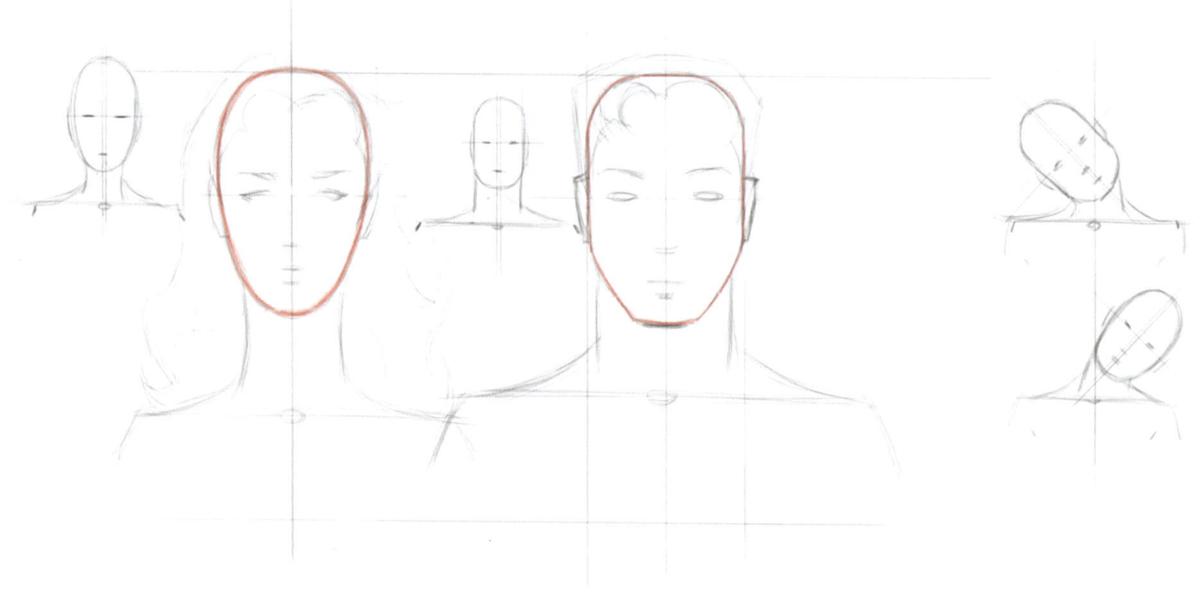

Fig. A. The centerline of the head

SIDE VIEW

In the Fig. B side-view sketch, drawing 1 (D1) risks being too rounded in the face, creating a sloping forehead and a weak chin. Drawing 2 is fine. Really. It distinguishes the round character of the skull from the angular planes of the face. That's a good thing. I prefer the triangular sail shape in drawing 3, however, because it's simpler. It's a little pointy in back, but I'll add a couple of bells and whistles and maybe you'll change your mind—or not.

Draw a small line back from the chin as it flows into the neck (this little underside plane keeps the mask of the face from looking like a paper cutout). The gesture line of the neck is generally a nice full curve that swings down over the omitted windpipe to the pit of the neck. The neck construction is completed by another curve coming off the back of the skull (more on that following).

Notice, in profile, how the gesture line in Fig. C has moved to the simplified contour of the head and is no longer straight like the front view (shown with red lines). Also notice the ear angles back a bit from that gesture line. Pay attention to how the long axis of the skull goes back and slightly up as it moves from front to back—a critical detail.

Even more important to drawing a successful profile is to make sure the back of the skull stays high compared to the placement of the chin. Looking straight ahead, use your fingers to feel the place in back where your skull meets the neck at the top of the spine. Now drag your finger around front, staying horizontal. Your finger should end up right over your eyeball. Whatever constructed shape(s) you use (and you could certainly find other solutions than these), make sure the skull sets high in back. Without that, the neck never fits as it should.

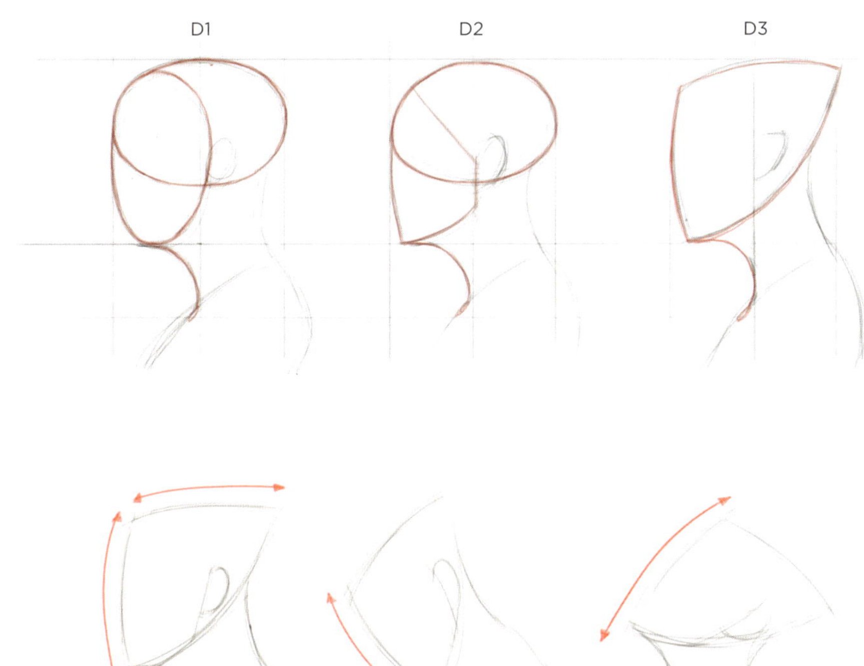

Fig. B. Simple yet characteristic. As long as you fulfill these two requirements, there are always choices for any given body part.

Fig. C. Everything looks a little flat without our trademark ends. The head is tough to get right. So, when in doubt, simplify.

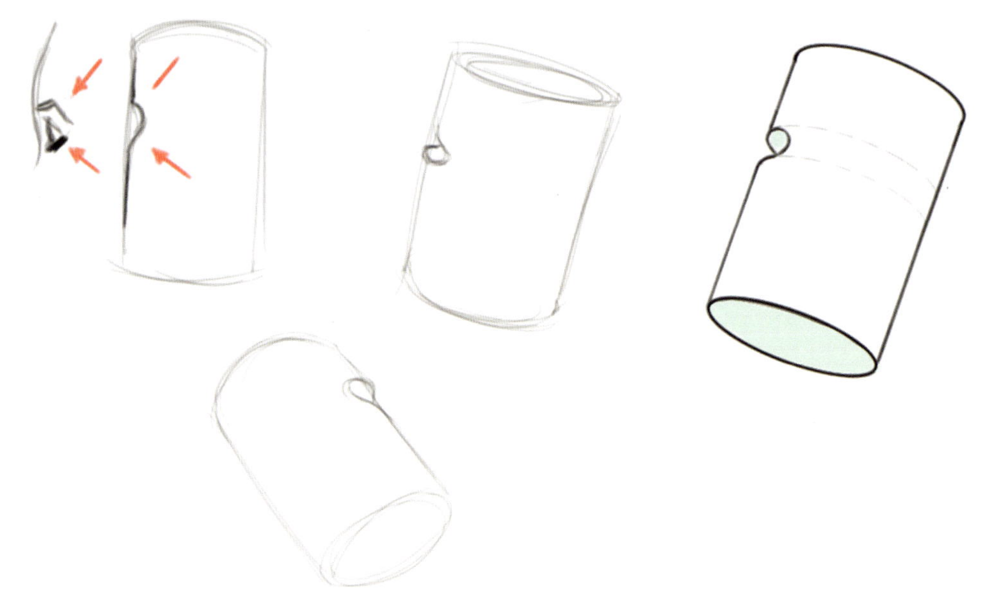

Whistle notch drawings

Adding specific features gets tricky so, first, let's learn how to draw "whistle notches" to represent them.

Whistle Notch

Imagine cutting a notch out of a tube. That's the whistle notch idea. This idea becomes the eye socket that houses the eyeball. We'll find that each feature has its own basic structure.

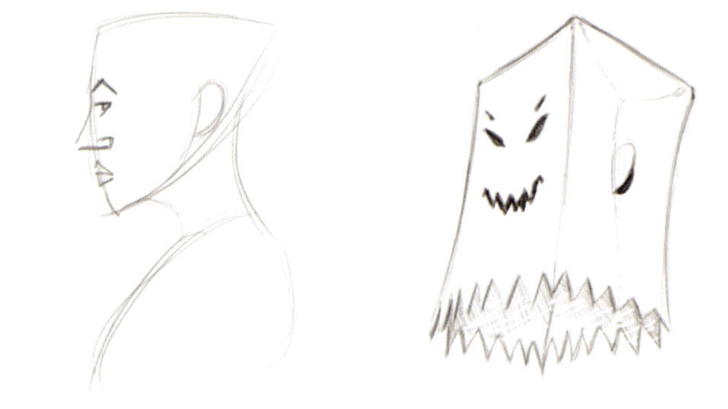

Cartoony drawing

The reason the whistle notch is so important is all features, except the ear, are on the front of the face. Drawing a face on a paper bag will give you the idea. When you just start drawing features of a basic profile, odds are they'll look flat and cartoony. Not good. Not structural. Remember: structure needs corners. The whistle notch acts as the corner for the face.

If you use the eyebrow and the cheek line as it meets the lower eyelid, that'll give you the notch. As the cheek descends, it suggests enough of the corner for the viewer to feel the frontal features are as they should be.

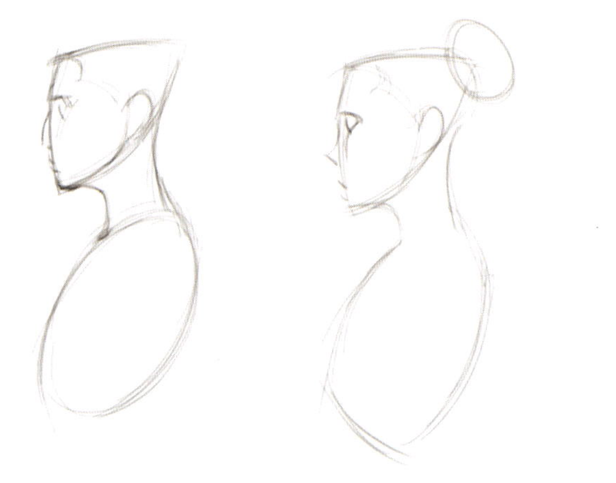

Eye sockets

THREE-QUARTER VIEW

As with the profile, the triangle construction also works great for a three-quarter view.

This back three-quarter view shows how those features are hiding around the front. Notice how the whistle notch has become the barest divot. Also, notice how the ear begins to crowd the front of the face. It's marking off these two landmarks that turn the head correctly.

What you have to be mindful of in a three-quarter front view is the centerline. Always measure how close it gets to the far side of the face.

Start with a "T" made from the centerline of the features and the eyebrow line. Then, mark off the features with appropriately placed construction lines ending with the chin to make sure the length is correct. All are on the front plane of the face, so make sure they're parallel to each other.

If you draw in the hairline (simply or more characteristically) to meet the jaw line, the ear attaches to the sideburn area. You're welcome to do this on the profile as well. The neck comes from behind the ear, both front and back views. If it feels too fat or too thin, you know the width of the face is off.

As the ears sit on the side of the face, relating them back to the eye or eyebrow line gets you a fairly accurate corner for dynamic positions of the head. Place the corner at the end or arch of the eyebrow for best results.

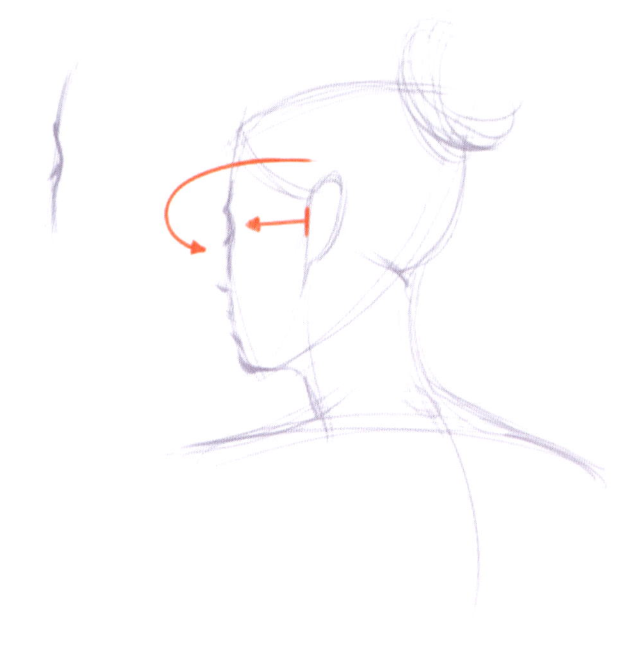

Back three-quarter view

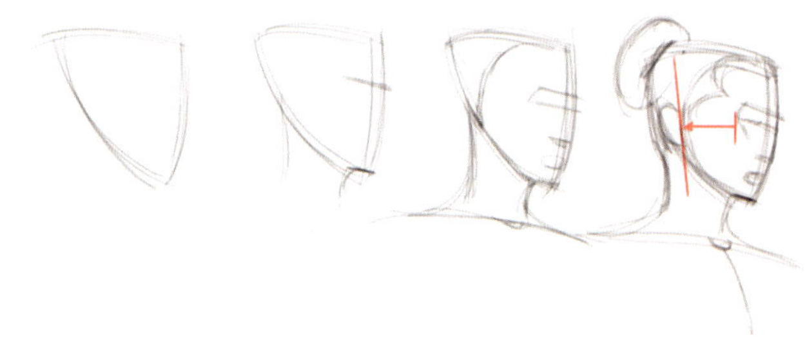

Front three-quarter view

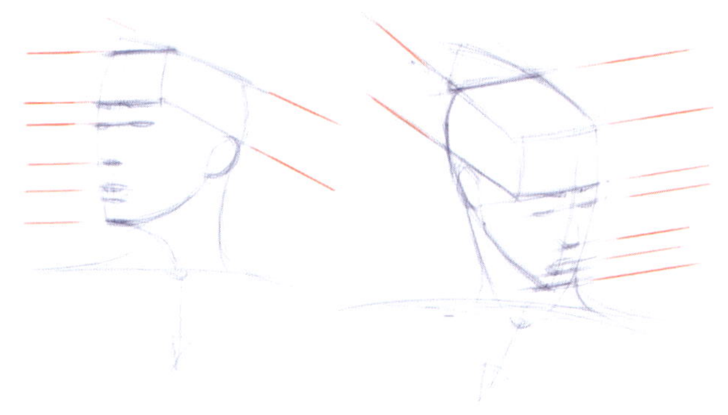

Two boxed-out heads

BACK VIEW

The back view may be the most difficult of any. You see very little of the face. The skull blocks it and the neck does, too. And the shrugging muscles that top the shoulder line overlap again.

As you can see in the image at right, the skull becomes a ball shape from the back. The neck is a simple tube (again without its 3-D ends). We see a wee bit of the face peeking out on either side of the neck. I've color-coded them with an ochre color. Finally, add a simple construction line for the shoulders and the sagging triangle for the shrugging muscles. That last can bend and change shape with various postures.

Eventually, the arms and torso will build off of the shoulder line, as in the drawing below. Make sure you take some time to get the head-neck-shoulder connection correct first.

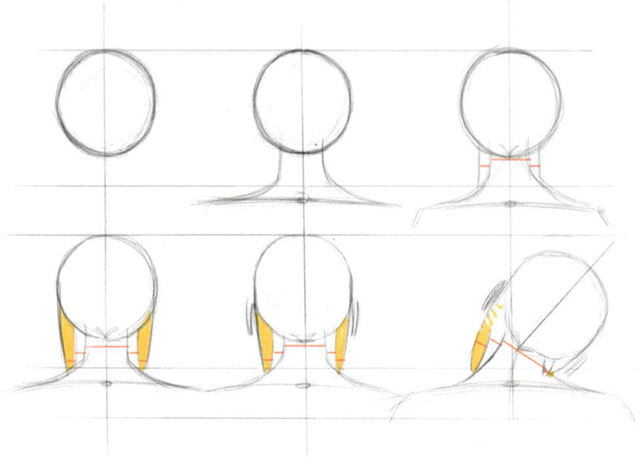

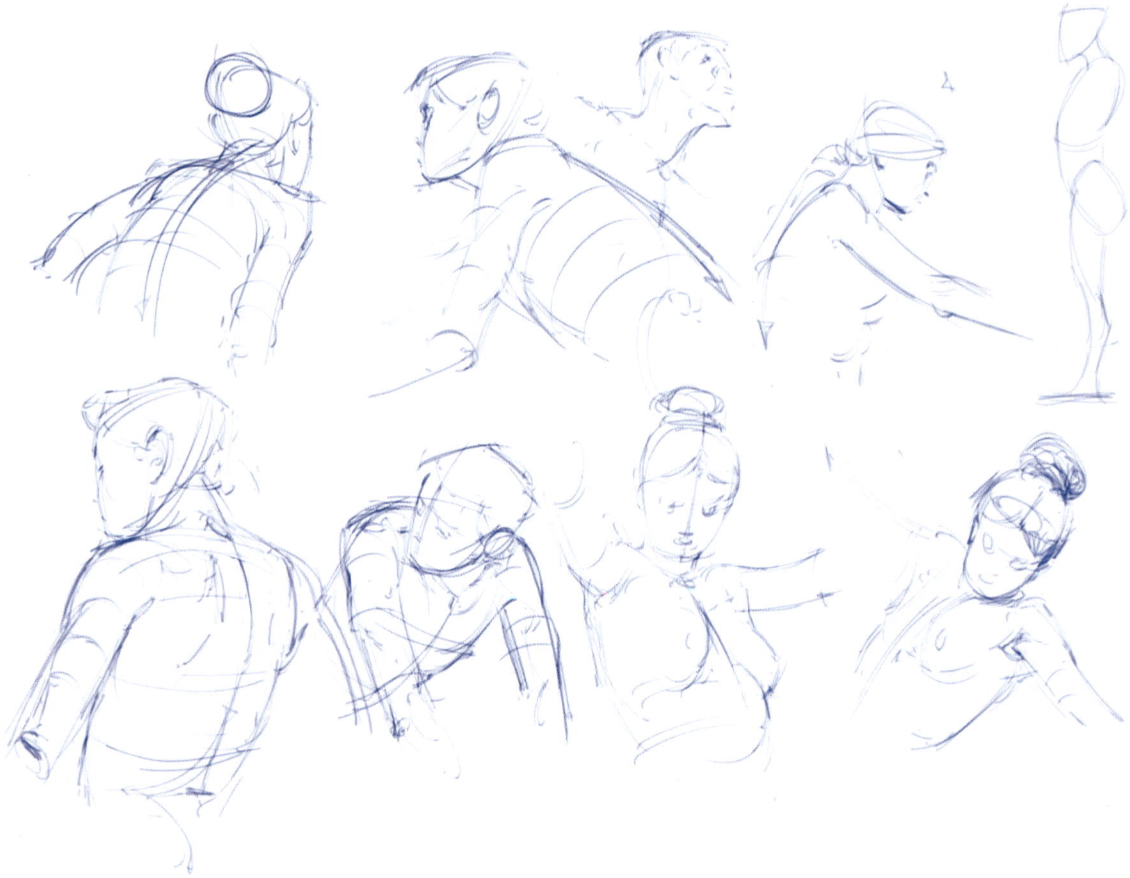

Step-by-step of the back view

Simple yet characteristic means, in part, any object you begin to sketch should be suggestive of the subtleties yet to come. It means you can move seamlessly from beginning construction to finished rendering.

The Torso

The torso includes the rib cage, waist, and hips. This is where the sexes show their clearest structural differences—again, with the qualifier, *on average*.

FRONT VIEW

There are multiple ways to conceive of the rib cage. It expands from the narrow neck to the wider waist. Beyond that, seeing a model with a rib cage that bulges away from the waist or seamlessly blends down into it guides me in choosing the most characteristic form for the job. See the images below and on the top of the next page.

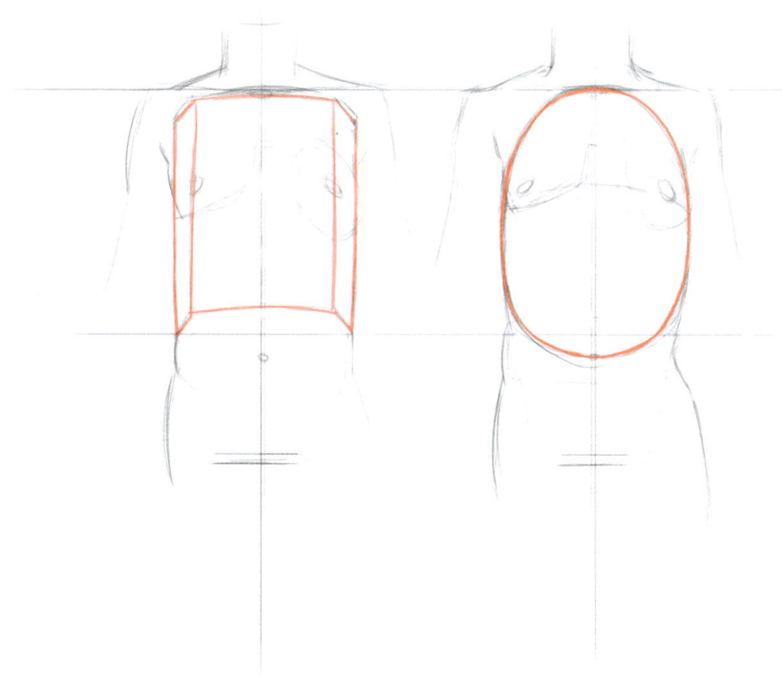

Start with a gesture line, straight and stiff as we did with the head, and have it touch the shoulder line. Just remember: simple yet characteristic.

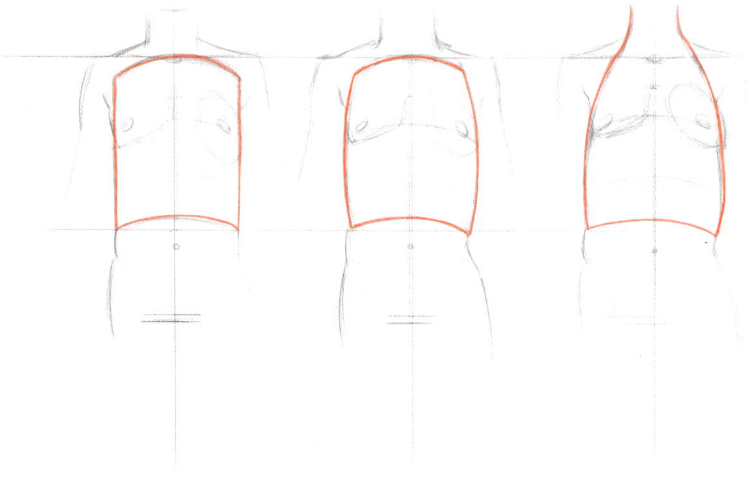

There is no structural difference between a male rib cage and a female rib cage. You may, of course, observe that the ribs on a particular female look small and a particular male's look big. It's a good generalization. In the classic ideal, the male is top heavy in ribs and shoulders and the female is fuller through the hips, by comparison.

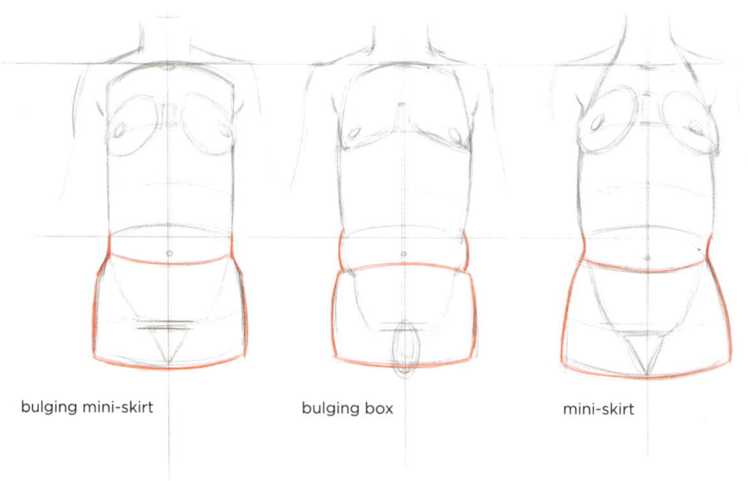

Male and female torsos

In the drawing of the torsos above, notice how I've drawn the waist as two simple lines without the constructed ends, very much as I did with the neck. Let the solid masses of the ribs and the hips do the work. The middle drawing with the bulging waist is more male in character, the other two, more female.

For the hips, the bulging box is the most typically male of the three, but it can be a good female solution in certain dynamic poses. The key difference between the sexes is the male tends to collect a little more muscle and a lot more fat at the waist—affectionately called love handles. The female has less bulk at the waist, but more at the lower hips. These often create clear structural differences between men and women, but not always. Again, pay attention to the specific model and how the model conforms to, or departs from, these generalities.

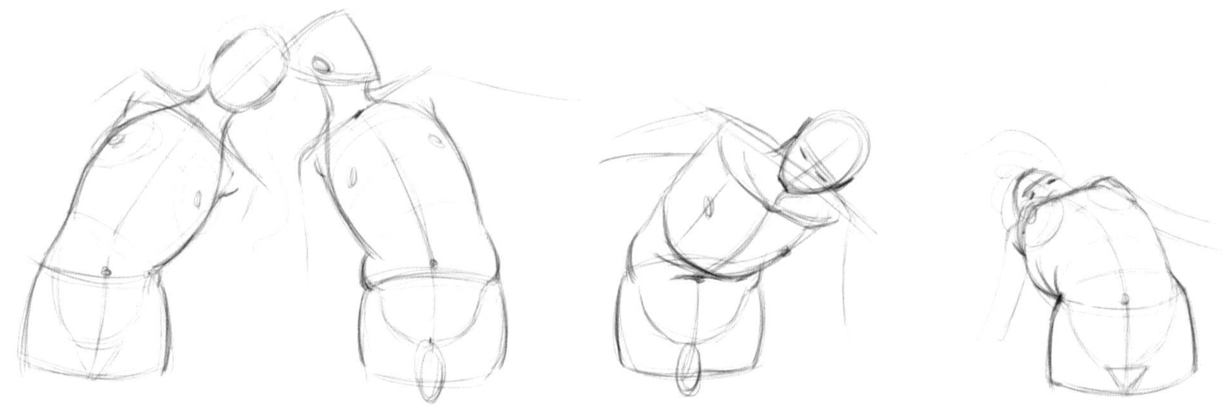

Front views of torso articulations with the bottle shape

One way to tighten the connection to the head-and-shoulder assembly is to use the bottleneck structure from the ribs up to around the nipple line. Notice how it takes you right through the shoulder-girdle interruption, which might otherwise fight you on constructing a cohesive whole. It creates a hidden connectivity that will be invisible in the finished drawing.

SIDE VIEW

One key to capturing the profile view is that the ribs-to-neck connection in back sits very high, while it's much lower in front (see the images on the next page). This is set up by that high back of the skull we talked about in the section on the head (see page 95). A shirt collar or necklace hangs in the same high-to-low manner. We must capture this at once if we want that gestural flow to keep on keeping on.

Notice the shoulders are lost inside the contour of the ribs in the profile position. The bottle shape that lets the neck flow into the wider ribs is particularly useful here. Key point: Make sure the bottle bends strongly into the neck from this position—an important difference from a front or back view.

Another key is to pay careful attention to the back of the ribs and, in an upright pose such as this, make sure the constructed rib cage has a vertical section to it that corresponds to the placement of the shoulder blades. The stomach and lower back also have that verticality before the dynamic tilt of the hips kicks in. I've added turquoise lines to call them out. Odds are your standing figure will feel like it's tipping off the page if these vertical moments aren't shown.

Any of the various shapes can work for male or female rib cages. I use a bulging box shape or an egg for the hips (notice the tilt). The bulging box tends to work for the female, and the egg for the male. But, a figure in a dynamic position can change that. In either case, make sure the hip tilts in opposition to the ribs. The curving gesture creates a balancing act. It is critical we capture it correctly.

As in the front view, Fig. A shows a few simple articulations with a mash-up of the basic shapes. If we simplify the profile a bit more, we see that staple of cute animal animation—the beanbag.

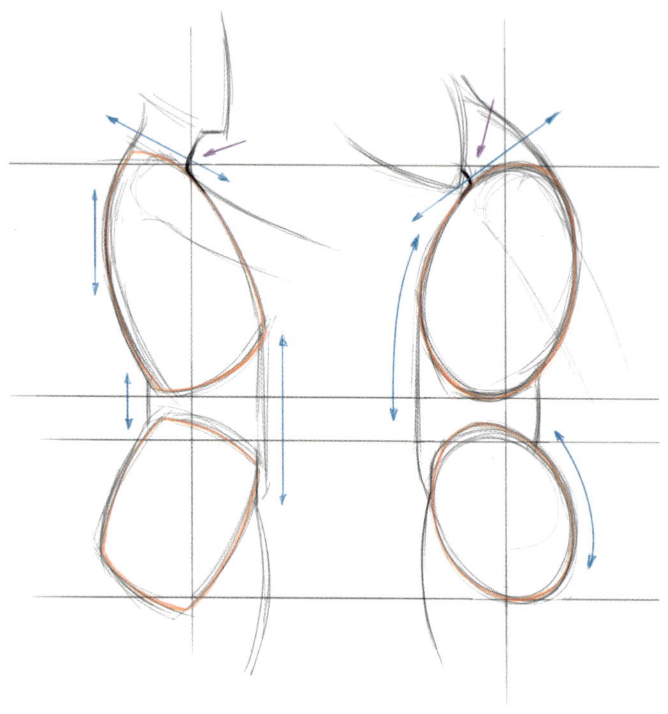

Make sure your drawings keep this corner at the pit of the neck (PoN) for a sharp change into the forward thrust of the ribs.

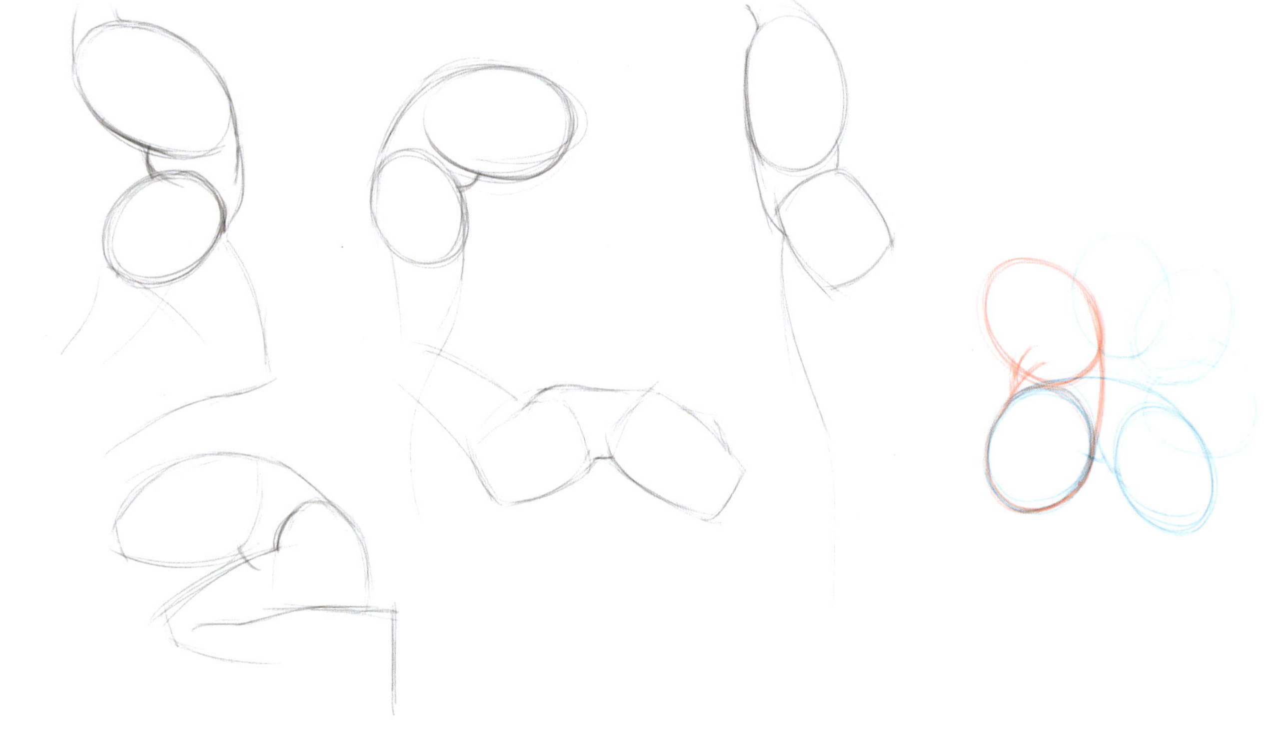

Fig. A. Side view articulation of the torso

BACK VIEW

Notice how that high back-to-neck connection we keep talking about shows up in Fig. B when the top of the rib cage ends slightly above the shoulder line. If you want, make the pit of the neck in front drop slightly below it.

Of course, all the silhouetted shapes for the back view are the same as those on the front. But, because of the curving spine, among other things, these are dealt with a little differently. For one, the stomach, legs, and pubic area don't block the hips as they do from the front. That makes life a lot easier. Also, notice how the hips tip up and the ribs tip down to bind into the lower back. The constructed ends curve accordingly.

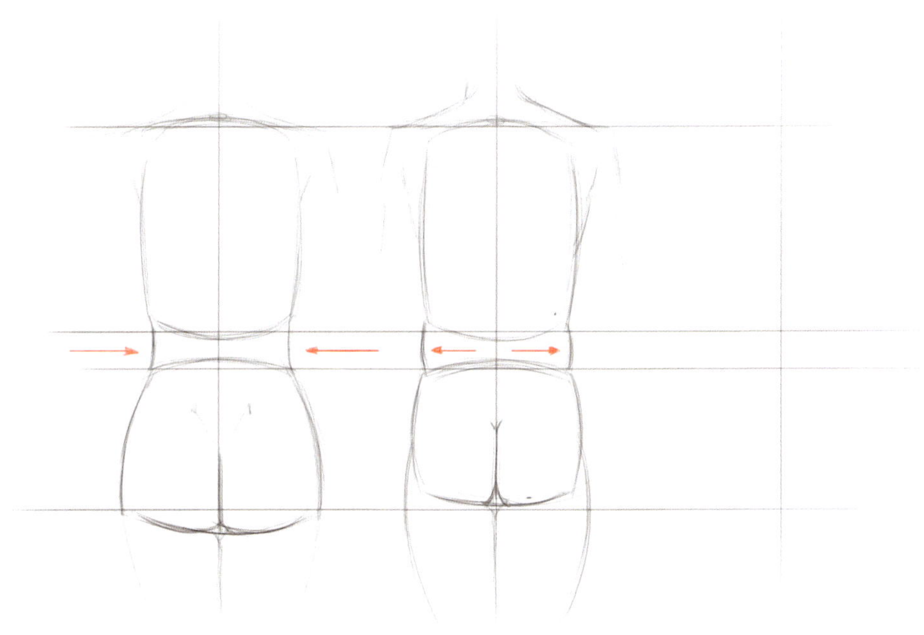

Fig. B. Torso back view with various hip shapes

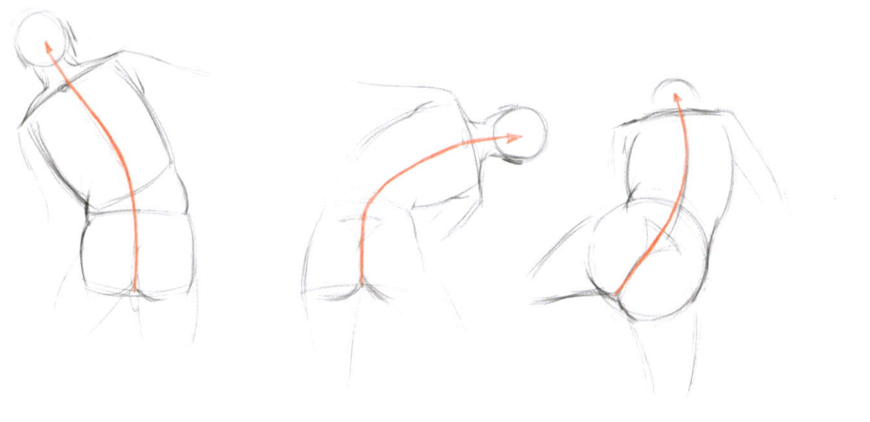

Here we see the accordion action of the unjointed spine and flexible waist.

The Arms and Hands

The arms originate in the torso, of course, and are engineered to do different jobs at different times. They need the flexibility to maneuver those fantastic tools we call hands into the right position to articulate what they need to articulate or move what they need to move. They need the span to, occasionally, help balance a particular body pose. And, they need a different kind of flexibility and strength to support or propel the full body from a dead-weight position into balance or even action. The design of the arms and hands shows a near miraculous mixture of these various necessities.

THE UPPER ARMS

For all its complexity (and later we'll see how complex), the shoulder assembly is primarily corners, to start the arms. When building the arms onto the torso, always, always, always make that corner connection strong. Later, in the rendering process, you can round it off.

You're probably well convinced by now that I don't like stiff and straight, especially when it comes to an asymmetrical form such as the arm. As you see on the drawn inserts, by capping the arm with the shoulder shape you get that nice flow back that we associate with the body.

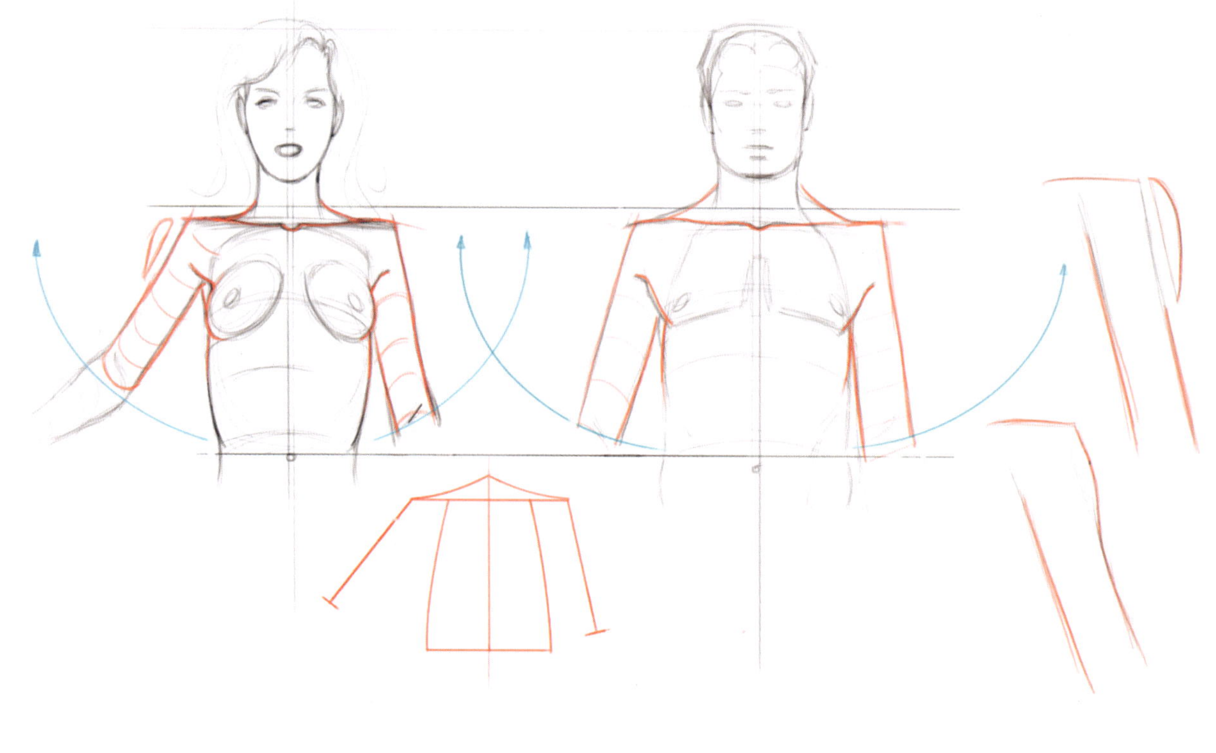

The front views (the back view, too) show arm constructions that are stiff and straight—a very rare occurrence as you should know by now. As you will see following, the side view takes us back to a nice curved gesture.

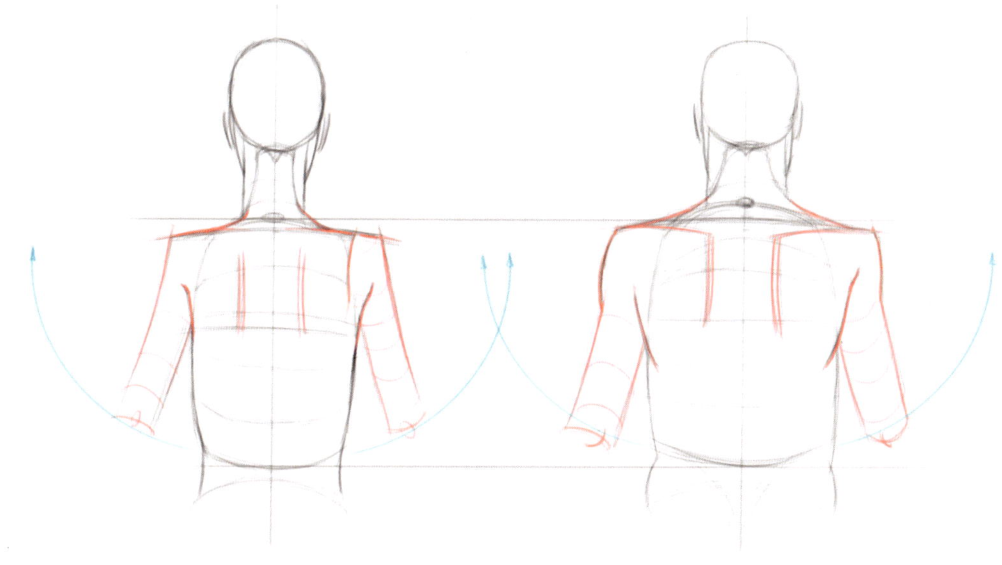

The upper arm is probably the easiest part to draw. It's just a tube with sides perfectly parallel from shoulder to elbow. You can see the shoulder cap minimized and maximized from arm to arm. Take your pick.

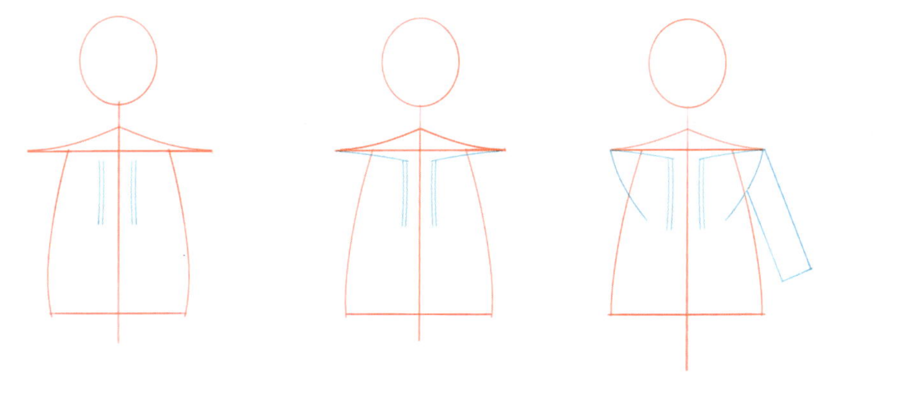

Here's a schematic of the shoulder girdle assembly just so it's clear.

One caveat: Sometimes you've drawn a figure with curve after curve and you just feel it might be nice to mix things up. On those occasions, finding a stubbornly straight gesture might be the very thing those carefully flexed lines need. Sometimes the aesthetic, the design, just wants something that all the wonderful theory has spent a lot of time fighting. Theory is great—but don't let it stop you from doing what your art needs.

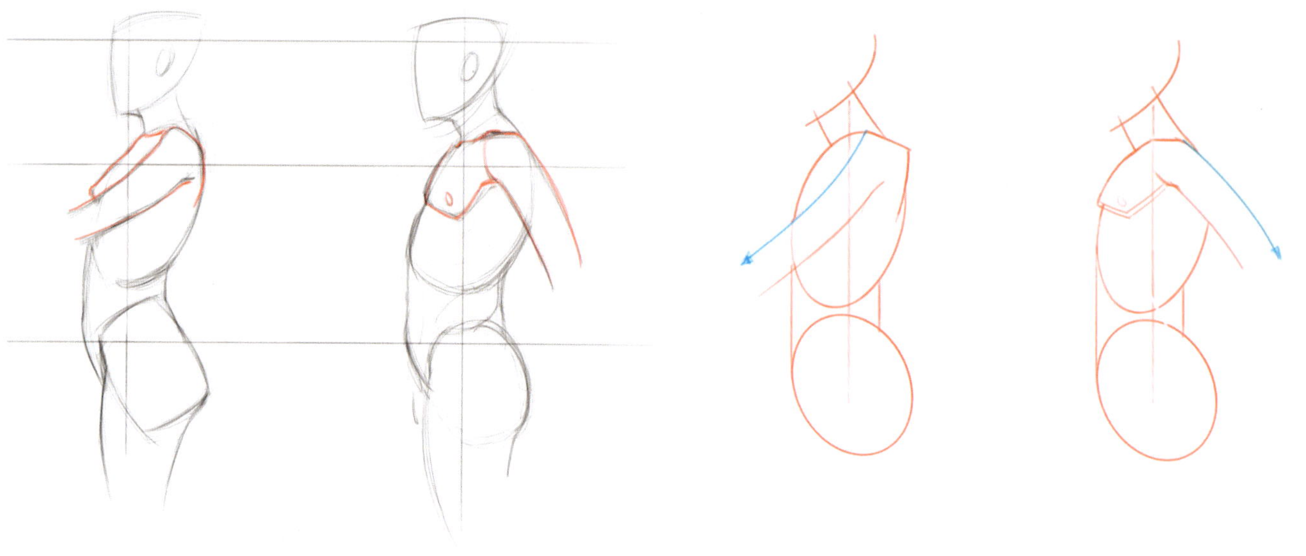

Here, the arm becomes naturally curved again. Remember, curves give us gestures; corners give us structures.

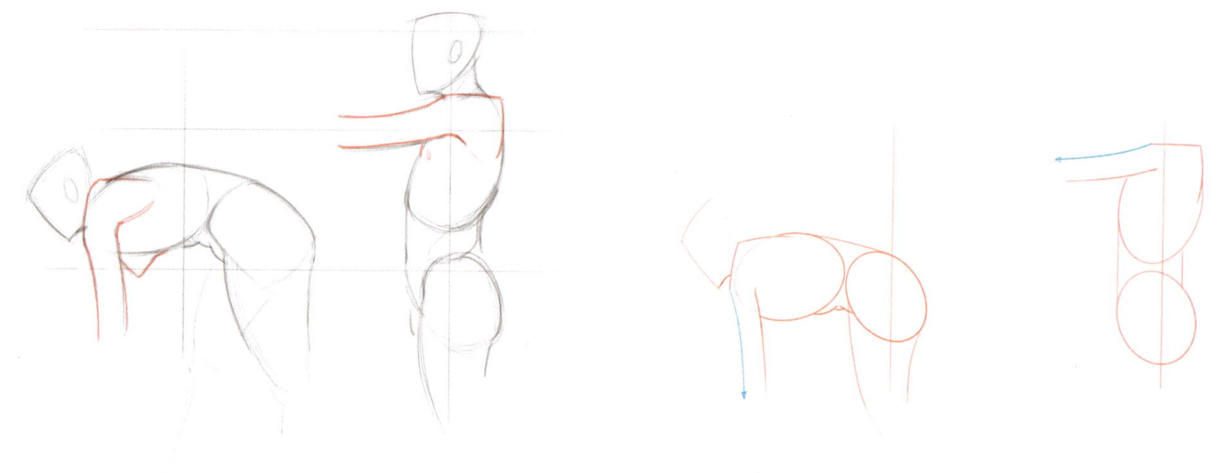

Notice how the shoulder blade unit creates a strong corner against the back of the rib cage and a subtle curve moving into the arms.

THE LOWER ARMS AND HANDS

Notice the addition of the forearm takes us right back to a curved gesture off the straight or straighter upper arm. I'm postponing the challenge of drawing hands by giving you a simplified version here. We will explore the hand in detail in chapter 9.

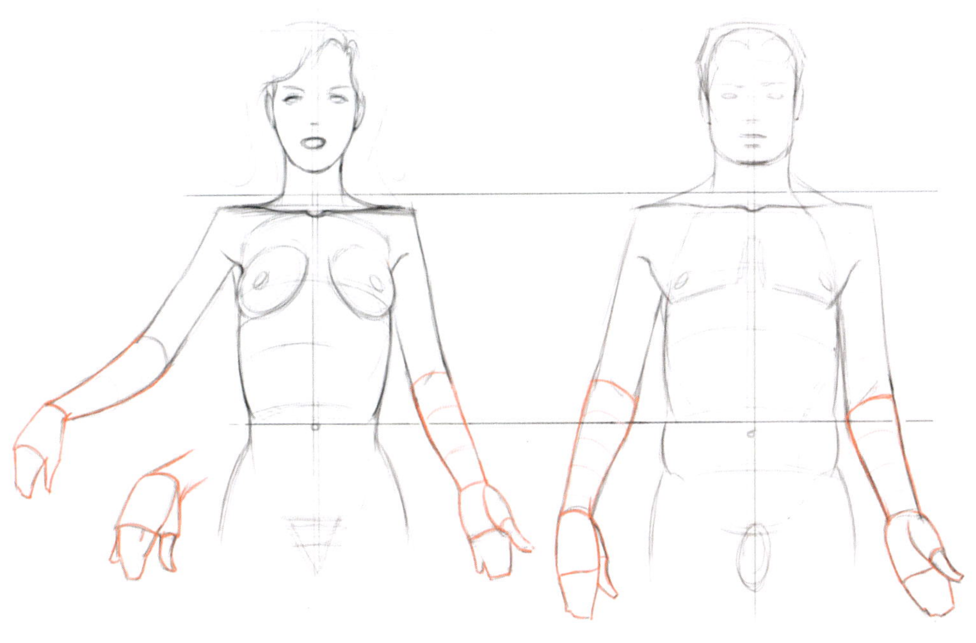

Arms and hands supinated and pronated

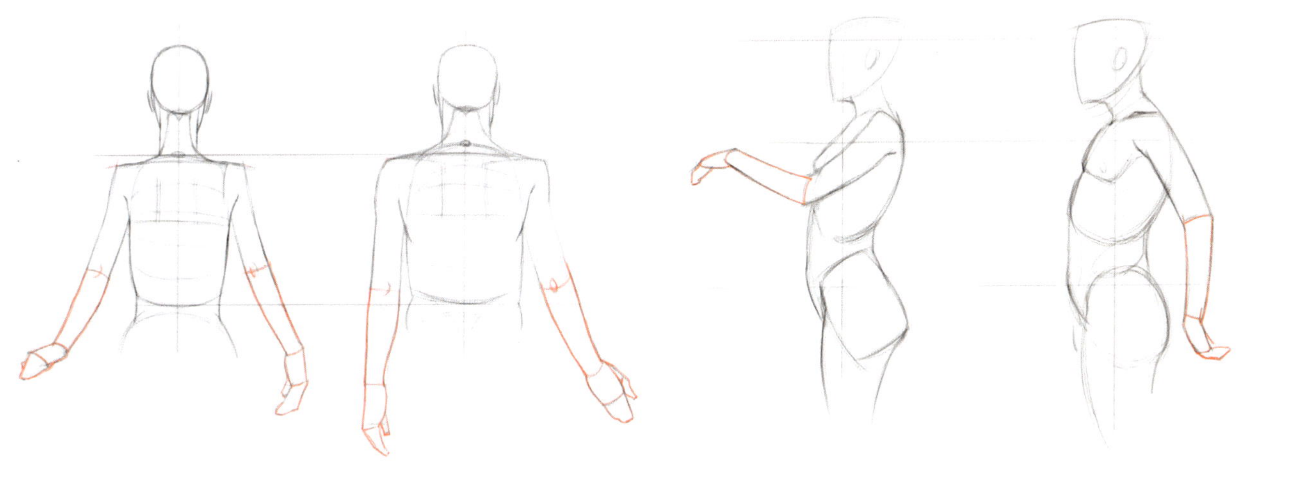

Back view variations

Profile view variations

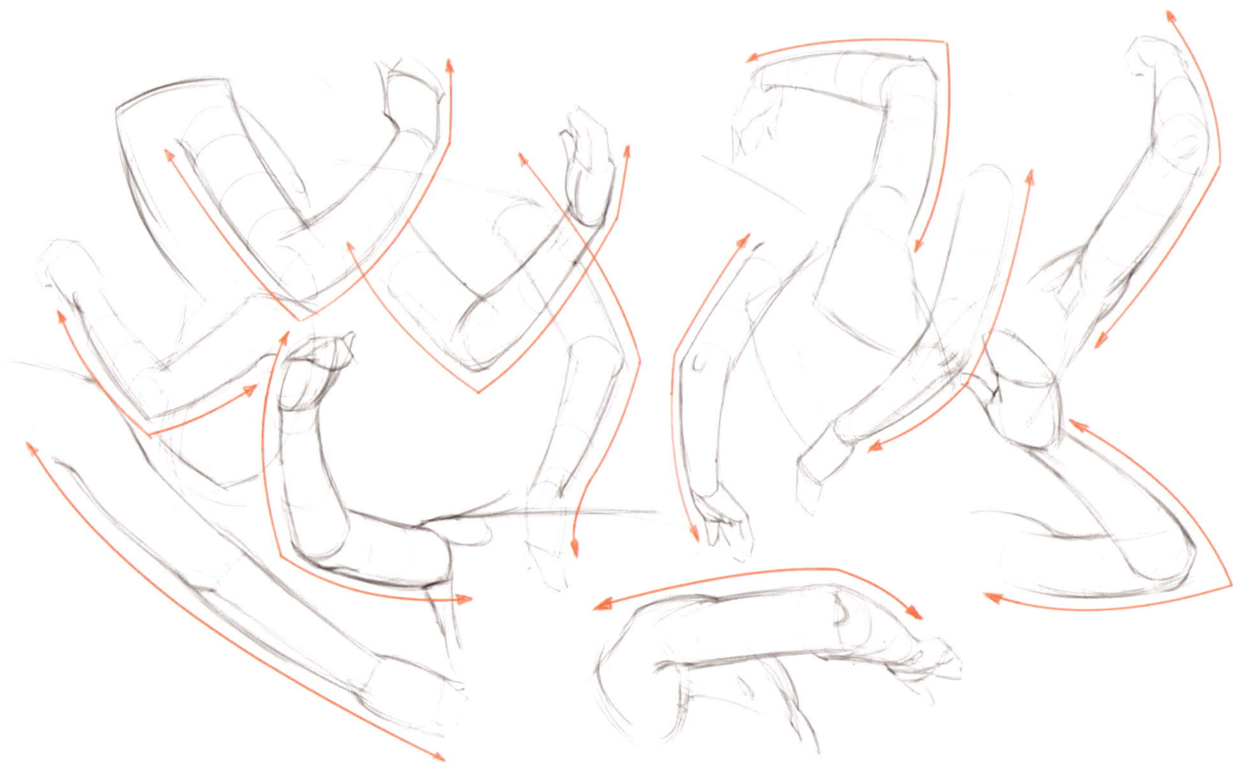

Study these drawings, then sketch various elbow articulations.

BASIC ARTICULATION AND THE ELBOW TEST

Once we've conceived of the jointed parts as simple gestures and structures, it's not a huge jump to be able to articulate them in basic ways. Notice when the elbow points down, both the upper and the lower arm swing up. When the elbow points up, the upper and the lower arm swing down. When the elbow is closer to the top contour, again, the upper and the lower arm swing down. And when the elbow is closer to the bottom, up

they go. That's the elbow test. Use it and you'll always get the gesture of the arm correct.

What is the real secret of success? Always complete the gesture/structure steps for the first part (G1/S1)—in this case, the upper arm—before beginning G2/S2 for the forearm. Don't fudge the connection. Then, and only then, go to the outside corner. The easiest place to connect the next gesture is usually the outside corner of the last structure.

The Legs and Feet

Although the arms can take up the task, usually the legs do the majority of work maintaining the body's stabile position or driving it into explosive action. The arms are able to move the body's weight, but only with great difficulty. The legs, however, easily handle that weight and plenty more besides. Any drawing of a leg must show the power to support and, yet, the potential energy to move quickly in any direction. All the while, the foot acts as both a platform of support and a shock absorber to soften the wear and tear from decades of action.

THE UPPER LEGS

The thighs come out of the middle to top area of the hips, depending on how the hips are conceived and how the legs are articulating. The thigh starts as a smooth flow out of or a subtle bump away from the hip. Either choice is good.

From a profile, see how the line drops off from the top of the constructed hip before curving into the meat of the thigh. Some very muscular thighs will do away with that drop. But if you see it on your model, it speaks to an anatomical connection, and for us gives a more nuanced and, therefore, more convincing connection.

More nuanced connection = good!

Always give extra attention to how you begin and end a constructed part. We want our audience to feel confident in how they move from one part to the next. Finishing the structure correctly makes for a better connection for the new gesture.

Compare the figures in the top two drawings at right. Notice how the differences between the male and female constructions show up, mainly, in the hips and not in the thighs.

Never stick the thigh onto the *bottom* of the hip. It will feel like it wants to break away when it tries to articulate against the hip. As you sit reading this, notice where your lap rests. It's close to the top of the hips, right? That is the way we need to draw it.

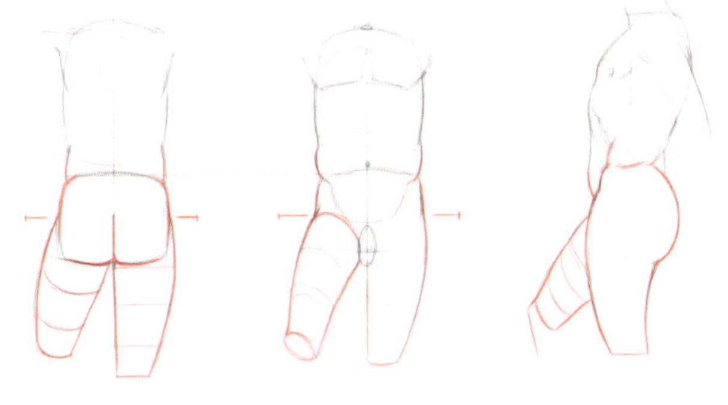

Male hips in back, front, and side positions

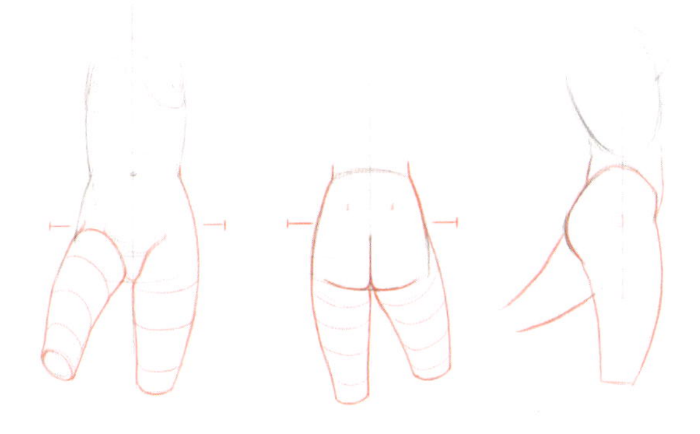

Female hips in front, back, and side positions

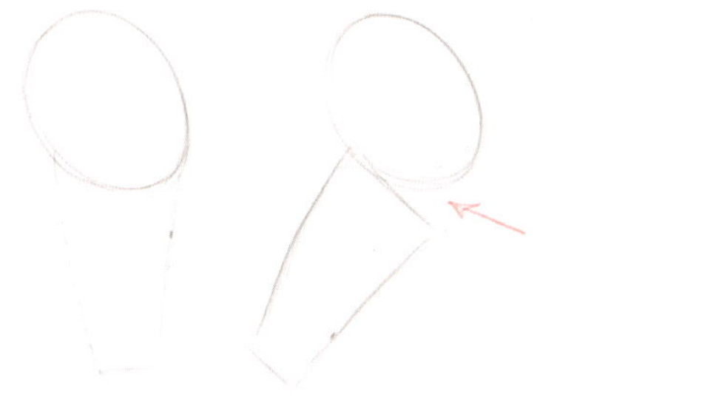

Incorrect attachment of the thigh to the hip

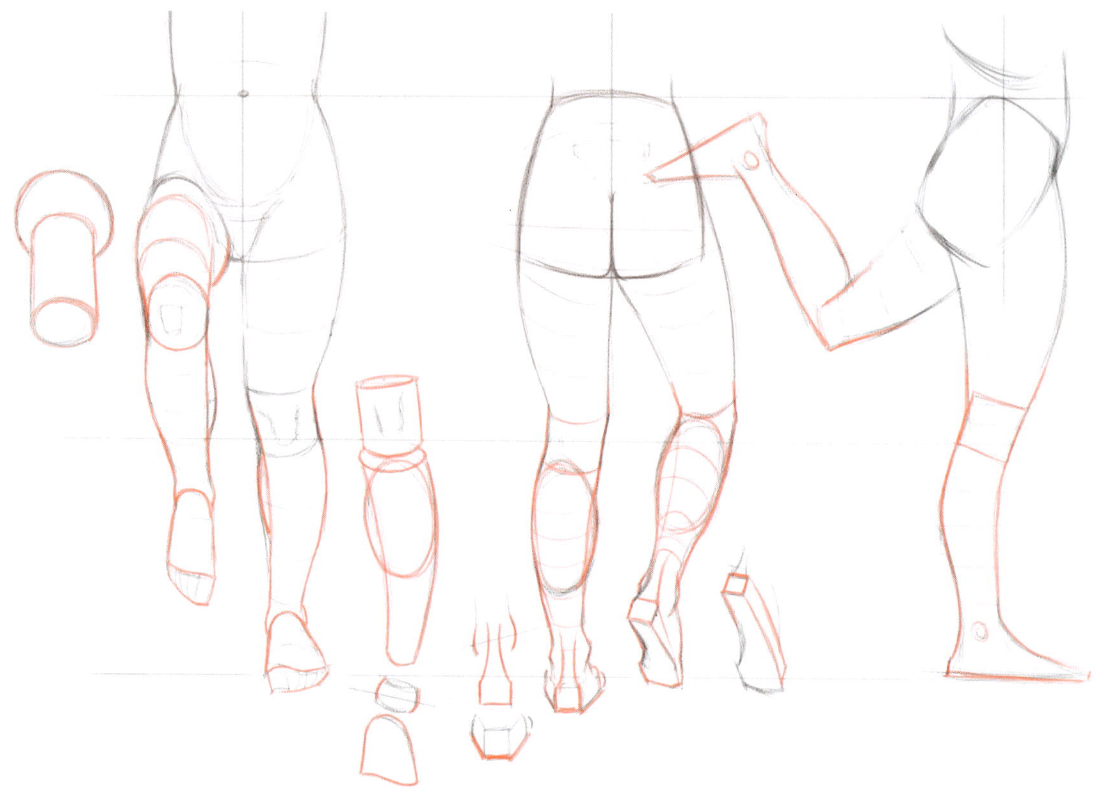

See how the lower leg has a mighty gestural curve from knee to ankle? This gesture is usually the most of any of the four limb sections. Almost everyone is a little bowlegged. Don't understate that.

THE LOWER LEGS AND FEET

From the profile, you see the full thigh curve thrusting forward, then a pull back to the thin shin. Full thigh, thin shin—that gives the simple gestural S-curve for the leg.

From the front or back, you can see the double-bump silhouette of standing legs. Draw a big, full, bulging curve from the middle or top of the hip to the knee—the gesture. Then, add another big, bulging, full curve from the knee to the ankle—another gesture. That gives you a "B" design.

And what about the knee? Does the knee belong to the upper leg or the lower leg? We'll explore that very important question in chapter 10. For now, group the knee area with either the upper or the lower leg, whichever seems more appropriate. And the appropriateness will vary depending on angles and articulations.

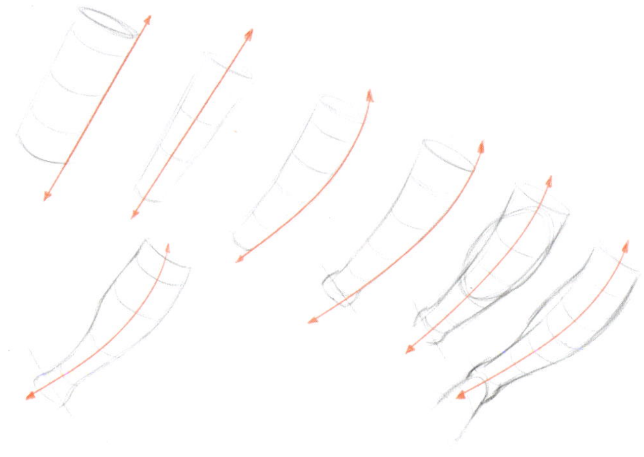

Fig. A. An ever-greater refined tube into a lower leg

FIGURE DRAWING FOR ARTISTS

Let's look at the lower leg a little more closely (see Fig. A on the opposite page). I've drawn it as just a tube. That's simple yet characteristic of what I see. But, by careful observation, I can get even more characteristic. And, of course, that is exactly what's happening in each successive drawing.

This is how we build our craft in structure. We want to find solutions to what we're seeing that are ever more characteristic. This is primarily why, when we look at the Old Masters, we seldom see lay-ins. They've done their homework. They knew the structures of the human body so well they went directly to the most characteristic choice—something close to a final contour.

Did they think it through exactly the way I've just described? In most cases, probably not. But this is the best way I know to understand their results. After all, the body is made of real volumes in real space, fitting together in a very specific way. That is why this method works for sculptors, animators, and chiaroscuro painters. It's the method behind the madness!

I studied with Burne Hogarth—an incredibly talented and very giving teacher. He taught me the B- and S-curve ideas for the gestural design of the legs. It's a great way to remember how to keep those legs nice and fluid.

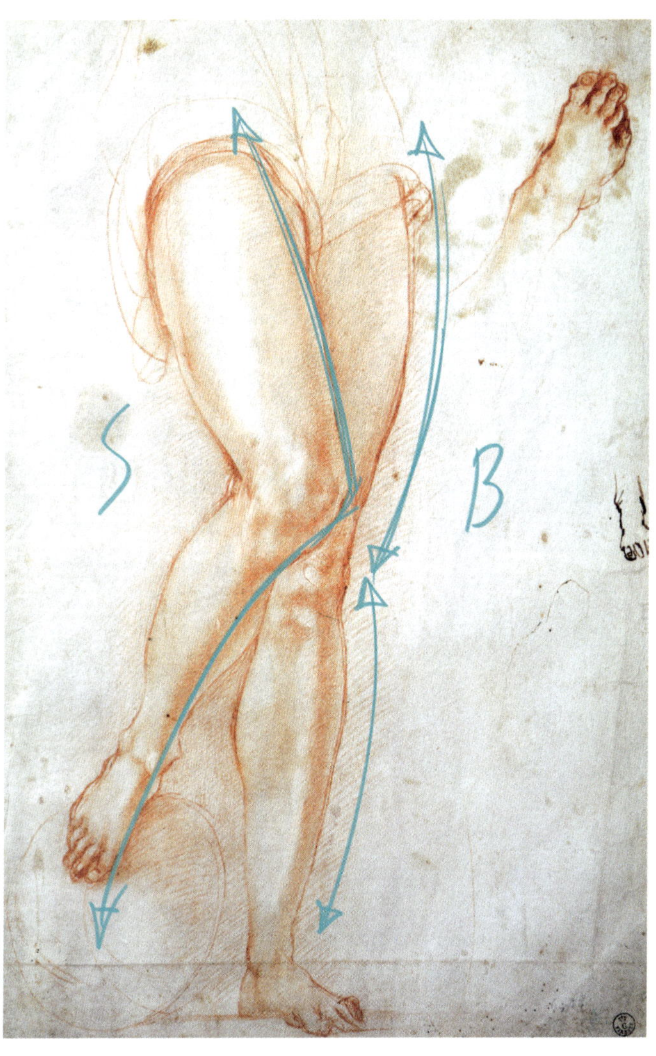

Study of Legs, c. sixteenth century, by Jacopo Carucci, known as Pontormo (1494–1557). Drawing. Uffizi Gallery Museum, Florence/ Bridgeman Images. Notice the B designs on these lovely legs. When the leg bends, that B (or S) will break against the knee's corner.

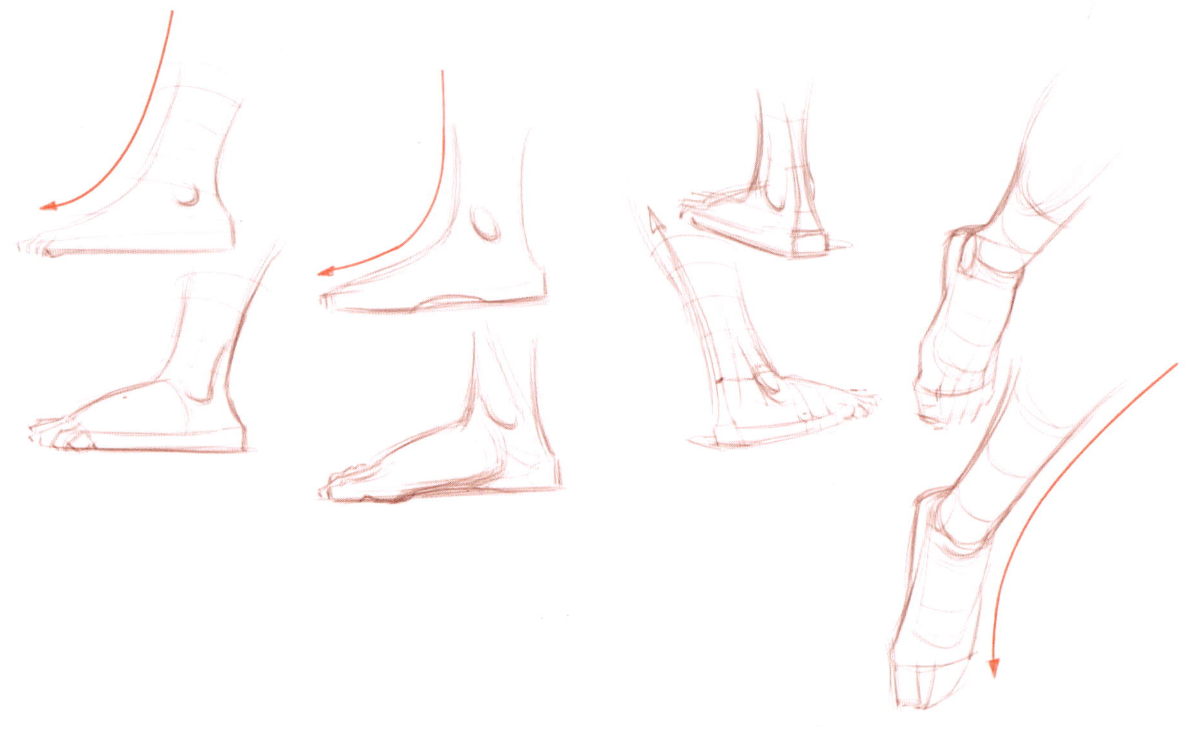

There's a terrific gestural transition from ankle to foot. Think of it as a bumpy or smooth ski slope taking the viewer's eye down to the finish line.

THE FEET

The foot is a simple sagging triangle from the profile angling briefly back at the heel and swinging forward to the toes. From the front, draw it as a simple tapering cone that cuts off at the toes. Add the toes grouped into a single shape. The back view has the heel and attaching tendon. It looks like a little chimneystack if you square the heel. The foot shape peeks from behind. This is good enough for now.

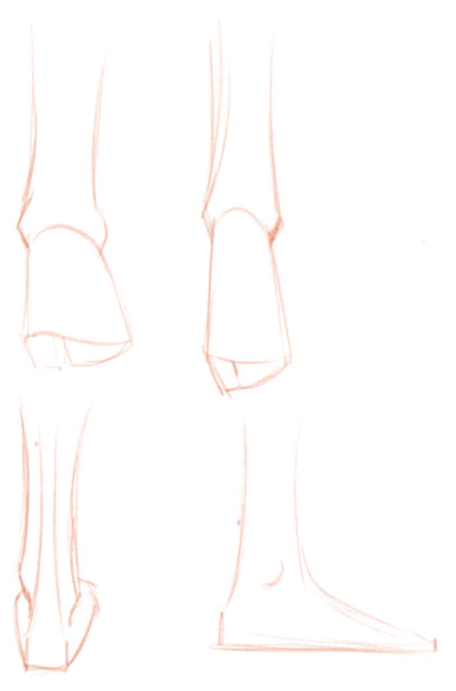

Foot constructions

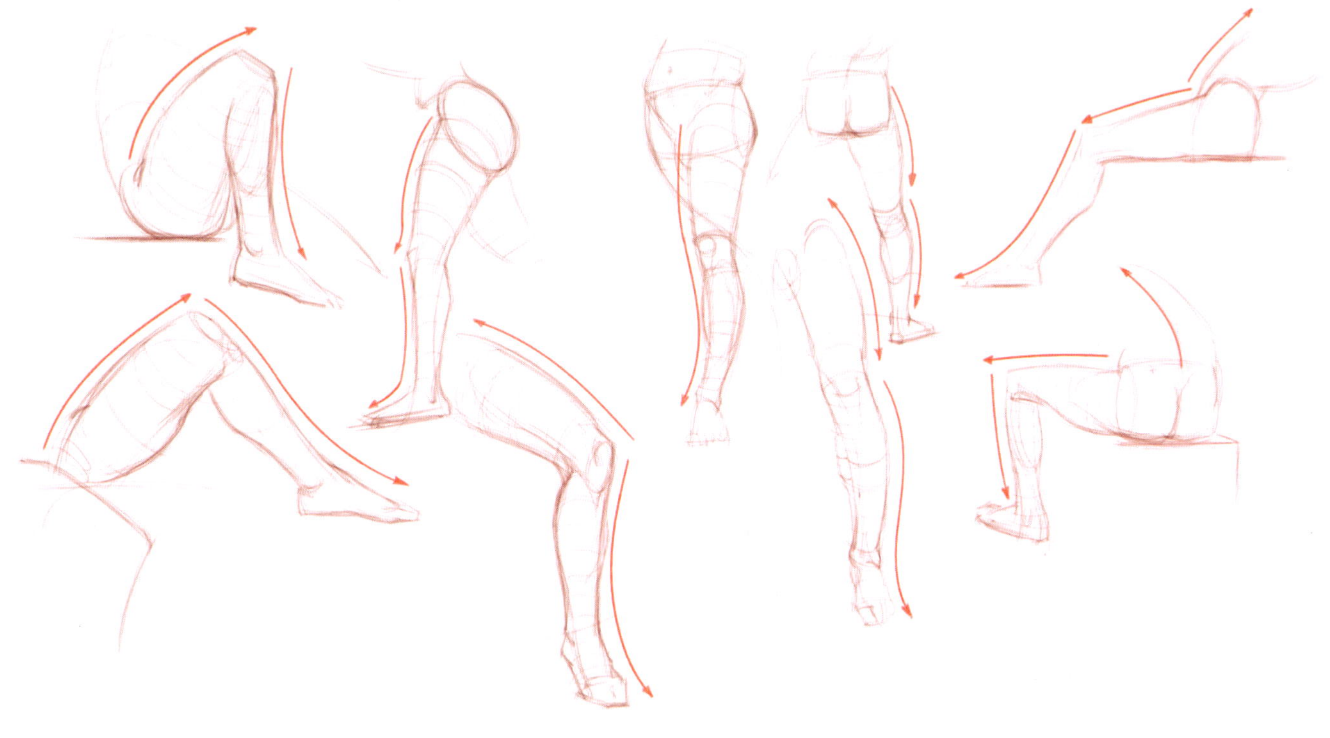

Legs flexing at the knee

ARTICULATING THE LEGS

The full-thigh, thin-shin trick works for most positions, even bent ones. I say "most" positions because if the leg bends so much that the back of the thigh pushes the mass of the calf forward, it can reverse that curve.

I've just thrown you a bit of a curve (pun intended). Notice these leg drawings are more complicated than the arms. Lay some tracing paper over them and find the simplest lay-in shapes you can. Lose the kneecap, the anklebones, the egg additions for the calves, and so on, and see how much you can distill it down. Then, take the simplest of the lay-ins and build it back up.

What you want is to find the happy medium between simple and characteristic. It will vary from person to person and from situation to situation. Your choices will evolve over time, as you become more and more the drawing ninja you are meant to be. It takes practice and a bit of experimentation. Here's the equation:

time in = craftsmanship out

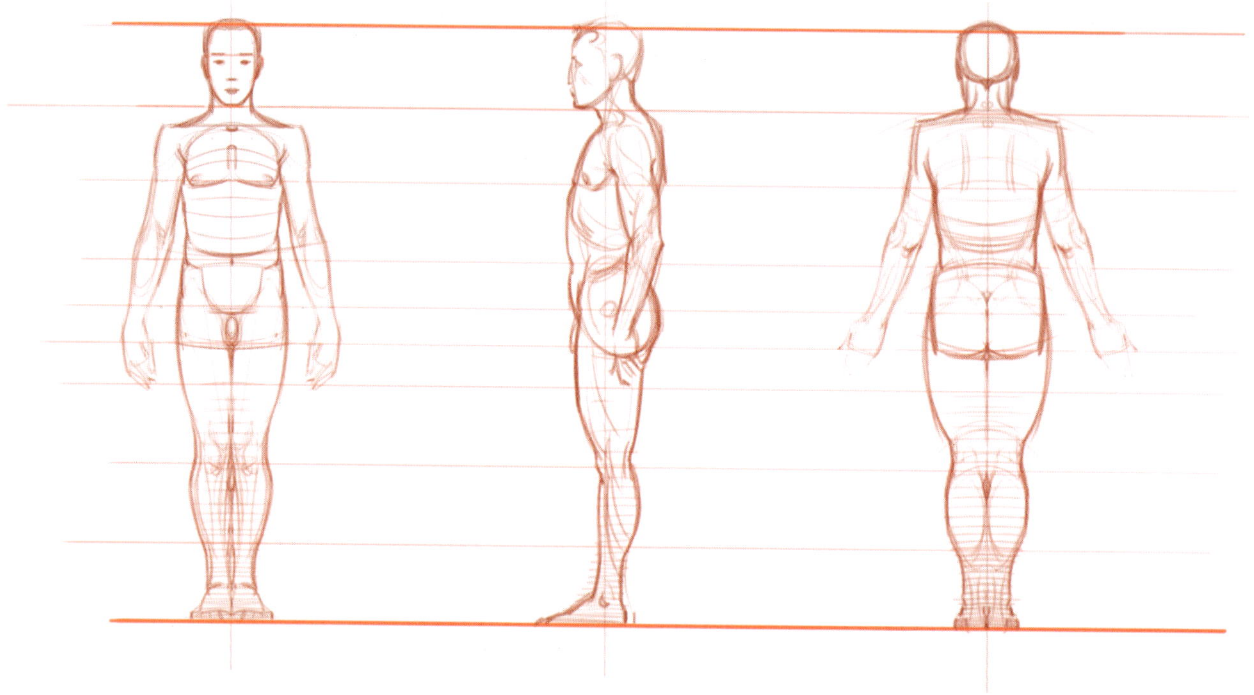

There are all sorts of ways to proportion the human body. There are all sorts of canons of beauty. I've picked one that uses the head as the yardstick and chosen proportions that fit reasonably well with most people's aesthetics. See the image on page 93 for the female equivalent.

Proportions

Proportions are very useful, especially as a means to double-check your drawing. They are also like good ethics: both are situational. A long, languid pose, such as Ingres's *La Grande Odalisque*, might need five extra vertebrae to make it work. The wealthy old woman of a John Singer Sargent portrait may have needed the long neck and deep eye sockets of Hera, Queen of the Gods, to fulfill the commission.

The artists I love don't "capture" life (as if such a thing were even possible). Instead, they translate it. They show something new about it. There is a rhythm to good proportion that makes It ring true in a way calipers and pinching fingers with one eye closed just can't.

So, even as I show you the pinching fingers stuff, trust your eye and your gut first. Draw it lightly first. Then, if it doesn't feel right—measure.

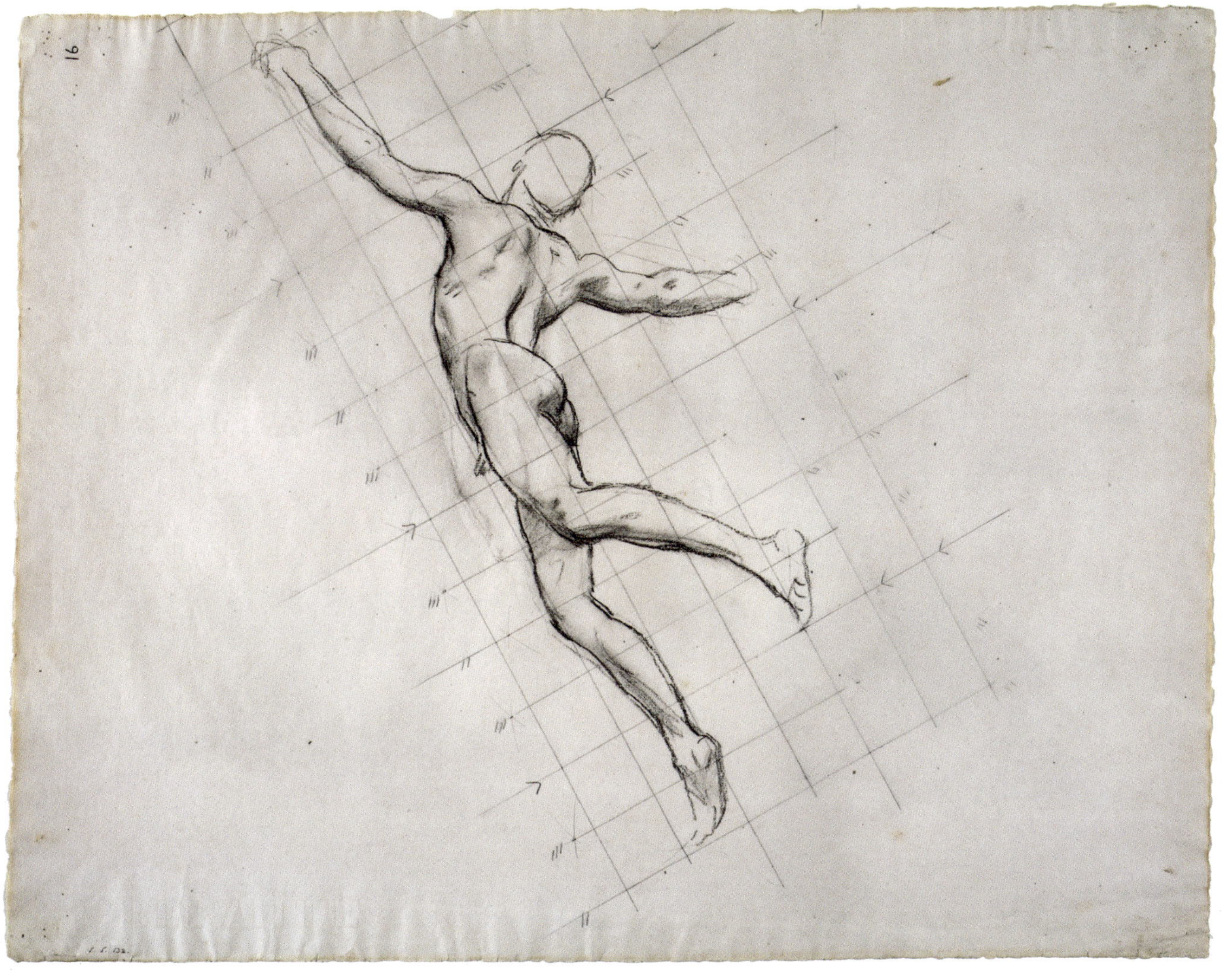

Nude in Action, John Singer Sargent (1856–1925). Charcoal on paper. Davis Museum and Cultural Center, Wellesley College, Massachusetts/ Bridgeman Images.

OLD MASTER *study*

What you see with our old friends like Raphael is they would compress. They would skip steps because they were, well, masters. But, when we look back at their work with grounded analysis, it's all there.

That brings up another point. You could just draw away—especially if you've internalized this stuff through practice. And then, when you need to go

back to troubleshoot a problem area, this method is ready to help. You don't have to draw this way—my way. But maybe you don't feel the solidity you should in the rib cage you sketched out. Now you know how to check it. If the connection from the neck doesn't feel as though it fits nicely into the ribs, you can fix it.

And that is the process for the whole human body . . . for now. Mastery comes through immersion. The more deeply you want to connect to this material, the more you need to live with it, become friends with it. Read, copy, and try to conceive it from memory. All that tests your knowledge and deepens your understanding. Then, when it has clicked, move on to the exercises opposite.

Battle Scene with Prisoners Being Pinioned, c. sixteenth century, Raphael Sanzio (1483–1520). Pen and ink over chalk on paper. University of Oxford, UK/ Bridgeman Images.

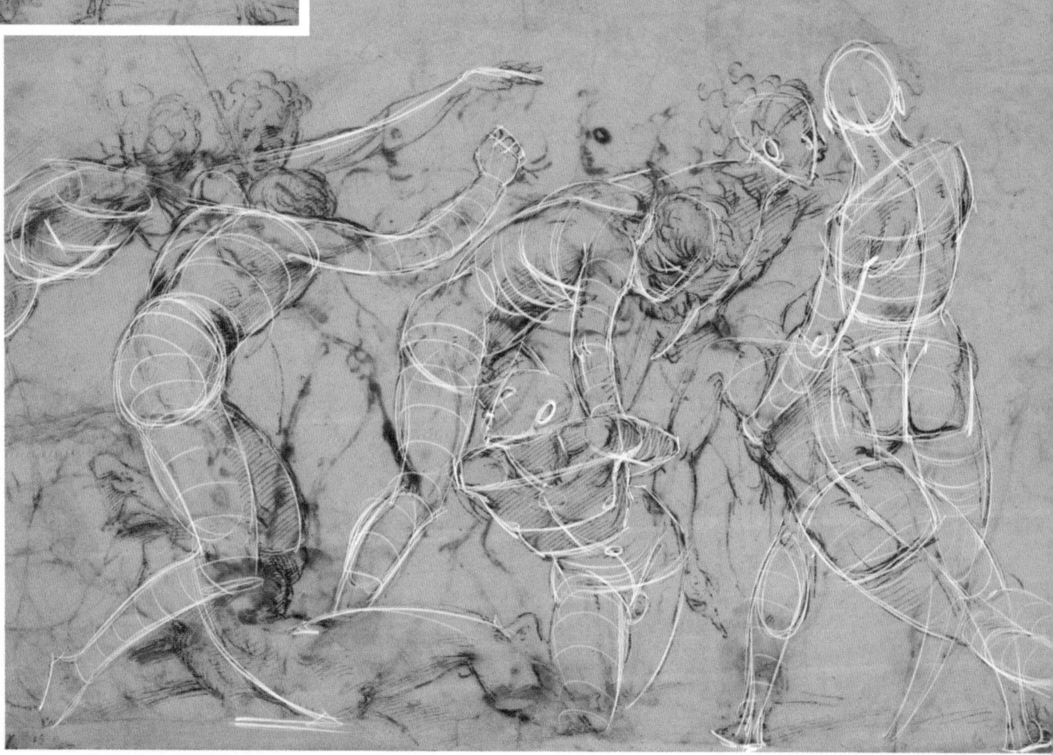

Raphael used constructed forms and gestural relationships in his art.

GIVE IT A TRY: *Exercise 1*

Lay tracing paper over the step-by-step drawings we studied in this chapter. Follow the process of making marks that are as simple and as clean as you can—that is, simple yet characteristic. Feel free to try other shapes. Look at your favorite artists and see how they solved this problem.

If you mess up, grab another sheet (or do it digitally). Start with the head and draw the simple constructions and simple positions until you do it without thinking. Then, start on a new body part.

It's like punching the bag in the gym or dancing. It's all about muscle memory. Know the moves. Know the forms. Work through this whole chapter for a month, maybe less, and you'll have it down.

Now, mix up the order. Start with the structure. Then, draw the gesture. Draw the ends before the sides. Invent your own shapes. Play with it.

I've said this before: Read and study this book; make it your own. Make your own method. Start with mine. Maybe keep a lot of it. But this has to fit *you*. It has to connect with you and flow out of you and onto the page like any beautifully fluid gesture must.

If you work hard, someday you'll find you don't agree with me on everything. *That* is where you want to be. That means you are finding your own voice. We need your voice.

As you go about it, be patient. Have fun. Cherish the little victories even when you sometimes lose the war. And keep at it, a little every day. It only has to be a little for that nest to quickly get too small.

GIVE IT A TRY: *Exercise 2*

Don't forget to do some object drawing. Keep building that mental warehouse of great and interesting shapes.

If you're a blubbering puddle of tears, go back to the chapters on gesture and start again. You'll get there.

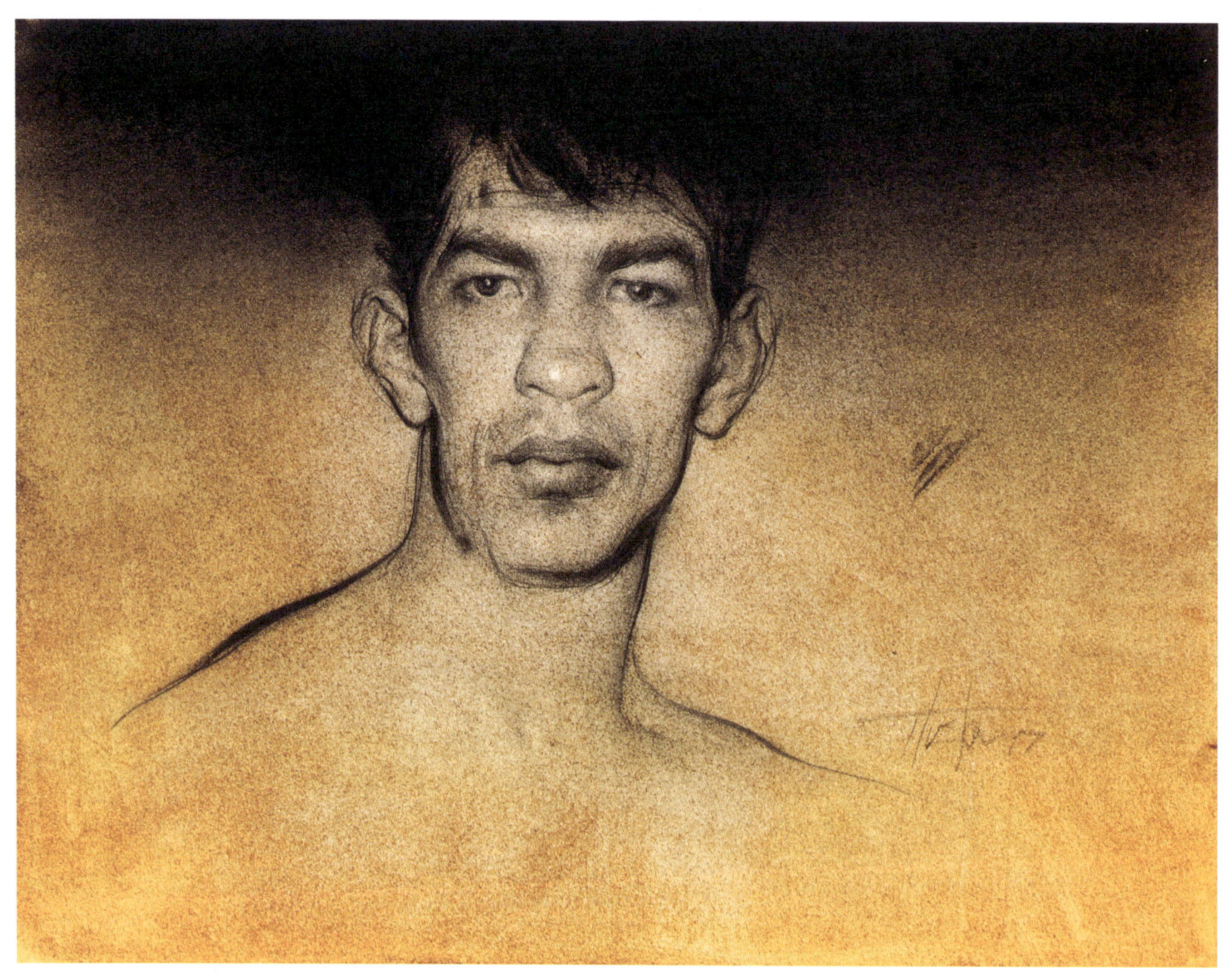

Gatti, 1997, by Steve Huston. Charcoal and Conté crayon on Strathmore Bristol paper. When it's time to take your drawing a little further, a well-structured head becomes a map for the details to come.

7 | THE HEAD

Now that we have enough structure, it's time to hang features on it.

Remeber that the best head drawing in the world is useless if it does not flow beautifully into the body. Make sure you track that lifeline we call *gesture*. It makes all the difference. Make a habit of sketching part of the neck and shoulders so you're always thinking about how to connect.

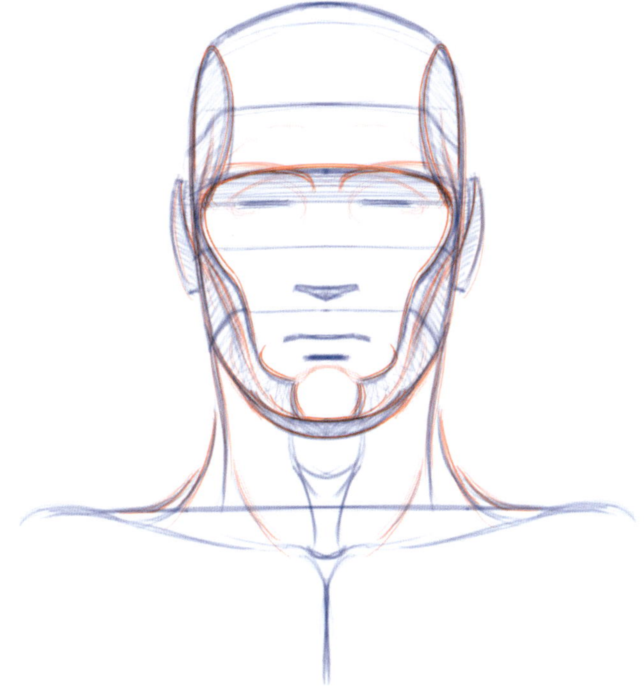

The big simple structures of the skull meet the big simple structures of the face, and we end with front planes, side planes, tops, and bottoms. That gives us what we need for the features.

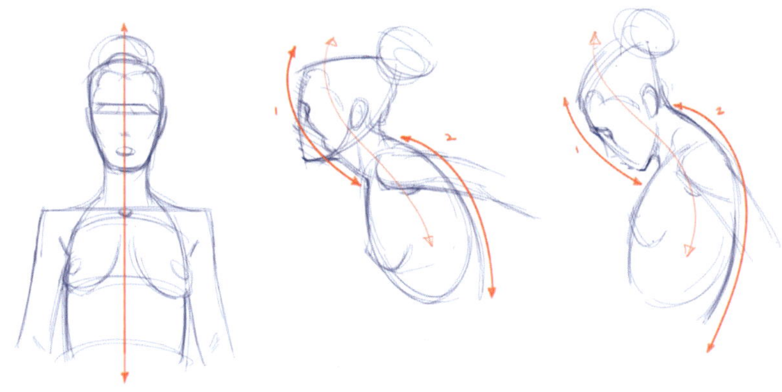

The shoulder girdle hides the much more important connection of head to rib cage. Let's consider that more carefully.

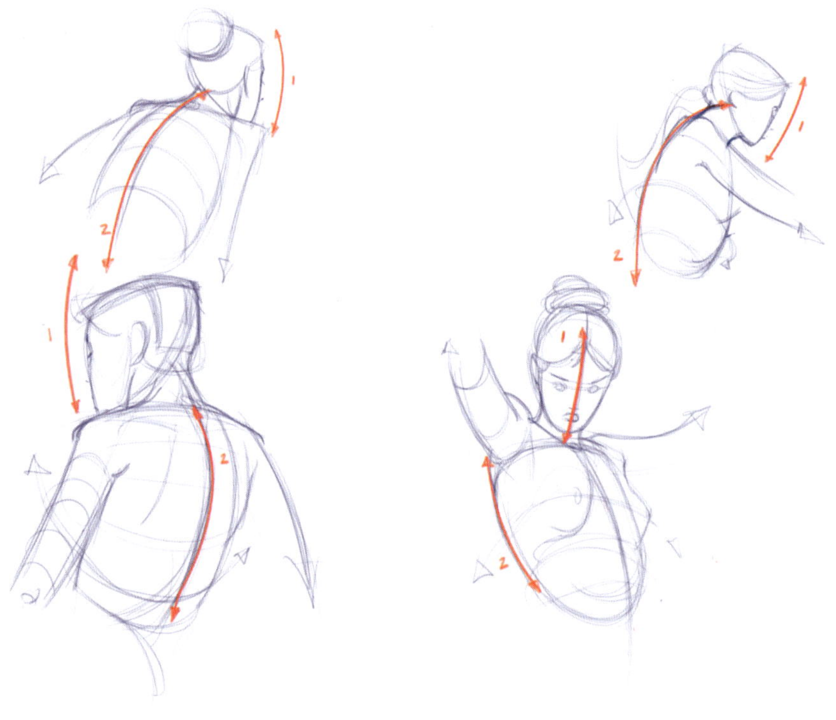

These poses are a bit more dynamic, but the principle is still the same.

In a formal frontal or back pose, there's nothing to consider. But, move toward the dynamic profile and—wow!—that wave action kicks in in a big way. In the images above, note how the neck joins the gesture of the front of the face when the chin lifts or the rib cage pulls back. Likewise, the neck joins the back of the rib cage when the chin moves toward the chest. Make sure you catch which bigger structure the neck gesture joins. It often makes or breaks the head to rib cage connection.

The Primary Structures of the Head

The head is a combination of two large masses: the cranium and the face. By first mapping the broader landscape—the cranium—we can then more easily conceive and place the features onto the face. Getting out the trusty measuring stick can help us plot the proportions, but it won't tell the whole story.

The trick for adding secondary detail to our work is the same trick we've used all along. We draw the big simple structures by starting with the big simple gestures. It doesn't change for the secondary structures. It never changes.

The lesser forms flow from their lesser gestures. The watery design of life composes a structure at every level, from a hangnail to a room of artists drawing the model. That's the great secret of the gesture and structure partnership and just another reason the gesture is the fundamental design line.

What we'll look for is the corner where two planes meet. Corners are structure. But, if we travel down a corner's long axis, it becomes a gesture. So, you can imagine we'll want to make those corners with curved lines, as shown at right.

Structure/gesture. Corners/curves. All the marks that will make up our interior detail will potentially be in the service of both ideas.

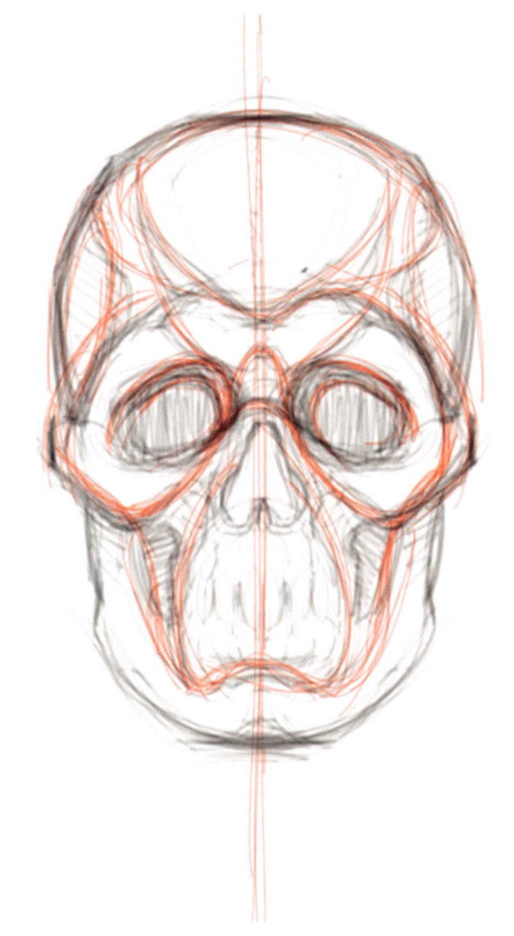

As you see by the red line gestures, there's a lot going on. We will look at each area.

The Secondary Structures of the Head

The cranium meets the face at the eye line/cheekbone area. This is as wide as the head generally gets.

The rising cheeks narrow slightly into the forehead and likewise cascade to the much narrower chin. This mask constitutes the multifaceted front planes of the face. And the long axes of those corners become the gestural movements between the forms. I've marked these in red in the figure at right.

The skullcap intrudes into the center of the forehead from above. This transitions the front plane into the top. The frontal cap may swell from or be completely submerged into the broader, squarer, brow ridge, depending on the character type.

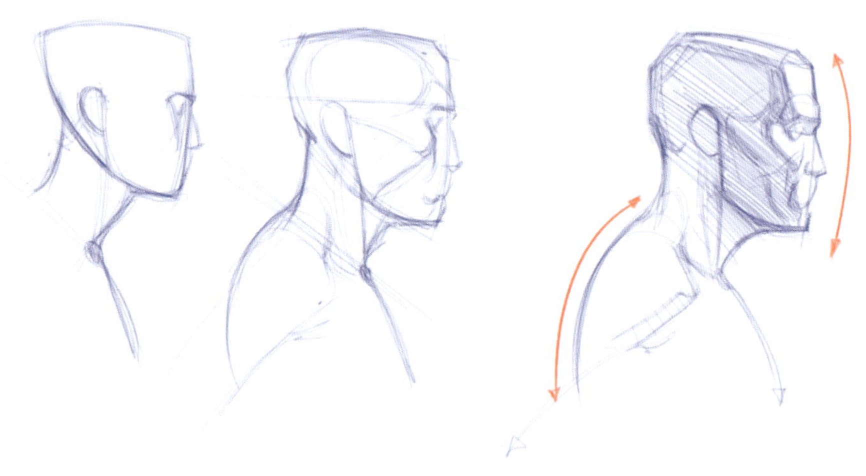

When we look closely, we see the face is built from an amazing set of forms that flow into and lock over each other.

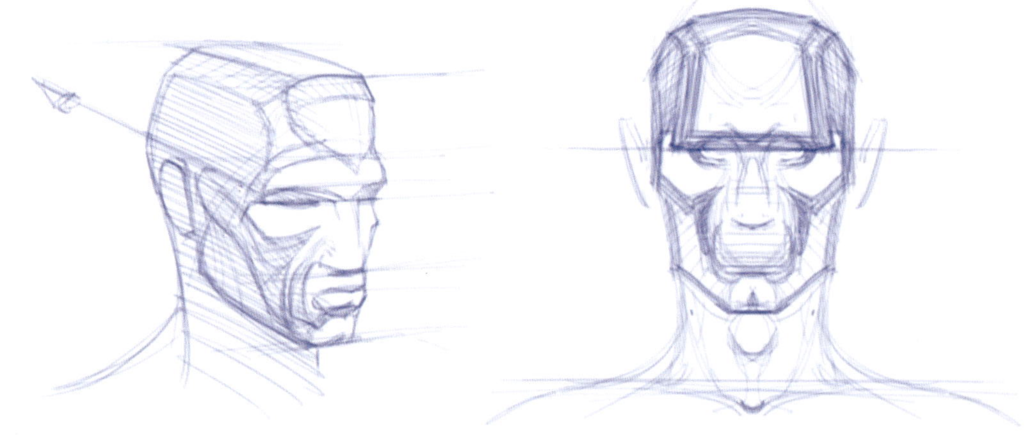

We can think of the forehead, cheek, and chin structures as rounder or squarer and simpler or more complicated. The more we play with those characteristics, the more opportunities open up.

The cheeks and chin transition back to the temple, ears, and jaw, creating the side planes. These can be rounded, chiseled, or even concave in character. Think of the cheeks as one wide rolling plane with the wedge of the nose and barrel of the mouth stacked on top.

Considering how each unique structure moves into the next is how gesture comes back into the mix. I'm sure you won't be surprised to learn that this step is critical. We never quit walking that tightrope between corners and curves no matter how detailed we get.

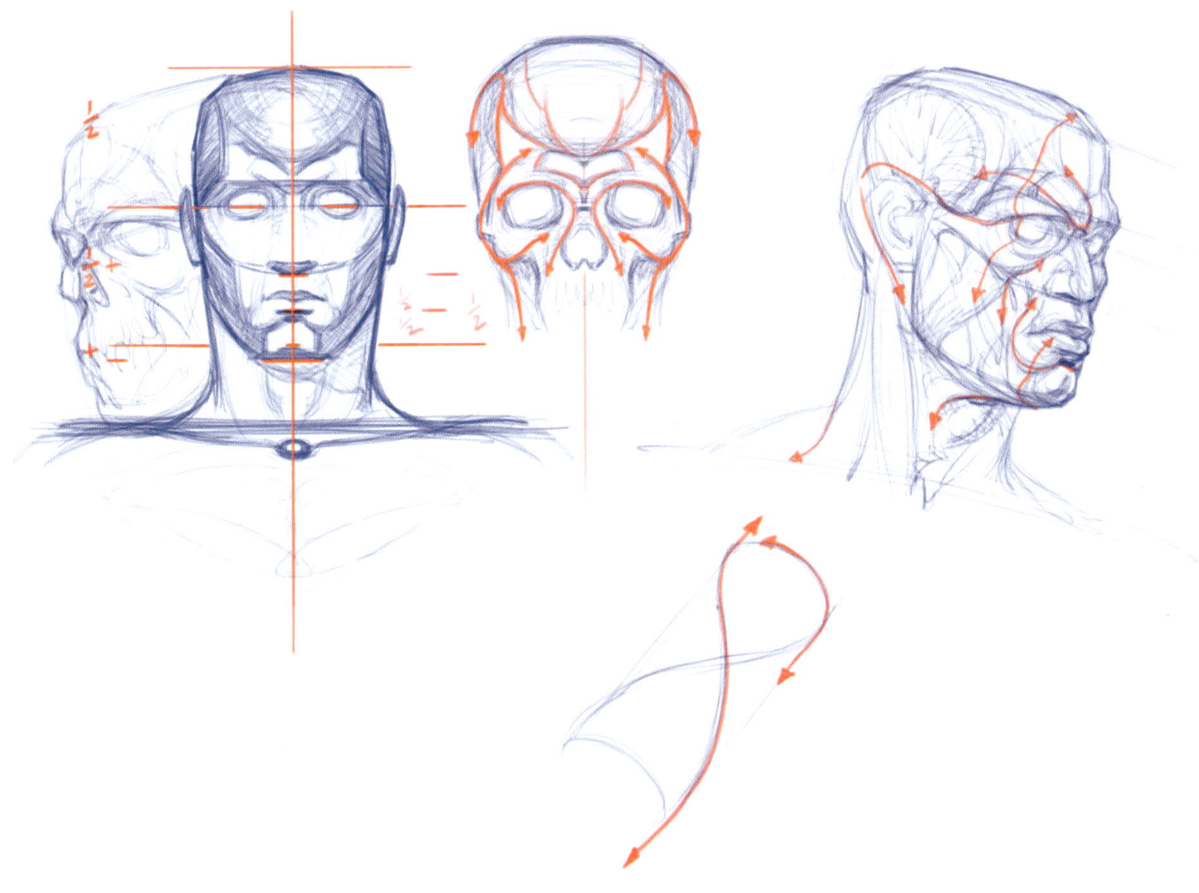

The gesture shouldn't just go over the form. It *rolls* over it. Think of drawing an S-curve on a roll of paper towels. As the S flows down the form, it also describes the round character of the form's volume.

Obviously, the skull has muscles, fat deposits, and skin clothing it, let alone hair, wrinkles, compression points, shadow shapes, and even pencil strokes. All can add subtle new gestures, but the key rhythms are created by the skull as described previously.

The gestural rhythms are often S-curves or even compound curves as opposed to the simple curves we experienced with the jointed body parts. That's because we're dealing with several subtle forms blending together. You decide how detailed you want it to be and how boxy or fluid. Just remember: when in doubt, simplify.

The gesture shows us new wondrous rhythms with every change of position. Drawing from life lets you tap that ever-changing source. Capturing these rhythms pulls our drawing together and makes it ring true on the deepest possible level.

When you look at photographs, anatomical drawings, or master works, try these kinds of red line analyses. You want a rich and diverse catalog of potential rhythms.

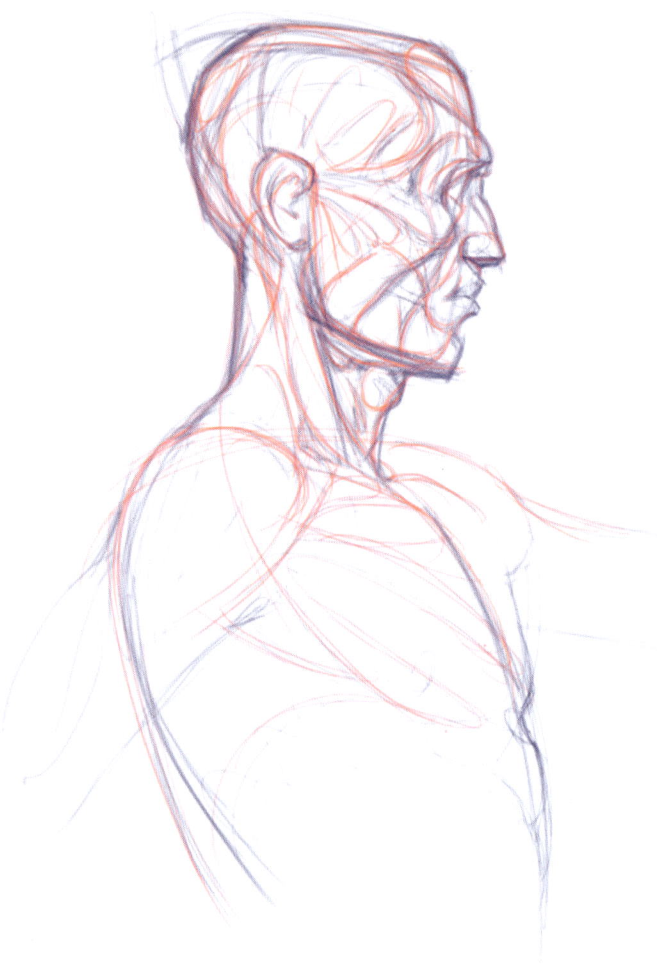

When you study anatomy, think of it as the source of gesture as well as structure. Follow the red lines to see what I mean. There are almost endless possibilities.

There are surprising numbers of gestural routes to chase depending on the style you want and the character you're after. However, it must follow the topography. And keep in mind, the more you separate the lesser structures, the more male-like and older the face will generally appear.

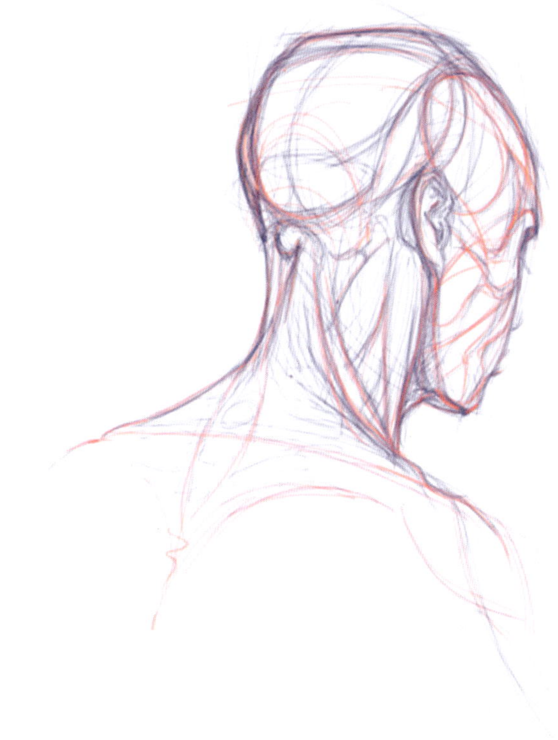

Here we see how those exquisite rhythms begin to shift as the pose shifts. They're still the same gestures. They simply look a little different now as they track over the forms.

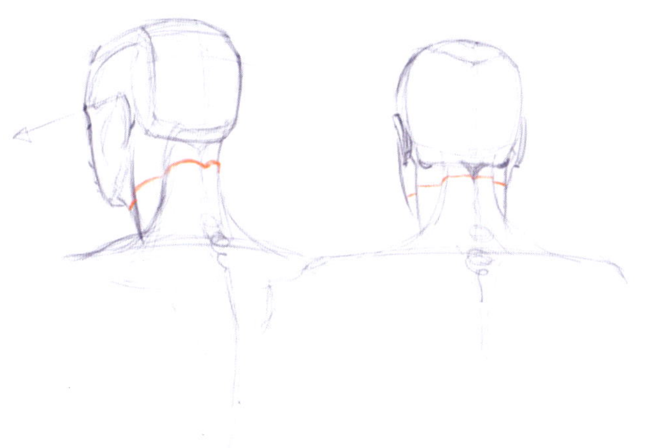

It's a good time to revisit those overlapping structures of shrugging muscles, neck, and head. The overlaps stay strong. This is just a more nuanced take than we've seen before.

A little disclaimer: The drawings here are my conceptions, with a little added flair, of basic anatomy for a book not predominately about anatomy. Meaning, an interested party could find a few anatomical "errors." I put errors in quotes because as long as the marks track gesture or structure, and as long as they're done with consistency, the audience won't read them as errors. They'll read them as the work of a stylist—which is exactly what you want. Bravo Buonarroti!

The Eyes

The key to constructing believable eyes is knowing they are, basically, balls in holes.

In fact, all features must be conceived as simple structures sitting on the bigger structure of the head. That's why it is so important to map out the facial architecture in particular.

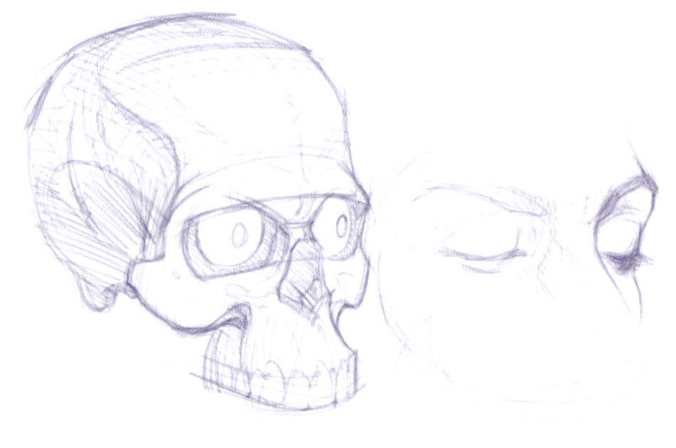

Something as pressure-packed as drawing the eyes is still primarily about structure and gesture. If you begin with those two fundamental ideas, even portraiture becomes more manageable.

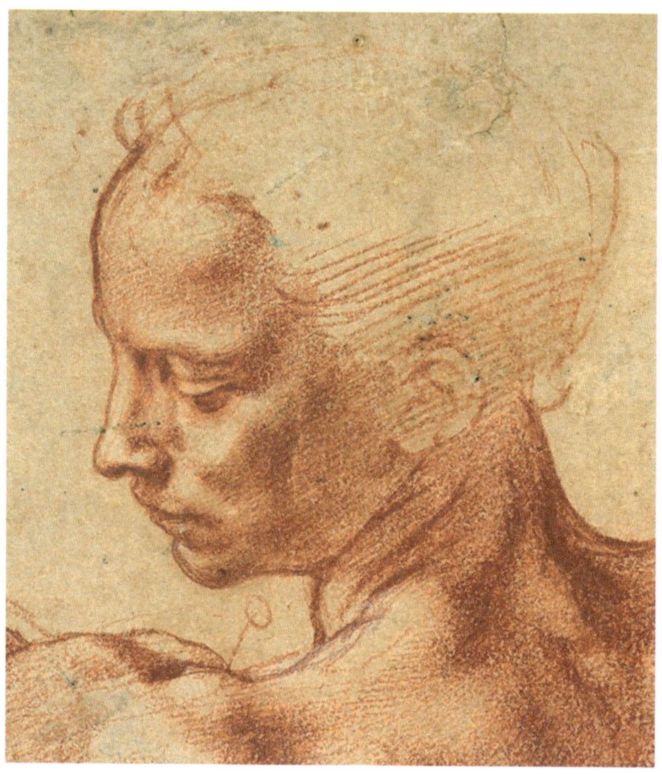

Studies for the Libyan Sibyl (recto), c. 1510–1511, Michelangelo Buonarroti (1475–1564). Chalk on paper. Metropolitan Museum of Art, New York/ Bridgeman Images. Michelangelo had to set his eye back into the plane of the face and away from the inside edge of the eyebrow. In other words, he had to give us subtle clues that the smaller eye structure rested in the landscape of the bigger face.

EYE STRUCTURE

We always work from the centerline outward to draw a well-constructed face.

Take a close look at the partial head in Fig. A. The red keystone steps back from the forehead to start the nose. It separates the eyebrows and, so, the eyes. The spherical shape of the eye shows itself clearly, whether the eyelid is open or closed. The eye socket is covered by the skin. The only real sense of its cave-like quality is how far back into the socket the eyeball sits.

Other things to notice: The sides of the nose end at the cheek. Some of the cheek is visible before the eyeballs start (marked in red). The inside corner of the eyelid angles down slightly because it is off the ball at that point. The lower lid nicely tracks over the bottom of the eyeball. Make sure there is plenty of cheek to the outside of the eyeballs (again, marked in red).

THE PROFILE OF THE EYE

We have to look for the thickness of the lids any time we can see them.

Notice in the drawing in Fig. B that I can easily fit another eye/eyelid shape (in red) in front before reaching the contour of the nose. Also notice how far back the eyeball sits from the eyelid. This is to show the great thickness of that awning structure.

In fact, from the eyebrow to the crease of the upper lid, to the upper lid, to the eyeball, everything steps back. This is because the brow ridge pushes forward to protect the eye as does the cheek to a lesser degree.

I exaggerated the thickness of the lids here and they look just fine, don't they? Always know which way to screw up—in other words, which way to push the idea!

Now look at those eyes in profile in Fig. C. The pupil and iris—the black and the colored circles that are, in effect, painted on the ball—become very thin ellipses when seen from the side.

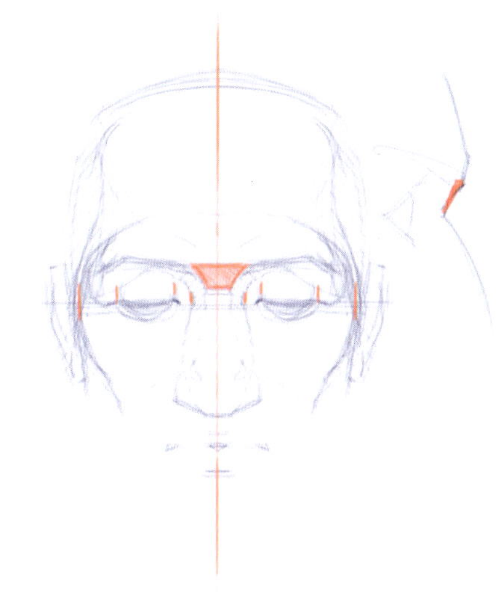

Fig. A. It starts with the most important landmark on the head. That's the keystone shape bringing the forehead and nose together and keeping the eyes apart.

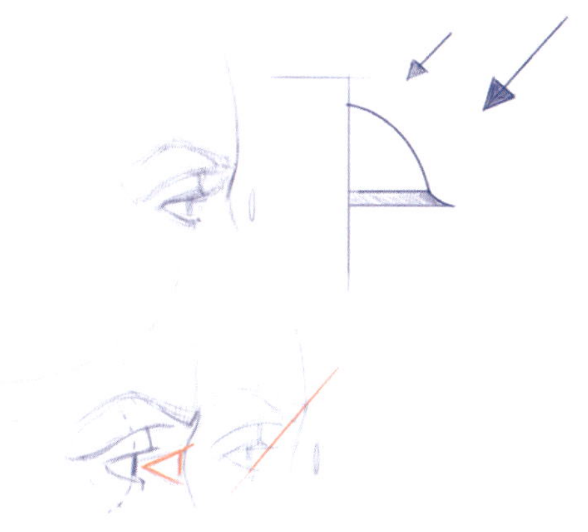

Fig. B. The upper lid and its lashes act like an awning dressing a store window. It shades and protects the eyeball.

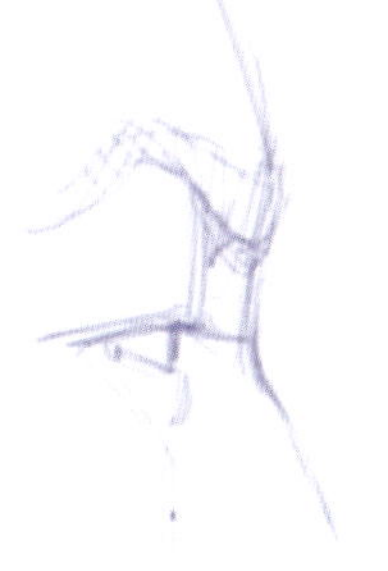

Fig. C. Here's an alternate structure when a thicker upper lid exists.

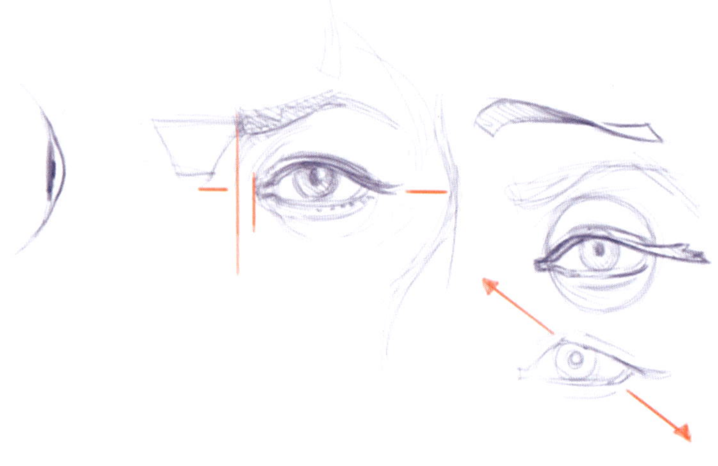

For being a simple ball in a hole, the eye displays some very interesting asymmetries. And as we'll see, sometimes less is more.

THE FRONT VIEW

In the front view of the eye, the lids, again, hint at the ball shape underneath. Careful, though—the more lines you add, the more you age your model. You can see I've aged this young woman above about ten years with my "extras."

Notice the inner eyelid steps to the outside of the placement of the eyebrow (shown with the two red vertical lines). This gives the feeling that the eye is back into that socket. The inner meeting of the eyelids is often a little lower than the outer meeting (shown with the two red horizontal lines).

It is usually best to draw the eyelashes as one mass rather than individual hairs. Notice the twisted ribbon

effect between the mass of lashes and the thickness of the upper lid. Notice also how in the rendering this awning often shades the iris and pupil into a grouping value of darkness, allowing the highlight to pop.

In the profile eyeball I've sketched (above left), you can see how our natural contact lens—the cornea—covers the pupil and iris. This distorts the upper lid, creating an apex to the lid's curve that shifts to the inside.

The lower lid sits too low to be affected, but rather tucks up tightly into the upper lid at the outside. In this way, it has an apex favoring that direction. The tilting red line shows this asymmetry.

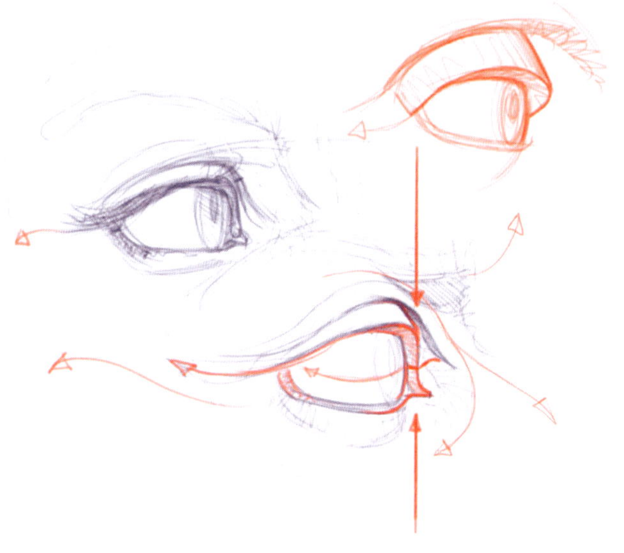

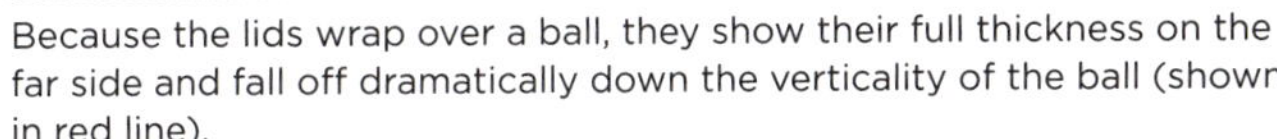

Because the lids wrap over a ball, they show their full thickness on the far side and fall off dramatically down the verticality of the ball (shown in red line).

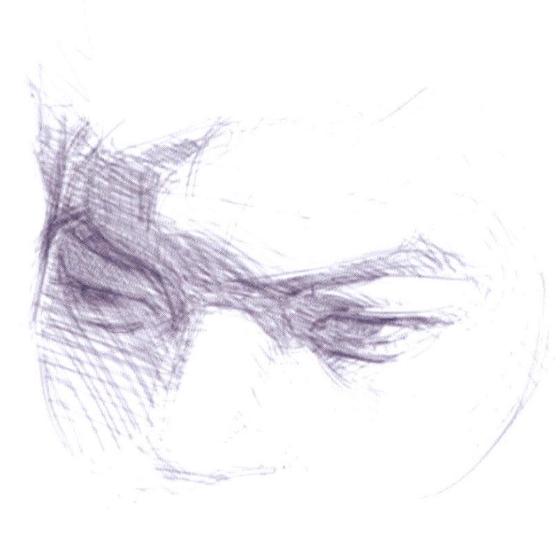

Here's another fuller-lidded model, meaning no dramatic crease to start the upper lid. I say fuller lid because it may not be an Asian character. For example, gravity pulls the upper lid crease lower as the character ages, and getting punched in the eye for your job builds scar tissue over it.

THE THREE-QUARTER VIEW

In the top red drawing in Fig. A, notice the thickness of the lid coming into view as it goes around the far side. I've taken away the vertical drop to make it more apparent in this three-quarter view.

We need at least one "out" from each feature. The "out" is the *gestural movement taking off from the feature and onto the surrounding structure*. The eye has a few. The S-curve of the eyelashes is one. It comes off the ball and onto the cheek with that graceful sweep. It works best on female models, as you can imagine.

There are several lines coming off the inside of the upper lid that sweep into the bridge of the nose, around the eyeball, and onto the cheek below it. Examine the red line arrows on the top left drawing. Another "out" is the eyebrow, which can take us into the furrowed brow line.

Whether it's the eyes or whatever detailed structure you're working on, make sure you plan for outs. It will look more sophisticated and less cartoon-like, guaranteed.

Notice how each eye is drawn with absolute fidelity to its structure and, yet, I make sure to show the visual pathway (the gesture) off the eye and back into the greater structure that supports it.

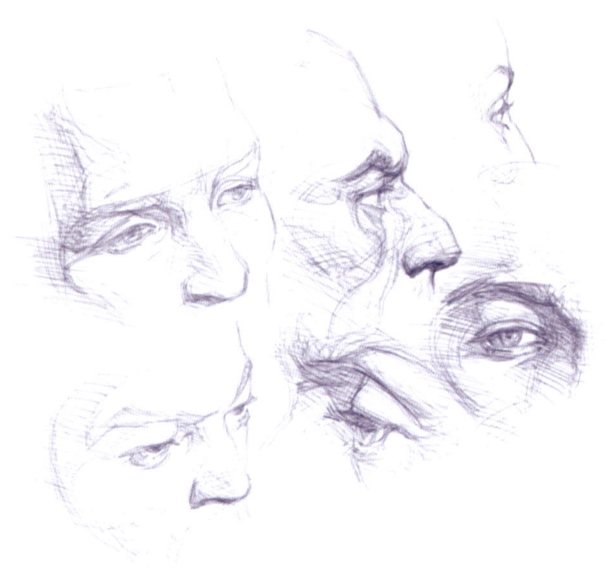

Any detail we choose to add must act as smaller gestures and structures that submit to the position and character of the face from which they originate.

The Nose

The nose and the barrel of the mouth together constitute the muzzle.

The gesture line of the face (G1) actually passes through the keystone and the point at which the barrel meets the chin (shown in red line in the drawing below). The silhouetted likeness of a person is based largely on how the muzzle builds and then recedes to the chin.

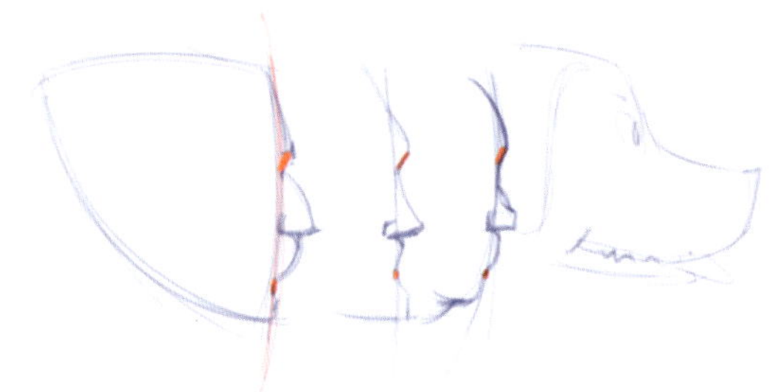

From a profile, we see that the nose starts on the plane of the face, but thrusts out from it once it moves down from the keystone.

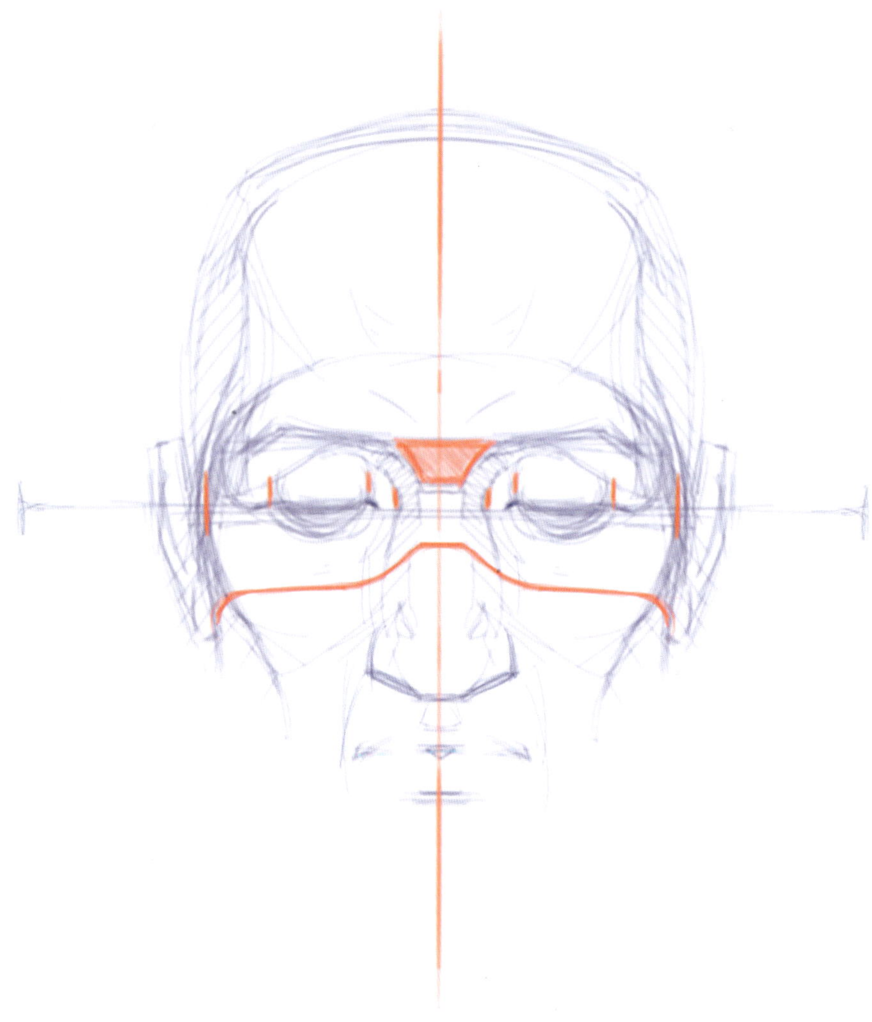

The nose is a wedge that sits on the bigger plane of the cheeks. It begins at the same keystone landmark from which we built the eyes.

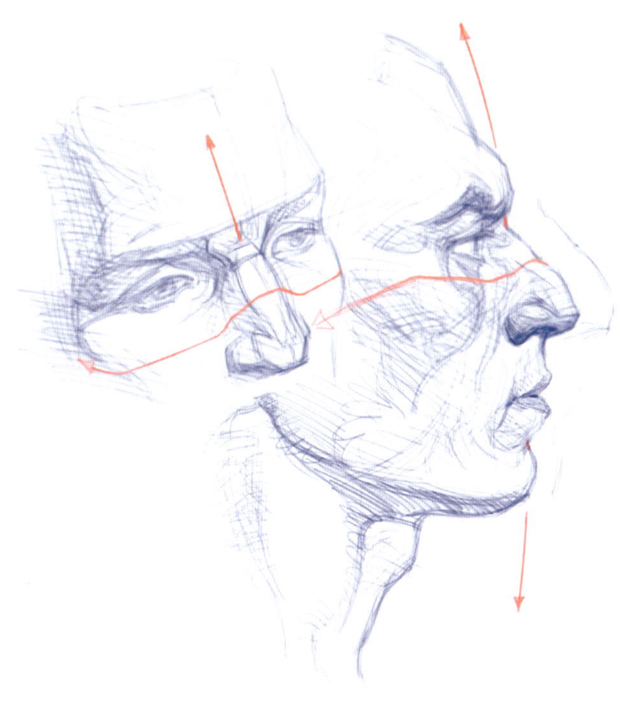

Let's revisit a couple of those more detailed drawings I showed you previously so we can understand how the parts of the nose converge.

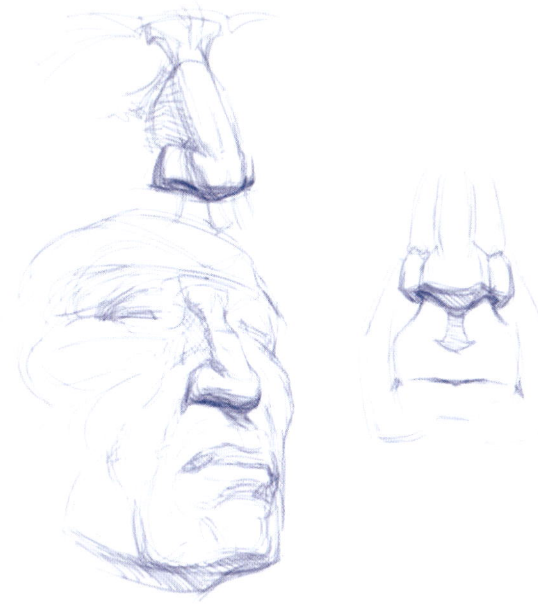

Here are some angles to show how strongly the mouth barrel affects the end of the nose.

The bridge of the nose begins from the keystone. It descends like a dagger blade, piercing the ball of the nose. The ball end can be rounder or squarer, but it can't be just a "tip." Meaning, it must have front, side, and bottom planes to become fully realized. With the ball, the wings of the nose span the barrel of the mouth, creating bridge-like structures the nostrils hide beneath.

Take special note of the red line arrows showing the mouth barrel emerging from under the wings in the fig-ure above (shown in ghosted lines to the right). The side planes of the bridge/wings bevel out, and both can be seen from a front view. They don't cut into the cheeks, but roll smoothly onto them.

The Mouth

We just saw how the start of the mouth is connected intimately to the end of the nose. As part of that muzzle, the mouth bulges out of its beginnings and separates, sometimes strongly and sometimes less so, from the lower cheek and jaw.

The chin pushes up from below and the bottom of the barrel sags over either side like a loose shirt over a big belt buckle (see Fig. A). On a mature or grinning face, the barrel ripples into each side of the jaw, creating the dimple lines (shown with red lines below). The philtrum is a small divot in the upper barrel and nicely marks its centerline.

The lips stair-step over the barrel while the line of the mouth tracks perfectly over its volume from whatever position you draw it (see Fig. B). The upper lip falls into shadow quickly, as does the plane from the bottom edge of the lower lip back to the chin.

The contour of the upper lip and the line of the mouth both tend to look like stretched-out capital Ms. (See Fig. C.) The center third or so of the bottom of the lower lip becomes a strong straight horizontal line or tilted to whatever angle the rest of the front plane features are constructed on.

You can see five dark accents along the lines of the mouth in the middle left in Fig. D. This is where the upper and lower lip shapes don't seal tightly. Drawing your line darker here is a good strategy.

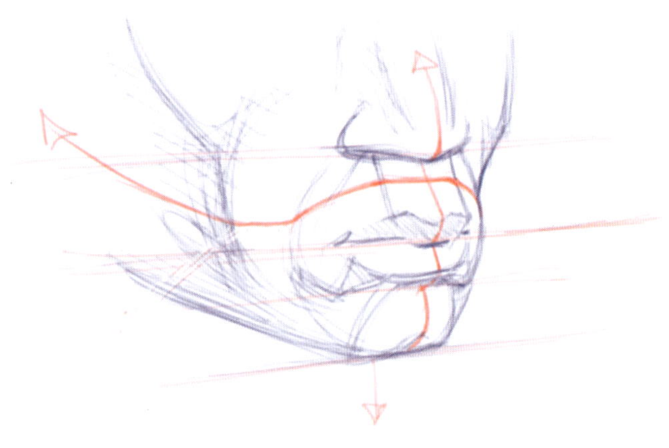

Fig. A. The key to the mouth is the barrel structure rounds over from left to right and from top to bottom. Seeing the rich variety of lip shapes can hide that bulging character if we aren't observant.

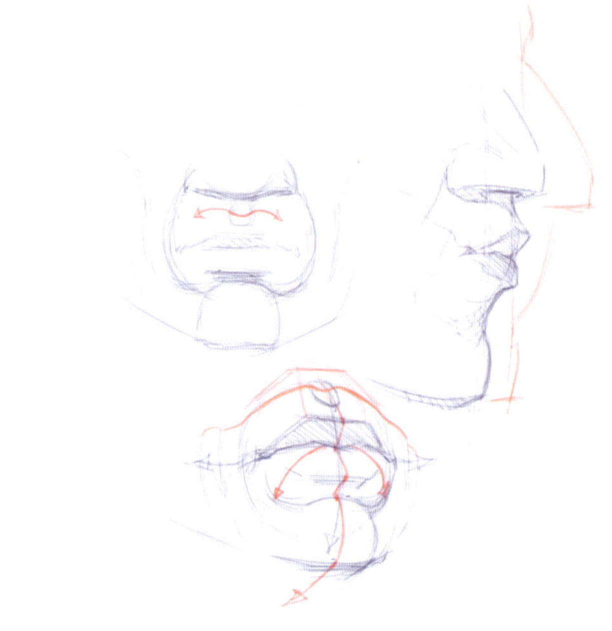

Fig. B. From every angle, the mouth barrel bulges off the plane of the face.

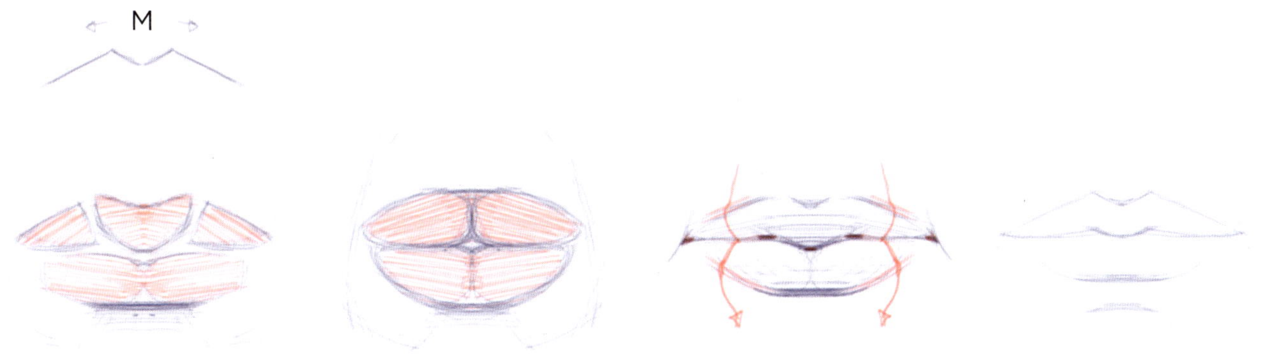

Fig. C. The lips are membranes and, so, have a deeper color and greater texture than skin. Their pillowy forms are full in youth, but thin with age. The upper lip can be broken into two or three distinct shapes (shown in red).

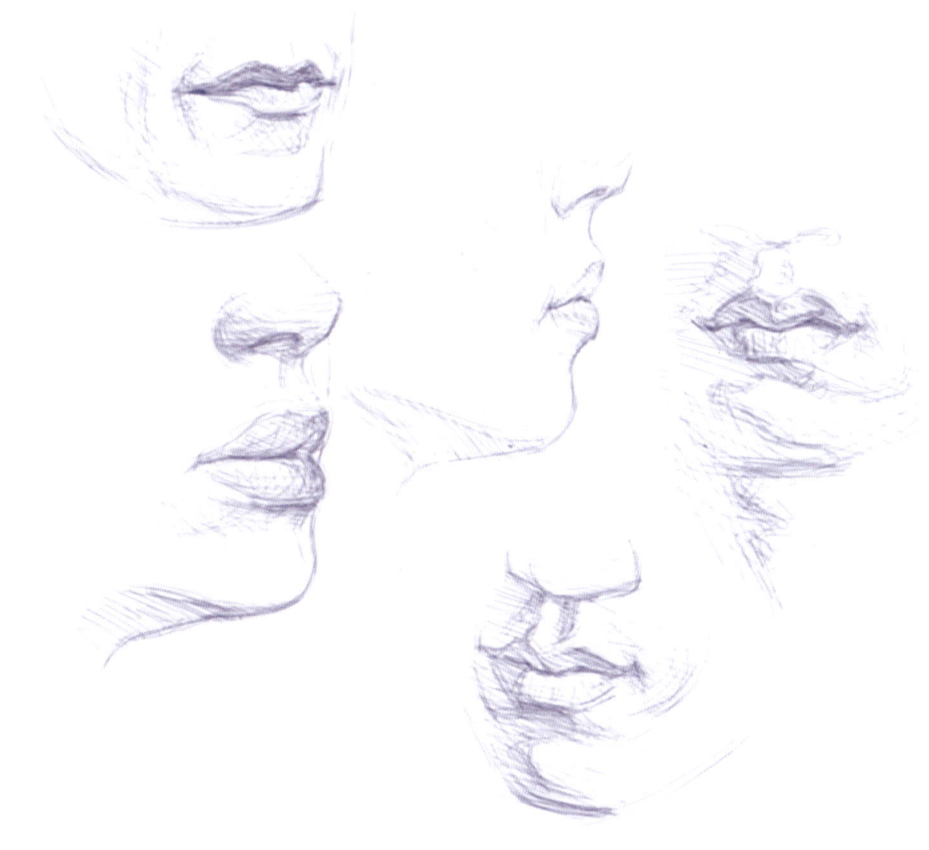

Fig. D. Practice finding the structures we just talked about under my careful rendering.

The Ear

The ear's shape can change radically, but the fundamental structure is surprisingly consistent. Think of it as a slice off the end of a cylinder and then cut a straight edge off that. It can be squarer, rounder, short, long, or wobbly. Whatever its character, it attaches and flows smoothly into the cheek plane (shown in red arrow line in Fig. A).

Now, what to do with all those convolutions that give an ear its character? Start with a C-shape that has the character you want. Add a question mark just inside it. Make sure it wanders a little. We don't want them to track in a parallel fashion. Rather, make it pinch and spread, as the red line segments show in Fig. B.

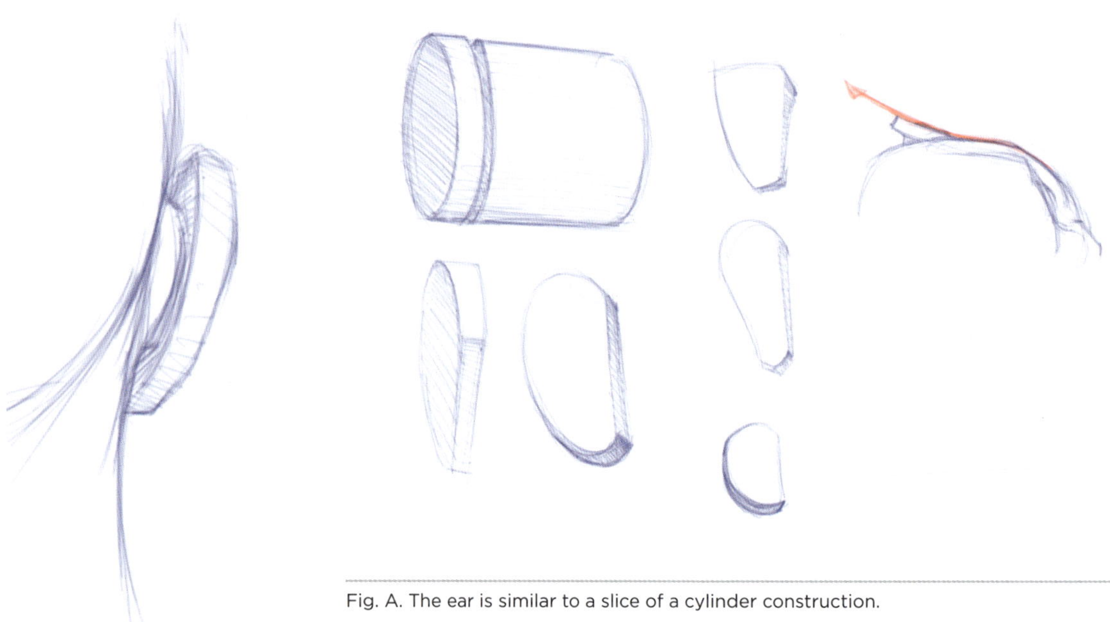

Fig. A. The ear is similar to a slice of a cylinder construction.

From the back, we see the big dish shape that funnels in the sound and the small bowl that connects it to the skull.

Add another question mark tight to the first. Add a third, but let it tilt forward. Don't give it a period. Instead, wrap the tail right into another little C-shape. This gives us an outer and an inner rim, and the little flap that blends into the cheek.

Lastly, take a little divot to make a *Y* out of the inner rim and wrap the outer rim down into the inside bowl.

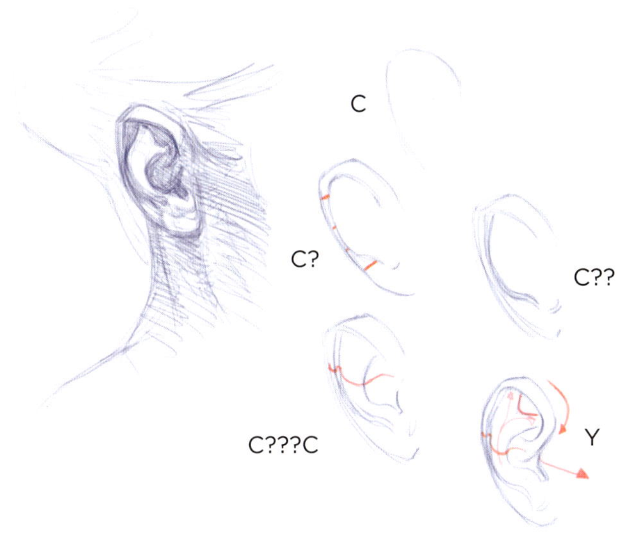

Fig. B. The ears are made up of *C*s and *?*s.

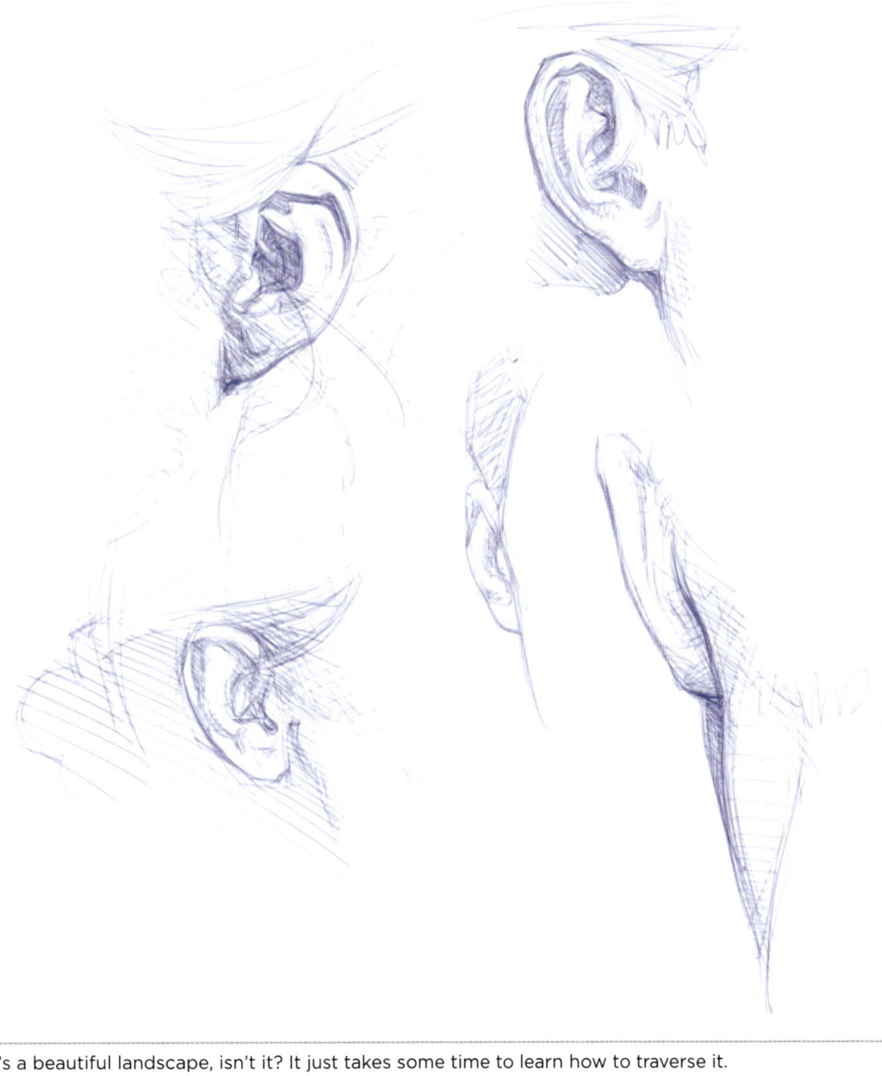

It's a beautiful landscape, isn't it? It just takes some time to learn how to traverse it.

OLD MASTER *study*

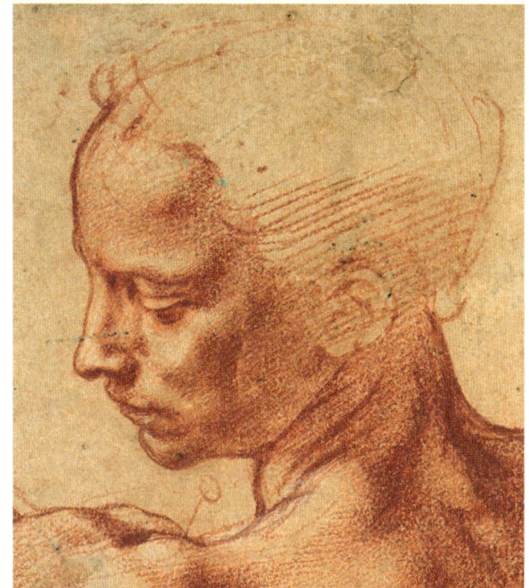

Studies for the Libyan Sibyl (recto),
c. 1510–1511, Michelangelo Buonarroti
(1475–1564). Chalk on paper.
Metropolitan Museum of Art,
New York/Bridgeman Images.

Michelangelo's *Study for the Libyan Sybil* is one of the most famous drawings in art history. Look at the absolute fidelity to structure and gesture. All the big and little front planes track almost perfectly. Because they're organic, they don't have to be perfect.

As is typical, the side planes wander around, but still respect the corner. That's box logic. The gestures go crazy getting one form to flow into the next. And look at those "outs." I love this guy!

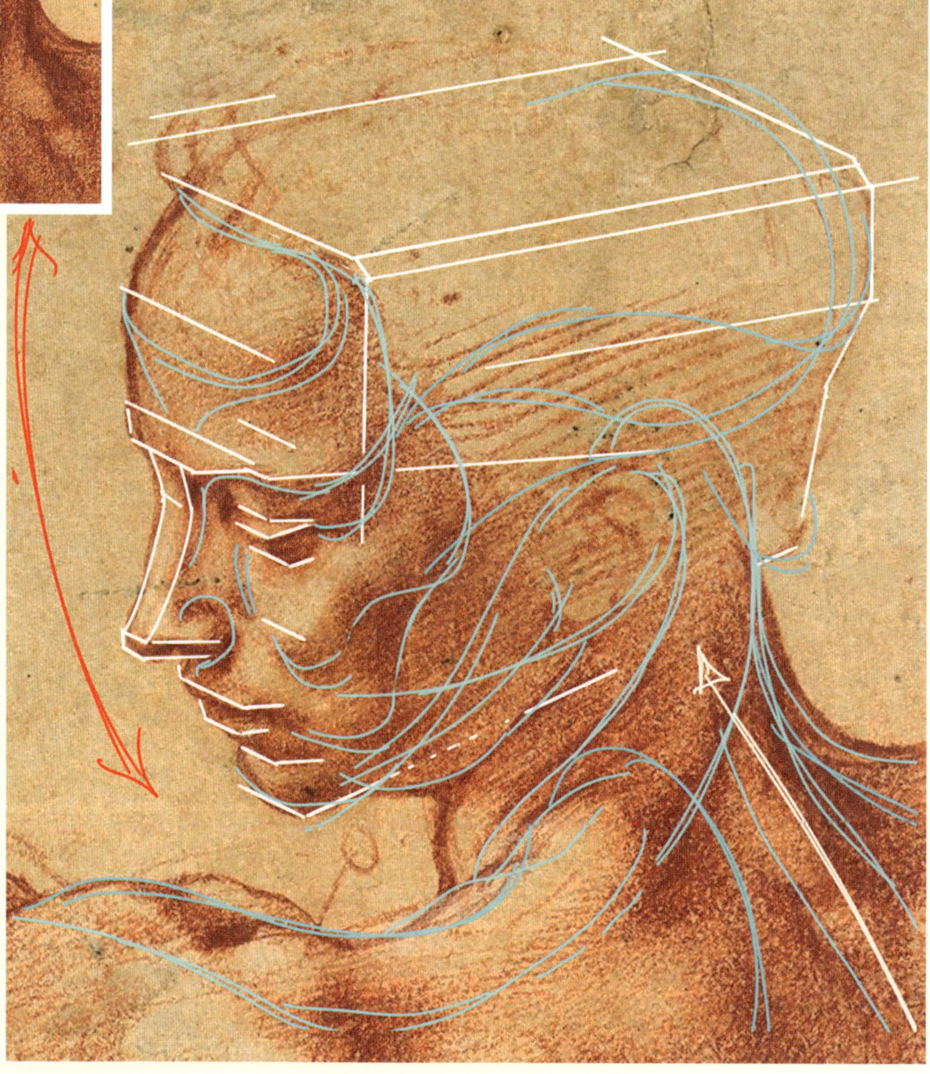

Is there a better drawing from which to learn about the head? It's a veritable master's class of knowledge and facility.

GIVE IT A TRY: *Exercise 1*

As I just did on the Michelangelo,
do your own structural and
gestural analyses on this fine
self-portrait by Fantin-Latour by
laying tracing paper over it.

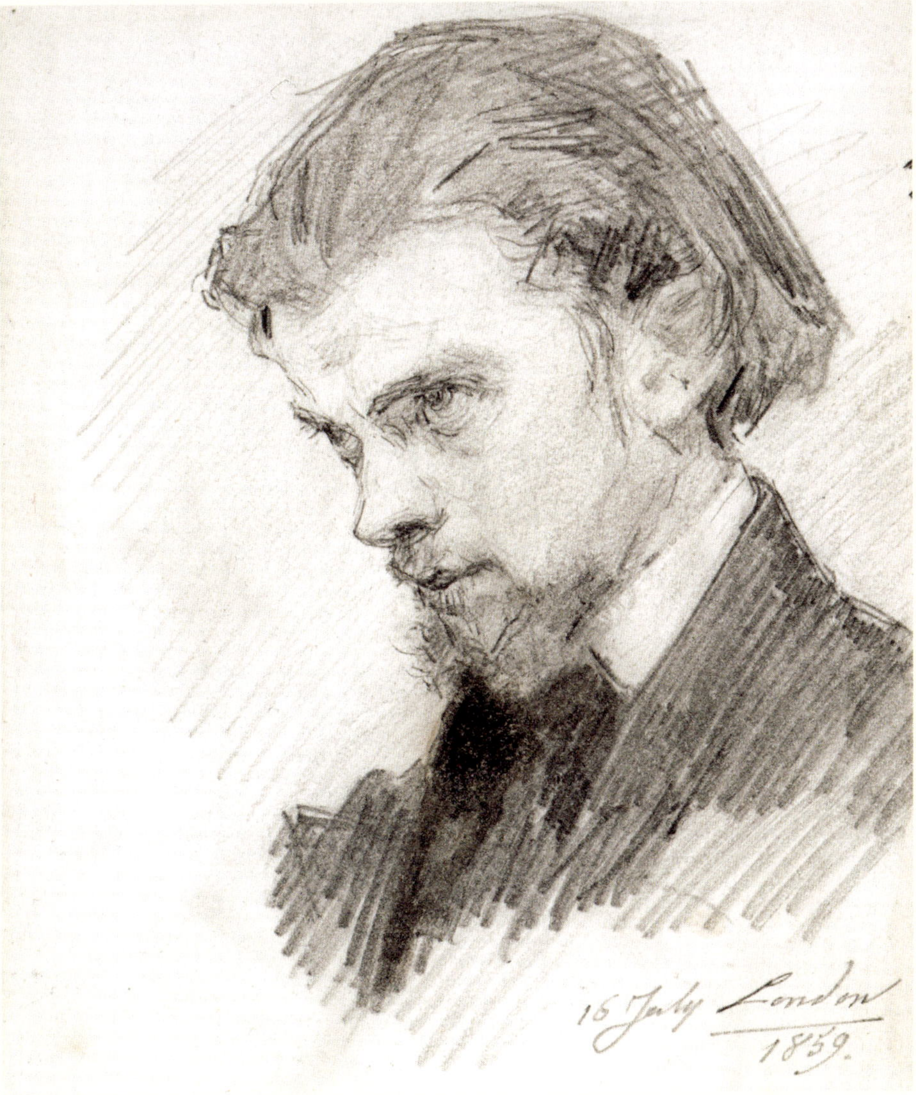

Self-Portrait, 1859, Ignace Henri Jean Fantin-Latour (1836–1904). Pencil on paper. University of
Cambridge, UK/Bridgeman Images.

GIVE IT A TRY: *Exercise 2*

Here is a page of sketches showing how I might begin
a drawing where the head construction is carefully tied
to the body gesture. Find those gestural lines and draw
some of your own.

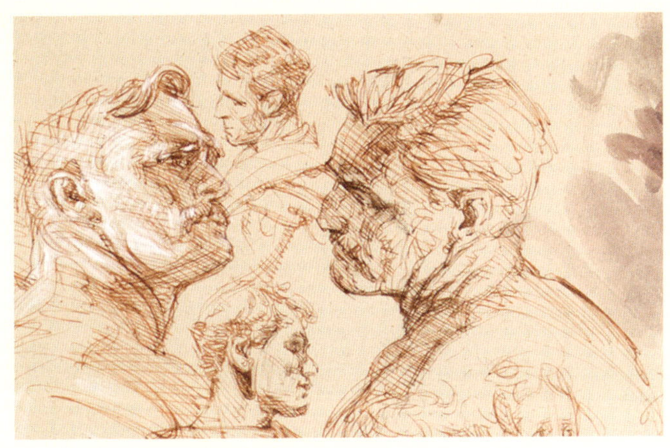

A page from my sketchbook. Fountain pen, brown ink, white
CarbOthello, and gouache on oatmeal-colored scrapbook paper.

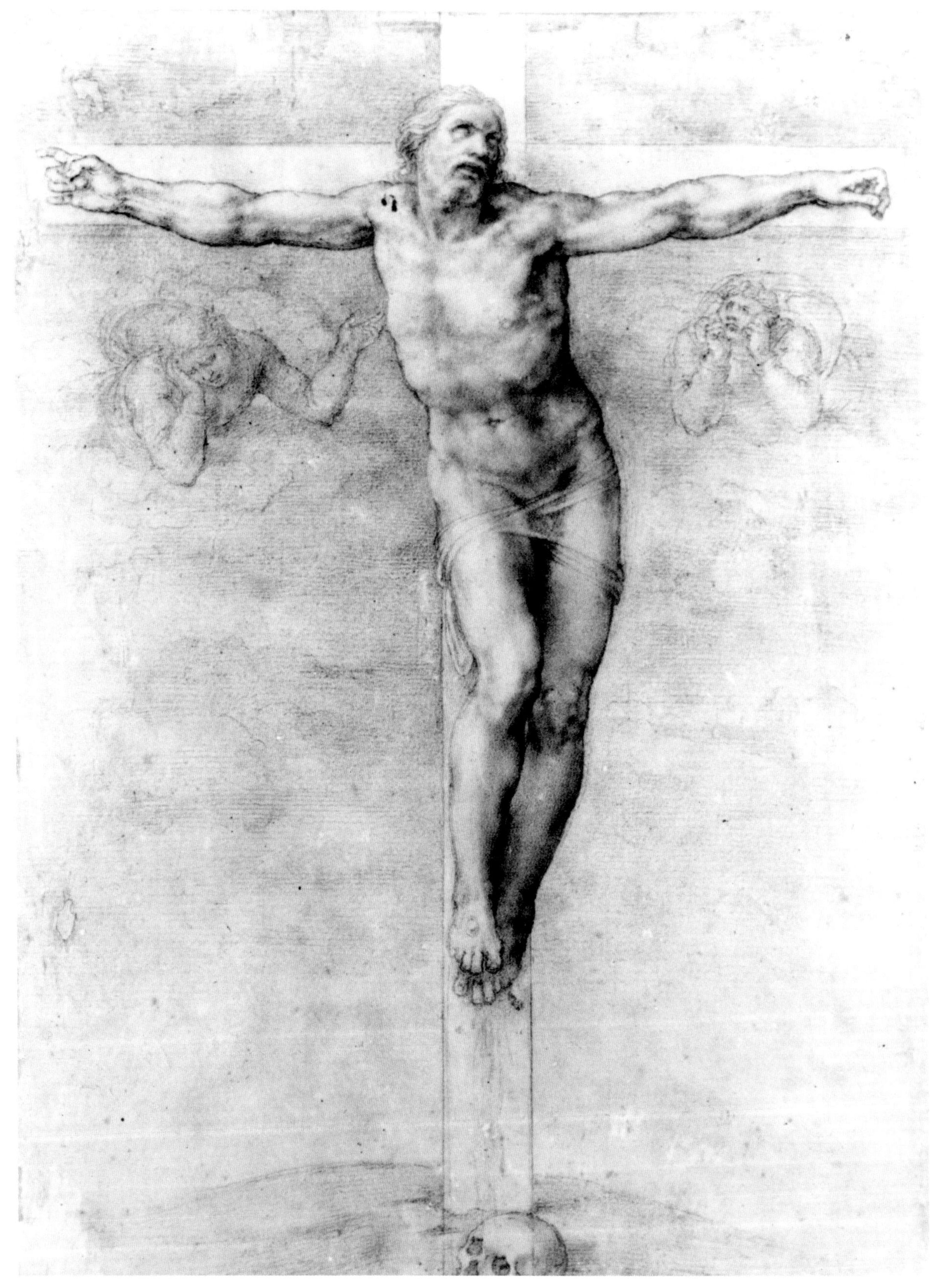

Christ on the Cross, c. sixteenth century, Michelangelo Buonarroti (1475–1564). Chalk on paper. Private collection/Bridgeman Images.

8 | THE TORSO

Let's talk gesture. Again.

Contrapposto: Opposing Positions

When artists use the term "contrapposto," it chiefly references the tilt of the shoulders against the opposing tilt of the hips. This is due to a shift in balance so one leg becomes the dominant support, letting the other leg relax. That hip, then, falls a bit with the relaxation, and the opposing shoulder rises in response.

The original idea of contrapposto was to bring a little asymmetry into the picture (or sculpture) to make the pose seem less formal—more natural. *Kritios Boy* is the first example in history we have of its use. Compare this to the *kouros* in chapter 3 (see page 53)—a subtle but powerful difference. In fact, you are looking at the most powerful idea in figurative art.

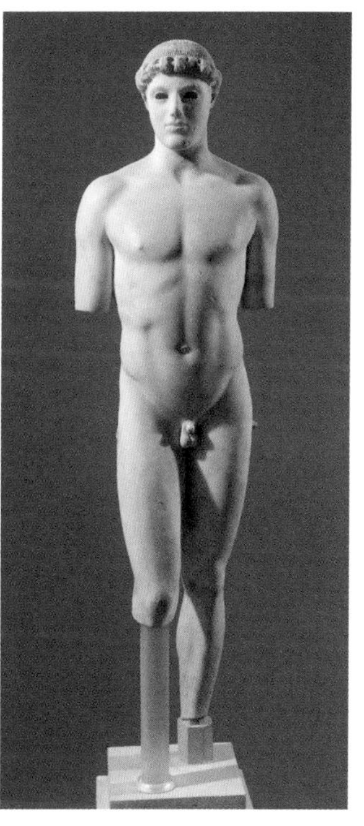

The Kritios Boy, c. fifth century BCE, Greek. Marble. Acropolis Museum, Athens/Bridgeman Images.

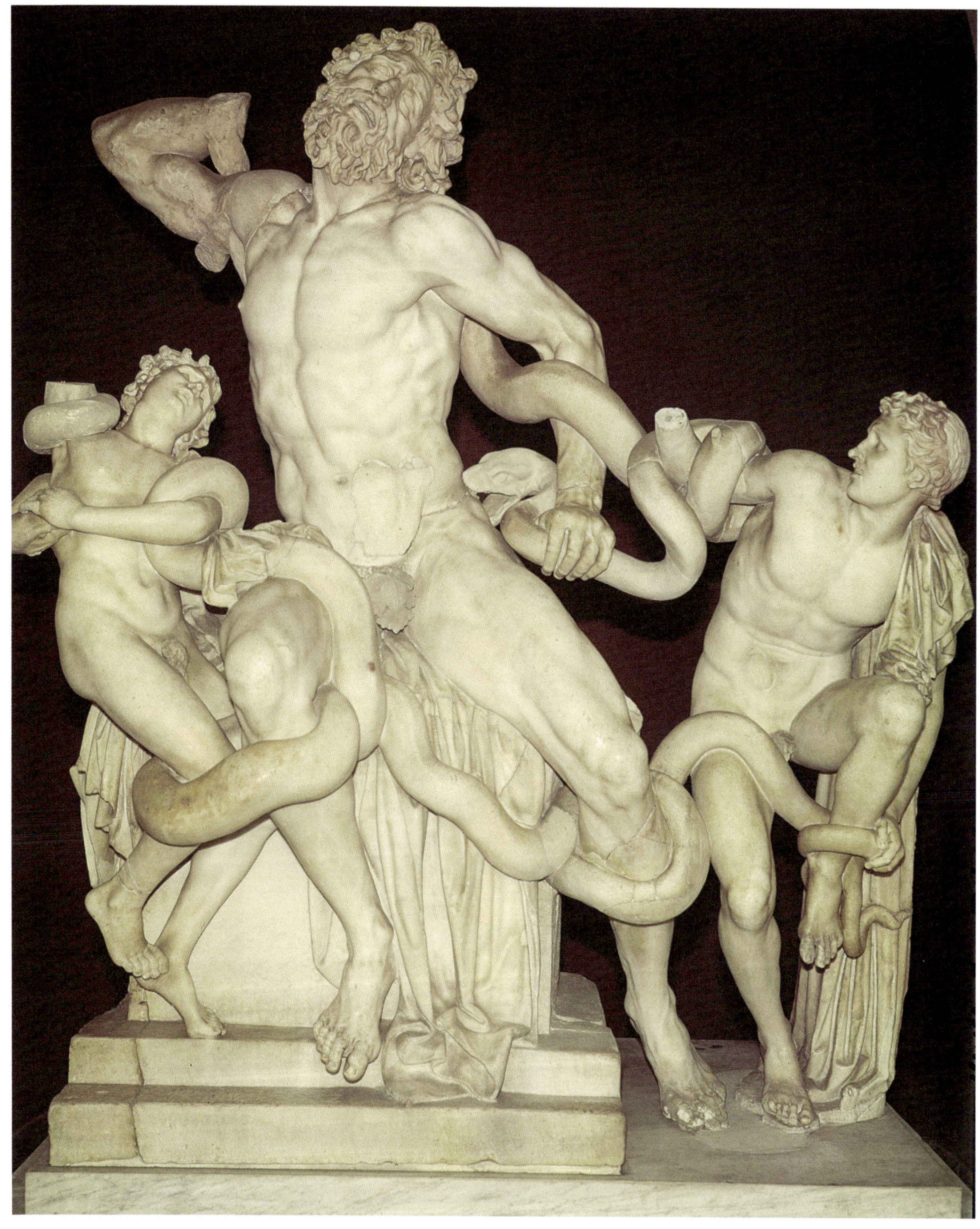

Laocoon, first century, Hellenistic original. Marble. Vatican Museums and Galleries, Vatican City/Bridgeman Images.

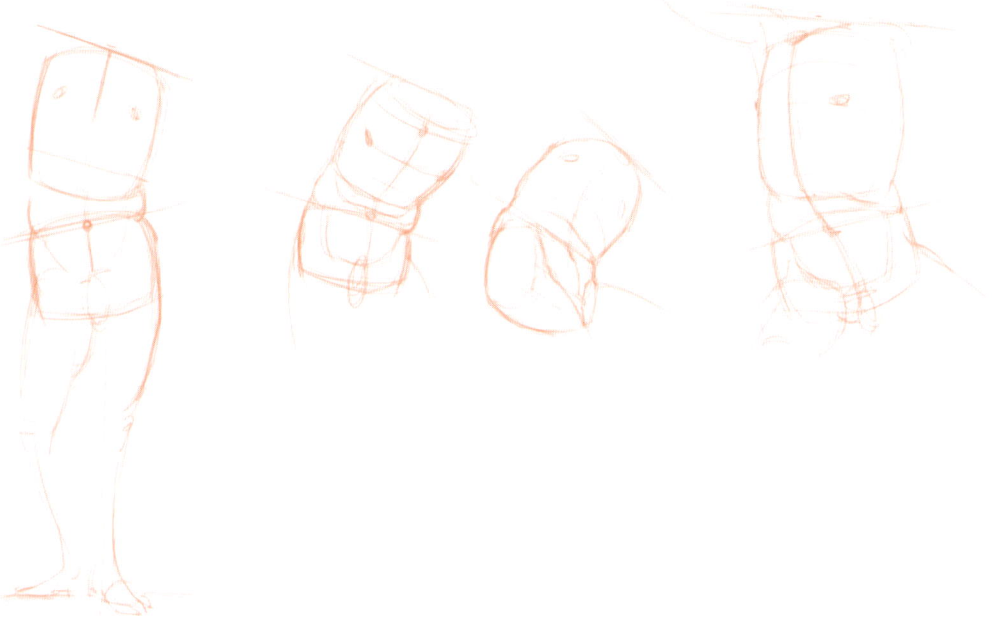

Here's a simple breakdown of the original "relaxed" contrapposto pose and more extreme possibilities.

As artists tend to do, they started playing with the possibilities. The "opposing positions" idea then became ever more dramatic, including the torso twisting left to right and front to back. Suddenly, the figure could break the picture plane. Artworks now had the power to break into our space or draw us into theirs. To see two of the most famous examples, look at *Laocoön* (left) or the tragically broken image of the *Belvedere Torso* from chapter 1 (see page 31).

Or just look at anything Michelangelo ever created!

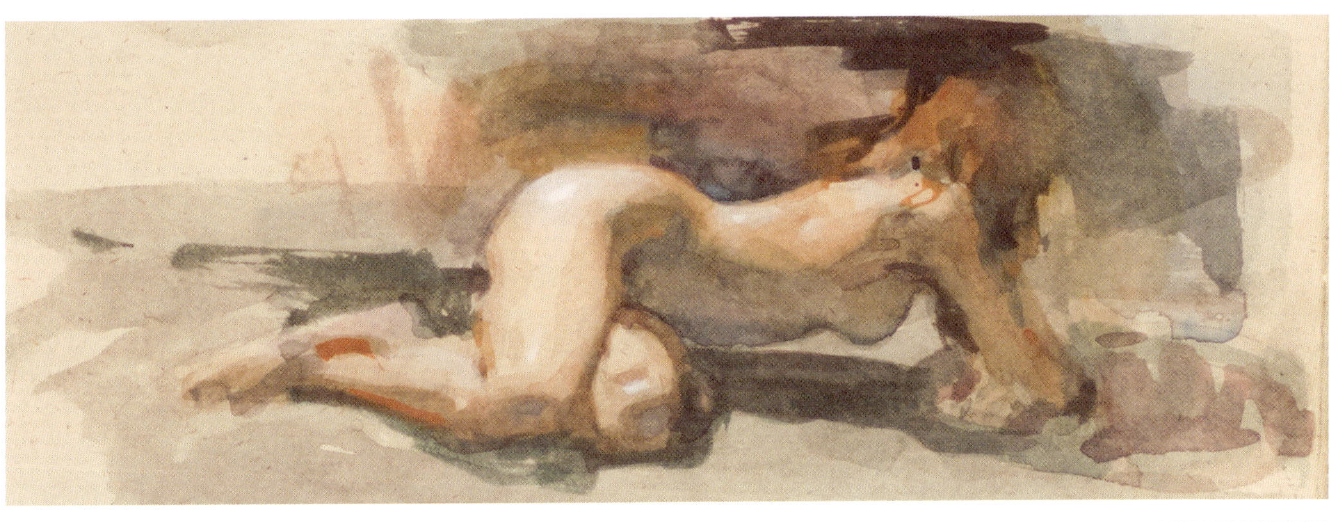

Contrapposto can show up in nearly unlimited ways.

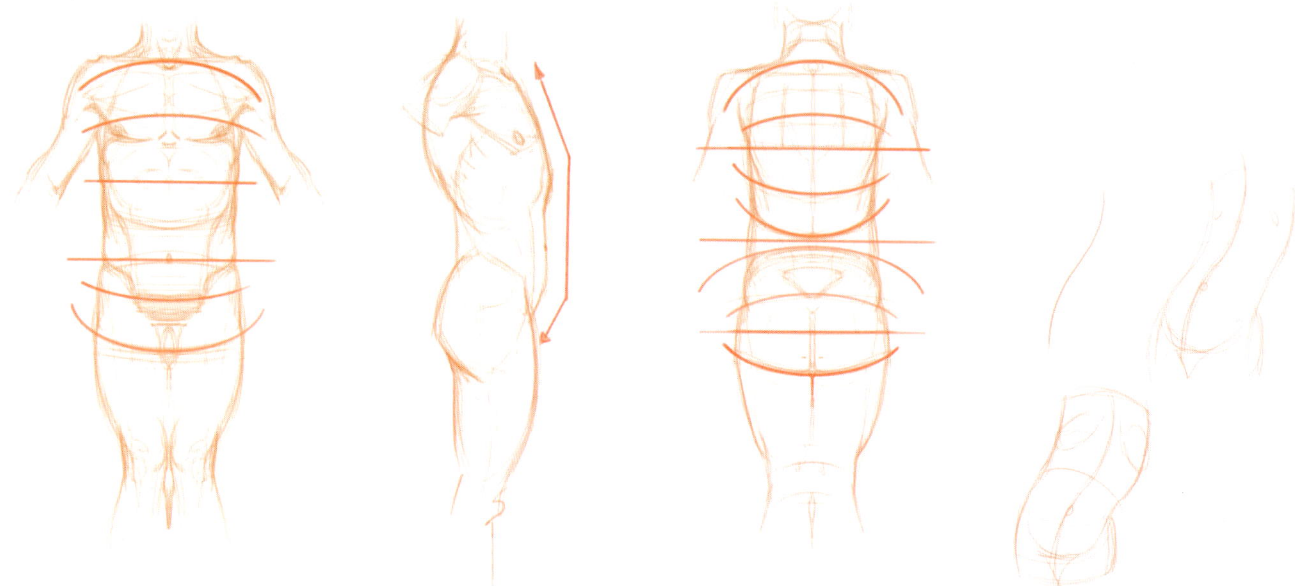

Because of the natural curve of the spine, even a stiff pose such as the *kouros* has a sort of contrapposto going on. The straight front view gives us a chest where the top tilts back into space, a stomach that is flat to the picture plane, and hips that tilt into space at the bottom. As the ribs and hips balance over the supporting legs, they tilt forward and back in opposing positions.

The spine could look rubbery and you could still miss getting the ribs facing in a different direction than the hips.

TWIST

It is, of course, the wonder of the spine that allows for contrapposto in all its variations. The twist is the ribs turning in a different direction from the hips. This plays fast and loose with our facing dimension and can be confusing to draw.

Here's the trick: An S-curve isn't always a twist, but a twist is always an S-curve. On the torso, you find it through the centerline. However, trying to draw the torso off an S-curve can make it look weird.

Make sure the centerline for the ribs stays close to the actual center or crowds one side. The hips, then, face the other way. That gets you the S-curve you want.

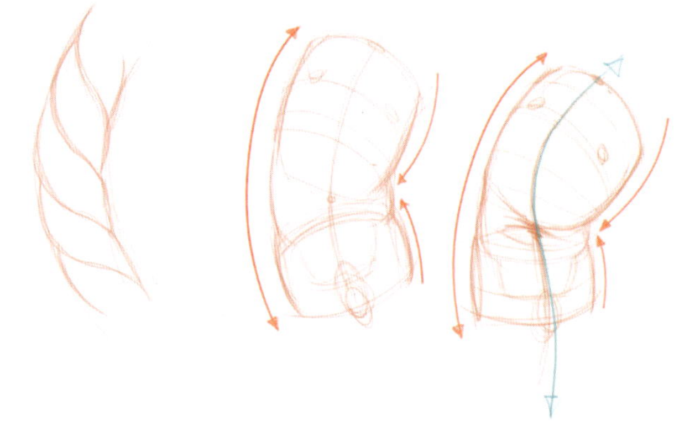

Think about a rope or wringing out a towel—the top goes one way, the bottom another, but the whole structure stays a simple curved tube.

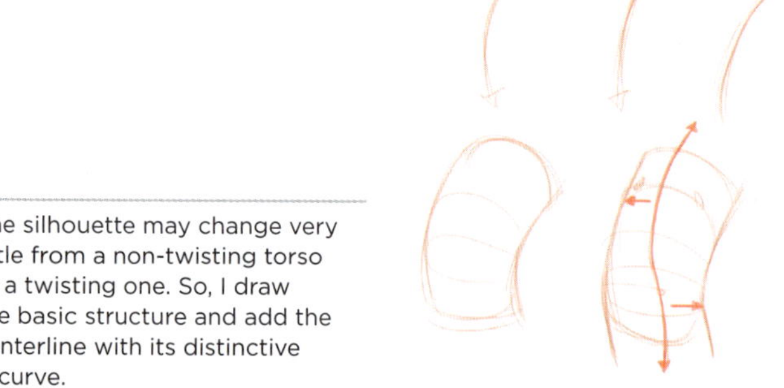

The silhouette may change very little from a non-twisting torso to a twisting one. So, I draw the basic structure and add the centerline with its distinctive S-curve.

We've talked about the torso as a beanbag conception (see Fig. A). Let's add the drumstick to it. The drumstick is a thin shape intruding into a thicker, more bulbous one. You'll see it all over the body: neck into head, thumb into hand, and ribs and waist into hips. It's very simple and very useful.

As shown in Fig. B, making a fuller mass at the base gives, generally, a more feminine look. Play it way down and step it in before it reaches the pubic area, and it becomes masculine.

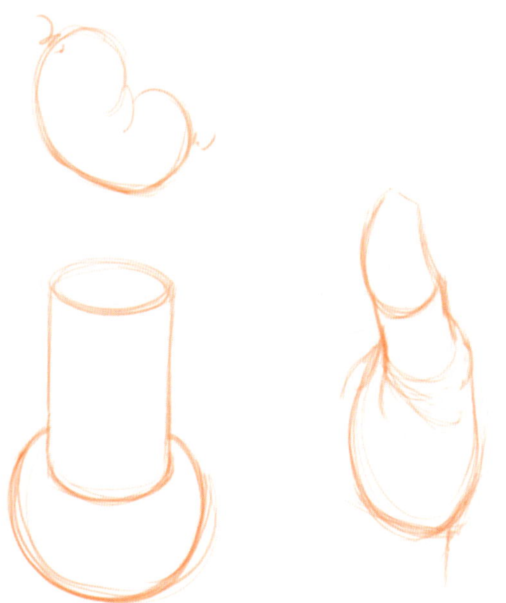

Fig. A. Beanbags and drumsticks. We find these constructs throughout the body, and they can make drawing the torso much easier.

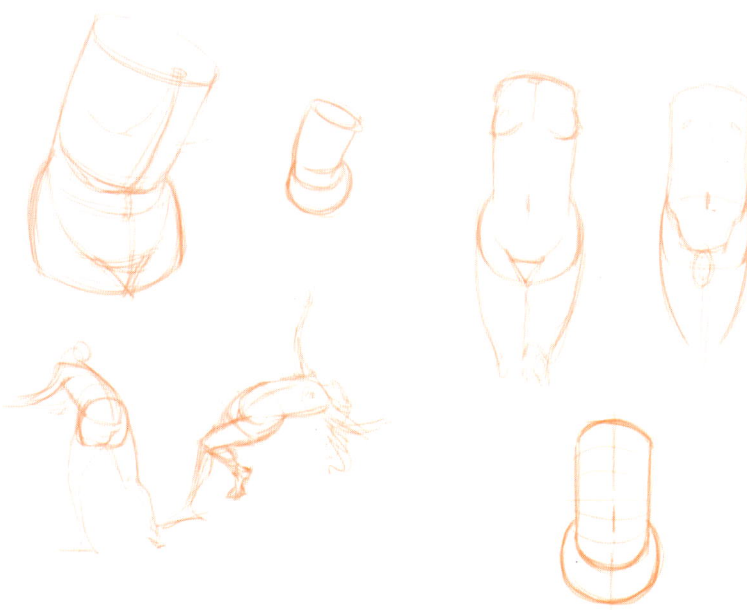

Fig. B. As always, the long axis of the stick part can be curved. Make sure that stomach goes way down into the hips.

INTERLOCKING

The other advantage of the drumstick is it creates an interlocking connection. Consider the three ways structures come together (as shown in the illustration at right):

1. They touch end to end.

2. They overlap.

3. They interlock.

Two structures interlocking is the best kind of connection. It's like a wrench locking onto a nut, or even better, a bolt in the nut. When one form intrudes and locks into another, it's good engineering—and anatomy is excellent engineering.

Bone meets bone at the joint. But muscle originates on one bone and intrudes into the muscle mass covering the other. It makes for a good fit and even better leverage. This happens all over the body. Find the interlocks. Use them whenever you can.

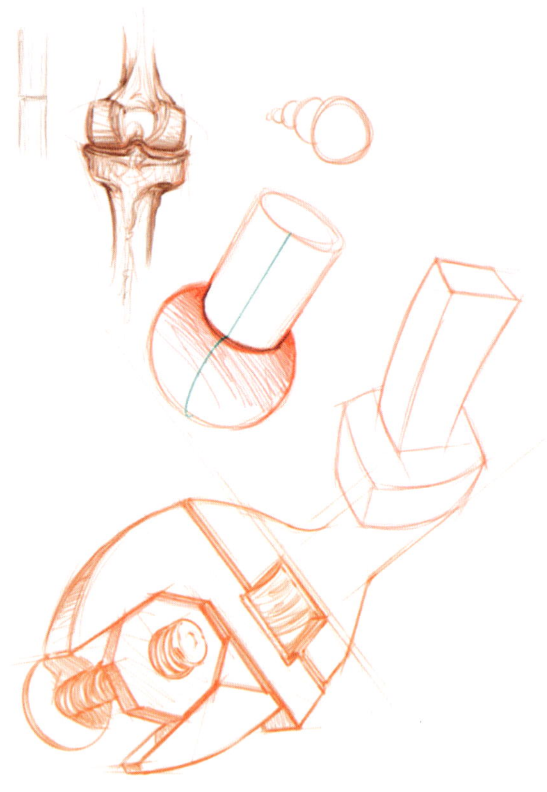

The drumstick shows up even more often in the secondary forms and locks those forms together.

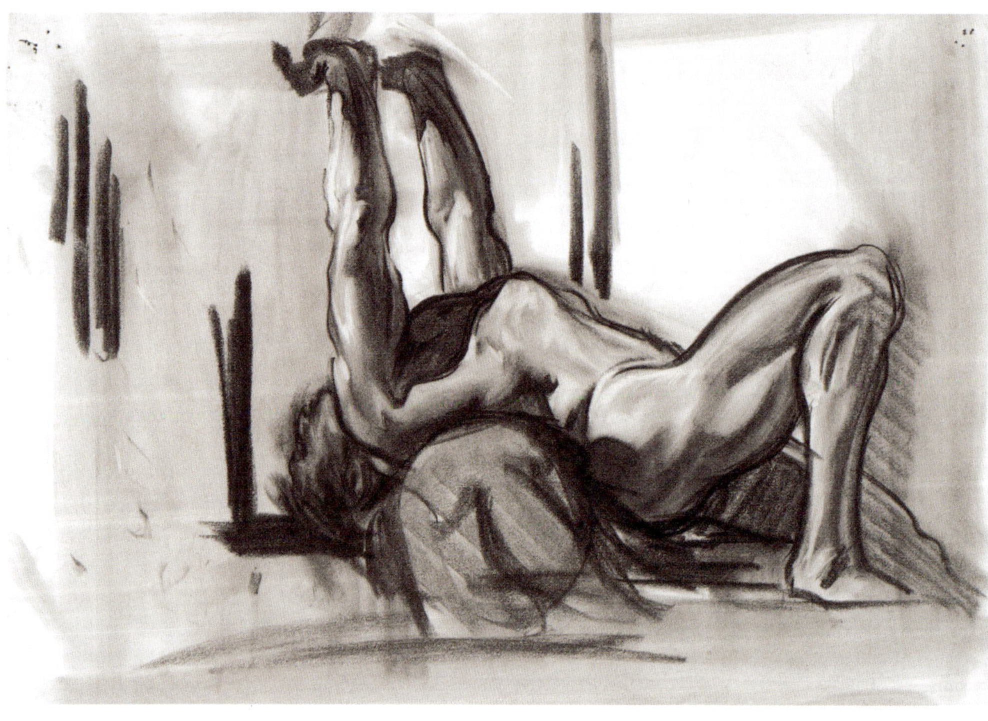

Find the interlocking connections in this drawing.

THE V-SHAPED MUSCLE

In fitness circles, it's called the "lats." It looks like the hood of a cobra. Starting at the armpits, it cuts across and contours over the ribs, descending into the cable muscles of the lower back. This is one of the most visible interlocks on the body. Careful, though—when drawn large they look very male.

The greatest thickness of the lats is from the mid-back up until the muscle reaches the armpits. Once it descends from the rib cage, it thins quickly and disappears into the base of the spine. It can be highly visible most of the way down or hinted at only by a very slight widening into the armpits.

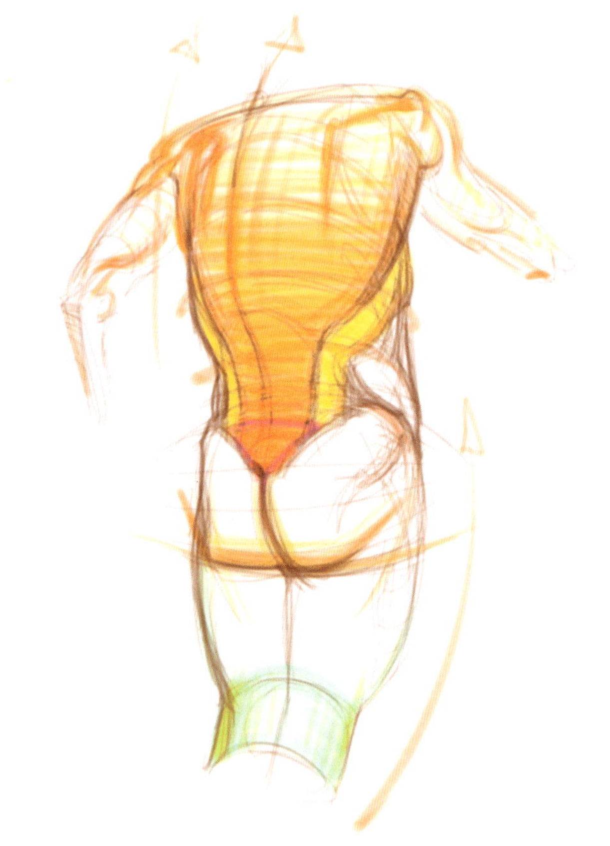

The latissimus dorsi muscle creates a V.

The lats cover more real estate than any other muscle—by far.

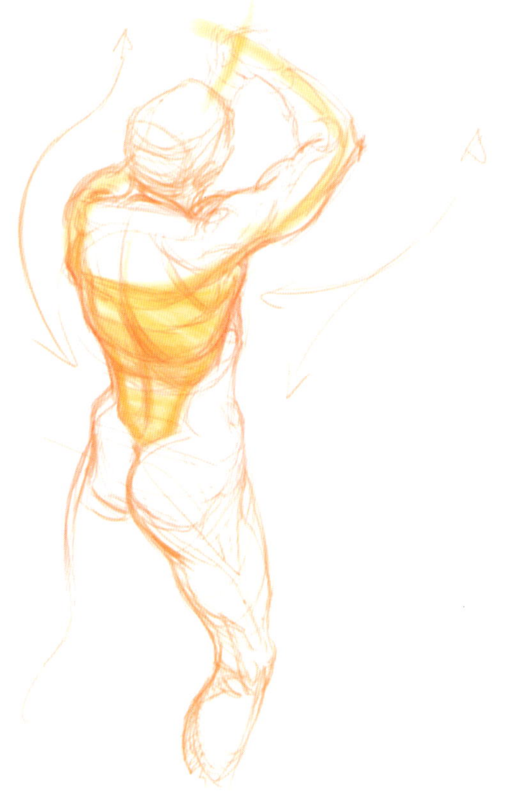

Making the lats visible is a terrific way to tie the arm gestures into the torso. However, you can see how it could quickly lean into comic book heroics.

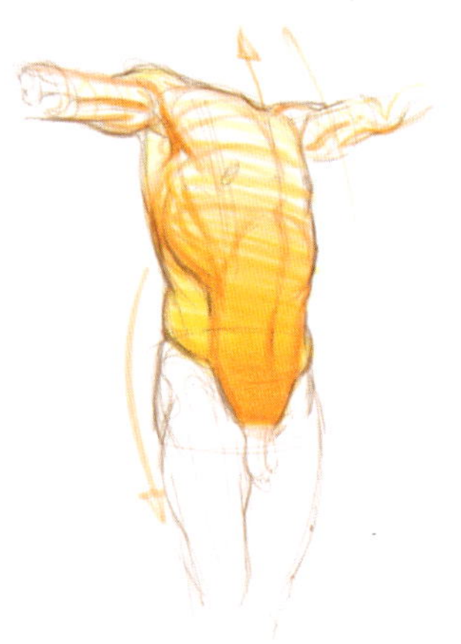

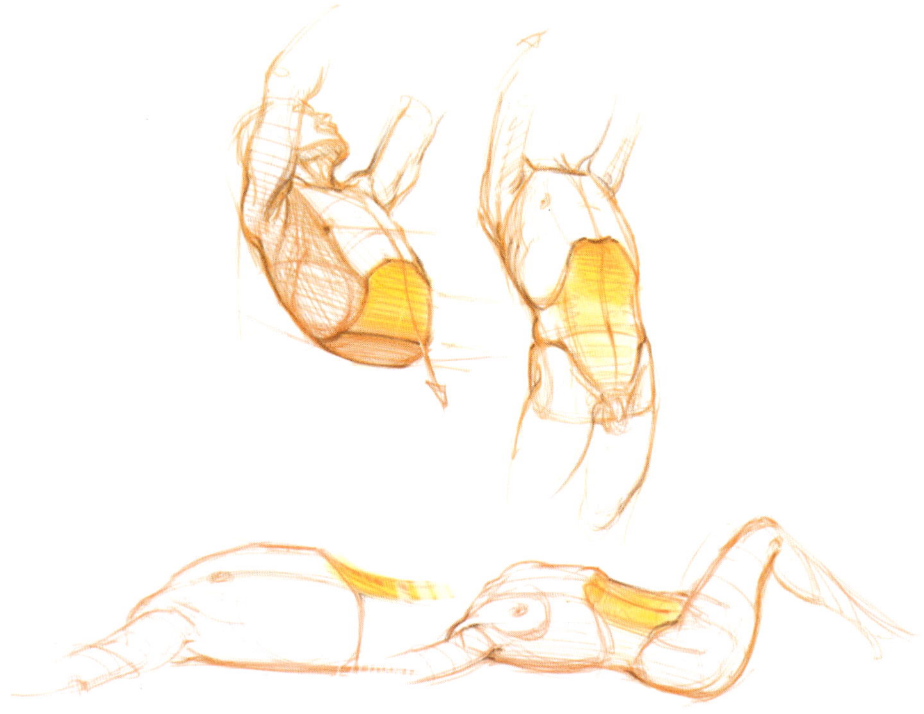

I actually sketched the interlocking-stomach-into-hips idea back in chapter 6, but never explained it. Here, it is realized more fully, and I've added a secondary interlock taking the ribs into the abdomen. Can you feel its absolute connectedness?

When your arms lift above your head or when you lie down, your rib cage wants to expand and the simple tube or egg shape changes like so.

THE FRONT OF THE RIB

You can see how, in many of the rib constructions, the nipples track the corner where the front plane meets two corner planes. However, in the reclining female sketch above, the breast has slipped to the side and misses the mark.

The point in choosing a structure is to find a solution that tracks the gestural path. As long as it is generally characteristic of the human form, it will ring true. Remember, you aren't drawing a rib cage. You're drawing your *idea* of a rib cage. It might feel intimidating at first, but it's actually liberating. If you let that be the motivation for the marks you make, it will set you free.

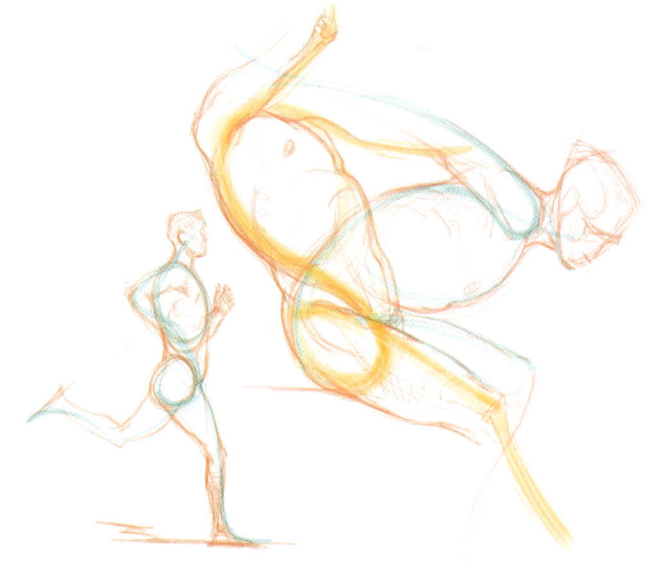

To review, gesture can give us these wonderful rollercoaster rides that viewers feel, but only subconsciously. Keep in mind these are several gestures strung together.

The Hips

The hips are the fulcrum of the body. They have the thickest muscles and the heaviest bones. The hips are the base for the articulating torso and the locomotive legs.

The hips are the only structure on the body that is wider than it is long. Squareness seems appropriate for its foundational strength. On the other hand, roundness suggests its pivotal qualities. The biggest difference in the male and female silhouette is seen often in the hips. A male's hips move smoothly into the legs while the female's resembles more of a diamond shape.

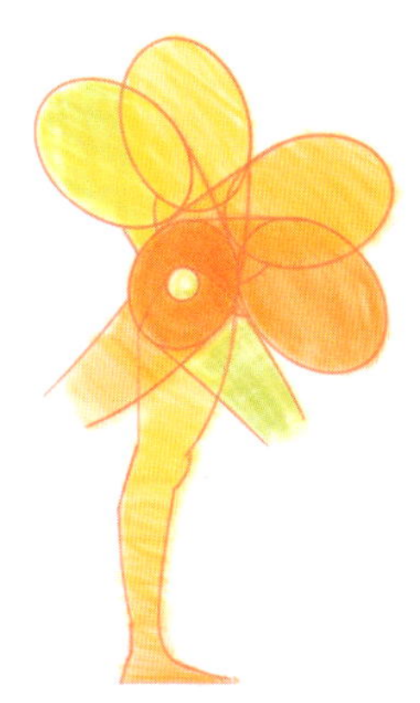

The hips are a pivot point for the upper and lower body.

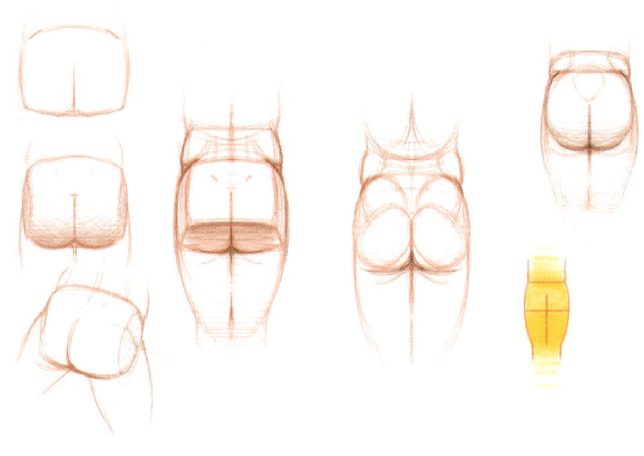

Several male hip structures

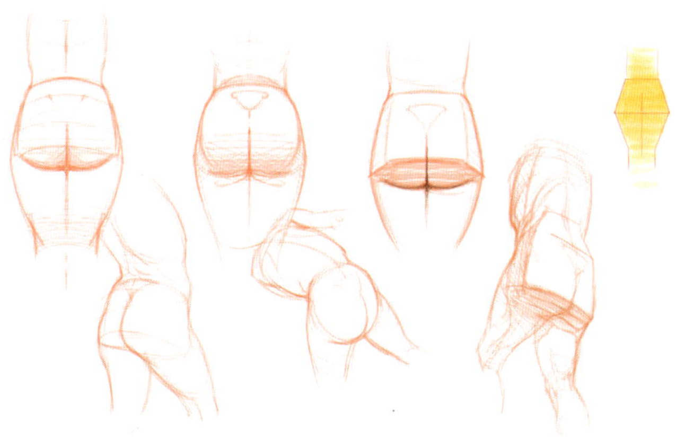

Several female hip structures

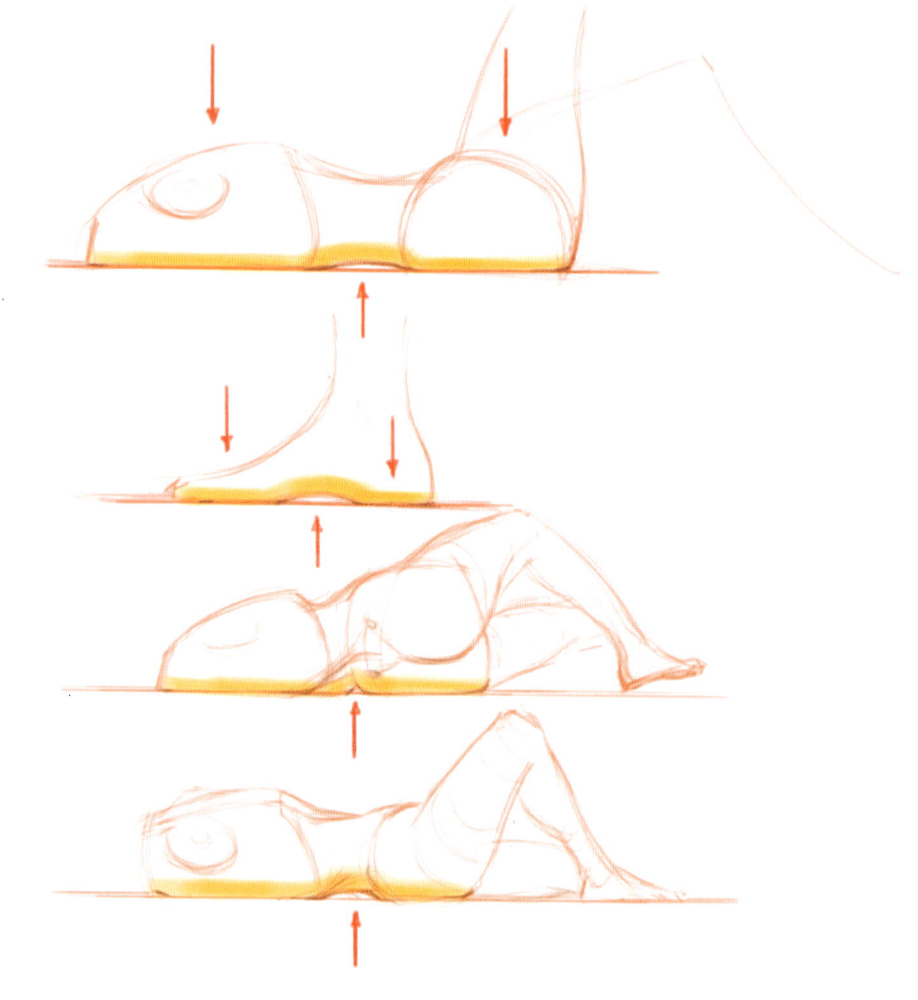

The hips in reclining positions

RECLINING

To help visualize this, think of a foot. The heel presses against the ground. The ball of the foot and the toes press against the ground. And the arch lifts off between.

That is, essentially, what happens with the hips, rib cage, and waist. In the figure above, notice where contact is made with the ground I cut off the tube or egg shape to show the weight compressing. This is very important. You can add some roundness in the rendering stage. You can also add a little contrapposto twist!

Pulling It Together

The torso has two major structures, three if you separate the waist. There are many variations (more than I've shown here), and, yet, they're all simple structures with symmetry around the centerline. As we've learned, secondary structures can be added, shadows can be added (we'll bring that back in chapter 11)—you can pack all sorts of extra details into your sketches. Stay simple, though. Get the basics down. It's like practicing scales on the piano. The rest follows naturally.

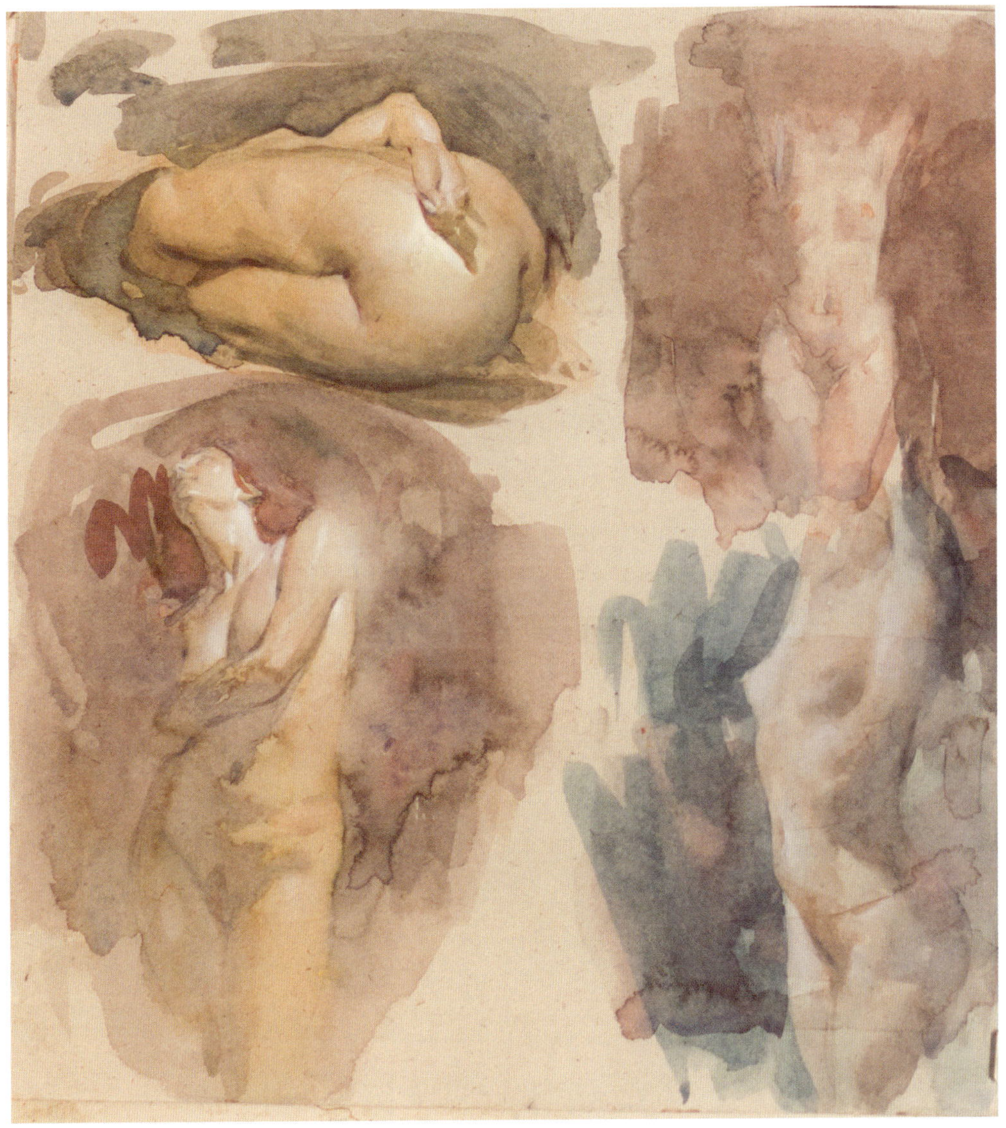

Various torso drawings in gouache and pen and ink on scrapbook paper

OLD MASTER *study*

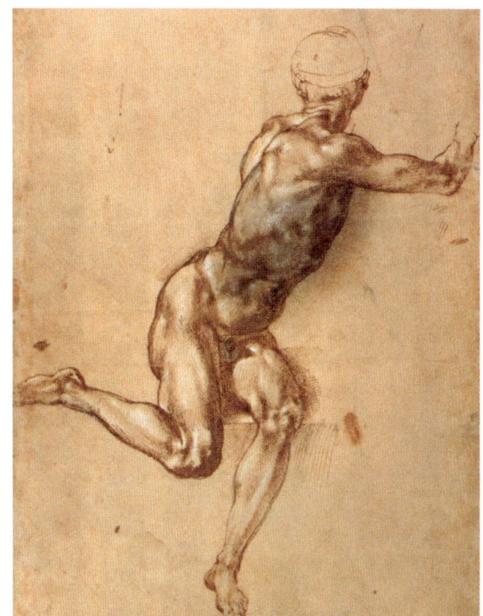

A Seated Male Nude Twisting Around, c. 1505, Michelangelo Buonarroti (1475–1564). Pen and ink with wash on paper. British Museum, London/ Bridgeman Images.

Notice how Michelangelo took the idea of contrapposto to the limit and maybe beyond. Michelangelo added extra length in the waist (as he liked to sometimes do) to give credence and emphasis to that mighty rotation.

Notice also how the legs are drawn a little small. Is that a problem? You decide. Should he have punched up the proportions or do the shorter legs keep the focus on that dynamic torso? It is quite all right to question the greats. That's how your vision becomes yours and not someone else's!

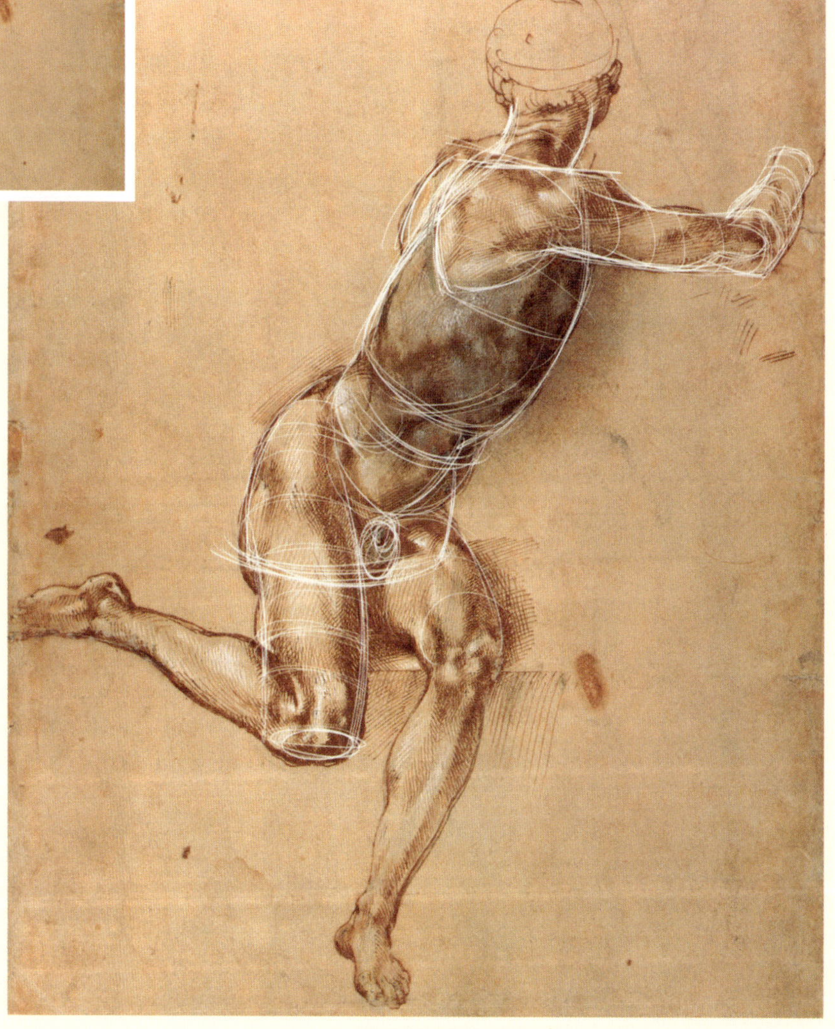

Look at the almost impossible contrapposo presented in Michelangelo's warrior figure as he turns toward the action. These ideas we're working with aren't just craft concepts. They can used to make emotionally powerful statements as Michelangelo has done here.

Every day for a week do a basic breakdown of one of my sketchbook drawings or gouache studies. You want to learn to see past the crosshatches, the shadow shapes, the color gradation, and all the rest and find our two foundational ideas that hold it together: gesture and structure.

GIVE IT A TRY: *Exercise 2*

Do a quick breakdown of one body part. Think how far you could get in a year by just committing five minutes a day.

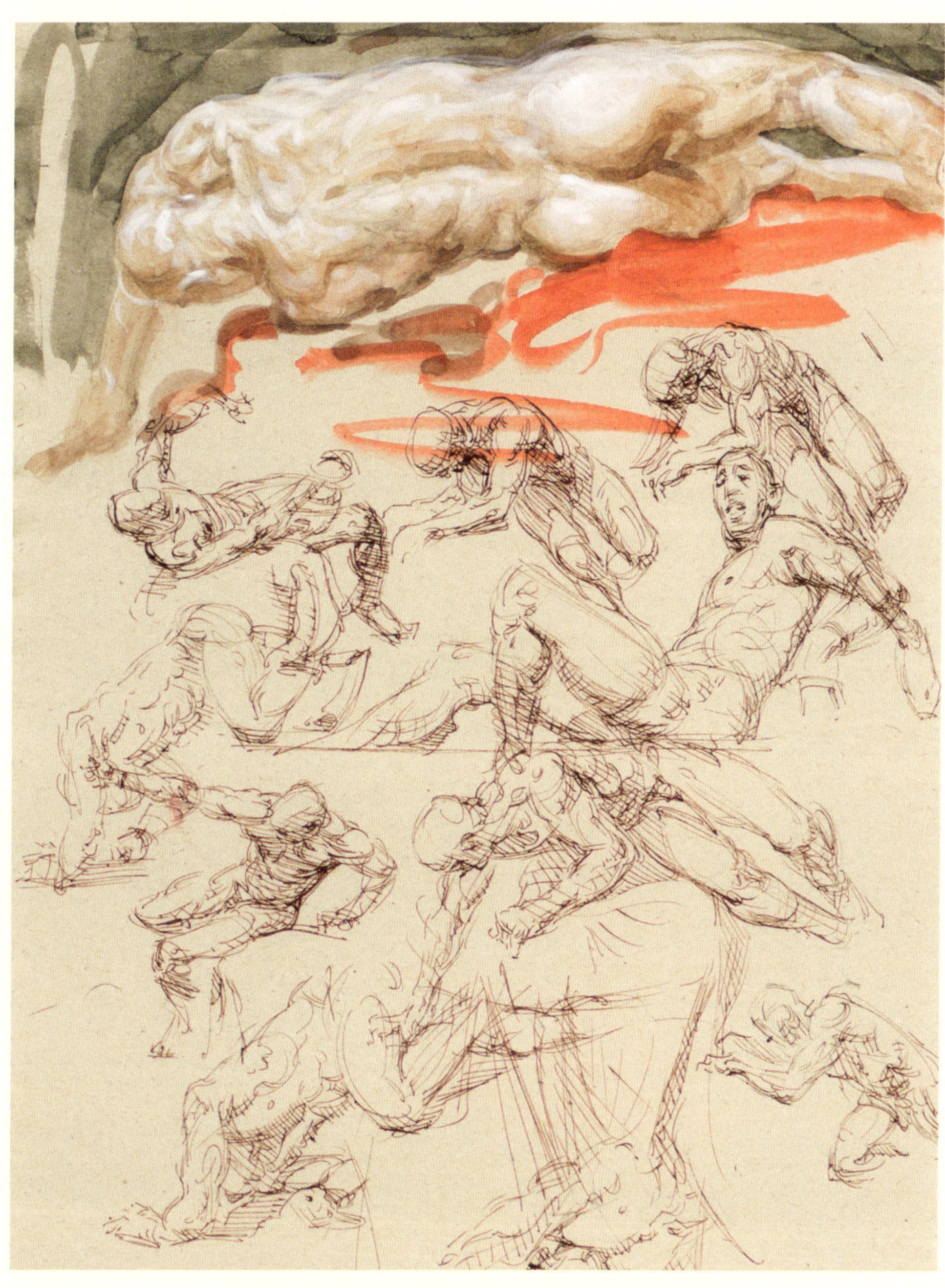

Mastering your craft is all about mileage, and there's no better way to gain mileage than by keeping a sketchbook. None of the work has to be perfect. Instead, just search for answers and have fun.

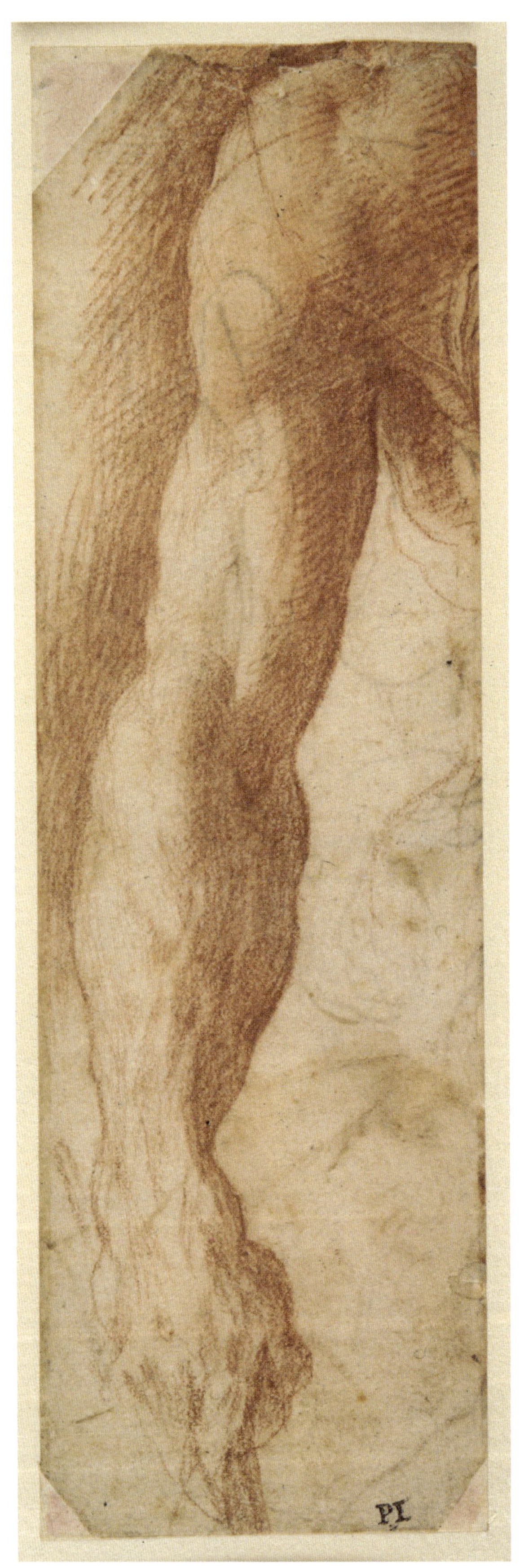

Study of a Man's Right Arm, His Hand Holding a Stick, c. sixteenth century, Francesco Parmigianino (1503–1540). Chalk on paper. Chatsworth House, Derbyshire, UK/Bridgeman Images.

9 | THE ARMS AND HANDS

To achieve the fullest range of motion, the arms have the most complicated engineering of the body. For the hapless artist, that means just knowing the structure of the arms won't cut it. We need to know a bit of anatomy for them to feel mobile and not just stuck on. Understanding the interlocking connections is crucial.

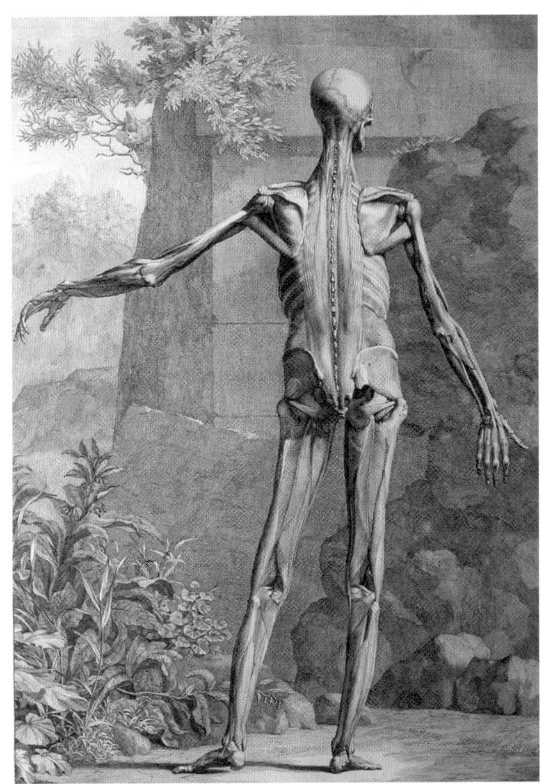

Musculature, illustration from Tabulae sceleti et musculorum corporis humani, 1740, by Bernhard Siegfried Albinus (1697–1770). Engraving. Humboldt University of Berlin/Bridgeman Images.

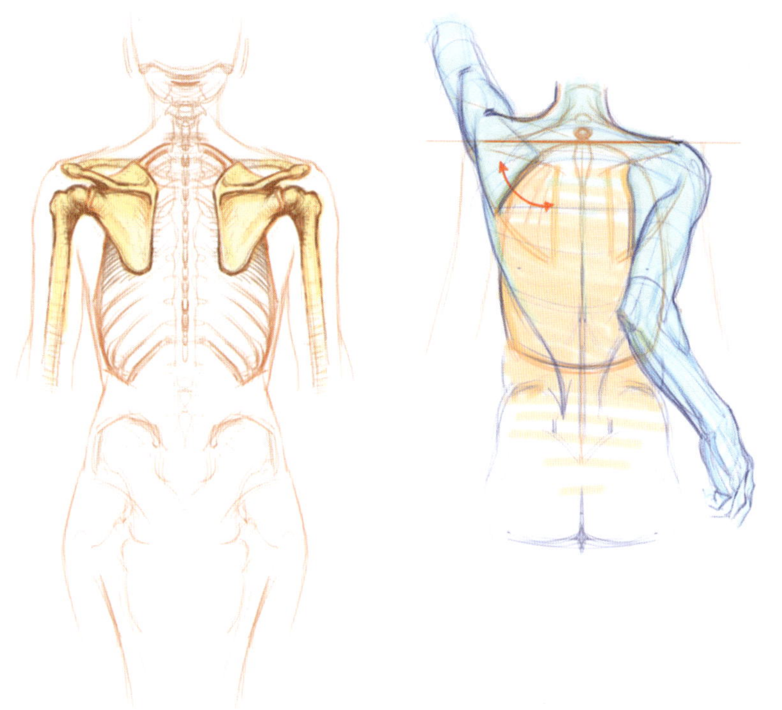

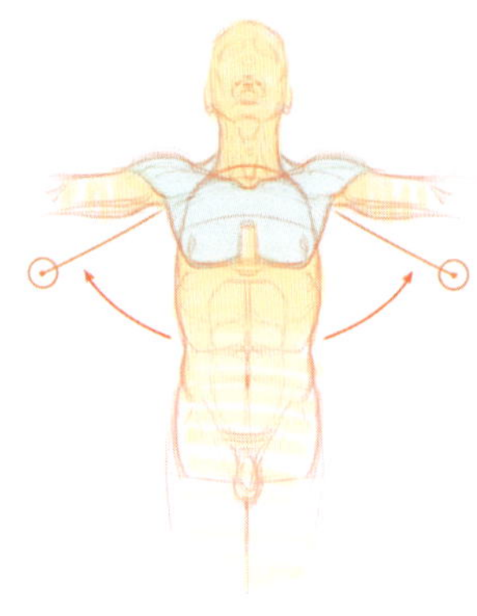

It doesn't matter how the shoulders move—the neck and rib cage don't necessarily move with them.

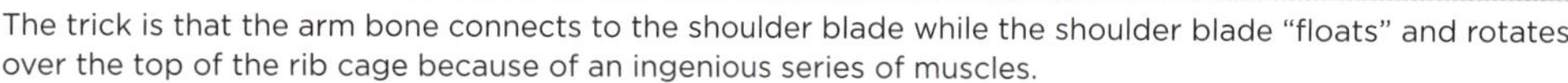

The trick is that the arm bone connects to the shoulder blade while the shoulder blade "floats" and rotates over the top of the rib cage because of an ingenious series of muscles.

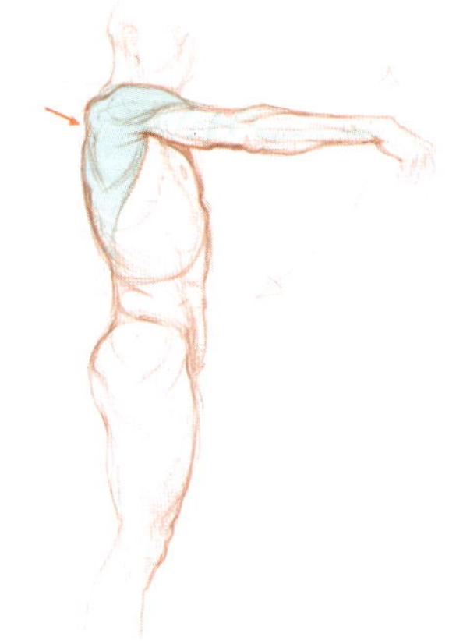

The red arrow indicates the shoulder blade has not rotated in this action.

The Shoulder Girdle

The chest and collarbones, the shoulders, and the shrugging muscles and shoulder blades together make up the shoulder girdle. Think of it as shoulder pads on a football player. The shoulder girdle is what creates the delicate balance between strapping the arms firmly to the rib cage and keeping them agile enough to scratch your nose or swing to the next tree.

The basic mechanism is this: When an arm has to exert force by positioning itself away from its relaxed positions against the torso, the shoulder blade muscles rotate over the ribs as the shoulder muscle raises the arm to the correct angle to do its work. It varies from person to person, but the rotation is part of lateral motions and begins as the arms lift toward a horizontal. The chest muscles move the arm in a hugging action. The lats move the arm in a yawning action.

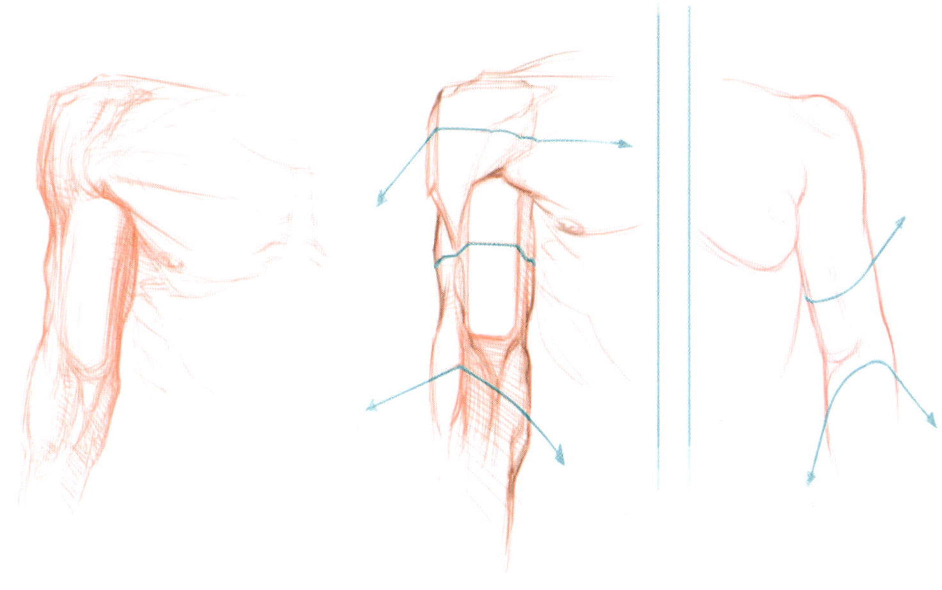

From this front view you can see how the triceps are wider than the bicep. Again, this difference is most apparent with a muscular arm. The bicep splits into the lower arm in much the same way the shoulder splits the upper arm, though it is usually less dramatic.

The Upper Arm

The upper arm can be treated as a simple tube with parallel sides. We learned this in chapter 6. Here we will take it further.

The shoulder muscle is called the deltoid because of its delta (Ð) shape below. It intrudes well into the arm and, on an athletic build, the axis of it to the upper arm criss-crosses, pushing out laterally as the upper arm moves forward and back. This concept is visualized best by turning the arm into a two-by-four (5 x 10 cm) board.

The forearm intrudes from below in much the same way the shoulder does from above. Notice how both shoulder and forearm split the biceps and triceps away. The more muscular the arm, the shorter the deltoid becomes. The bulky bicep and triceps rise up the shoulder like a rising tide on the beach.

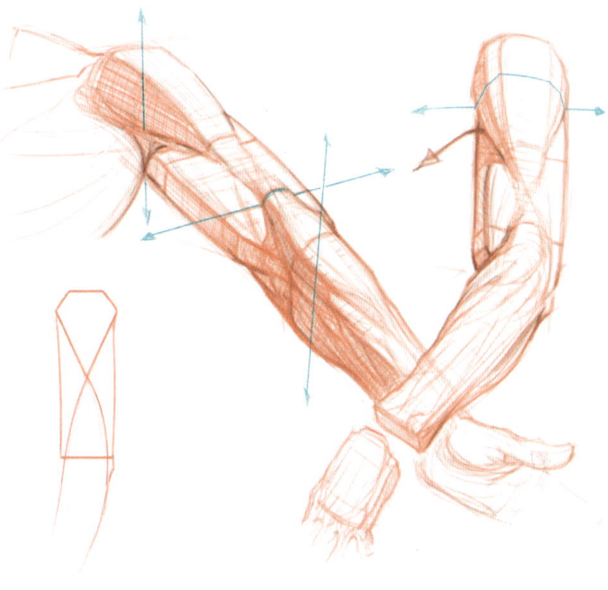

The rich variety of choices for the upper arm comes from the deltoid muscle above and supinator/extensor group below.

The Elbow

The elbow is structurally the corner between the upper and lower arm. Whatever bone comes to the surface is relatively rounded. During the Renaissance, and for a long time after, the elbow was drawn just that way. The drawing on the left in Fig. A goes that way.

Modern convention, as the other three drawings shows, often ties a couple of the rounded heads together to make a square. It speaks to the idea that hard bone should be squarer (and many times darker in line) and soft muscle rounder (with a touch lighter line). These kinds of visual metaphors are useful for creating an aesthetic "worldview," so to speak.

Whatever you do, if you can see the elbow, distinguish it from the rest of the arm.

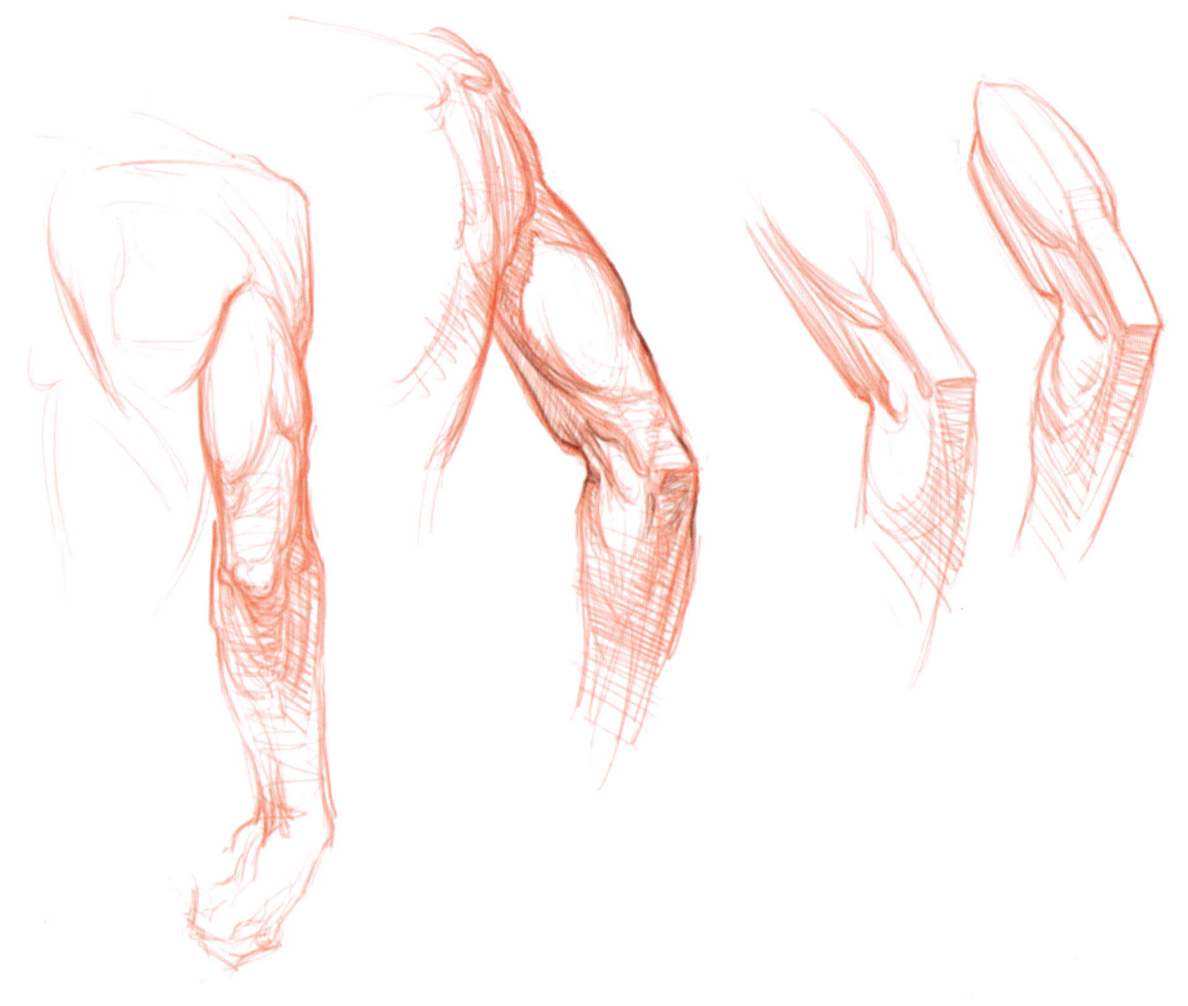

Fig. A. Part of my process includes working on joints whenever I have more time to draw. Finding those secondary structures makes the two primaries connect. Of course, bringing the piece into a well-conceived whole is the hard part.

The Forearm

When the palm of the hand turns forward or up, the forearm gets wide across the front and narrow across the side. When the palm turns back or down, the forearm becomes more egg- or tube-like. The wrist never changes shape and tends to be like the two-by-four (5 x 10 cm) board shape.

Remember that the front of the upper arm is stiff and straight, and so is the forearm for about a third or so of its length. You can see that on the inside contour and the red gesture line just inside it in the arm at left in Fig. B. After that initial continuation of the upper arm's straight design, the forearm takes off, flowing away from the body.

You can see in all conceptions that the upper half of the forearm is more bulbous and the wrist is sleeker—notice the drumstick shape—following the flow of the gesture.

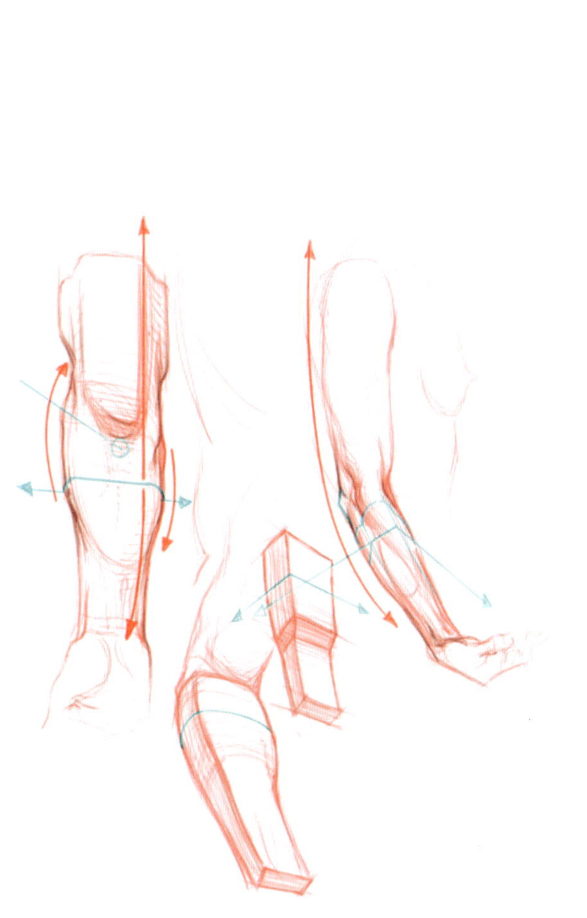

Fig. B. Supinated view of the forearm

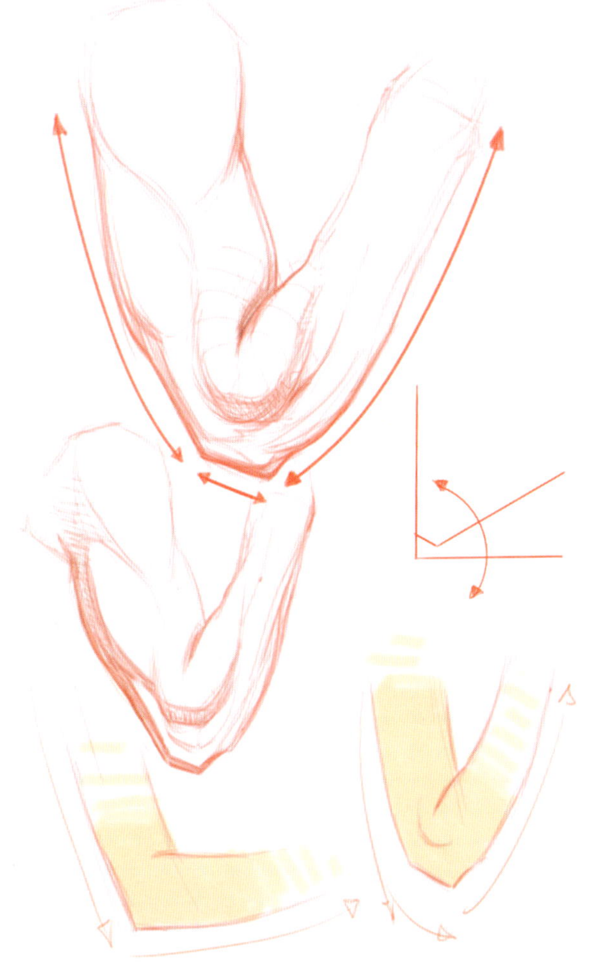

When the arm bends more than 90 degrees, the elbow corner becomes two corners as the two parts of the arm make that tight turn. We'll see something very similar with the knee.

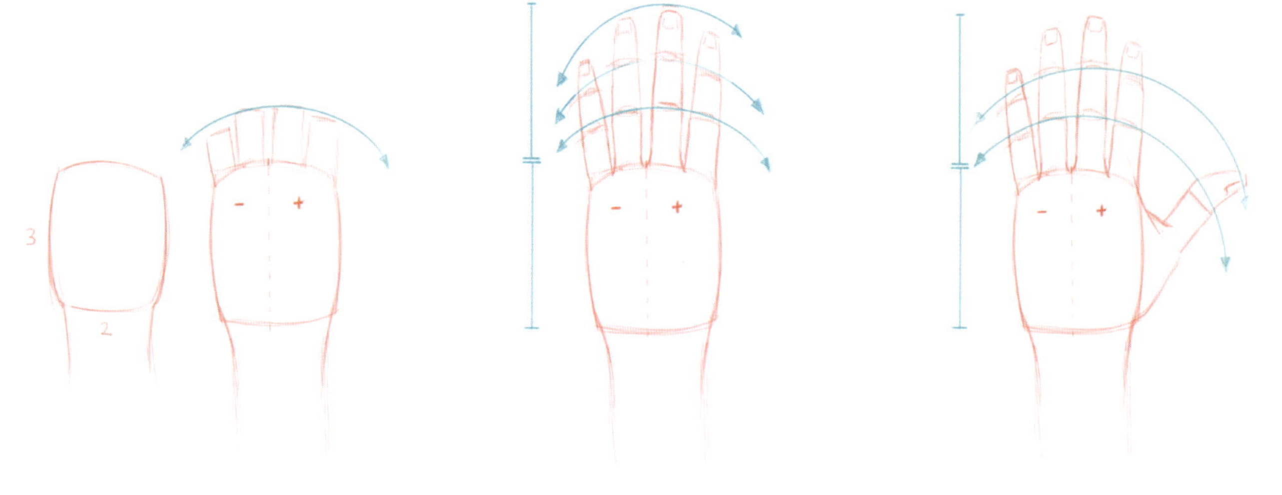

Follow the hand construction joint by joint.

The Hand

The gestural connection of wrist to hand happens by way of the tendons in the wrist. Tendons are great. They're lines that take you well into one part from another. The relationship between the parts—that's gesture. Tendons are tailor made to help with gestures. The places they are most evident are in the hands, wrists, ankles, and feet.

THE LAY-IN OF THE HAND

The back of the hand is generally wider than the wrist and about the same shape and proportion as the rib cage. The knuckle line of the hand and each jointed section flows off a gestural curve. The more widespread the fingers are, the better they align. Watch for this in subsequent drawings. It goes a long way toward organizing the wiggly digits.

Mark the halfway point on the hand (shown by dotted lines in illustrations above), making the thumb side a little fatter than the little finger side. Add the first joint of each finger.

As you build from the knuckles to the end of the finger, each finger joint is about one-quarter shorter than the last. The thumb starts with a triangular webbing instead of the first tube shape the fingers have. Add a tube on that and a hooking tube to finish it.

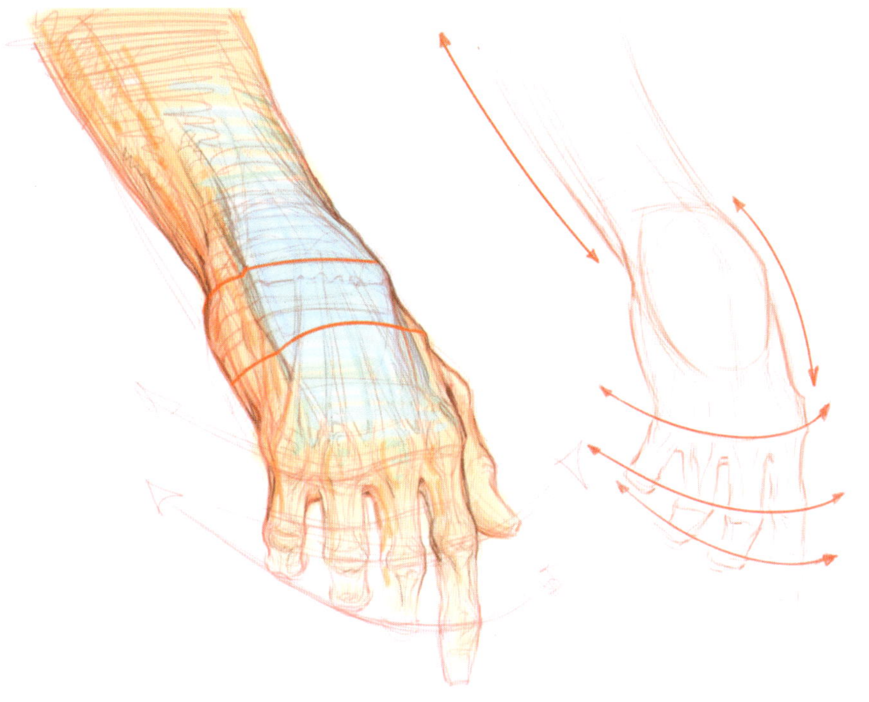

Back of the hand in two colors

The palm side has three soft pads with the finger and thumb sections having their own. These protect the delicate joints and create traction for grip.

The back of the hand has a transitional wedge-like form as shown by the blue tint on the hand above. We'll see a much more pronounced version in the foot. This wedge was an egg in Renaissance works. Christian art being all the rage back then, the egg had the added benefit of connoting the birth and rebirth idea. Art is a language as rich as any other.

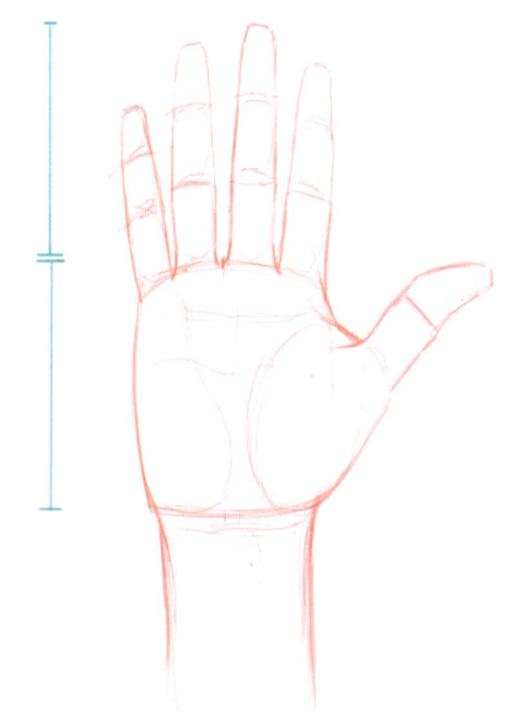

Palm side of the hand

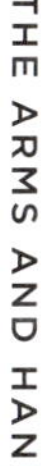

THE FINGERS

The fingers are simple tubes until you get to the tips. These taper into more conical or more wedge-like structures. As always, you can make rounder or squarer choices. And let that padded side sag a touch to show their soft character.

Start with a simple tube to understand the fingertip. Sketch the nail at the top end of the tube. The key is not to have the neatly trimmed nail intrude into the front of the tube. If it does, it will look like the poor drawing off to the right in Fig. A.

The bottom drawing in the same figure, the one with the red arrow, takes it a bit farther. Here, I've distorted the end of the nail into the contour of the end of the tube. Look at the end of your own trimmed nails and you'll see, at some point, the nail does curve that way. I've just made it happen a little sooner. As I've said before, err on the side of the more dynamic; push things as much as you can toward your idea. You'll seldom be disappointed.

What about the gesture of the fingers themselves? After all, they're short, straight tubes. A bent finger makes a chiseled gesture (see Fig. B). Better, we get this wonderful wave action when we add the knuckles—their rise and fall reinforced by the sagging pads. Make the knuckles squared or more dome-like. It's very much like the wedge shape that takes us from the wrist to the back of the hand.

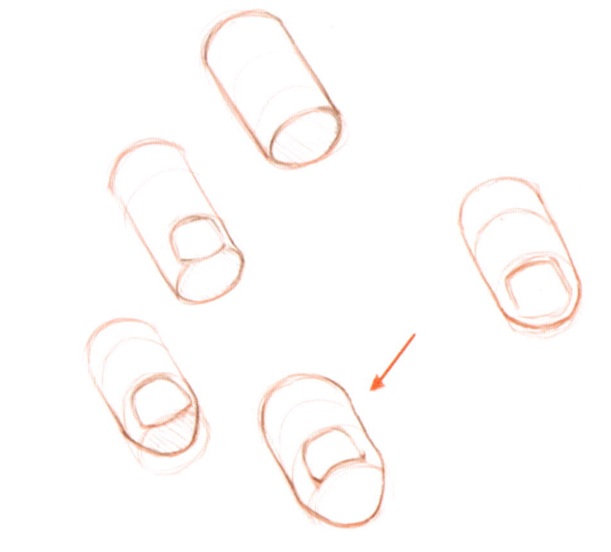

Fig. A. Structure in the fingernails

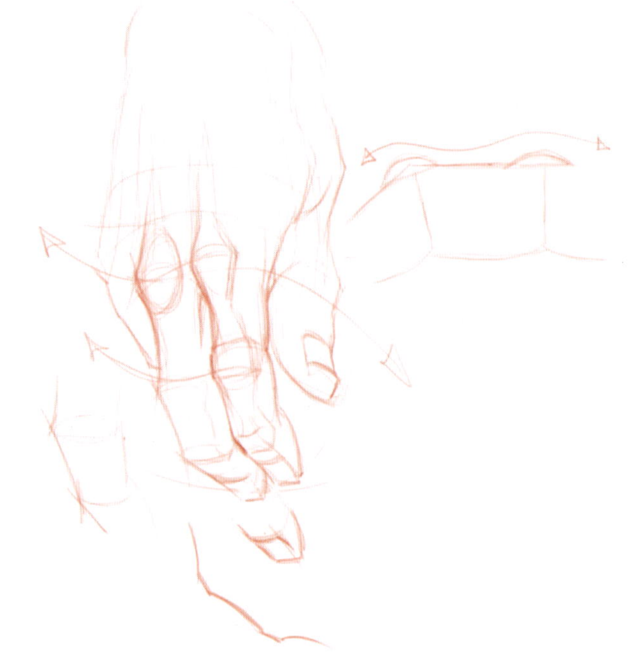

Fig. B. Gesture in the knuckles

THE THUMB

Puppy dog head, spoon, and kidney bean are the three shapes the thumb can take on, depending on the angle. The more choices you have throughout the body, the more successful the lay-in and the less work any refinement will be.

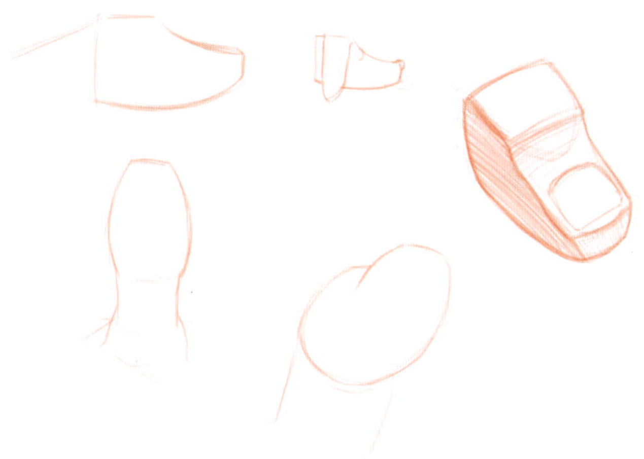

Thumb shapes

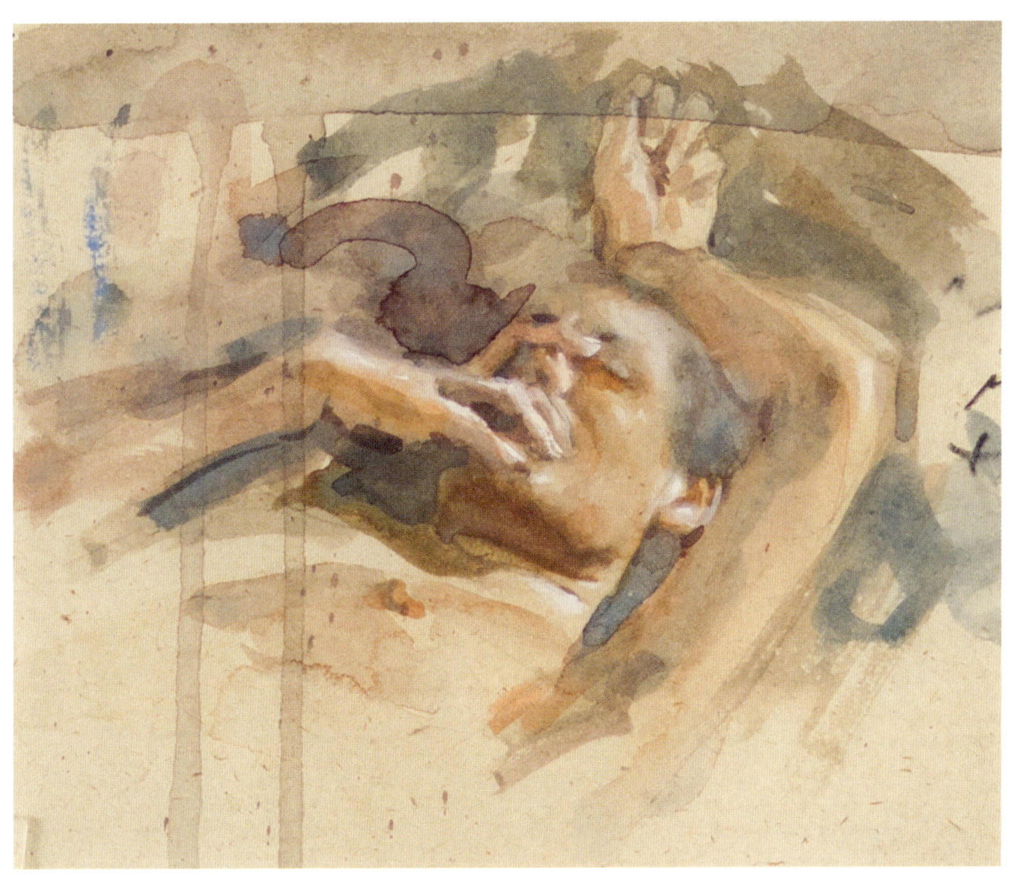

Hands across the face in gouache on scrapbook paper.

OLD MASTER *study*

As round, soft, and feminine as Lely's drawings are, he uses a surprising amount of boxes. Notice in particular how the highlights pick out those boxy corners while moving fluidly down the long axis curves. For the masterful artisan, that's his job! The bent wrist he's treated in two ways. In the top drawing, he's gone for the Renaissance eggs; for the lower left, it's the box.

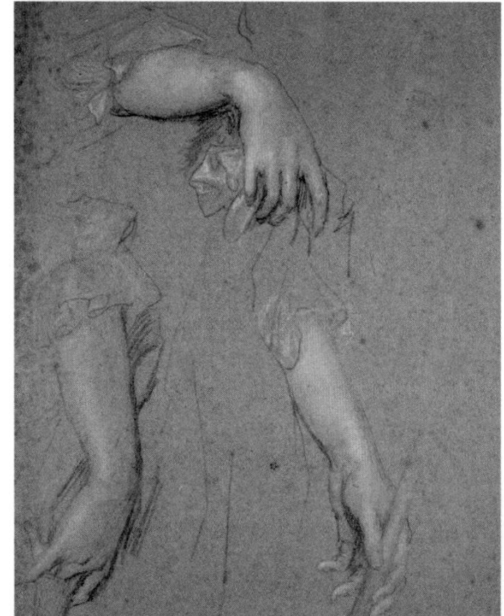

Studies of Hands, seventeenth century, by Sir Peter Lely (1618–1680). Chalk on paper. University of Oxford, UK/ Bridgeman Images.

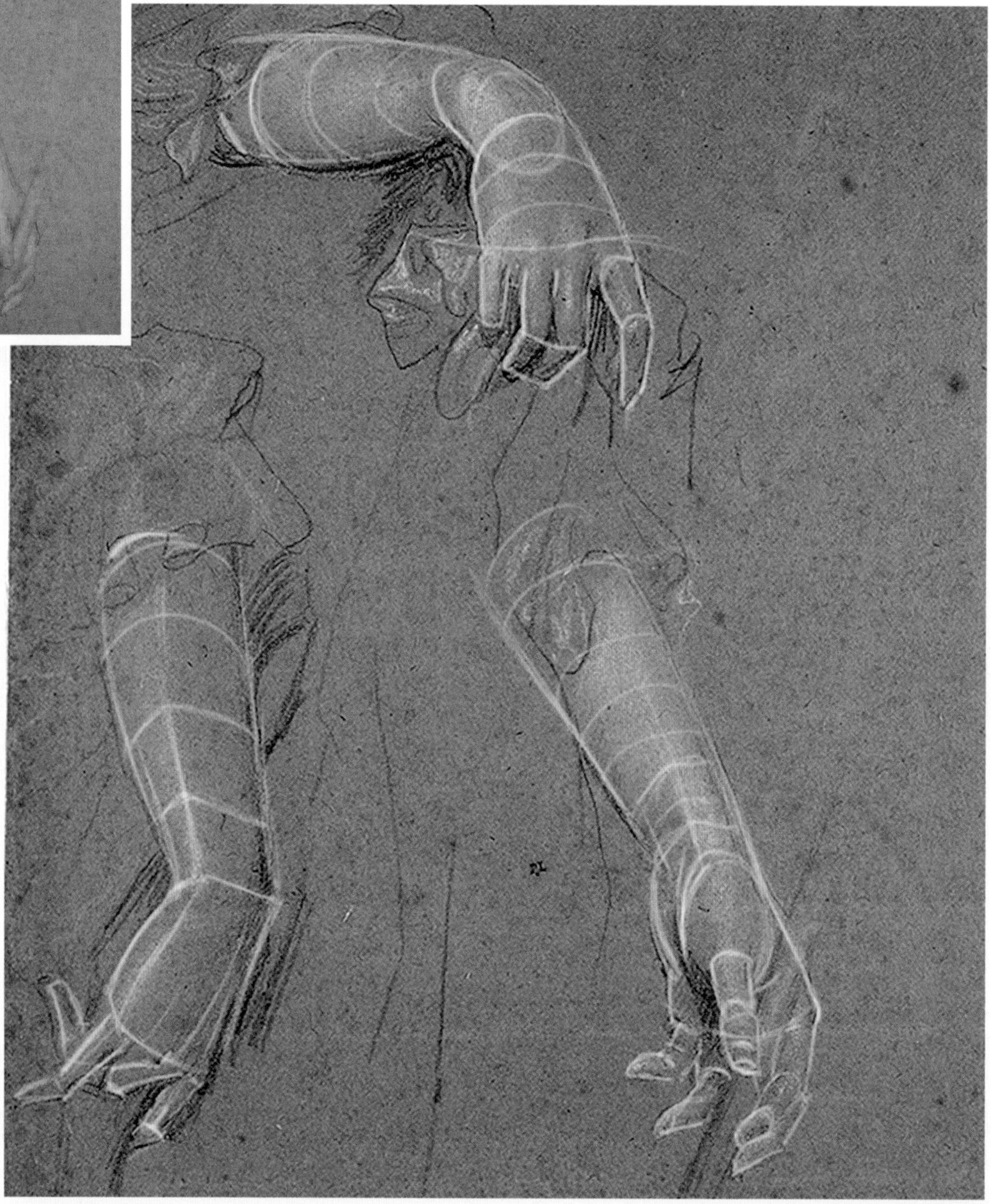

Remember, no matter how complicated a structure is, just work it out one jointed part at a time.

GIVE IT A TRY: *Exercise 1*

Break down some of the hand and arm studies, such as
in the example on this page. Pay special attention to the
joints. Look to the interlocks and work on the swelling
knuckles.

GIVE IT A TRY: *Exercise 2*

Once a week, draw your own hand, looking at it
directly or in a mirror. Don't always just draw the whole
complex. Sometimes draw the finger and thumb.
See how many conceptions you can discover as you
turn them this way and that—building that catalog of
shapes, always building!

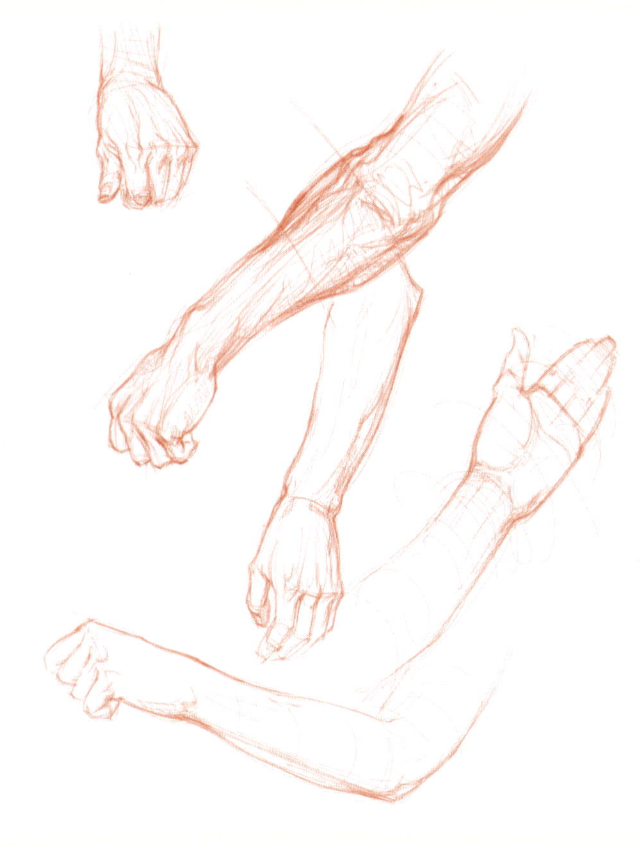

Studies of hands

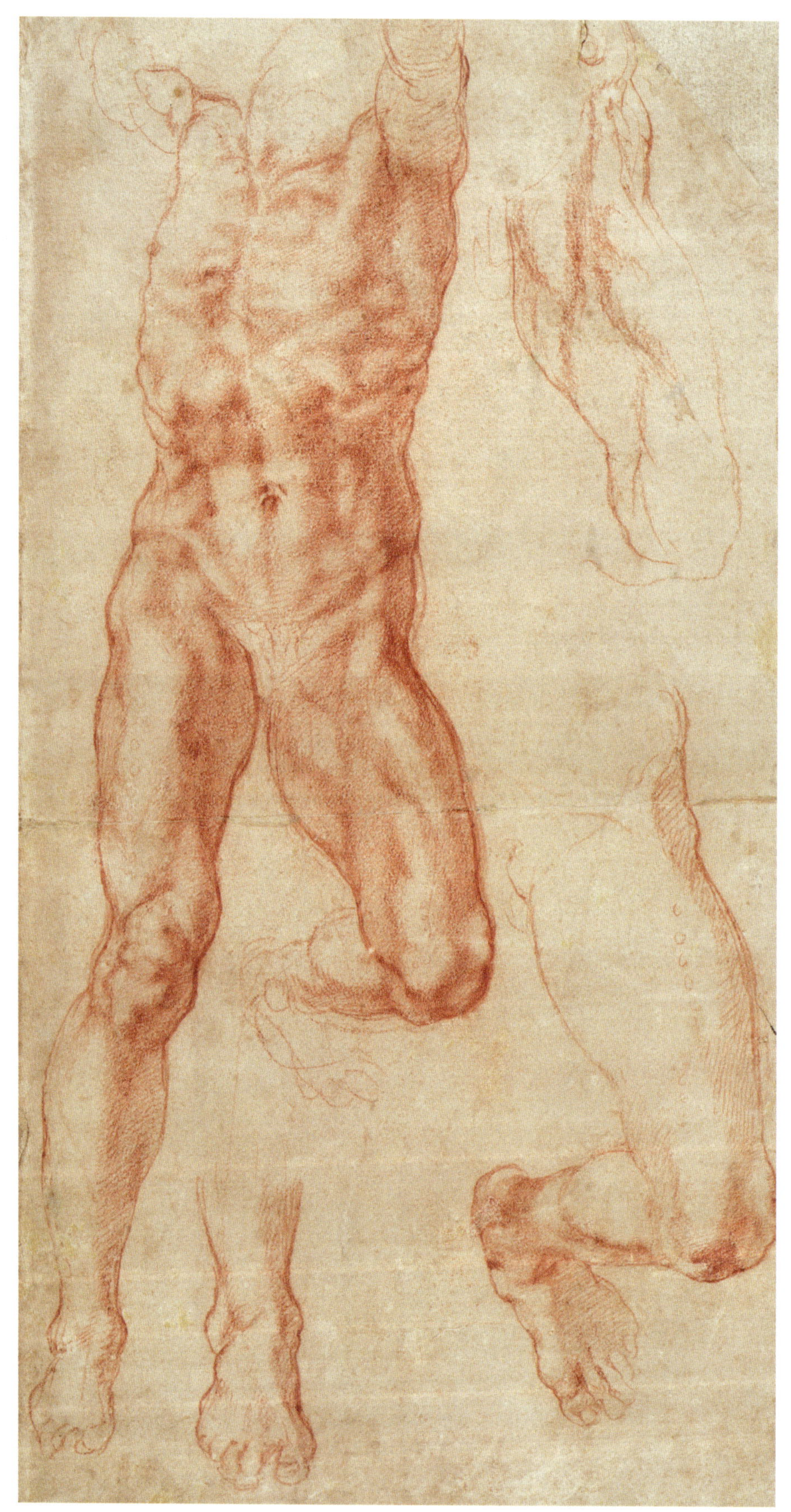

Study of a Male Nude, Stretching Upwards, c. sixteenth century, Michelangelo Buonarroti (1475–1564). Chalk on paper. British Museum, London/Bridgeman Images.

10 | THE LEGS AND FEET

Imagine if the standing stones of Stonehenge, after holding still for so long, simply decided to walk off. That just begins to describe the marvel of our hip and leg design. Further, imagine those stones rooted into small flying buttresses that not only distribute the weight, but also soften the impact of that active/inactive dynamic. That describes the feet. The legs and feet are beautiful, powerful, and can be a challenge to capture on the page. Let's see how we can refine those strategies we've already discussed as we explore the lower extremities.

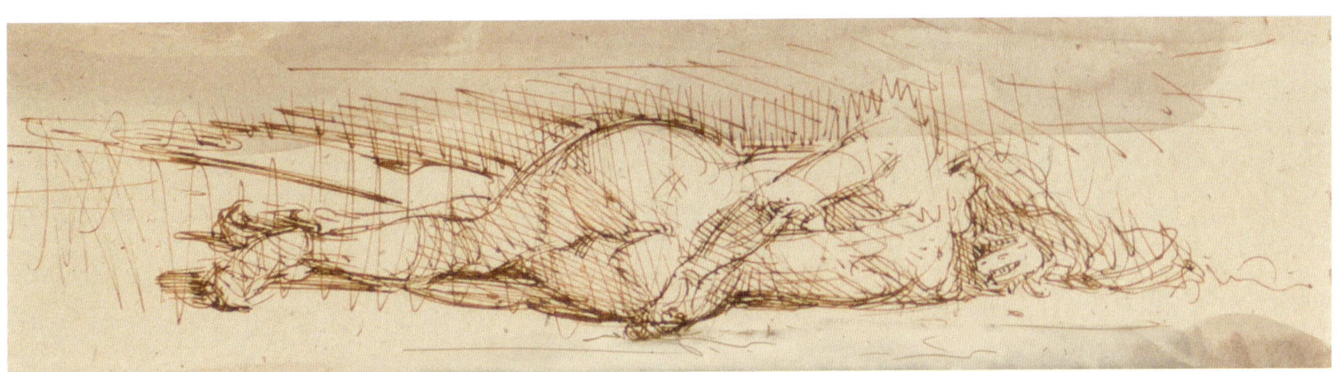

You've got to make the legs and the hips a team when you draw them. Together, they accomplish amazing things.

Post and Lintel

How to support great weight and still imbue it with the power of quick and decisive motion? Enter the post and lintel system. Think Stonehenge without the cracks. Notice how the pelvis in the left figure below accepts the leg bones from the sides instead of the bottom. The single column of head and torso still sits comfortably on the twin pillars of the legs.

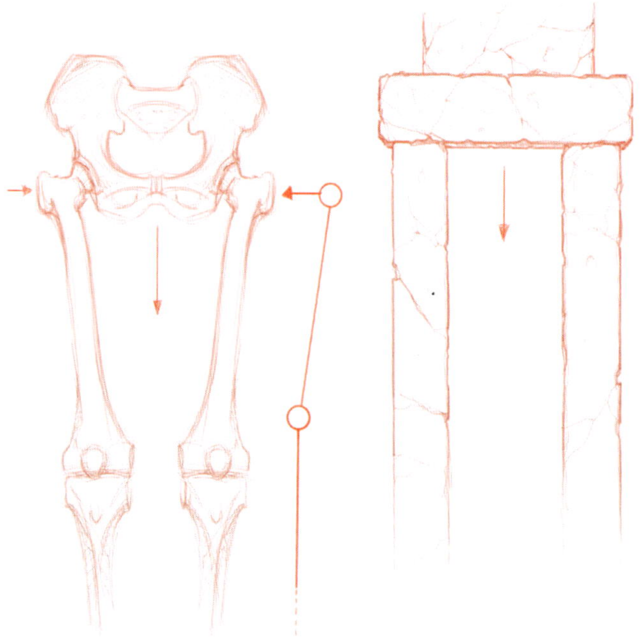

The body needs a relatively wide base to be able to hold its position indefinitely. That's where this modified post and lintel system comes in.

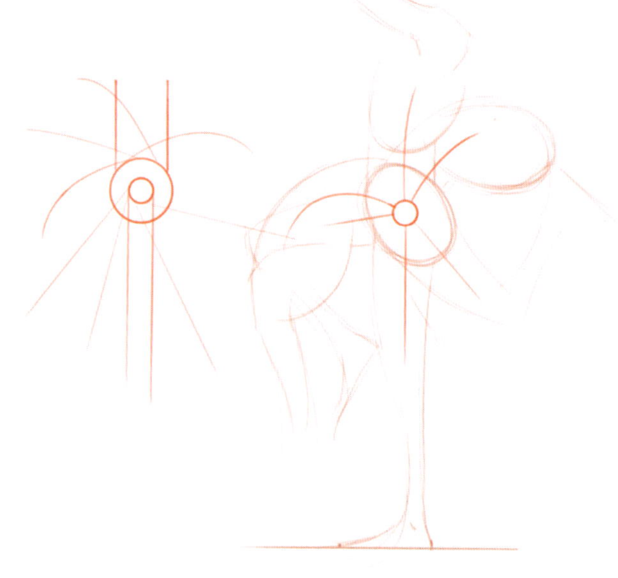

Profile schematic. By forgoing bottom joinery for side, the legs are able to articulate off the hip fulcrum and move the upper body as needed.

Gesture and Structure

There are only subtle variations of form on the inside of the legs so they can come together without disruption. The outside goes a little crazy to allow for the big sweeping gestures of the lower leg. This is true right down through the feet.

The tube structure that holds the knee in Fig. A and makes for an easier transition from thigh to shin (see pages 109–111) also leads us into important secondary gestures—one up into the hip and the other down to the inside anklebone. Follow the turquoise lines in Fig. B.

The leg must show both the strength to support its body's weight and a fluid grace to be able to move it. Observe this important balancing act in your favorite artists' works.

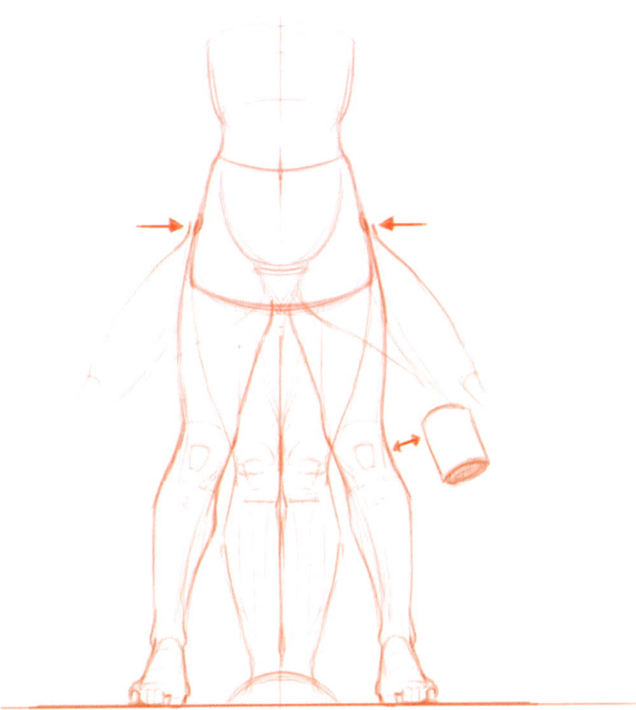

Fig. A. Front view articulation

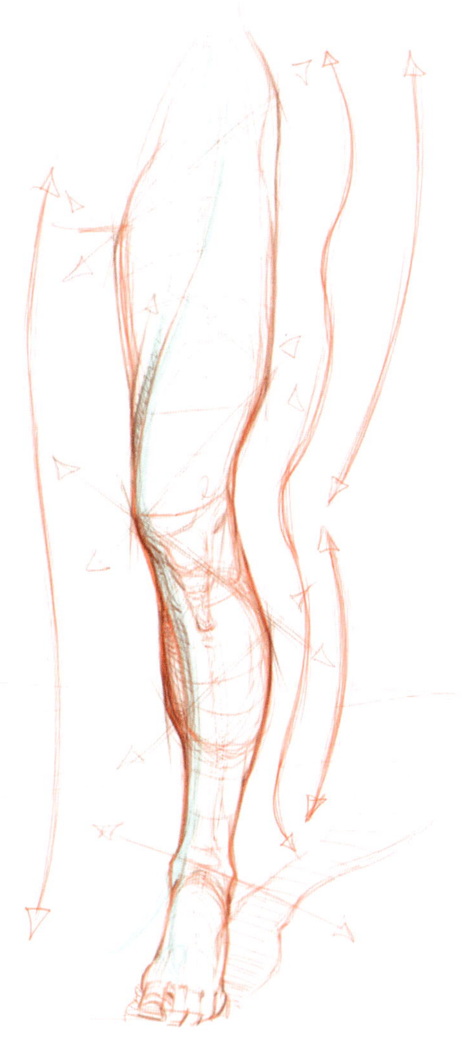

Fig. B. Construction of the leg with gesture lines

THE CORNERS IN THE CURVES

Because the curved gestures are organic curves, they are imperfect. Some of those imperfect curves speed up, turn more quickly, and give us apexes. That equals corners. What I'm saying is there are corners in the curves that will keep any contour line from looking like rubber. It will make them feel organic, sophisticated—and real. The turquoise arrows in Fig. 1 show the major corners in the curves.

Wherever you see a bulging contour, look for the corners, and see whether you can make an egg shape out of it against the opposing contour. I've marked them in Fig. 1 with turquoise eggs.

The corners-in-the-curves idea is something to look for throughout the body and, for that matter, throughout nature. We talk about rounding off constructed corners all the time. In fact, that's the key task of gradation. Now, we can square up the curves if we like.

Notice how the different ideas of structure and gesture have something in common. That's a good thing. There are corners in the curves and curves in the corners. As artists with unique voices, we shall play wonderful games bringing our two ideas closer together or pushing them farther apart.

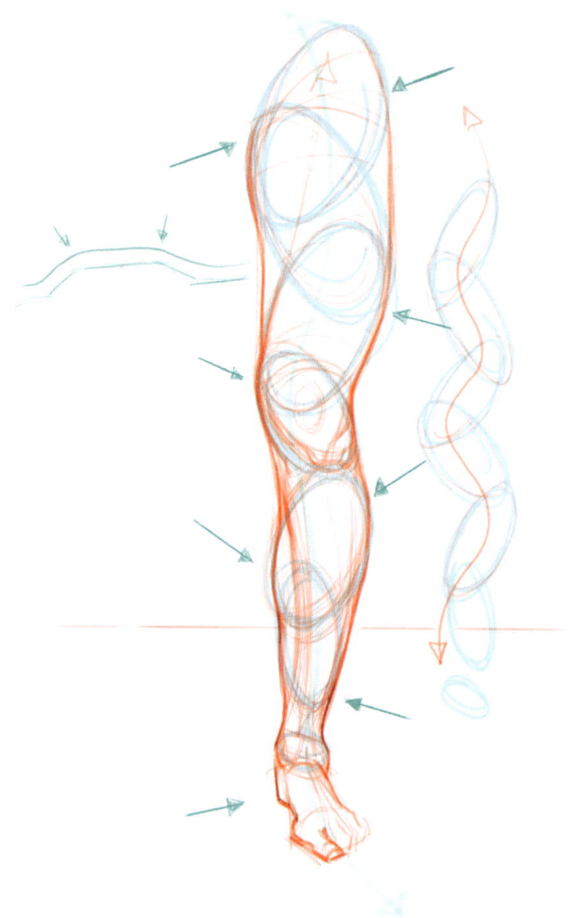

Fig. 1. Nature's little imperfections give us a chance to play with wonderful secondary gestures.

The Knee

The knee nestles into the greater forms in straight-legged positions (see Fig. 2). The relaxed forms in a leg with the joint locked ripple over the knee like waves washing over a pebble in the sand.

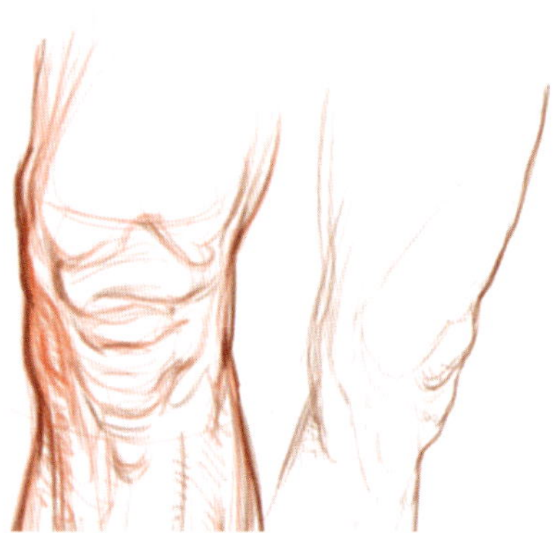

Fig. 2. A locked knee joint

When those relaxed forms just begin to flex, the knee becomes a corner. But also, it shows off its tendinous connections into those upper and lower forms. Notice every line you make flows up or down, tying the lesser structures around the knee into the greater leg structures.

The knee becomes the full-fledged corner we know and love when the leg bends decisively, as in Fig. 4. And like the elbow, a boxy construction can be a good way to go.

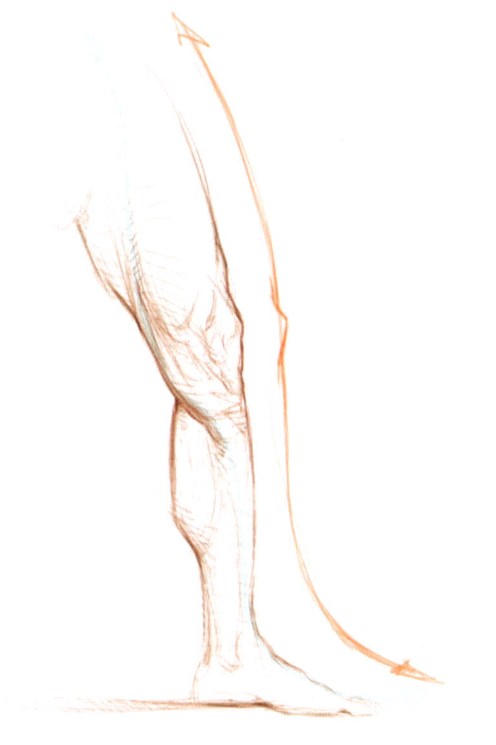

Fig. 3. A slightly flexed knee

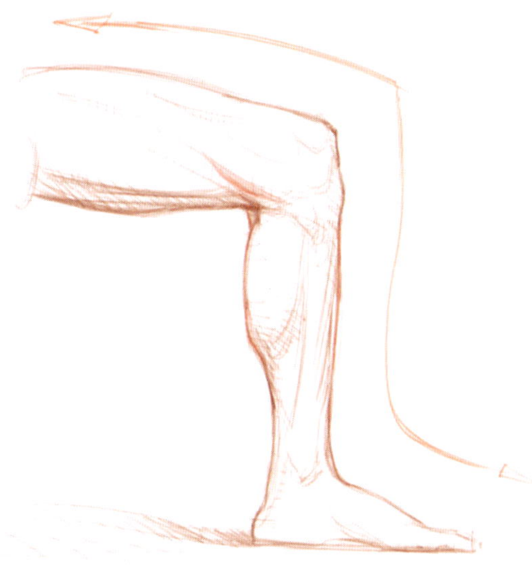

The kneecap and its surrounding structures can separate from the bigger thigh structure. Draw the full tube or box structure for the thigh and then cap that full thickness with the knee. Don't let the thigh deflate down to a tiny knee ending, as shown in Fig. 5.

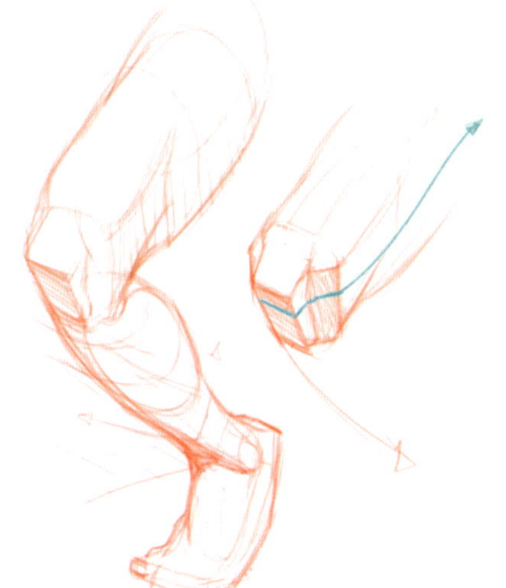

Fig. 4. Bent legs

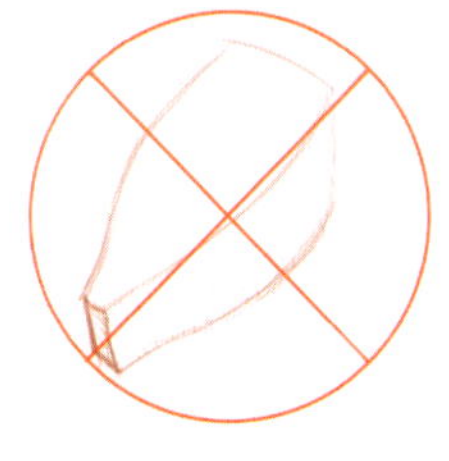

Fig. 5. Incorrect structure

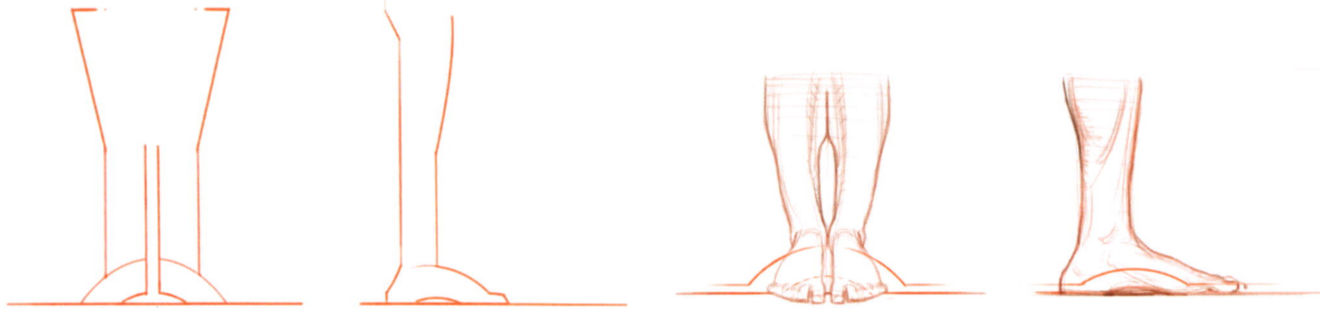

Schematics and sketches of front and profile views

The Foot

The foot is a snowshoe for the ankle, a wide platform of support—with a twist. It needs stability and mobility like the rest of the body. So that the entire broad base can flex, it has an arch. The arch is also a shock absorber for the impact the foot takes when all that weight comes down on it in a leap, sprint, or walk. (See the images above.)

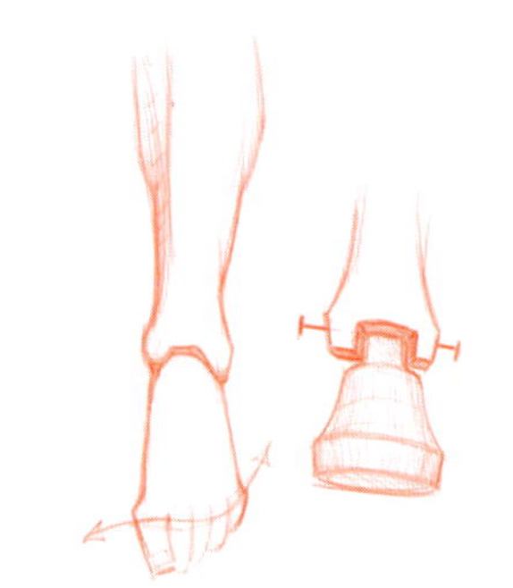

Fig. A. Ankle connection

The arch works front to back. But it also works side to side, expanding or contracting as the feet spread wide or close together.

The ankle locks around the foot like a yoke around a bell—and "rings" the same way (see Fig. A).

Think of the bill of a cartoon duck. That's what the wedge of the foot looks like from the front (see Fig. B). To refine it, the wedge is high to the big toe side and angles lower to the little toe side (shown with the red line arrows). Both the big toe and little toe knuckles flare widely to suggest that platform idea.

Drawing the back of the foot is similar to drawing the back of the head. There are a series of subtle overlaps that are critical, even more so for the foot because a back view thrusts the toes deep into the picture plane.

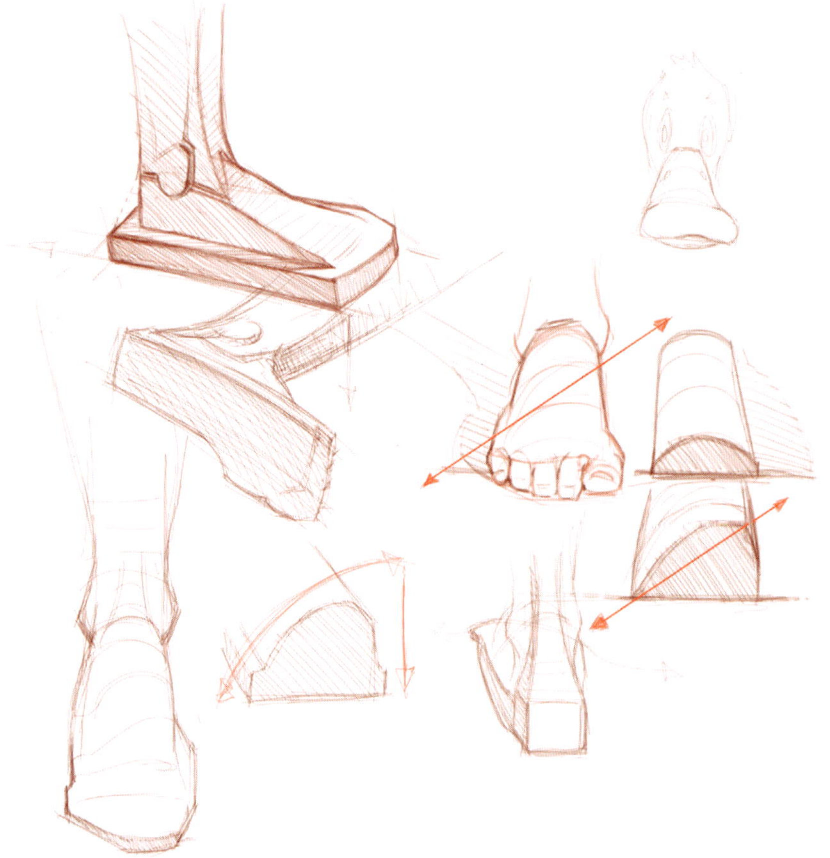

Fig. B. The platform and wedge of the foot

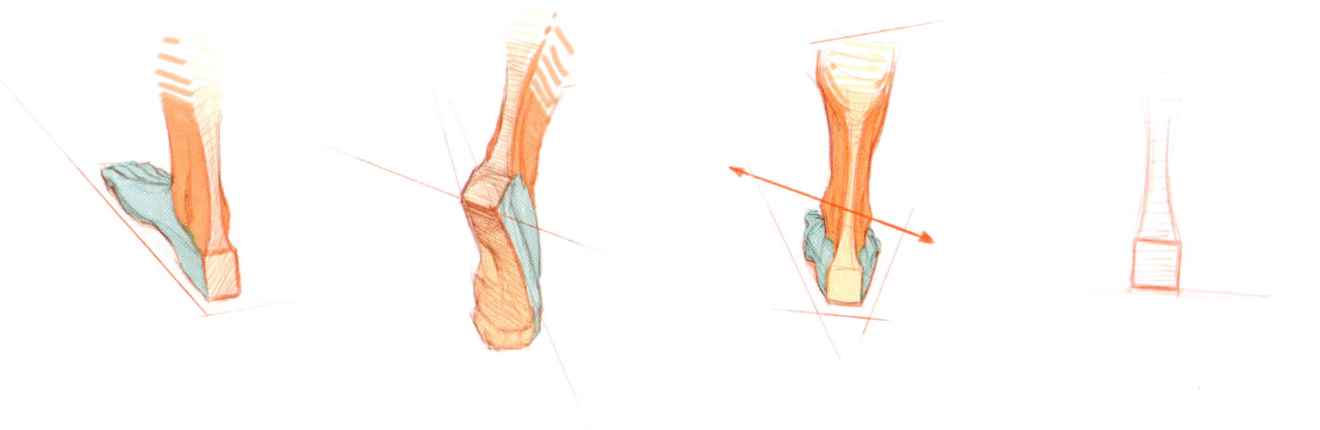

Back views of the foot

The heel and Achilles tendon make a fireplace and chimney structure (marked in pale yellow in the figure above). Behind that is the ankle and anklebone section (marked in orange). Make sure the anklebones orient high/low to each other, as shown by the red line with arrows. The turquoise section is the body of the foot.

THE TOES

Unlike the fingers, the toes have only a narrow ability to articulate, so they stay grouped closely together and we have only three basic structures. When any of those structures presses the ground as they usually do, really flatten your line to show the compression.

We construct the toes very much like the fingers. They have a pad on the underside for gripping and protection. Imagine the whole weight of your body slapping those poor little digits hard on the ground and you see why the pads are even more robust than the fingers. This makes the toe ends very rounded in shape; with the nail inserted, they look like cartoon faces with parkas on! They have a certain asymmetry as the toes converge on the centerline of the foot.

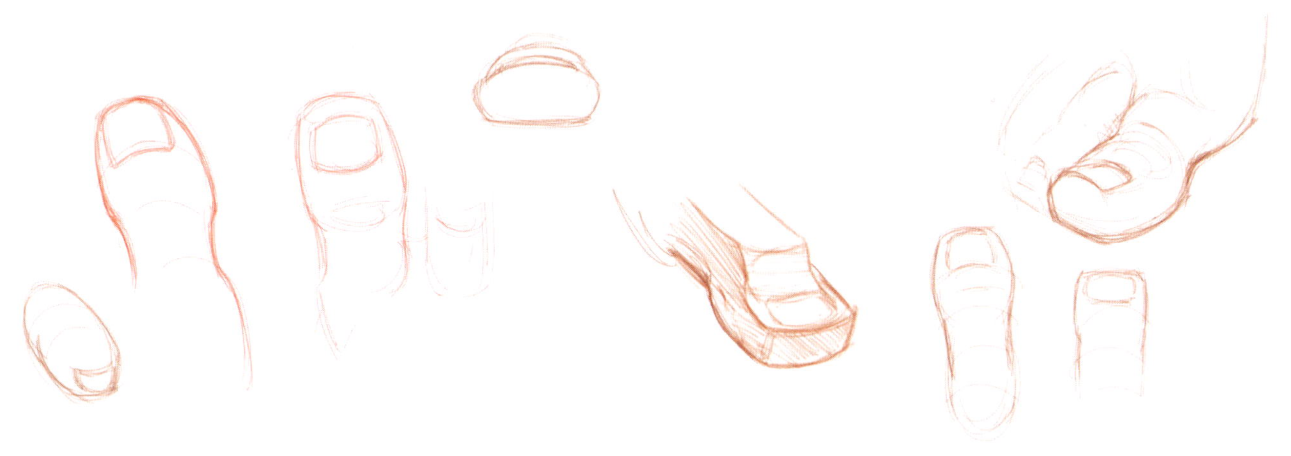

Constructions of the toes

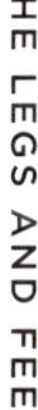

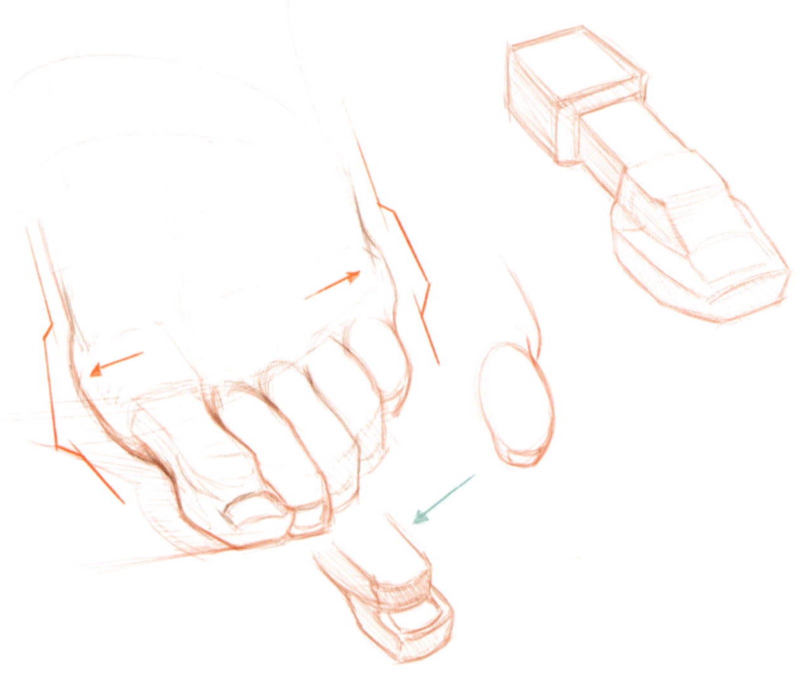

Toe connections

Unlike the others, the big toe has a knuckle, generally, that is closer in character to the thumb, and it is often squarer in character. When you add the originating knuckle of the foot, you get a kind of arch between the planting ball of the foot and the toe's end, as seen in the top figure, opposite. Then, when we line up the toes together, we see their three structures.

Notice in the figure above how the knuckles push out on either side of the big and little toes. This is that snowshoe platform spread wide below the wedge of the foot. I've marked it with red lines. The toes exhibit nice interlocking to the foot structure.

The big toe with its arch looks like a boxy barbell. The three middle toes are more like fingers. Long and simple, they curve down or step down to the toe tips. If they grip the ground, they take on a strong stair-stepping appearance (the turquoise arrow in the figure above). The little toe can look like a shorter version of the middle three. But, more often, it looks like an egg.

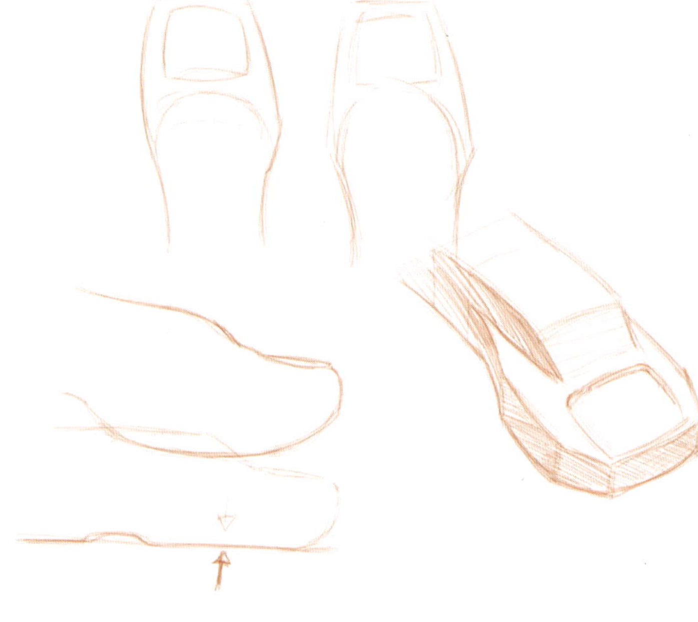

The big toe

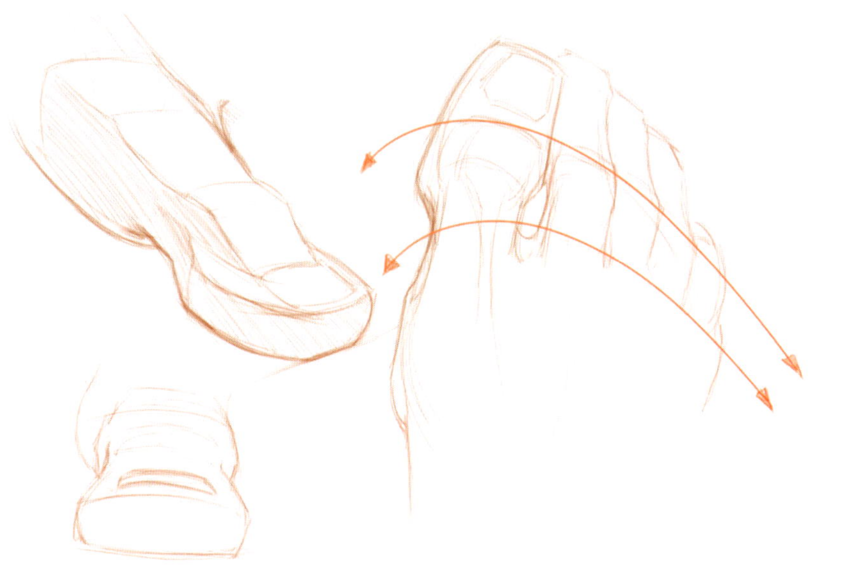

Big toe knuckle

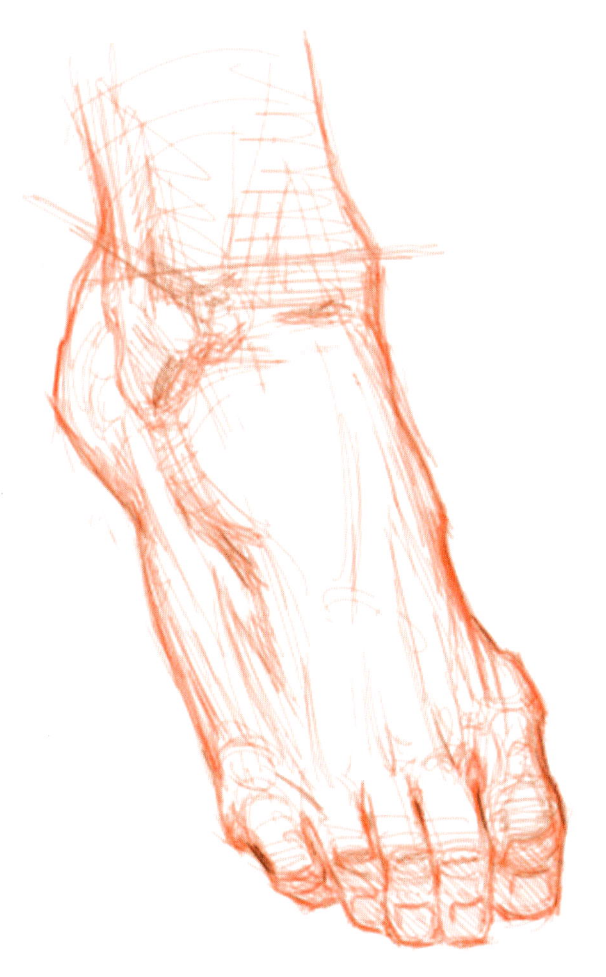

Finished drawing of a foot

OLD MASTER *study*

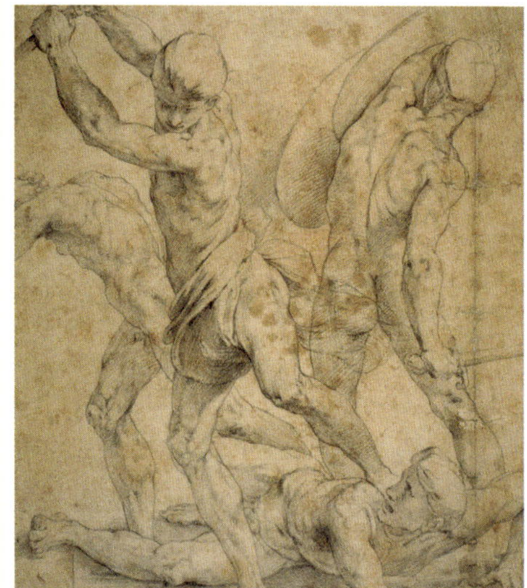

The Panel Beneath the Statue of Apollo in "The School of Athens," after a drawing by Raphael, c. sixteenth century, Raphael Sanzio (1483–1520). Chalk on paper. Chatsworth House, Derbyshire, UK/Bridgeman Images.

In this image from Raphael's *School of Athens*, there is contrapposto everywhere (follow my white lines). I couldn't resist calling out a few examples. Particularly, notice the wild gesture lines going every which way on the sprawling figure at the bottom. The horror of his situation comes across much more strongly from his pose than from the expression on his face.

Notice how, as the legs bend in support and action, the back hamstring tendons stretch around the legs and attach below the knee like reins on a horse. I've marked these with red arrows. That kind of cutting across attachment gives a sense of power, something you don't want to miss in these kinds of poses.

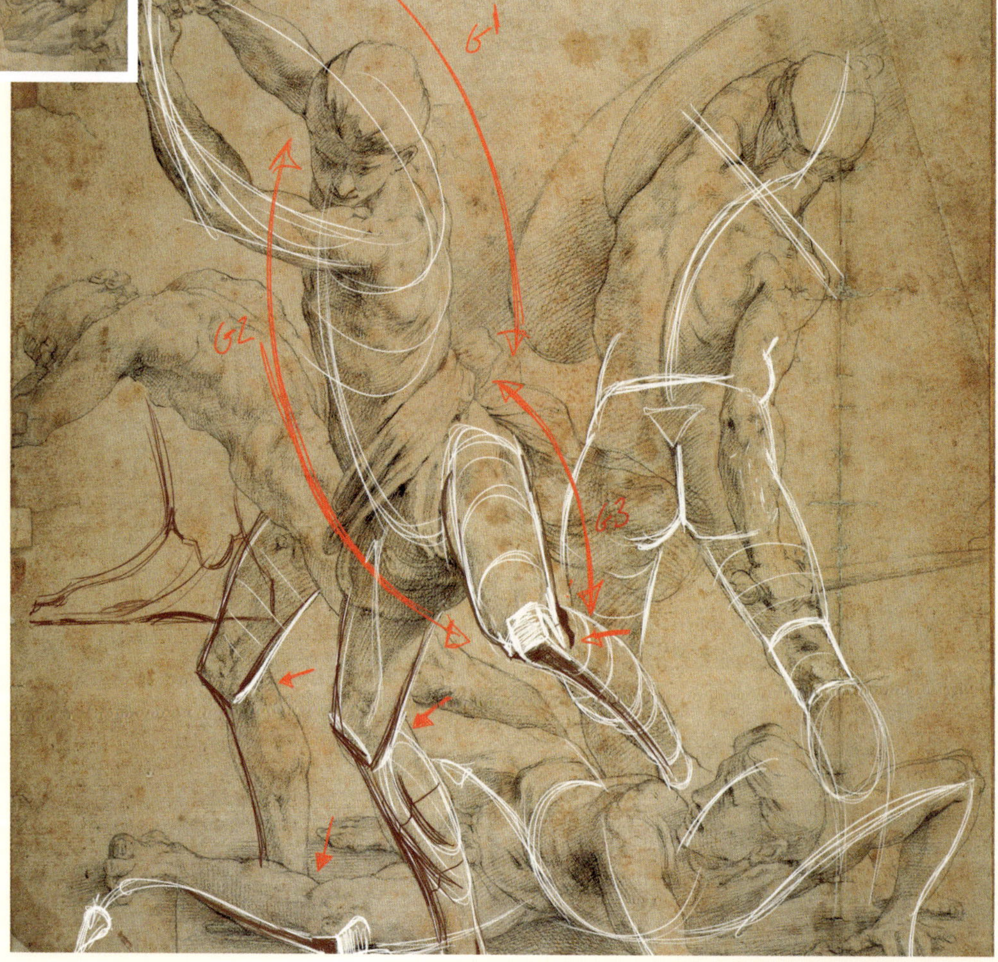

As you follow my marks, don't just look at each individual long axis curve. Look at the whole complex of curves. Gesture in its greatest sense is a wondrous dance of rhythms, each one needing the others to make it all come together. Now, look at the construction of the legs and how they are smaller, but every bit as beautiful as the gestures in those lesser forms. Art is all about the relationships.

GIVE IT A TRY: *Exercise 1*

Redraw the Michelangelo (see page 164) from the
beginning of the chapter. Pay special attention to his
own redraw of the right-side leg and consider why it's
so much better. Look at how nicely he's connecting the
feet to the ankles.

GIVE IT A TRY: *Exercise 2*

Find the opposing eggs in the *School of Athens*,
opposite. Remember, if you see a bulging contour on
the left side, find an opposing bulge (either higher or
lower) on the right. You should be able to find several
in each leg.

Are you still drawing in your object sketchbook?
Congratulations! I knew you were.

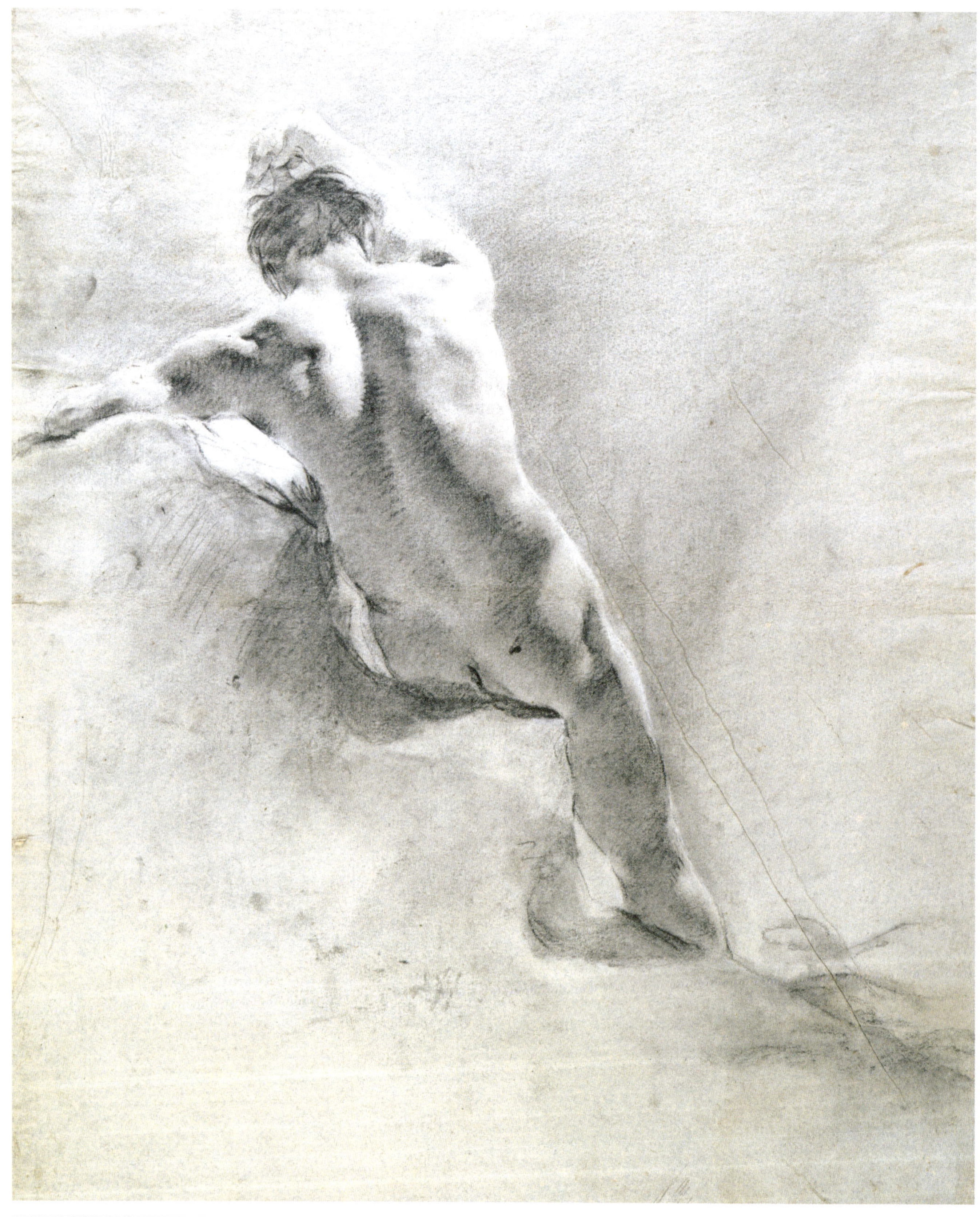

Study of a Male Nude, c. 1715, Giambattista Piazzetta (1683–754). Black chalk heightened with white on paper. Detroit Institute of Arts/Bridgeman Images.

Chapter after chapter of gesture and structure practice, and still we haven't done much with shadows. It's time.

Shadows are corners. Their dark values tie the elements of a composition together and give it weight.

different value = different plane

The Darks Stay Dark

Remember, the darks stay dark and the lights stay light, and the two don't compete. We use the squint test to see the model (or the reference) in the same manner.

The artist is limited to flat paper. Nature has no such limitations. In addition, the white value of the paper is nowhere near the value of sunlight or a spotlight. We can't match nature's scope and we certainly can't "capture" it on paper. All we can do is find a value range that rings true to nature's relative light and dark relationship.

Put that relationship in solid planes describing solid forms, tie it together with curved gesture lines, and we have something worth hanging on the wall. That's what people respond to in a chiaroscuro piece.

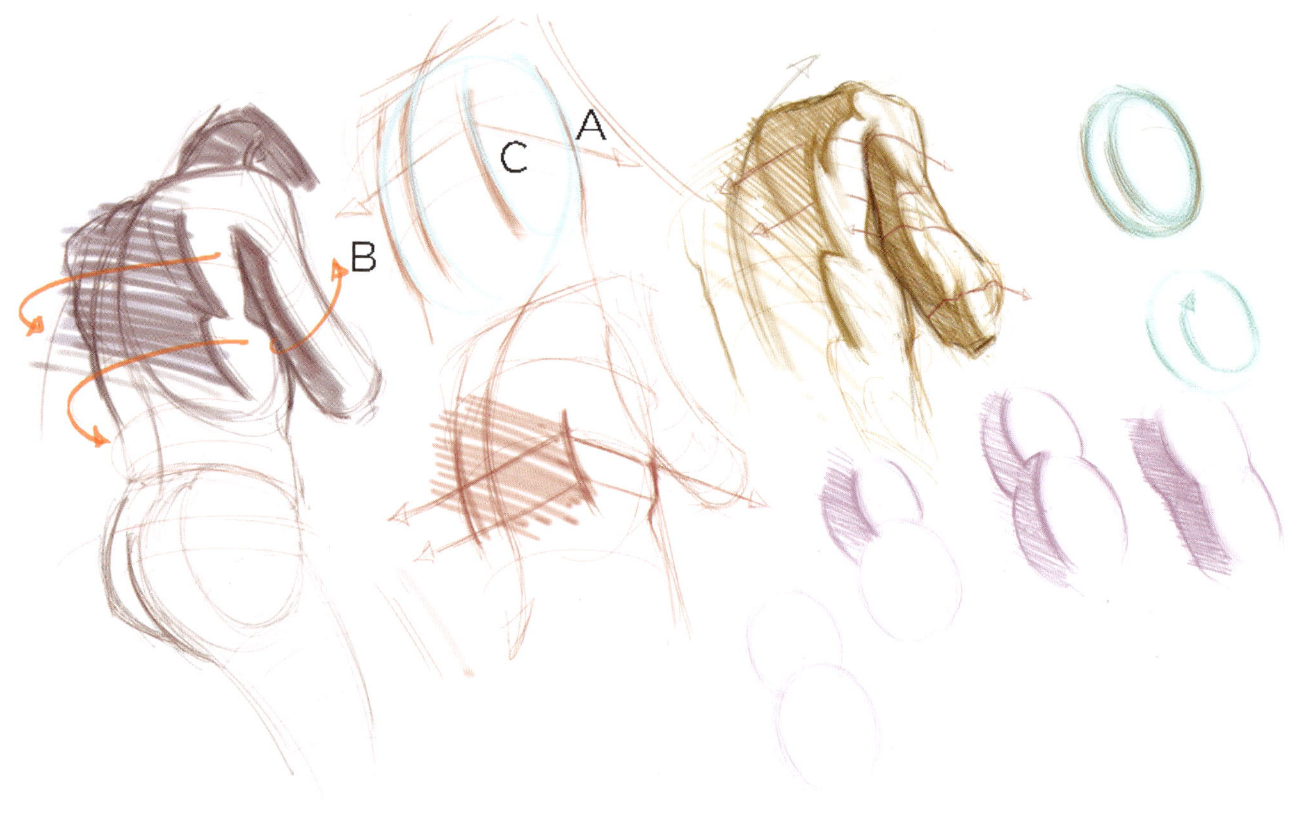

Use this process to work across a small cross section and then move up or down to a new cross section. I've marked that section-by-section process with A, B, and C above.

BIG AND SIMPLE TO SMALL AND COMPLEX

We get confused, lost, and frustrated chasing these theories. Remember, when in doubt, simplify. Focus on the big stuff. Find the forms that take you across the whole width of that body part. That's the foundation. That's all you need. The medium and small structures follow (or not).

A great way to practice is with two or three big simple forms and how they connect—like the hip and thigh or the rib cage, waist, and hips. Let me show you.

To review: draw the long axis gesture (G1) and then follow our process. I've slowed it down even more:

1. Connecting off the gesture, draw the beginning of the form.

2. Draw the end of the form.

3. Draw the shape of the shadow in the middle of the form.

Think of it as telling a story with a beginning, an end, and a middle in between: Start the form, end the form, and find the middle of the form.

Use this process to work across a small cross section, and then move up or down to a new cross section. I've marked that section-by-section process with A, B, and C in the drawing above. You can see it play out on the middle set of figures with the three-step process outlined previously, and in more detail on the far right figure.

A single 1 (connecting gesture), can play against several 2s (end of the form) and 3s (shape of the shadow in the middle of the form).

Sometimes a side may be hidden—say, behind the arm. That's okay. What is key is finding the rhythm from side to side and from side to shadow.

In the same figure, look at the turquoise balls to see how those rhythms move like a loop-the-loop roller coaster through the beginning, middle, and end sequence—that's very important. Very.

Gesture is defined by the long axis because all body parts connect end to end. Things don't last long side to side, and they have definite endings there. That's across the form.

Going down the form, a stomach muscle rises up, submerges, then another rises up, and so on. You have to build the volume, and then explain it away. Making those transitions from one form to the next is tricky. So, work across, then down, then across again, and then down again.

Work your way through the entire body, big simple form by big simple form, or start with the big form across and then construct all the lesser forms across on top of it. When you've finished, move on to the next big simple form.

The breakdowns from Fig. A, right, follow on the next two pages. Notice how the proportions in the break-downs vary from the source drawing. I like to mix things up as I go—searching for greater heroic proportions in one or more length in another. Lean the figure back more, tilt things into deeper space—I'll do anything to find an interesting take on the material. In other words, I'm doing my best not to copy it. I'm trying to give it a vision.

When people see your drawing in a book or online, you want them to know immediately that it's yours.

That's a lot of information. Let's take another look.

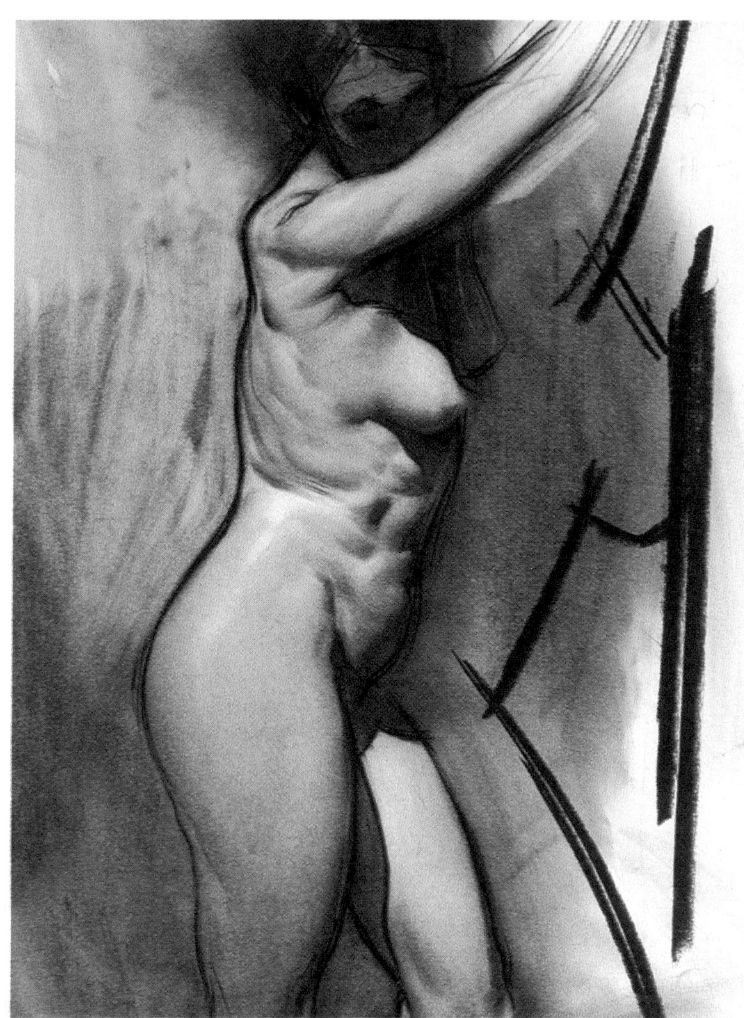

Fig. A. *Figure Study*, c. 2001, by Steve Huston. Alphacolor and Conté chalk on Strathmore, Bristol finish. (1) Find the shape of the form; (2) find the shape of the shadow on the form; (3) give the shadow a darker value; and (4) add halftone gradations. That's our four-step process.

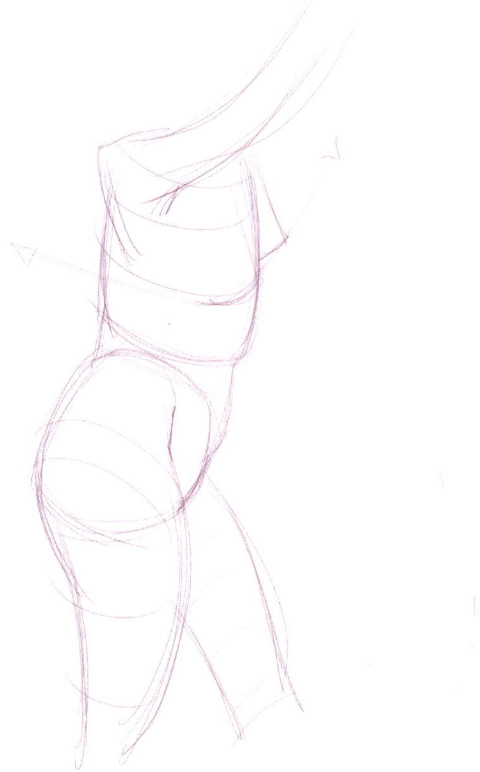

Fig. B. Always start with a solidly constructed figure.

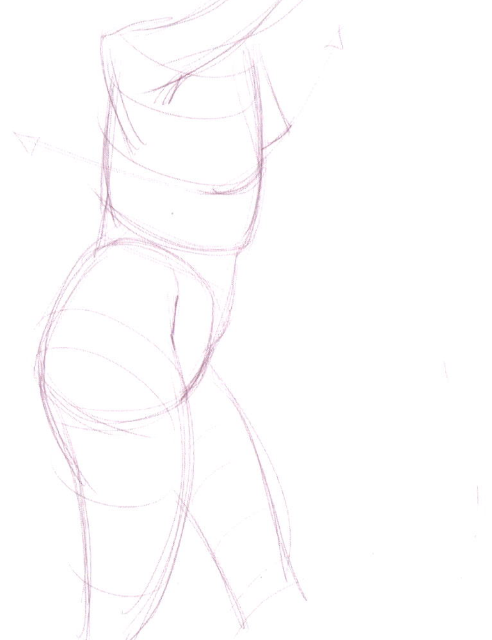

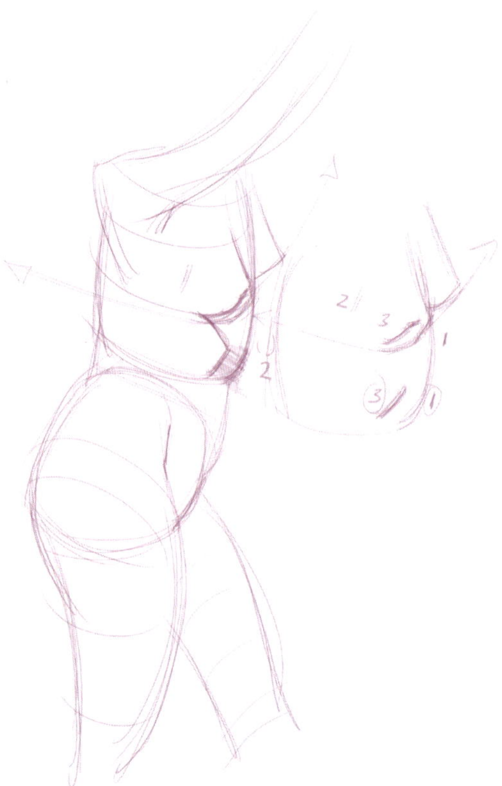

Fig. C. Beginning to add the shadows

I'm working from Fig. A and removing all those intimidating lumps and bumps. I'm just going big and simple (see Fig. B). The rest will follow if I have the time and inclination. Keep in mind, I've done a careful lay-in of the whole body (or as much as I plan to draw of it) before beginning my shading work.

A. I start with the big simple rib cage (see Fig. C). I only see a bit of it under the breast. That's all I need. Follow it with 1, 2, and 3 (see the right-side drawing), then fill it in with 4 (the shadow), and move on.

B. I'm adding the breast because it's in the way. I could have started with it because it is interrupting the big simple structure I needed. Follow with 1, 2, and 3—cast its shadow over the ribs. Make sure it tracks over that simplified surface like an ant over a picnic cloth. I'm leaving out the shadow value on step B to distinguish it from step A.

Hint: Notice that I wobble the shadow (#3) of the breast to suggest the nipple. I don't have to structure out the nipple because the foundational structure of the breast is solid. If you get the big stuff, wobble away, and the little stuff will usually take care of itself. But the step-by-step process is always there when you need it.

Now, I can keep rendering across to find the lesser structures. I've added some more ribs. The egg-like rhythms in turquoise in Fig. D show how they tie back into the greater rib cage. Everything connects. That is the idea of gesture.

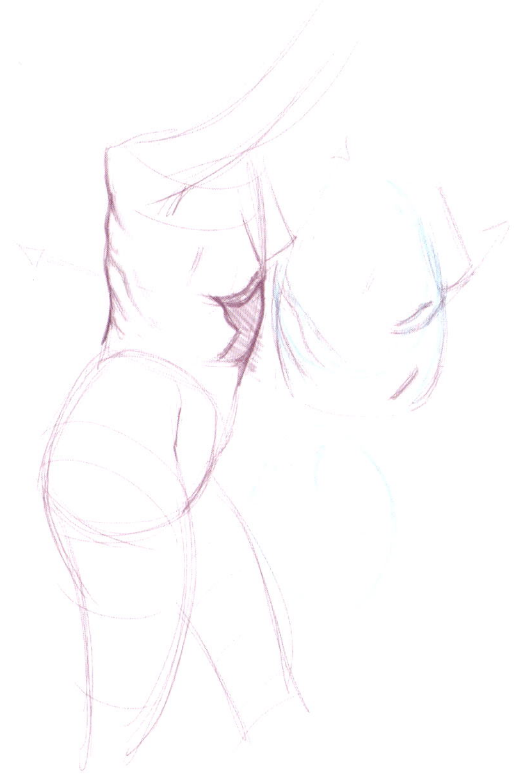

Fig. D. Getting the lesser structures

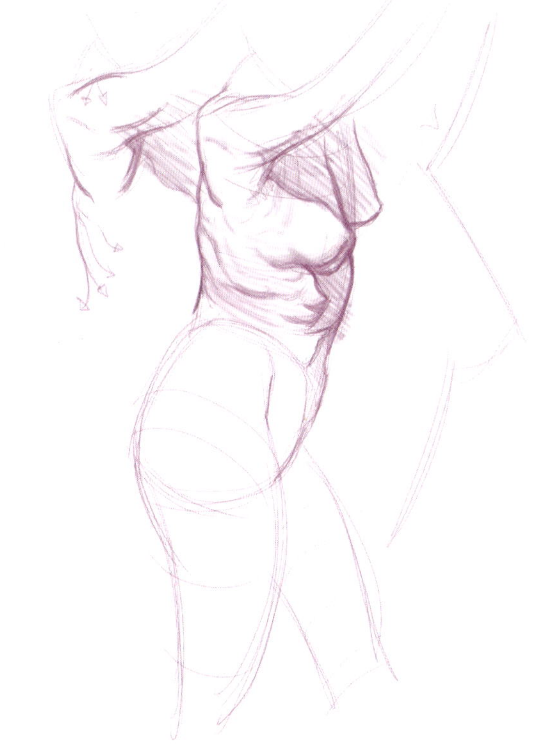

Fig. E. Adding the shoulder blade

I've erased or lightened the lay-in lines. Normally, I'd just leave them, but I wanted the new additions to be clear. I've also darkened and refined the contours. Notice the added ribs wobble and so does the cast shadow off the breast. For the cast shadow, I just drew a dark line over the lighter one. No need to erase.

Stay light with your lines for as long as possible. It pays off.

On to the shoulder and shoulder blade (see Fig. E). I refine my lay-in a little, making sure everything tracks. Then, it's back to my process. Always trust the process. You can always shortcut later when you feel confident. The tiny stuff between shoulder blade and breast I can pick up as subtle detail. Give them a connective rhythm to some greater structure and you'll be fine.

The safest thing to do, until you've really nailed the chiaroscuro idea, is keep the shadow detail simple. Use line. Stay away from the reflected light stuff. It just makes drawing harder in the beginning. Who needs that?

Highlights and Lighter Halftones

Using middle-value paper (not a bright, colored one) gives us a ground on which to add highlights and lighter halftones. They perform many functions for the artist. They increase the contrast between light and dark. Pushing the chiaroscuro effect is usually a good idea. They add nuance and, potentially, more roundness and, even possibly, texture to the light side. And highlights find more corners.

Corner highlights have the most benefit. To repeat what I've said previously, the core shadow is the primary corner for the structure. It's where the planes in light meet the planes in shadow. A highlight is where at least two planes meet, but all planes are in light. Highlights give us more structure.

Make sure the highlight stays away from the darker halftone and the core shadow edge. Think of the tone as the color value. If you are drawing a figure, then the toned paper is the skin tone.

It helps the effect if you add a slight gradation to the highlight as it moves down the form. It might be the drop-off of light or a flaring effect from the angle viewed. Even that subtle change moves the viewer's eye and he will feel more volume.

If the object is backlit, the highlight might blast out the lights with little or no gradation. Typically, the artist then puts the rendering into the shadow side. Joaquín Sorolla's backlit figures on the beach are probably the most famous examples of this.

As I've mentioned, highlights can be used to push the contrast. In the top left object in the drawing above, notice how the highlight snuggles right up to the cast shadow edge on the box, popping the value change. This is totally different from the idea of keeping the highlight away from the core shadow edges, as demonstrated everywhere else.

You can see in the fountain pen sketch at right in the bottom left figure, that highlights can be used even in quick sketches. Just chase the corners.

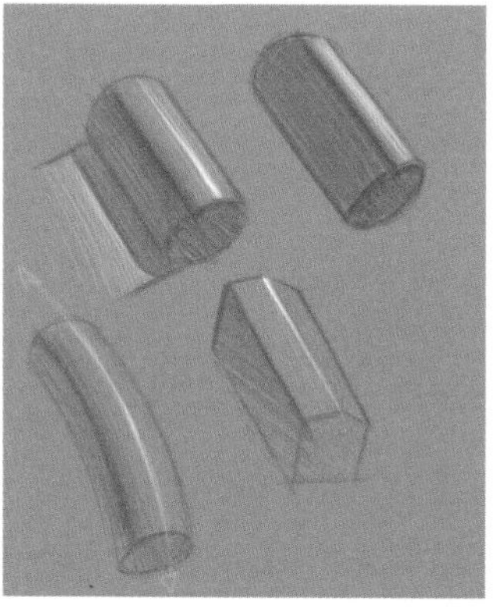

Toned paper objects

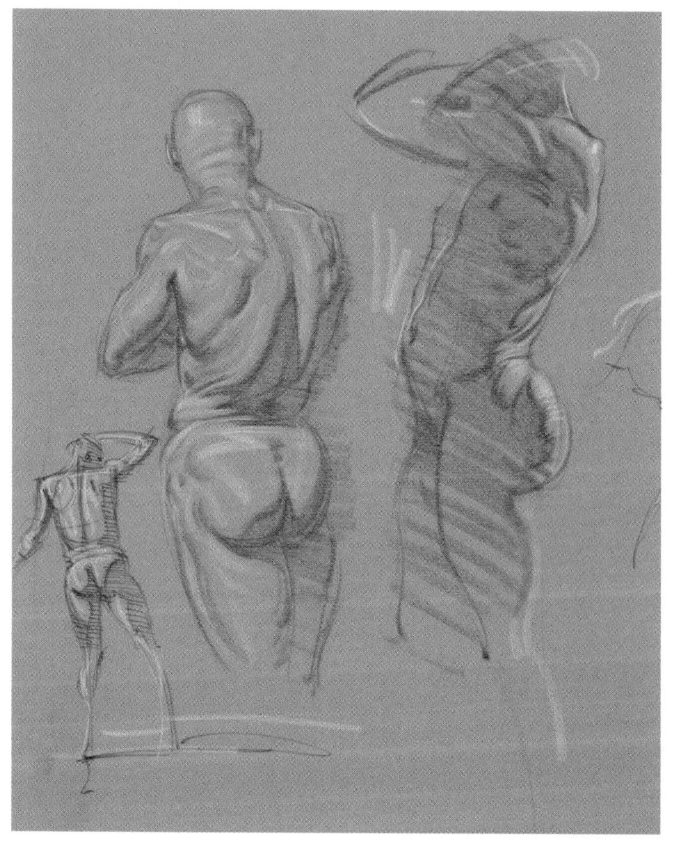

Toned paper figures

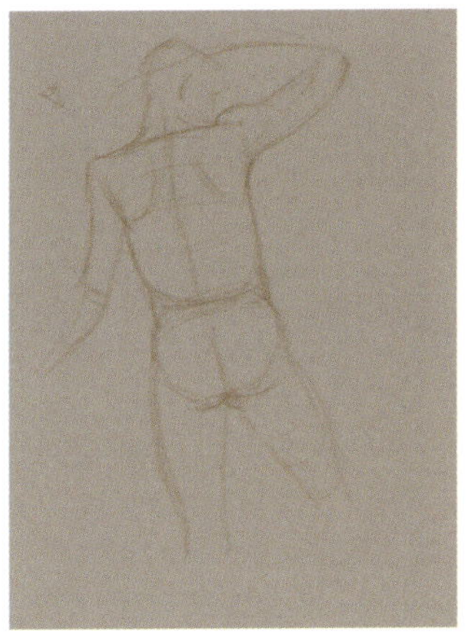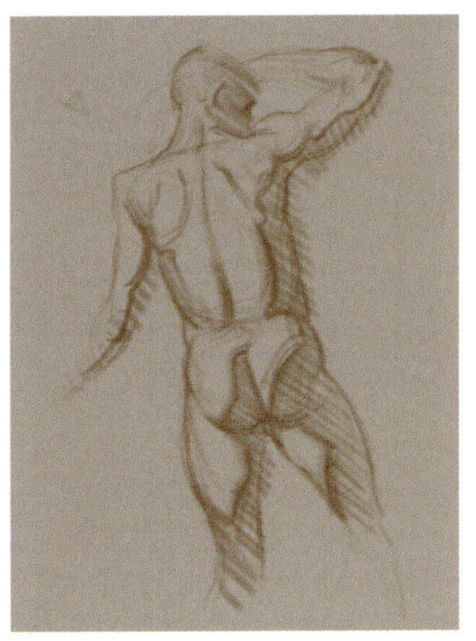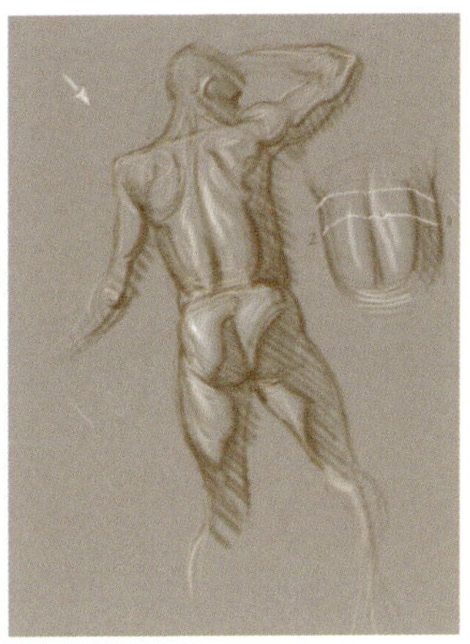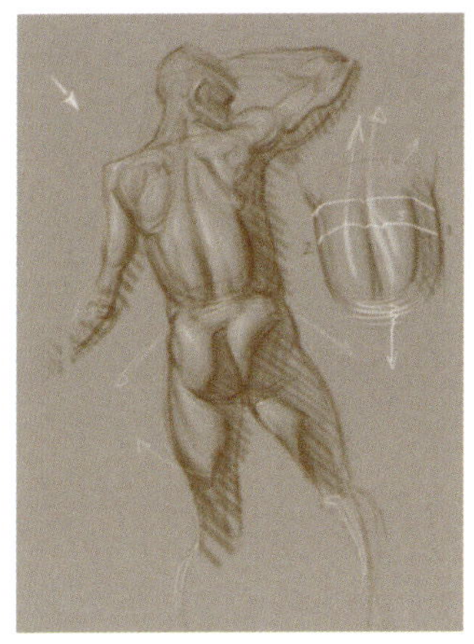

Step-by-step for rendering shadows on toned paper. Always start with the basic construction.

The same drawing with new highlights

Remember to follow the gestures. That's right. Highlights are gestures, too, as they track the corner down its long axis. If they follow the curved character of the form (and we hope they always do), that's the definition of a gesture.

Did you already figure that out? If not, don't fret. This book is about only two ideas—but they're big ideas. They are a lot to hold on to.

Be aware of the direction of the light source. If it's coming from the upper left, everything turning down and/or to the right will get darker. Look where the highlights push up against cast shadows, creating new corners away from core shadows, and they work great for creating zigzag pinches.

I use this style a lot—almost exclusively—in life drawing. It's an overblown style in terms of shape design and highlight use. Typically, you want to submerge both into a more cohesive whole. However, I have a big-budget,

Baroque-kind of style. And I'm really exaggerating in the sketch as notations for an eventual painting. Making the mark "loud" acts as a reminder.

In fact, the toned paper technique is a great transition into painting. You start with a middle-value ground (the paper), knock down the darks, and accent with the lights. That is how most chiaroscuro painters such as van Dyke, Rembrandt, and Sargent worked.

Here is the same figure again (top right) with tamed-down highlights and halftones. Even here, they're still quite strong. Look at the Piazzetta at the start of the chapter (see page 176) to see how tame the Old Masters made them.

Every highlight is doing its structural work of creating or accenting corners and its gestural work of moving down the long axis or finding an "out" from one form to the next. We're trying to make every mark count, remember?

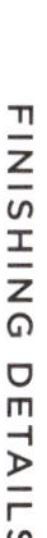

OLD MASTER *study*

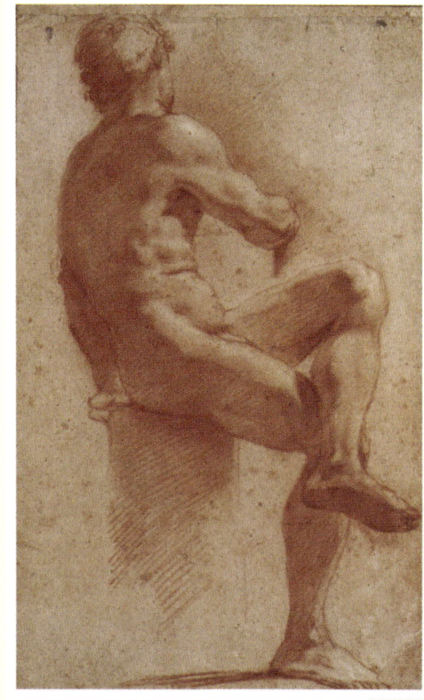

A Male Nude Seated with His Back Turned, Annibale Carracci (1560–1609). Chalk on paper. Private collection/Bridgeman Images.

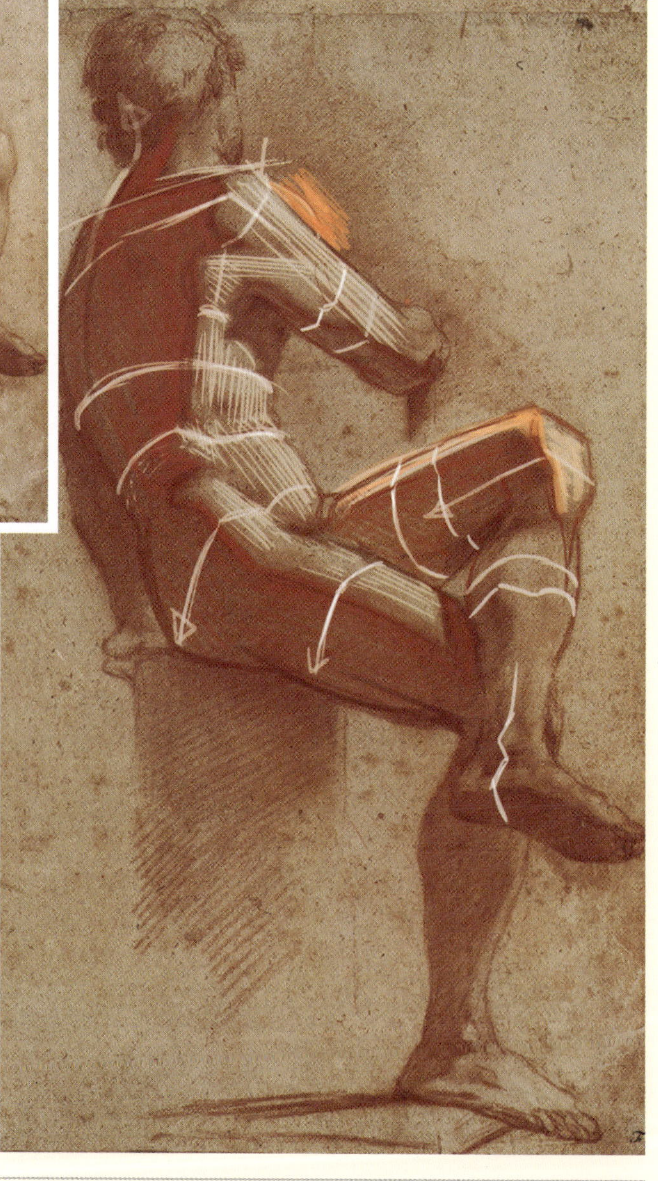

Solid shadows give weight to the many varied positions of this difficult and nuanced pose.

Let's look at the shadow pattern from this Carracci masterpiece from chapter 5 (see page 68). Notice the incredible restraint in the use of highlights. I've removed most of the secondary forms to make the analysis crystal clear.

Carracci was one of the greatest draftsmen in history, and this piece shows it. Look at how faithful the shadow shapes are in terms of gesture and structure. Here we get a much clearer example of how shadows show corners.

I dusted back the bulge of the shoulder muscle to make that corner obvious and did something similar to the knee. But there are corners everywhere if you know how to look. And by now, you do!

GIVE IT A TRY: *Exercise 1*

Warm up by drawing the shadow shapes of balls, boxes,
and tubes from memory or from my earlier attempts.
Add shadow shapes to them. Now, go back to the step-
by-step analyses we worked through and select only
one constructed shape from that drawing—say,
an egg for the rib cage. Do our 1-2-3 process: (1) Draw
the beginning of the egg. (2) Draw the end of the egg.
(3) Draw the middle shadow shape of the egg.
Do this with several drawings. That should help the
process sink in.

GIVE IT A TRY: *Exercise 2*

Using toned paper and picking two or three body parts
from any of the drawings from this chapter, do a careful
lay-in. Then, break down the big simple shadow shapes
on the big simple forms. Do it again. This time, add
some secondary forms. Do it again. Add the highlights.

FIVE MINUTES

How to Start

I hope for you countless little improvements throughout a long and fruitful life.

Art wants you for the long haul. Pace yourself. An athlete is old at thirty-four. Artists are catching their stride at sixty.

There's a famous anecdote about Anders Zorn. It may be apocryphal. Zorn went to art school eight hours a day, so the story goes. Not enough for this prodigious talent, so he went home and painted for four more. Twelve hours a day: that's how much dedication Zorn put into his craft.

Good for him, and good for you if you can do it. And you may be the type that can. But, if you're not . . .

You'll try it for a week—fail miserably. You'll give up your dream, convinced you never had it, whatever *it* is.

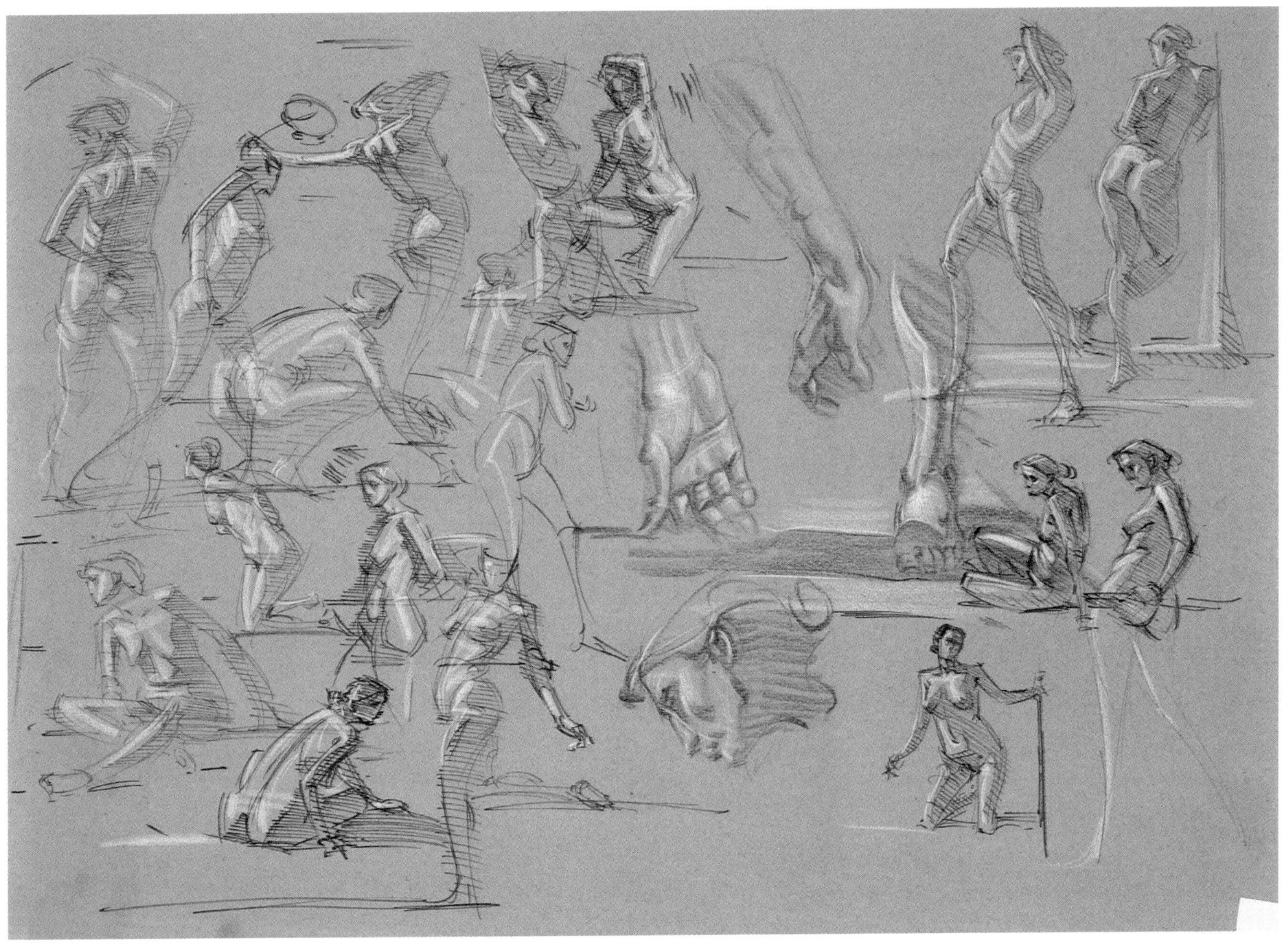

Various figures in marker pen and brown and white CarbOthello pencil on toned paper

Just as there's an art to drawing a beautiful figure, there's also an art to reinventing yourself. Both need a process to build on.

- I want to be a fine artist.

- I want to be an animator.

- I want a hobby other than surfing the Internet.

- I want to draw my grandchild or grandparent and be proud enough to frame it.

Whatever your dream is, try this: Draw for five minutes a day. Draw a tube. Draw a figure. Draw the eye of a figure or whatever you can draw in five minutes. Do that for two weeks and only that. If you miss a day or two, forgive yourself and start again.

When you've accomplished those, make it ten minutes a day. Do that for another week.

The strange and wondrous thing about the human condition is each of us needs to motivate ourselves to become the person we really want to be. Motivate! It's usually about forming good habits and building on countless little improvements: improvements in craft, in work habits, in cutting ourselves a break every once in a while. So . . .

- five minutes

- ten minutes

- fifteen minutes

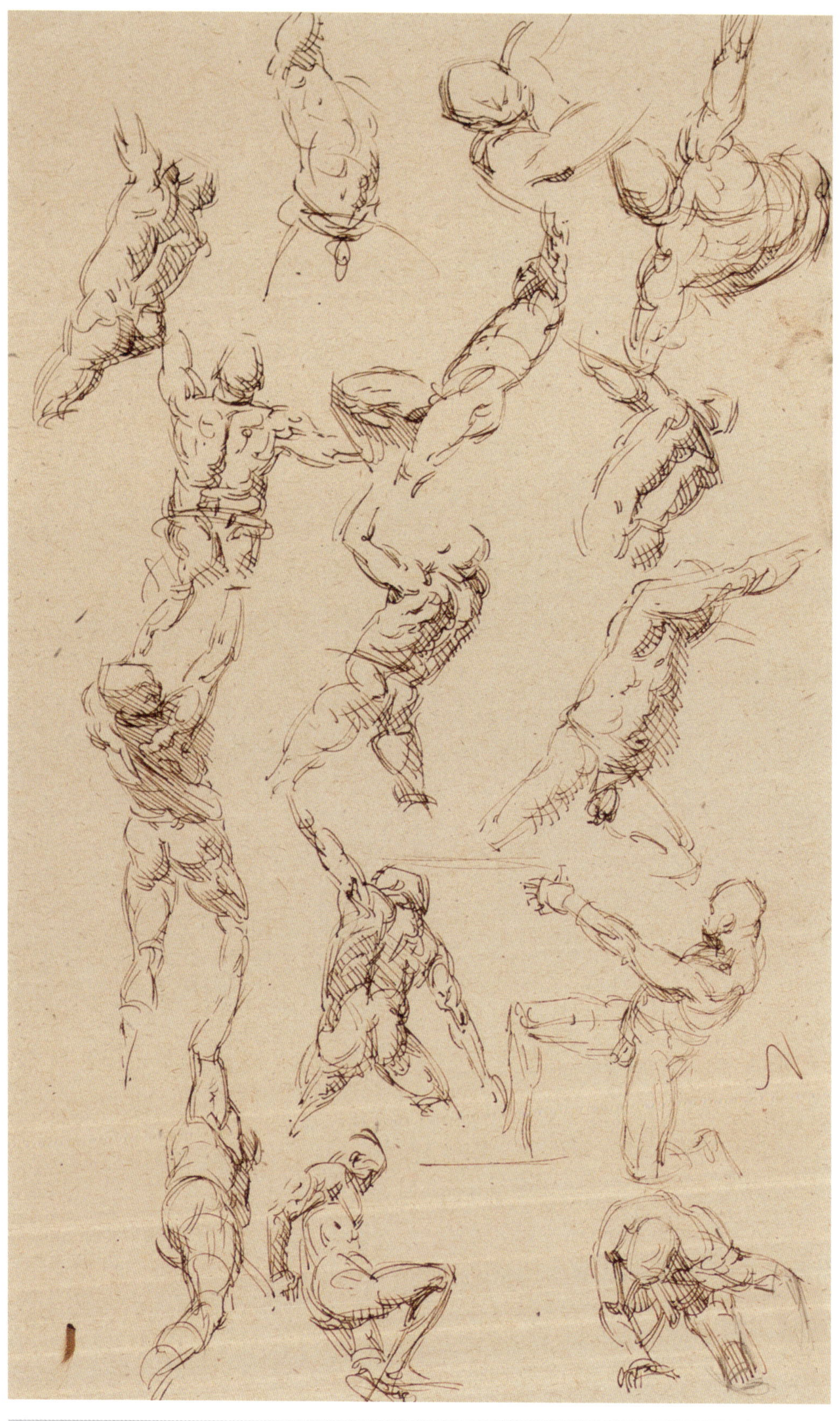

Focus on gesture and structure with every mark you make and it will lead you to great things.

Eventually, you'll find a good habit has formed, and you no longer have to fool yourself into doing what you really wanted to do all along. You'll also find the five or ten minutes often turn into ten or fifteen minutes without even realizing it.

Now, how are you feeling? Like a winner? An artist? You should. Artists do art, and you've been doing it every single day.

How many hours do five minutes every day over twenty years equal? A lot. Be in it for the long term. And when you're not drawing with a pencil, draw with your eyes.

See the world as an artist because you are an artist. Be modest in your goals, at first.

Five minutes a day and soon you'll be putting in the long hours without even thinking about it. Why? Because you proved weeks ago who you really are!

So, I wish for you those small improvements. Because, then, I know you'll be making new ones next year and the year after that, just like I will be.

I'll know both of us are making our world a little more beautiful, five minutes at a time.

How to Keep Going

I hope this process of making things come together beautifully has been an enriching experience for you. Making things come together beautifully—that's a metaphor, isn't it? Metaphor is part of the mythic idea that I spoke about on the very first page of this book. Metaphors and myth connect straight to the heart and bypass the head. And that is art's great power, as well. Having a vision of how things should come together, and then doing it, is an endeavor that can seep into the soul and whisper little wisdoms about life, wisdoms we don't even have the words to ask about.

Don't get me wrong. In between the meditative moments you might be tempted to tear your hair out. Art can be hard. But, oh, when those sublime moments come, it is you who feels connected, and the hair loss is easily worth it.

"Come together." That aesthetic wisdom deserves its own school of philosophy, it seems to me. Well, at least we can preach it with our pencils! And that is not such a bad deal.

I've spent my life being an artist, most of it as a professional. I wish that for you, as well, if you wish it for yourself. Many of us may just want to have fun and improve a little, or use the process as a lovely release of tension. And that is as it should be. On whatever level you choose to participate, art enriches you. And when you have the courage to do a drawing, whether it's from time to time or all the time, well, the world is better for it.

It's been a privilege "talking" art with you. Thank you. I feel richer for it as well. Please let me know on my Facebook page where your new adventure takes you. On whatever level you choose to participate, I've experienced what you're about to and, I must say, I'm a little jealous about what's in store for you as I think back to those old feelings.

Go have fun. Go have the time of your life and make us all better by doing so.

About the Author

Steve Huston is a native of Alaska who received his degree from the
Art Center College of Design in Pasadena, California. He first established
himself as a successful illustrator, commissioned by such high-profile
clients as Paramount Pictures, MGM, and Warner Brothers.

After holding a faculty position at the Art Center, in addition to teaching courses in life drawing, anatomy, and composition for the artists and animators of Disney and Dreamworks SKG studios, Huston earnestly began his career as a fine artist, winning top prizes at the California Art Club Gold Medal Show two years in a row. A string of gallery shows followed, first in Los Angeles and then in New York and elsewhere.

Huston continues exhibiting his work widely. His works are poetic, poignant, and masterfully powerful, and his figures are iconic archetypes of masculine and feminine line and form. His work is much sought after by prestigious private collectors, distinguished fellow artists, and other cognoscenti of the contemporary art world. He has been an extraordinarily effective mentor whose instruction and guidance have produced an impressive number of accomplished acolytes.

Acknowledgments

As I offer this book as a teaching guide to you, I want to take a moment to thank those who were at least as generous in their guidance of me. First to Vernon Wilson, the kindest teacher I ever had the pleasure of studying under. Vern is the only artist I've ever seen draw with the rhythm and grace of an orchestra conductor. Vern, the image of you drawing has been an inspiration to me my whole career. Thanks, my friend. You're a good man!

Thanks to Dan McCaw. He started as my teacher and quickly became cheerleader and friend. Dan is the kind of soul who would give you the shirt off his back. His keen guidance during the years has given me gifts far greater. I also want to thank Harry Carmean for his masterful demonstration of not only how to draw, but also how to remain a student of art even into your nineties. David Mocarski for giving generously of his time critiquing my work a good year after I left school. Thanks, David. And to Richard Bunkall. Richard died far too young, but was a philosophical coach for me in his last months. Thank you Richard.

And you, my readers, will benefit immensely by exploring each of these fine artist's work on the web.

Last, I want to thank my family, my dear family, including but not limited to my parents, my lovely children, and the love of my life, my wife Jen. Thank you most of all, sweetheart. For me, the honeymoon has never ended!

Also Available

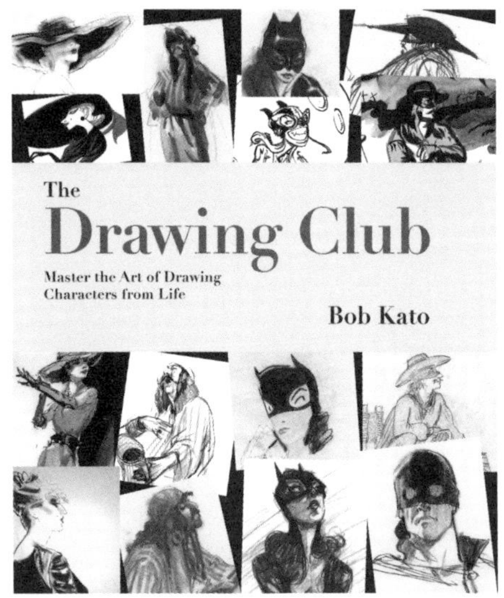

The Drawing Club
978-1-59253-911-6

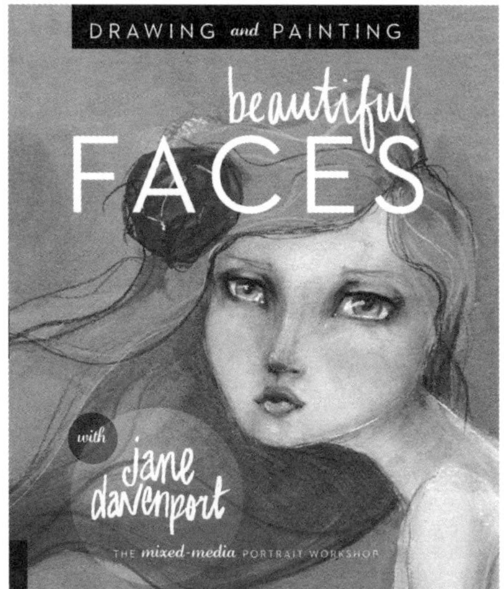

Drawing and Painting Beautiful Faces
978-1-59253-986-4

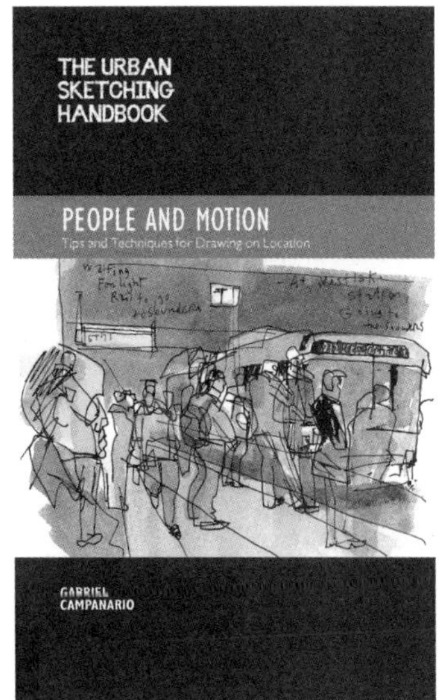

The Urban Sketching Handbook:
People and Motion
978-1-59253-962-8